Codex 40

FIAT

FIAT

Michael Sedgwick

B. T. BATSFORD LTD LONDON

For Helen, the perfect co-driver

First published 1974
© Michael Sedgwick and Helen Marshall 1974
Made and Printed in Great Britain by
Tinling (1973) Ltd, Prescot, Lancs
for the publishers B. T. Batsford Ltd
4 Fitzhardinge Street, London W1

ISBN 0 7134 0473 6

For convenience the name is spelt
FIAT throughout this book. It is,
however, the case that up to the end
of 1906 the spelling F.I.A.T. was
invariably used.

Contents

The Plates

(The source of each plate is given after its description, and the author and publisher thank the owners of the photographs for permission to reproduce them. Where no source is given the photograph is from the author's own collection.)

Acknowledgements

A FIAT is not a committee job. Every example I have driven in the past quarter of a century bears the stamp of its designer, and there is no confusing a Giacosa with a Montabone.

A history of the *marque* is quite another thing. Any fool can sort out a 124 from a 124 Special or a 124 Sport Coupé 1600. Only a little more proficiency is needed to quote all Nazzaro's winning average speeds, or to know which of Rosatelli's fighter biplanes boasted a four-gun armament. But knowledge without understanding or interpretation is so much verbiage, and consequently I have leant heavily on countless friends, colleagues and even total strangers. All were pestered, and all responded nobly. Some have since become personal friends, which speaks volumes for their patience.

First of all, my thanks must go to Augusto Costantino and all at FIAT's *Centro Storico* in Turin. For a whole week we sat round a table in his office, discussing the *minutiae* of the FIAT story, and never once did his enthusiasm or interest flag, albeit we were using French as a conversational medium. The Costantino method has to be experienced to be believed. Mention an obscure model, and with a quick '*bien entendu*' the whole saga unfolds in words and photostats at one's elbow. Next come Alfred Woolf and his associates Biddy Laing and Tom Walkerley, who look after FIAT public relations in Britain, and also look after FIAT-minded historians. Nothing was ever too much trouble for them, be it South American export statistics, 1965 O.M. catalogues, the loan of a new 125 Special, or an elusive spare part for our own 850 coupé. George Liston Young, founder and Hon. Secretary of the FIAT Register, kindly read the manuscript for me, and contributed much information, while the Register's *topolino* specialists, Derek

Pearce and Tony Prins, gave generously of their experience with this lovable and infuriating little car.

My fellow historians and scribes have also been most generous and sympathetic, and I must single out Anthony Bird, John Bolster, S. C. H. Davis, Dennis C. Field, M.I.E.E., G. N. Georgano, Lytton P. Jarman, F. Wilson McComb, Keith Marvin, the late St John C. Nixon, Michael Worthington-Williams, and R. J. Wyatt, at the same time paying tribute to the memory of Henry Knox, who taught me more about Edwardian motoring that I could have hoped to acquire from mere book-learning. Thanks are also due to the countless P.R.O.s of rival firms who furnished a wealth of assorted information, usually by return mail—'though it were to their own hindrance'. As ever, Eric Bellamy, the Librarian of the National Motor Museum at Beaulieu, gave me the free run of his superb archives, never refusing to help in the search for an unlikely reference.

FIAT is, of course, 'The Car of International Reputation', and a mere Englishman must cast his net wide to gain full perspective. In Europe Ivan Mahy covered Belgium, while Vaclav Petrik and Marian Suman-Hreblay contributed a wealth of data from Czechoslovakia. Ole E. Riisager seems to know every FIAT in Denmark by name, and was a tireless correspondent, as was Jacques Dorizon on matters French, with which J. P. Chambault also helped mightily. I could wish for no better mentor on FIAT in Germany and Austria than that distinguished historian Hans Heinrich von Fersen, and across the border in the Democratic Republic Dr Hans Mai was immensely helpful. Lajos Haris of Budapest weighed in with more Austro-Hungarian information, and among my many Italian friends Angelo Tito Anselmi and Count Giovanni Lurani-Cernuschi filled in numerous gaps. Bart Vanderveen not only gave generously of his immense knowledge of commercial vehicles, but also went hunting for FIAT lore in his native Netherlands. To J. M. Fischer I owe the story of FIAT in pre-War Poland, Russia and Japan were, as ever, the province of Bill Emery, with some further Russian assistance from Alec Ulmann, and to my good friend Ferdinand Hediger I owe enough information on matters Swiss to fill a good-sized book. The same goes for Portugal, where Ing. Norberto Pedroso, himself the owner of a Garavini-bodied 508 cabriolet, worked tirelessly on our behalf.

Outside Europe another very faithful correspondent, Roni K. Khan, filled in the Indian story. For Australia I relied on Edward du Cros (also a mine of information on D'Arcy Baker), Bruce Lindsay and Tony Parkinson, and my main New Zealand source was Harold Kidd. The American FIAT saga would have been woefully sketchy but for the endeavours of Dr Alfred S. Lewerenz of the Horseless Carriage Club and Frank Robinson Jr of Bellevue, Washington, who spent hours in libraries tracking early references. Hugh Durnford responded nobly to a request for Canadian information, and in Uruguay Alvaro Casal Tatlock opened up a whole vista hitherto unsuspected by a mere Limey.

There are also the specialists who saved me from floundering in unfamiliar waters. Nobody knows more about the European racing scene between the Wars than Cyril Posthumus, and nobody could have been more generous with help. Across the Atlantic Jerry Gebby and Peter Helck went to untold trouble to plumb the obscurities of American racing, William Boddy of *Motor Sport* guided me through the 'Mephistopheles' maze, and V. H. Tuson contributed his memories of racing and tuning 508s and 509s. The modern Formulae are a nightmare, but David Filsell made my exploration of Formula III and Formula Junior a relatively painless process. Horace A. Beale III sent me reams of fascinating notes on the adventures of a FIAT-owning family in Pennsylvania before 1914, B. T. White was my mentor on hard-skinned military vehicles, and John H. Blake of the British Light Aviation Centre turned me loose in his library, as well as answering the tiresome aeronautical queries of a confirmed land animal.

But above all, my thanks go to my friend and partner Helen Marshall. Much of the early 'hard slog' behind a two-year research campaign was Helen's, and so was much of the driving. She has logged many hours behind the wheels of pretty nearly every current FIAT model. Her encouragement, humour and compassion have made light of what would otherwise have been a mammoth task.

Introduction:
The Colossus of Piedmont

*Volkswagen has been an eighth wonder of the world long
enough to have a request for official status considered.
Yet, interestingly enough, some of the shrewdest people
in the British car industry are rather more apprehensive
about the competition they are likely to meet from* FIAT
of Italy.

Graham Turner, *The Car Makers,* 1963

Thus wrote one of the motor industry's most perceptive critics
some ten years ago, when British entry to the Common Market
was but a pipe-dream obstructed by the monolithic Charles de
Gaulle, and FIAT's annual vehicle production was still below the
million mark. The statement must sound even more remarkable
when one considers that in 1963, Italy, for many years a closed
shop, was fast becoming a viable market for foreign manufacturers: the first seven months of the year saw 29,285 new Volkswagen registered on FIAT's home territory. In Britain, B.M.C. were
riding the crest of the Issigonis wave with the well-established
Mini backed by the Hydrolastic 1100, and Rootes were essaying
a come-back with the equally advanced Hillman 'Imp'. FIAT's
'1963 English sales of 5,515 units represented a drop in the
bucket, and in other export fields the outlook could have been
brighter. The *marque* was seventh best seller in Belgium, seventh
among America's foreign imports, and trailing in third place on
the key Swiss market, behind Volkswagen and Opel.

But by 1971 Mr Turner's prophecy rang true. Company
President Gianni Agnelli might confess sadly in his Turin Show

speech that labour disputes had lost FIAT three million working hours and 160,000 vehicles. 'These cars', he observed, 'were built and sold all the same—by other manufacturers.' FIAT's traditional 90-per-cent share of the home market (a statistical constant from the 1920s to the early 1960s) had shrunk to less than 65 per cent, but in terms of hard finance the colossus of Turin was sitting pretty, with 1,589,000 cars and commercial vehicles, representing a solid £1,250,000,000 worth of cash, delivered in the calendar year. Exports were down on 1970, but a total of 616,000 units was not to be despised, especially as this equalled more than three-quarters of B.M.C.'s *total* private-car production in 1969. To domestic production one could add something like half a million vehicles put together by *filiali*, associated companies and concessionaires in 28 foreign countries. Not all these firms made private cars, of course: protectionist Japan might allow tractor manufacture, but it would never do for the 127 to confront Datsun's 'Cherry' in a home match. Against this, however, FIAT was the first foreign organisation to establish a foothold in the Soviet Union since Henry Ford's engineers masterminded the great white elephant of Gorki in 1931, and nurtured a generation of Russian motorists of Model-A derivatives.

Not that foreign assembly was a prerequisite for good sales. If Turin had learnt not to place undue reliance on the capricious North American market, they were trying hard in Canada with a new depot at Scarborough, Ontario. They were top of the league table in countries as diverse as Belgium and Uruguay, and the associated SEAT plant in Barcelona had long been Spain's number one manufacturer of private cars. In West Germany, Portugal and Switzerland they were never far behind the leaders, and even in places where currency restrictions bred frightful prices (at the official rate of exchange a Czech buyer had to pay £2,570 for a 500) sales were still encouraging. If British figures for 1971 were somewhat artificial—inflated by the prolonged and bitter Ford strike, and then affected by labour unrest in Turin—a sale of 13,009 cars between January and May was still impressive.

How have FIAT arrived at this commanding position? When the first Tipo-A chugged through the streets of Turin at a sedate 20 m.p.h., Italy was not regarded as a serious industrial nation. Her train service was a standing joke, and a shrugged *domani* was the order of the day. Even as a nation she was young. Yet today FIAT probably ranks fifth among the motor manufacturers of the world, behind America's Big Three and Volkswagen— though Toyota of Japan is beginning to challenge the Torinese giant.

Until the late 1950s, the rise of FIAT was steady rather than spectacular. FIAT might be world-ranking in the 1930s, on the strength of a long and distinguished record and a vast range of industrial interests, but their 1935 total of 32,000-odd units compared unfavourably with Morris's 96,000 and Chevrolet's 775,950. Even Vauxhall, only just getting into their stride as a division of General Motors, delivered 26,240 private cars, despite a range that offered nothing smaller than an undis- tinguished 1,500 c.c. 'six'. Where FIAT scored was in their widespread chain of sales outlets, probably unsurpassed by any maker outside the U.S.A. As yet the Nazi-inspired German export drive was barely gathering momentum, and British cars were seldom seen outside red-coloured areas of the map. But the simple 'Balilla' 4 *porte* 4 *marce* was (and still is) en- countered throughout Europe, as well as in South America, Asia and Australasia. At various times it was built under licence in France, Germany, Czechoslovakia and Poland. The 1930s might be an uneasy era, but well over 30 per cent of Italian car output went abroad, and a good 90 per cent of this hailed from FIAT's Lingotto plant.

What is the secret of FIAT success, apart from sheer size? First of all, of course, there is the financial strength that spells independence. Of the big British names of the 1930s, Austin and Morris have succumbed to mergers and the Rootes Group to American ownership. In Germany Auto Union's chequered career has ended in fusion with N.S.U., and in France only Peugeot has remained independent: Renault was nationalised in 1945, and Citroën is now partly owned by FIAT, whose car-making interests embrace Lancia, Ferrari, and (indirectly) Maserati at home, not to mention the role of fairy godmother to the Soviet and Polish private-car industries. For every take-over in the complex history of Europe's car-makers, there has been talk of at least 20 others. General Motors investigated Austin and Morris before plumping for Vauxhall in 1925, and about the same time their name was linked with Mathis of France, whom Ford eventually absorbed. Ford tried to buy Isotta Fraschini in 1930. But nobody has sought to acquire FIAT. The empire founded by Giovanni Agnelli in 1899 remains inviolate.

FIAT has always been a family firm. Agnelli, a Piedmontese and a former cavalry officer, founded the Fabbrica Italiana Automobili Torino on 1 July 1899, and he and his descendants have directed the company's destinies ever since, surviving the 'work-in' of 1920, the German occupation of Northern Italy in 1943, and the political and economic chaos that followed the fall of the Axis Powers. This record is equalled only by Peugeot of France: and though FIAT is much younger (Jean-Pierre Peugeot was cold-rolling steel in 1810) it is also far bigger. It is also fair to say that Italy's twentieth-century history has been even less stable than France's, while south of the Alps regionalism counts for more. A citizen of Turin will not readily admit to being Italian: he is Piedmontese, and one ignores this statement of 'nationality' at one's peril. FIAT's reluctance to commit themselves as whole-heartedly in the south as have Alfa-Romeo may well have its roots in this deep regional feeling.

A family tradition can breed a destructive paternalism, but to dismiss the three Agnellis—Giovanni, Edoardo, and Gianni—as mere paternalists is to introduce a totally erroneous conception. Too many writers have tended to stress FIAT's role as that of a relentless octopus, sucking manufacturer after manufacturer into its insatiable maw. It is certainly true to say that there are now only two independent producers of any size in the Italian Republic: Alfa-Romeo, who have been state-owned since 1933, and Innocenti, whose products are British in all but name.

Since FIAT purchased Lancia in 1969, the group enjoys a monopoly of domestic heavy truck production. Though Ansaldo, Ceirano and Isotta Fraschini went to their graves as independents, their departures were all accelerated by their inability to compete with FIAT in a narrow market, and by capital reserves insufficient for the rainy days of the inter-War years and Mussolini's imperialist sprees.

Giovanni Agnelli, however, was no monopolist. Rich he certainly was, while he combined in equal proportions business and engineering ability. He was also an intellectual socialist and a disciple of the legendary Don Bosco. If his contributions to charity received less publicity than those of his British contemporary, Lord Nuffield, he was a pioneer of industrial welfare, and FIAT's formidable present-day social programmes (which in 1972 alone were scheduled to embrace the construction of 25,000 homes for workers in and around Turin) date from 1920, when the company opened its first holiday camp for children. The Common Market is generally regarded as a post-1945 phenomenon, but Agnelli was already propounding his views on a federal Europe in 1916. Nor did his lifelong love affair with the automobile blind him to the prime duty of an employer: to provide work. When FIAT bought a company, they were not seeking monopoly: their objective was to safeguard jobs, and when Abarth was threatened with liquidation in the autumn of 1971 only an injection of funds from the colossus kept things going. Once again one can see in FIAT's cautious southern policy a fear of the widespread unemployment that would follow the sort of gaffe that can happen, when a labour force, unaccustomed to specialist engineering, is suddenly harnessed to such a project.

Politically, the Agnellis seem to have been a power behind the throne. Since 1945, it has been fashionable to claim an 'anti-Fascist' record in the 1930s, but there can be little doubt about FIAT's performance—or lack of it. How else to explain a company which could disseminate *Topolino* and *Millecento* throughout the world in 1938, and yet consistently fall behind with war production from 1940 onwards? FIAT made a first-class job of

'Italianising' the inverted-vee Daimler-Benz aero-engine, but there were never enough of these to go round, while Lingotto and Mirafiori were the first Italian factories to come out on strike (in the early spring of 1945) against German occupation. In the last year of War the Axis lost 35 million man-hours at the hands of Italy's biggest industrial enterprise.

The Agnelli viewpoint also manifested itself in one of the characteristics that distinguishes FIAT from all its competitors—diversification. If FIAT spells private cars to the vast majority, the firm's current slogan—*terra, mare, cielo* (land, sea and air)—is the strict truth. Their range of commercial vehicles extends from the diminutive Bianchina van up to vast 100-tonners, while other land-based products include fork-lift trucks, earth-moving machinery, and agricultural tractors. Other FIAT divisions produce all forms of railway rolling-stock, aircraft, aero engines, and vast marine diesel units with outputs of up to 42,000 b.h.p. The firm has a stake in such ultra-modern industries as electronics and nuclear energy. Their Building and Plant Division is involved in civil engineering projects as far afield as Colombia, where FIAT engineers were erecting a hydro-electric power station in 1972. FIAT make their own steel, machine tools, and lubricating oils, as well as running insurance and hire-purchase companies, and controlling more than one 'bus network. *La Stampa*, Turin's principal newspaper, is owned by I.F.I., FIAT's principal shareholder, and at times the complex has made bicycles, refrigerators, and even complete merchant ships.

What is more, these outside activities are neither also-rans nor attempts at monopoly. They stemmed from Giovanni Agnelli's determination to save his company during the world-wide slump of 1907. While Isotta Fraschini sought refuge in an alliance with Lorraine-Dietrich of France, FIAT branched out into marine engines, aero-motors, and later aircraft. Agricultural tractors followed in 1919. As for the firm's achievements outside the realm of the private car, what of the four-square *Tipo* 15TER army lorries which underscore Ernest Hemingway's *A Farewell To Arms*, the early submarines

powered by FIAT diesel engines, and the FIAT-engined M.V.
Vulcania, pride of the Italian merchant fleet in the 1930s?
A FIAT-powered Macchi MC72 floatplane did 441 m.p.h. in
1934, and this speed has never been bettered by a piston-
engined marine aircraft. So far from creating new 'corners'
in Italian industry, FIAT has even loosened its hold on outside
activities: the firm's nuclear interests are undertaken as a
partner in the SORIN consortium, and during the 1969–71
period they have altered the status of the railway, *grandi motori*
and aircraft divisions from *sezioni* to jointly-owned companies
in which FIAT has a 50-per-cent interest. Thus FIAT's *sezione
aeronautica* is now part of Aeritalia, not that this will prevent
aircraft enthusiasts from calling the end-product anything but a
FIAT.

As to the cars, these are both national and international.
Since 1919 FIAT have been general providers of automobiles to
Italy, and until the booming 'sixties a middle-class Italian in
quest of four-wheeled transport had a simple choice—FIAT
or abstinence. The most important consequence, as everyone
knows, has been the creation of the most imaginative custom-
coachwork industry of all time. But it must not be forgotten
that while Italians have long had to be content with what FIAT
gave them, they have seldom had much cause for complaint.
There have been the mistakes: the 509 of 1925 was liable to
rev its guts out, the 1.4-litre 514 of 1929 was the wrong car at
the wrong time, the post-war 1400 was impossibly overgeared,
and only a hurried up-rating saved 1957's 'Nuova 500' from a
slow handclap. It is characteristic of FIAT that they rose to the
challenge, and turned this potential lemon into a best-seller
which, at the ripe old age of 16, is still being turned out at a
rate of 1,500 a day.

The role of national provider might have tempted FIAT into
painful orthodoxy—those dreadful 'average saloons' which are
the fleet-operator's dream and the technical journalist's nightmare. Not that there was much incentive to pander specifically
to Italian tastes when ninety per cent of raw materials had to be
imported, foreign exchange was short, and private cars were

beyond the means of even the professional classes. Today there is one car to every $5\frac{1}{2}$ Italians and the ubiquitous 500 has decimated the ranks of the scooters, but in 1938, when one in every twenty Britons had a car, the corresponding ratio in Italy was one in 112. FIATs may be unmistakably Italian—a recent critic has slated the 127's driving position as 'designed for the standard Italian Ape'—and even after owning four of the breed I still find it hard to reconcile myself to a dipped beam with a cut-off so sharp as to be uncomfortable. Raucous exhaust notes characterise the smaller species, but no FIAT has been as insular as some British bread-and-butter models; and here I am not thinking of the home-market-only types that proliferated in the 1930s. More interesting still, no FIAT has felt like a committee design, a label all too easily attached to models from other world-ranking factories. The chief designer's personality has always shone through, from the pioneering efforts of the ultra-conservative Faccioli to the era of Dante Giacosa. Pretty well every big name in the story of Italian motor engineering has worked for FIAT at one time or another: if Fornaca, Cavalli and Zerbi are indelibly associated with the Agnelli interests, Vittorio Jano will always be remembered for his Alfa-Romeos, Bertarione for his work at Sunbeam and Hotchkiss, and Fessia for his f.w.d. Lancias. Vincenzzo Lancia himself was for many years the pacemaker of the FIAT works team before he set up on his own, and Pininfarina got his first break as a stylist from FIAT's special-body division.

'Export or bust' has always been the Italian motor industry's slogan, hence the fact that FIAT were already promoting their product as 'The Car of International Reputation' in 1910. Kaiser Wilhelm II of Germany owned one, licence-production was already under way in Vienna, and in Poughkeepsie a group of American businessmen had started the manufacture of *Tipo* 4s for the local carriage trade. Ten years later FIAT ushered in the age of mass-production with the indestructible 501: in its fifth year this doughty machine helped the company sell 8,000 cars abroad in a season when total output was under 14,000.

Post-war prosperity has seen a return to the role of general provider in any market where the European type of car is viable. To-day FIAT offers everything from minimal town transport (the 500) up to the 130, a luxurious executive sedan with automatic transmission. Sports cars, long a half-hearted if interesting sideline, are now a regular item in a programme which embraces high-performance 'personal' versions of the 124, 128 and 130, not to mention the ferocious 'Dino', almost a Ferrari. Until 1920, every vehicle was put together in the original works in the Corso Dante, but in 1972 home production alone was divided between three major plants in the Turin area (Mirafiori, Rivalta and Lingotto), one in Milan (Autobianchi), the Ferrari works at Maranello which takes care of 'Dinos', and a new branch in Naples which assembles some 500s as well as being responsible for light commercials and the 850T minibus. Sometimes strikes can force a big group to fall back on their overseas plants, but sheer pressure of demand has had the same effect on FIAT, and now not only the 850 *berlina* but also the aged 600D are the responsibility of SEAT in Barcelona. Even then there are not enough of these 'outmoded' models to satisfy every customer. Just about the only sector that FIAT does not cover (though America's Big Three, British Leyland, Mercedes-Benz, Nissan and Toyota do) is the head-of-State market typified by the 600 Mercedes-Benz and the 'Phantom VI' Rolls-Royce. One cannot blame them, for their last two contributions—the V-12 'SuperFIAT' of 1921 and the monstrous 530 straight-eight of 1930—both coincided with world-wide depressions, and were stillborn. In any case, in the computerised world of industrial Turin, no model that cannot be made at the rate of at leasty fifty a day is viable.

Perhaps the one thing that singles FIAT out from the rest is the incredible city of Turin. More than ten per cent of its 1,150,000 citizens are engaged directly in the motor industry: FIAT itself has a payroll of around 180,000 albeit not all of these work in Piedmont. Turin is often considered to be the 'company town' *par excellence*, if one excepts that Hitlerian creation called Wolfsburg. It may not be so wholly committed to the internal-combustion engine as Detroit or even Coventry: it furnishes ten per cent of Italy's paper, and rates as the nation's printing capital, as well as being prominent in such diverse products as textiles, tanning, office machinery, cosmetics and vermouth. Nevertheless it is dominated by FIAT.

The dominance is an unobtrusive one. Admittedly the kilometre 'stones' on the *autostrada* which links the city with Milan proclaim the magic initials with monotonous regularity, if one arrives by rail one rides in a FIAT-built carriage behind a FIAT-built locomotive, and a goodly proportion of the hangars at Caselle International Airport are occupied by FIAT's flight-test department, while the firm's showrooms occupy an important site in the Via Roma, Turin's Regent Street. It is fatal to try and enumerate the FIAT establishments in Turin and its environs without the aid of a computer. FIAT-owned companies produce paint and plastics, FIAT have a seven-per-cent interest in the Olivetti typewriter empire at nearby Ivrea, and outside the realm of cars there are vast operations like the *sezione* S.P.A. (trucks) at Stura and its next-door neighbour, the *sezione ricambi* (spare parts) which calmly processes 600 tons of bits and pieces a day, undaunted by a regular stock-list embracing 110,000 items.

As for the welfare schemes, these are limitless. The old Corso Dante works now house a Technical Training School, there are FIAT housing schemes, a FIAT health service with 21 centres in Turin alone, 27 social service centres, and a sports club with facilities for tennis, basketball, bowls, soccer, athletics, and swimming. Nor are the old forgotten, for the firm's Long Service Scheme rewards veteran employees after 25 years' service, and a man who retires at the 30-year mark is assured of a monthly pension of 58,000 lire. If he dies, his widow receives 48,500 lire. There are creches for the children of workers who would otherwise be left unattended, and FIAT send 14,000 of their *bimbi* to holiday camps every summer.

Even the historian, that tedious annotator of other men's flowers, is treated with a sympathy and efficiency that belies the proverbial dourness of the Piedmontese. At the *Centro Storico*, in the Via Chiabrera, just round the corner from the original Corso Dante block, is a factory museum where complete cars range from an 1899 3½ h.p. to a 2300S coupé of the 1960s. Faultless scale models cover every aspect of the company's wares, from marine engines to nuclear power plants. The *Centro* is also a mine of information. A seeker after truth may well be disconcerted by catalogues and instruction manuals for every sub-type of the 501 in six languages, but he is likely to feel much humbler when he poses a knotty question on exports to Australia or the impossible ramifications of the Ceirano dynasty. A shrug and a '*non lo so*' would be permissible: instead, the bewildered researcher is bombarded with photostats giving chapter and verse, and within minutes, too. If he is prepared to wait another half-hour, he will probably get them in his own language.

This is no 'company' book. It is one Englishman's attempt to appraise the career of a *marque* more consistently international than any of the five thousand odd that have jockeyed for the favour of the world's automobile-lovers. It spans seventy years of experiment and consolidation, and the story ranges from the dusty circuits of the early 1900s to the traffic jams of the 1970s, from the muddy farm-lands of the Po Valley to the embattled skies of the Western Desert.

Inevitably corners must be cut, and racing enthusiasts may be disappointed if this aspect of the FIAT saga does not bulk large enough. FIAT, they will argue were a major force on the circuits for a quarter of a century, and their departure was much mourned when Giovanni Agnelli closed the competition department for good in 1927. Among FIAT's contribution to the *grandes épreuves* were four-wheel brakes in 1914, the *pointe Bordino* in 1917, and the supercharger in 1923. Though Agnelli's decision of 1927 has never officially been rescinded (one must not allude to to-day's 124 rally cars as 'works FIATs'), the influence has continued, and the 508CMM of 1938 shares with Hans-George Röhr's front-wheel drive Adlers the distinction of pioneering the closed sports-racer.

I must also apologise for using English measurements and Italian type designations throughout the book. This may be irritating for our American friends, but cars are known internationally by their type-numbers, and if one plunges into English notation one is confronted with some dreadful problems. Early 525s were sold in London as 20–70 h.p. models—so were 1932–33 522S sports cars!

Perspective, however, must be kept, and the story of FIAT is the story of modern Italy, from the *Risorgimento* of Garibaldi and Cavour to the modern nation architected out of chaos by Alcide de Gasperi and his successors. Who has not heard the old cliché?: 'The French Government owns Renault, and nobody knows who owns Volkswagen, but FIAT owns Italy'. The latter part is untrue: in fact an unpleasant fate awaits the journalist who whispers such heresies within earshot of Mirafiori. But can one be surprised at such talk, when one reflects that currently FIAT command 21 per cent of all private-car sales in Common Market countries, and 16.5 per cent of combined Common Market and E.F.T.A. sales? One in every seven Portuguese, and one in every ten Dutchmen who buy a new car opt for a FIAT. In spite of this, I prefer my own definition of the breed, which reflects that 'extreme particularity' once ascribed to Texas by John Gunther. Whenever I return to the wheel of a FIAT after a spell with other *marques*, I spend the first quarter of an hour wondering why anyone buys one. The next half-hour leaves me wondering why I have strayed from the fold for so long, while within a couple of hours with the car I am puzzled why everyone doesn't go out and shop in Turin.

This book is an attempt to explain the why and the wherefore.

1 Ceiranos and Others

Solidity, elegance, lightness, no worries, no noise,
minimum consumption, prices which fear no competition,
normal and de luxe bodywork, a vehicle for outings, for
racing, and for the mountain

FIAT advertisement, 1900

On 1 July 1899, a group of well-to-do young Piedmontese
gathered round a table in Turin's Palazzo Bricherasio. Their
host, Emanuele Cacherano di Bricherasio, wore a white
dressing-gown with white lapels and cuffs, and among his companions were Giovanni Agnelli, a 33-year-old cavalry officer
turned amateur engineer: Cesare Goria-Gatti, a distinguished
criminal lawyer whose cycling exploits had earned him the
nickname of 'The Black Cat': and Roberto Biscaretti di Ruffia,
father of the founder of the city's *Museo dell'Automobile*. They
were bound by more than one interest: most of them were keen
horsemen, but they were also intellectual socialists of a type un-
common in upper-class Italian circles. It was said of Bricherasio
that he kept 'an annotated copy of the Credo of Karl Marx'
open on his desk.

They had not, however, assembled in order to change the
world, though the ultimate consequence of their deliberations
was to have a far greater effect on their country than any left-
wing congress, from the early days of Benito Mussolini to those
of Palmiro Togliatti. Their object was to draw up the articles of
a car-making venture. This, with portentous verbosity, they
proposed to christen *La Società Italiana per la Costruzione e il*
Comercio dello Automobili Torino. Fortunately this answer to the
initial-monger's prayer was nipped in the bud by Biscaretti,

whose suggestion of *Fabbrica Italiana Automobili Torino*, or
FIAT for short, was adopted, over the protests of the free-
thinking Bricherasio. He considered that it was 'altogether too
biblical', but FIAT it was, and FIAT it has remained ever since,
albeit the periods were scrapped at the end of 1906. Even when
the company opened an aircraft department in 1915, some
front-office humorist quietly translated the scriptural Latin
into Italian as '*sia*' (let it be). It was lucky for all concerned that
these initials also stood for Societa Italiana Aeronautica!

Not that this meeting attracted any more attention than the
one five years later that was to introduce Charles Stewart Rolls
to Frederick Henry Royce. Italy was not 'car country' and to
the mainstream enthusiasts of France, Germany and Britain
Agnelli's activities in Turin were as remote as Marc Birkigt's
prentice efforts in Barcelona. 'No details are available', ran a
British report, 'as to the type of car to be turned out or as to the
motive power'. Young bloods drove Panhards of the sort that
were establishing Fernand Charron as the Tazio Nuvolari of his
day: sedater folk were content with the leisured 12 m.p.h.
afforded by Karl Benz's 'Velo'. Nobody expected much from
Italy. The Government knew precious little of motor-cars, and
cared little for what it saw. While the first FIATs were being
assembled in their new factory, a Royal Commission 'for the
regulation of automobiles' was propounding the kind of suggestions one might expect of a panel composed entirely of railway
engineers. The monarch was, as yet, equally unenthusiastic, dis-
missing the new locomotion as 'hideous, dangerous, and
abominations altogether.'

In any case the future 'nation of enthusiasts' was barely a
nation in 1899. Italy as an entity was a mere thirty-eight years
old, and it was only in 1870 that the capture of Rome put paid to
the Papacy as a temporal power. In a mountainous and infertile
country sorely lacking in minerals, unity alone could not spell
prosperity, while the upper-class Liberals who governed Italy
until the advent of Fascism in 1922 had little contact with either
the populace or their problems. This state of affairs was felt
especially in the South, which had no primary schools as late as

1870; thirty years later nearly 79 per cent of the population of Calabria was illiterate, by contrast with a national average of 48.5 per cent. The last quarter of the old century saw three major insurrections in Sicily. The reforming zeal of the socialists was impeded by the attitude of the Church towards 'politics', which it reinforced by an encyclical issued in 1895. To make matters worse, the powers that be in Rome insisted on playing first-division diplomacy, and while Italy's alliance with Germany and Austria, signed in 1882, helped her trade, the same could not be said of her expansionist adventures in Africa. Britain, France, Germany, Belgium and Portugal filled their exchequers at the native's expense; Italy was saddled with a diet of rocks and desert, not to mention the humiliating defeat that ended her first attempt to annex Ethiopia. No wonder Adolf Hitler felt disinclined to back Mussolini's Abyssinian campaign in 1935.

The Italian social structure, with a great gulf fixed between rich and poor, did not make for a healthy economy, while Italy's prospects in the realm of heavy industry were equally discouraging. Coal, iron and lead were all mined near Turin in the early nineteenth century, but though these helped to make the city a manufacturing centre, supplies were limited. At the height of the Fascist era in 1937 the country had to import 99 per cent of its mineral oil, 95 per cent of its coal, and 80 per cent of its iron and steel. *Ergo*, industrialisation had to be financed by an energetic export policy.

The growth of modern Turin can be traced from the installation of gas lighting in 1837, when engineering works started to supplement the existing textile industry. The unification of Italy in 1861 accelerated the process, but a survey made four years later shows that the State was still the principal local employer. The Royal Arsenal, the Valdocco arms factory, and the railway workshops all had payrolls of over three hundred, but while private enterprise was moving in (Ansaldo had been founded in 1852) the biggest independent concerns were small affairs with 120–130 hands apiece.

The landed aristocracy were slower to accept the motor car

than their British counterparts. Undoubtedly the mountainous nature of the terrain contributed to this slow start, but the roads were notoriously bad, and contemporary travellers such as Konody could find little good to say of them. As late as 1908 the Italian commercial-vehicle market was regarded as sterile, most of FIAT's 'heavies' going abroad. There was no national automobile club before 1905, a state of affairs which accentuated the traditional rivalry between Milan and Turin. Inevitably this bickering added to the general acrimony that surrounded the Gorden Bennett Cup, and matters might have come to blows had any Italian factory essayed a racing car of international calibre before 1904. In 1900 France boasted 1,200 agents, 1,400 repairers and 7,000 licenced drivers; but a year later the entire Italian industry delivered a mere 300 cars. Petrol supplies were a continuing headache, and regional clubs planned to organise dumps at twenty-mile intervals on some of the more important roads. The only portent of things to come had been in May, 1895, when a race was staged between Turin and Asti. Italians claim that this was the first real motor-race in the world—Paris-Rouen was, after all, strictly a 'trial'. Be that as it may, it attracted five starters, one of which (a Savigliano steamer) was actually of Italian manufacture. A second contest (Arona-Stresa) followed in 1897, this being won by Cobianchi's Panhard from a de Dion tricycle ridden by Ricordi.

By this time, however, the nucleus of a motoring movement had emerged, in the form of a band of enthusiasts based in Turin. Their stamping ground was Signora Burello's café, once a haunt of horse-copers. Prominent among them was Giovanni Agnelli. Born a Piedmontese at Villar Perosa in 1866, of landowning stock, he passed from a 'classical education' to the Pinerolo Cavalry School, whence he was commissioned into the Savoia Regiment in 1886. His army career lasted only six years, during which he made the acquaintance of a kindred spirit, Giulio Gropello. As a consequence some odd experiments were conducted in the military workshops. Initially Agnelli expended much thought on that time-honoured chimera, the perpetual motion machine, but he soon fell under the spell of Enrico Bernardi, one of the pioneers of the internal-combustion engine. A former professor of physics at Vicenza, Bernardi patented his first motor in 1882, and by 1889 he had produced a small four-stroke horizontal unit. 1894 saw a primitive motorcycle, and two years later he was responsible for the first all-Italian petrol car, a three-wheeler with single, chain-driven rear wheel, built at Padua by Miari e Giusti.

Not that Agnelli was as yet interested in locomotion: he was thinking in terms of stationary engines for agricultural use. Nor did he aspire to design from scratch; instead he acquired the best that was possible on a subaltern's pay, an old Daimler engine that had come from Germany in a consignment of scrap iron. This he harnessed to a dynamo to provide electric light in his workshop, but the illuminations were short-lived. The improvised coupling snapped, and broke the shoulder of Scotto, the *tenente's* faithful batman. This disaster marked the end of Agnelli's experiments for the time being.

Along with aristocratic socialists of the stamp of Bricherasio and Goria-Gatti there was Biscaretti, described as a 'jack of all trades', and already the owner of two motor-tricycles and a Benz. There was Michele Lanza, chandler and compulsive experimenter, still too empirical in his outlook to countenance what he termed 'the industrialisation of the motor-car'. There was Gustave Deslex, Swiss-born banker who was later to help finance FIAT, and Giovanni Battista Ceirano, eldest son of a watchmaker from Cuneo who was the unwitting godfather of Italy's motor industry.

Old Ceirano seems to have stayed faithful to horology: not so his offspring. With a thoughtlessness that has been cursed by motoring historians ever since, he christened his two elder sons (born in 1860 and 1865) Giovanni. Both of them, as well as their younger brother Matteo, were duly involved in the manufacture of cars, but it was Giovanni Battista whose prentice efforts had aroused the interest and support of Goria-Gatti, and with the lawyer's assistance he raised 6,000 lire to open a cycle factory in October, 1898. He also planned to build light cars to the designs of Aristide Faccioli. Ceirano, as a Rudge agent, had been cashing in on the British cycle boom: this may explain why he chose the name of 'Welleyes' for his wares, even though its pronunciation was beyond the average Italian. Giovanni Battista's new works also boasted one of Turin's first telephones. To complete the circle there was another cycle agent, Luigi Storero, later to join the FIAT racing team, and to be closely connected with the company for many years.

From the beginning Agnelli was the driving force. As Biscaretti's son Carlo later wrote:

> We were all young and enthusiastic, and obsessed by the motor-car. Instinctively we felt that Giovanni Agnelli was our leader. He made us turn up to all his discussions, in which he gave a clear indication of the future he envisaged, and of his great ability.

He had no patience with Lanza's tinkerings. 'Thank God', he informed that wayward genius, 'you make candles in your factory. You'd go bankrupt if you manufactured only motor-cars.' Hence the chandler was by-passed, and vanished from the scene about 1902, though Agnelli would probably have bid for his patents had the opposition (which already existed) beaten him to Ceirano's door. On the practical side the young Italian, like Edge, Jarrott and Rolls in England, flirted with the motor-tricycle; its simplicity and excellent power-to-weight ratio appealed to him, and he took his own de Dion to pieces to discover what made it tick. He accompanied Storero on a purchasing trip to Paris, where he made the acquaintance of Giuseppe Prunello, an expatriate Piedmontese who was already building tricycles under the gallicised name of Prunel. These Prunels sold in fair numbers in Turin under yet another name, Phoenix, but their maker's car business prospered little better than Lanza's. Prunels were still on the market as late as 1907, and some quite hefty four-cylinder machinery was offered, but to the end they remained scissors-and-paste jobs, relying heavily on those Parisian general providers, MM. Lacoste and Battmann.

In any case it is unlikely that Agnelli's independent Piedmontese spirit would have acquiesced in a policy of importation, even if the raw materials came from a compatriot. Ceirano was the best bet, and by the summer of 1899 a deal had been arranged whereby the new FIAT concern acquired the Ceirano patents and the services of Aristide Faccioli as their chief engineer. They also inherited the Welleyes prototype, which had been built for Ceirano by the Martina company. Ceirano himself was left with his factory and his bicycle business, and in due course he re-entered the fray as a car maker, producing a single-cylinder Ceirano *voiturette* which was at least eighty per cent Renault. As by this time Isotta Fraschini were assembling crypto-Renaults in Milan, the story becomes complicated.

Agnelli's first step was to scrap the Welleyes' belt drive. In his characteristically progressive way, he also tried to set up his new factory away from the centre of town, on the Stupinigi road. It seems probable that the Agrelli family owned some land in that quarter, since FIAT later operated an airfield on the site of what is now the vast Mirafiori plant opened in 1939. But the municipal authorities vetoed the idea, and a factory with an area of 12,000 square metres was erected in the Corso Danta, not far from the River Po. Here fifty workmen transferred from the Welleyes venture produced the *Tipo*-A, first car to bear the name of FIAT.

Though he did not realise it, Agnelli had also inherited two of his greatest racing drivers, architects of the *annus mirabilis* of 1907. He was at the same time training a man who was to rank second only to himself as a car maker in Turin. Vincenzo Lancia's was no rags-to-riches story; his father was a soup canner who had made his pile out of Crimean War contracts. Felice Nazzaro was the son of a local coal merchant. The young Lancia was nominally in charge of the Ceirano stores, but his flair for machinery was soon recognised, and he gravitated to the test shop, leaving Gallo, the book-keeper, to cope with all the clerical work. A love of music made him sensitive to 'sounds which jarred on his ears', which makes his reputation as a car-breaker all the more surprising. His passion for opera could triumph over a somewhat histrionic nature: Vincenzo

Lancia, who wept tears of frustration after his FIAT expired on the Auvergne Circuit in 1905, actually enjoyed being beaten at Brescia in 1900 by Franchetti's Panhard. His conqueror was an orchestra leader by profession; that was enough.

The less spectacular Nazzaro started as a general factotum, but was promoted to the rank of 'specialist mechanic'. In this capacity he also dealt with difficult customers and V.I.P.s, a position which led to a meeting with Vincenzo Florio. Both Lancia and Nazzaro were destined to become manufacturers in their own right, though the latter's venture never prospered, and he sold out in 1916 to return to FIAT. Neither lost their affection for their *alma mater:* Lancia actually drove for Agnelli after he started to make cars in competition with his former boss.

The first FIAT was an effective little car, though it scarcely lived up to the flowery phraseology of the infant press department. Outwardly it resembled a baby Benz. The 65 × 99 mm (697 c.c.) horizontal-twin engine had automatic inlet valves, and lived at the rear of a simple flitch-plate frame, with an untidy tubular cooler hung at the front. It rode on full-elliptic springs at the front, and on conventional semi-elliptics at the rear, and inevitably the practical Agnelli preferred trembler coils to the vagaries of burner ignition. The sliding-type gearbox had three forward ratios, selected by a central, floor-mounted lever; no reverse was provided, though it had become an optional extra by 1900. The clutch was a leather cone, and power was transmitted to the rear wheels by side chains. There were contracting band brakes on transmission and rear wheels. Already the company's claims were conservative; the car was sold as a 3½ h.p., but the actual output was 4.2 b.h.p., and the unit would run up to 1,000 r.p.m. Top speed was in the region of 22 m.p.h., while the 'minimum consumption' was no idle boast, contemporary reports speaking of a 35 m.p.g. thirst which matched that of early de Dions. All the mechanical elements were made in the factory: understandably, as Italy had no ancillary industries like France, and was never destined to father any kind of proprietary-engine business.

1. Count Roberto Biscaretti and his family take the air in a 3½ h.p. FIAT, 1899.

(FIAT)

2. Early racing days: Biscaretti's 12 h.p. in the *Giro d'Italia*, 1901. One wonders where they kept the (necessary) spare tyre.

(FIAT)

3. Towards a modern shape. The 1901 12 h.p. 'tonneau' (top) is pure Panhard, with tubular radiator, central raised panel on the bonnet and quadrant change.

(FIAT)

4. (centre) Of similar vintage is the 8 h.p. 'Duc', first of the front-engined types.

(FIAT)

5. By 1902 (bottom) the 12 h.p., though still with automatic inlet valves and reinforced wood frame, has acquired a 'modern' bonnet and honeycomb radiator.

(FIAT)

There were, however, no body shops in the Corso Dante, early coachwork in the *vis-à-vis* or *duc* styles being commissioned from Alessio or Locati *e* Torretta. FIAT's own coachwork division would not be opened for another ten years, and standard bodies in the American sense did not come until the advent of *Tipo* Zero in 1912. Later models sold had 5½ h.p. 837 c.c. engines, and eight of these primordial FIATs were built. Astonishingly, four of them have survived.

Inevitably, both car and company took some time to get off the ground, and FIAT lost more than 18,000 lire on their first year's trading, though two dozen vehicles were made between January and December, 1900. The deliberations of the Royal Commission in Rome can scarcely have helped, especially when they came up with a recommended speed limit of 6 kilometres an hour (3¾ m.p.h.) in towns, which made post-Emancipation Britain sound like a scorcher's utopia. The country limit of 20 k.p.h., however, approximated closely to prevailing British rules, but the motoring fraternity was not amused, and the fiery Countess Lina Sforza-Corsini reminded the authorities that the *minimum* speed of her 8 h.p. machine was well in excess of the statutory urban rate. It was to be some time before official Italy came to terms with the motorcar: as late as 1902 they could still infuriate the French by suddenly cancelling the Nice-Abbazia race, while one wonders what their reaction would have been had they known that within ten years Felice Nazzaro would be exercising 28 litres of racing FIAT on the streets of Turin!

For the first Turin Show of May, 1900 the FIAT was enlarged to 1,082 c.c. and eight nominal horse-power, and wheel steering made its appearance, replacing handlebars on the company's first racer. The 8 h.p. *corsa* was an ingenious experiment, being blessed with an infinitely variable belt drive not unlike that of to-day's D.A.F. Alas!, the simplicity and low weight of such an arrangement was paid for in terms of a lethargic performance on hills, and the *corsa* went the way of subsequent essays in gearlessness by Winton and C.G.V.

Not, however, before it had won FIAT their first major success.

Though Goria-Gatti had finished second in the 400-kg category of Limone-Cuneo-Turin (1899) his mount had been a belt-driven Welleyes, and it was left to Lancia to trounce the Panhard opposition in Padua-Bassano-Vicenza-Padua. Nazzaro on another FIAT was third. To show that this was no fluke, the Italian cars repeated their success in Turin-Asti, Castore being the outright winner and Biscaretti taking the 'tourist' honours. Panhard, as we have seen, had their revenge when the musician Franchetti annexed Brescia-Cremona-Brescia, and the latter city's 75-kilometre *riunione* is chiefly memorable for the triumph of a young Milanese, Ettore Bugatti, who rode a Prinetti *e* Stucchi tricycle of his own design. In the four-wheeler category Agnelli himself had to give best to Ginori's Bolide.

It is almost certain that the founder had already set his sights on world markets, though scarcely any cars were exported before 1902. Be that as it may, he was determined that the FIATS he was making should be equal to Italian roads. Cooling difficulties rather than lack of creative ability would lead him to adopt the Mercédès honeycomb radiator, and already Faccioli's obstinate conservatism was infuriating him, as Herbert Austin was to exasperate the Wolseley directors a few years later. FIATS might be able to beat Panhards on occasion, but Panhards were the coming thing, and Agnelli instructed his chief engineer that future cars must have front-mounted vertical engines. Faccioli was also required to brush up his knowledge of the latest foreign models.

He acceded to the first request, coming up in 1901 with a new 8 h.p., still of 1,082 c.c. The central chain drive apart, it closely resembled a small Panhard, and the gear lever was mounted in a right-hand quadrant. Fifty-six were produced alongside the last of the old type, and it survived into the Enrico era, ultimately benefiting from his progressive influence to the tune of a Mercédès-type radiator.

On foreign designs, however, Faccioli was adamant, and in April, 1901 he was eased out of FIAT. Giovanni Enrico reigned in his stead. To the end of his days Faccioli never forgave

Agnelli, for whom his hatred was almost obsessional, and unlike Austin he never prospered. He worked his way round the various ventures of the Ceirano clan, making engines for Giovanni Battista and then being associated with Matteo in the Itala and S.P.A. ventures. Latterly he designed a series of unsuccessful S.P.A. aero-engines.

Agnelli had no occasion to regret the change. With Enrico came the four-cylinder engine, the Mercédès idiom, and the first taste of international acclaim. 73 cars were sold in 1901, 107 in 1902, and 134 in 1903, which time FIAT was the leading Italian maker, even though at peak their output did not exceed 30 per cent of the national total. By the end of 1902, carriage folk in the U.S.A. and Portugal had seen their first FIATs and a year later there were customers in Britain, France and Germany as well. Piedmontese industry was acquiring champions of the stamp of C. V. Tangeman, Emile Mathis and D'Arcy Baker. No matter what happened on the circuits, FIAT would soon be mentioned in the same breath as Panhard, Berliet, Rochet-Schneider, de Dietrich, Mercédès and Napier.

2 Expansion and Enrico

When you drive a FIAT *you Find It All There, and use your hands for steering only. There are no levers and handles of any description, either on the dashboard or steering pillar of this famous Italian car. Every function of the motor is controlled absolutely by pressure on the small foot pedal.*

FIAT advertisement, *Motor Age*, April 1904

If the dismissal of Aristide Faccioli marked a turning-point in the story of FIAT, it was followed by a period of consolidation which lasted until 1906.

During those five seasons FIAT graduated from local obscurity to the big league, along with Daimler and Napier in Britain, Mercédès and the rejuvenated Benz in Germany, and the *grandes marques* of France: Panhard, Mors, Lorraine-Dietrich, Hotchkiss, Berliet, Rochet-Schneider and Delaunay-Belleville. In 1906 *The Automotor Journal* rated FIAT as Italy's no. 1 manufacturer; though their production estimate of 1,800 cars per annum erred on the side of optimism, the company was to make over 1,000 that season, whereas their closest rivals, Isotta Fraschini, had a capacity of a paltry 300. Earlier in the year Giovanni Enrico had retired from the post of chief engineer after a reign which had seen the advent of a strong Mercédès influence, while as the big chain-driven cars approached their zenith the birth of a new generation was to be observed in Cesare Momo's FIAT-Brevetti, built in Ansaldi's Via Cuneo works. On the circuits, an uneasy dominance of Italian sprints gave way to a force to be reckoned with wherever the big red cars ventured. True, FIAT's solitary 1904 victory was an empty one, and the *marque* won not a single classic in 1905 or 1906, but they were always in the running, even if Nazzaro had yet to reach the peak of his form, and Lancia suffered from a built-in hoodoo. The power behind the Italian challenge was reflected in the A.C.I.'s continuing support for the dying Gordon Bennett Cup, this in spite of the fact that at a pinch Milan and Turin could field three works teams between them. As his empire grew, so Giovanni Agnelli's shrewdness became apparent. FIAT stood out from all their rivals, with the possible exception of the Daimler Motoren Gesellschaft, by virtue of the deliberate nature of their diversification. Admittedly motor-boat racing was a cheap way of testing next year's racing-car engines, and everyone tried their hand at the game, but where Panhard or Brasier confined their maritime interests to mere sport, depositing valuable chunks of machinery at the bottom of Monaco Harbour in the process, FIAT were busy on power units for the new-fangled and despised submarines, and even had a stake in a shipyard. Commercial vehicles were taken seriously, and at the 1906 Milan Exhibition the company displayed its first railcar.

Many a writer, past and present, has asserted that this was an imitative era for FIAT. *The Car Illustrated* called their 1905 models 'Italian editions of the Mercédès;' at Homburg in 1904 those commentators who waxed malicious over Emil Jellinek's attempts to underwrite the Gordon Bennett Cup with identical Mercédès from Untertürkheim and Wiener-Neustadt even hinted that the three FIATs were just another Teutonic insurance policy. Granted, the cars bore a close resemblance to their German counterparts, and certain FIAT features—notably the sight-feed lubricator with the oil floating on the surface of the cooling water—suggested that someone in Turin had his eye on infringement suits. But then car design was still largely imitative in 1904, and an analysis taken at that year's Paris Salon shows that the FIAT's main features (four-cylinder engine, mechanically-operated inlet valves, low-tension magneto ignition, honeycomb radiator, and pressed-steel frame) were favoured by the majority of exhibitors. From 1902 onwards Wilhelm Maybach's Mercédès became the exemplar, backed by Eliot

Zborowski's impressive showing in Paris-Vienna and Jenatzy's victory at Athy in 1903. Erstwhile copiers of the Panhard switched to gate change and T-head engines, hallmarks of Germany's leading car. Berliet, Rochet-Schneider, Martini and Star, all manufacturers of some standing, produced crypto-Mercédès, and so, for a while, did Peugeot. Their conversions were more immediate and wholesale than anything that happened in the Corso Dante. The definitive 35 h.p. Mercédès was in production by 1901, but FIAT did not offer a T-head engine until 1903, while quadrant change and armoured wood frames persisted for another season. Further, Enrico anticipated his German rivals with full overhead valves in his 1905 racers. If some FIATs used a crib of the Mercédès scroll clutch, Momo's excellent multi-plate affair, which had nothing in common with anything German, was on the market by the end of 1904. Mercédès were hardened advocates of side chains—shaft driven models did not reach the public until 1909. If FIAT did not share Itala's faith in bevels, their live-axle 'Brevetti' appeared in 1906. Much has been made of the evidence of British tourists who had their Mercédès serviced in the Corso Dante, but this is no more than a tribute to good practical engineers.

In any case, Agnelli's attitude approximated to Henry Royce's, in that he was not unwilling to copy an idea if it helped him achieve his objective. Faccioli's Sinatrian insistence on 'doing it my way' had terminated his career at FIAT, but his successor, Enrico, proved much more receptive. In some ways his early career paralleled that of the Swiss Birkigt, though the Italian had run his own steam-engine works until forced out of business by lack of funds. Thereafter he had made his name as a civil engineer, as well as installing electric light at the 1884 Turin Exhibition. In person he was neat and meticulous, with a waxed moustache and piercing eyes, while his capacity for lucid explanation and lightning pencilled diagrams was also reminiscent of Birkigt. Like Agnelli, he owed his internal-combustion background to the clan Bernardi, in this case the professor's son Lauro. Further, he was an inventor in his own right, who devised a constant-mesh gearbox, a method of gear-changing by oil pressure which eliminated the conventional clutch, and a form of servo brake which was tested on a couple of FIAT lorries and a special racing car commissioned by Vincenzo Florio.

Enrico's career was of course furthered by the healthier climate of Italian motoring. The country was no richer, but it was far more receptive to the motor-car. The inefficiency of the railways had at last broken the King's resistance, and when he was marooned at Ostia 'Prince Colonna whisked him into the city at express speed, that is, in less than an hour when he had been accustomed to take three or four'. The process was completed when a motor-car enabled him to beat the stork to his Queen's second confinement, and by the autumn of 1901 he owned a stud of ten vehicles. As yet his taste ran to Panhards, but the frugal monarch can scarcely have appreciated being asked to pay duty on his car when he inadvertently crossed the French frontier at Ventimiglia. Thereafter, like the Kaiser, he divided his favours evenly between the major Italian manufacturers. A far keener motorist was the Queen Mother Mergherita, whose stable of elegant Italas chauffeured by the great Alessandro Cagno became an institution. She was, however, also one of Agnelli's clients, buying a Lanza-bodied 24 h.p. waggonnette in 1903, and a landaulette of similar horse-power in 1906.

This royal patronage was reflected in a more liberal attitude to the automobile, and by 1904 the out-of-town speed limit had gone for good, though drivers were still restricted to 9 m.p.h. in towns. (Italians already drove on the right-hand side; the industry was, however, slower to adopt l.h.d. than either France or Germany). Agnelli himself demonstrated one of his new four-cylinder cars by covering 1,382 miles at a running average of 24 m.p.h., while the famous Abruzzi-Coltelletti match of 1901, usually regarded as the beginning of Italy's racing and *granturismo* traditions, was another moral victory for FIAT.

Racing sold cars, and exports rose. A mere twenty were sent abroad in 1901, but this had risen to 52 by 1903, and to 257 in 1905, after Lancia and Nazzaro had scared the living daylights out of the French *grandes voitures* at Clermont-Ferrand.

Imports also rose, from 199 cars in 1900 to 688 in 1905, though this was the inevitable consequence of a manufacturing policy geared to a small aristocratic home market and a 'snob' export business, which favoured large, powerful and expensive vehicles. Already FIAT's runs were quite big—557 of the 7.4-litre 24–40 h.p. model were made in 1906 alone—but everything was on a bespoke basis, and purchasers of some types had a choice of four wheelbase lengths. Hence anything small and cheap had to be imported, because domestic production did not pay: when the A.L.F.A. firm attempted to support itself on the assembly of Alexandre Darracq's 'singles' and 'twins', these proved unequal to the hilly Italian roads, thus occasioning a *volte face* which brought Giuseppe Merosi into the story, and founded the Alfa Romeo line. As late as 1914, Fornaca of FIAT was unwilling to chance his arm at anything smaller than the 1.8-litre Zero.

But the company prospered. Though Italy lagged far behind France—where car production had passed the 8,000 mark in 1902—FIAT's original factory had tripled in size by 1904, and a year later the directors declared a dividend of 20 per cent. What is more, Agnelli could justly regard himself as the sponsor of a 'car of international reputation.'

Much of this success was owed to racing. A 12 h.p. FIAT won Portugal's first motor race in 1902: within a few months the Queen Mother owned a *coupé de Ville* and her son's Ministry of War ordered five vehicles. To this day neither Ford nor the Japanese have been able to undermine the company's position in the Iberian Peninsula. When the FIATs showed a clean pair of wheels to the much-fancied Mercédès in the 1905 Gordon Bennett Cup, Germans started to shop in the Corso Dante; they still do. In Britain, where road-racing was strictly off limits, the irrepressible D'Arcy Baker expended many a column-inch on his favourite car's continental triumphs; in the golden year of 1907 his advertising gave hardly a clue to the sort of cars one could buy off the showroom floor. In the autumn of 1902 a FIAT made an undistinguished appearance in a reliability trial staged by the Automobile Club of America, but by the time Enrico retired in 1906 his creations were to be seen in unlikely places. Among the season's more off-beat performances were an outright win in the Swedish Winter Cup, and class victories in India's Bombay-Mahableshwar Trial and Portugal's Valada sprint.

Agnelli's foreign aides were an energetic crew. In those days Britain was the spiritual home of the high-powered publicist. This was the era of Napier's S. F. Edge, Martini's H. H. P. Deasy, White's Frederick Coleman, Rolls-Royce's Charlie Rolls, Oldsmobile's William Letts, and Crossley's Charles Jarrott, who also had a stake in Lorraine-Dietrich. If FIAT's man in London, D'Arcy Baker, was not in the Edge class, he was a ruthless promoter who took care that for every six inches of paid advertising in the weekly press, there were another three free inches in the correspondence columns. In the manner of his kind, he would happily contradict himself if it suited his book. After the Opening Meeting at Brooklands in 1907 (at which neither the great Louis Wagner nor the Japanese amateur Okura distinguished themselves for FIAT) a pontifical Mr Baker came out against track racing, 'as it cannot bring out the sterling qualities of a car in the same way as a race like the Kaiserpreis or the Grand Prix over a difficult course', but when Felice Nazzaro trounced Frank Newton's Napier in the celebrated match of 1908, 'Mr FIAT' led the jubilation. He even promoted a race for *Tipo* 1 FIAT taxicabs when these modish yellow-and-black vehicles began to grace London's streets, and he would surely have approved of the 'battle of the Mice' which enlivened Brooklands in April 1938. He launched a FIAT double-decker 'bus in 1906 by taking a party of selected journalists from London to Edinburgh at an average speed of 14.7 m.p.h. which was probably illegal.

Like Agnelli, Baker had been intended for an army career, and he served through the Boer War before resigning his commission in 1903. At this time he was already the owner of a Wolseley, but he preferred the FIAT belonging to a brother officer, Victor Miller. Before the year was out he and Miller had formed FIAT Motors Ltd. with a capital of £15,000, increased two years later to £60,000. Baker's friends have described him as a 'man about town' rather than a practical businessman, and he lived in considerable state at Hedsor, Bucks, where he kept a stud of racehorses as well as the largest and most expensive models FIAT could provide. He was also something of an autocrat: FIAT Motors was not, and never became a Turin-owned *filiale*, and Baker remained firmly at the helm until his death in 1932. The absence of documentation on FIAT of England during the Baker era suggests that he felt no obligation to explain his methods to his opposite numbers in Italy. Not that Agnelli had cause for complaint; Baker maintained a large and efficient repair depot at Willesden and an associated garage business in Brighton, he did a brisk trade in re-exports, English-bodied FIATs being despatched to customers in Portugal, Japan, and South America, while in 1906 his second-in-command Victor Miller drove a new 24 h.p. chassis from Turin to Dieppe at a mean average speed of 31.95 m.p.h. Baker had his maharajahs, too. H.H. of Scindia took delivery of a 16–24 h.p. landaulette that August, and FIAT Motors let it be known that the car was to be used by the Prince and Princess of Wales on their forthcoming tour of India. The Maharajah was luckier than Lord Willoughby de Eresby, who received a 40 h.p. as a wedding present, only to lose it in a 'coach-house fire' at Lincoln a few weeks later.

More spectacular was Baker's counterpart across the North Sea in Germany, the Alsatian Emile Mathis. This son of a Strasbourg hotelier combined an intense Gallicism with the ability to turn his enforced German nationality to good account, and in the early 'teens he commanded Germany's largest car-sales organisation. These operations continued after he set up as a serious manufacturer in 1911, and Mathis subsequently became Deputy Chairman of DAHV, the German motor trade association. His tastes were catholic—Panhard, Mors, Lorraine-Dietrich, Rochet-Schneider, Minerva, the Sizaire-Naudin *voiturette* and the obscure Rebour all passed through his hands as well as FIATs, and his territory embraced a goodly chunk of Austria. He was an active and successful driver who supported events in Germany, France and Switzerland, and managed to sell two FIATs to the All-Highest himself. One of these, a 1905 24–40 h.p., embarrassed the native manufacturers by wafting the Emperor from Hanover to Hamburg at an average speed of close on 60 m.p.h. English motoring magazines duly recorded this fact, but nearer home the Swiss *Automobile Revue* was more tactful, publishing a picture of '*l'automobile favorite de l'empéreur*' without identifying the make! A 50–60 h.p. six-cylinder delivered in 1907 was the only foreign model in the Imperial stable by 1909, unless the 'Mercédès Electric' also on the strength was in fact a product of Wiener-Neustadt.

Mathis and FIAT parted company in 1911. It is tempting to relate this severance to some of the Alsatian's peculiar business practices, such as selling thinly-disguised Stoewers with Mathis radiators and hub-caps at a considerable mark-up, and fabricating 'instant Knights' out of four-cylinder Minervas similarly camouflaged. When he sold his personal S61 FIAT in London, this also became a temporary Mathis, only to revert to its true identity at Brooklands Track a few years later. One wonders how such tactics were received in Turin, though curiously Agnelli and Mathis remained on excellent terms.

The American scene was a little quieter, if only because the imported-car market was strictly a snob affair, and was to become even more rarefied once European-type four-cylinder models became one of Detroit's regular lines. The man willing to expend $14,000 on a 60 h.p. FIAT had little interest in flashy salesmanship, albeit Hollander and Tangeman, the New York agents, tried to persuade clients that the magic initials stood for 'Find It All There'. 'As simple to operate as a stem winding watch: as comfortable as a parlor car', they proclaimed. But within its narrow limits, the market was a promising one. In 1903 the United States imported 267 cars, valued at over three-and-a-half million dollars, and while this was a drop in the ocean beside the 4,000 Oldsmobiles, 1,708 Fords and 1,698 Cadillacs delivered that year, it represented a staggering 18 per cent of native production's total value. In 1906 imports were up to 1,433 cars worth nearly $6,000,000 and FIAT enjoyed a respectable share of the pickings. In the ten Eastern Seaboard states alone they registered 35 new cars, as against 116 Panhards, 114 Mercédès, 51 Renaults and 40 Darracqs—and this when their cheapest model retailed at $7,000, or close on ten times the list price of a single-cylinder Cadillac roadster.

Nobody, however, had contemplated distribution on such a scale when Enrico's first model—the 12 h.p. *corsa*—appeared in 1901. This was much more Panhard than Mercédès, with a tubular frontal radiator inherited from the last Faccioli cars, automatic inlet valves, and a flitch-plate frame. The four pair-cast cylinders had a bore and stroke of 100 × 120 mm (3,770 c.c.), ignition was by low-tension magneto, and there was a reversion to the side-chain drive of the original rear-engined types. The new car was first seen in the 1,000-mile *Giro d'Italia* a month after Faccioli's departure, so one wonders if Enrico had been keeping it up his sleeve for some time.

The *Giro*'s entry list reads like a *Who's Who* of contemporary Italian motoring, with Giulio Fraschini at the wheel of one of his Isotta Fraschinis (*alias* Renault) and Marchand, Bernardi, Lanza and FIAT upholding national prestige against the usual bevy of Panhards, Mors, Renaults, Peugeots and Delahayes. Bricherasio and Goria-Gatti drove the old 'twins', the 'four' making its début in Biscaretti's hands. FIAT's own racing history tersely summarises the *marque*'s performance in two words, '*tutte arrivate*', and that is all the cars achieved, though twenty-eight of the 55 starters could not claim even that distinction. At Padua, however, the 12 h.p. recorded 45 m.p.h. in a ten-mile event, Nazzaro won the Piumbino-Grosseto contest, and in the Saluzzo Trials Storero was the victor, finishing ahead of Cagno on an 8 h.p. FIAT. The Padua meeting also incorporated the Coppa Italia, the world's second closed-circuit race, but this proved a Panhard benefit, and there was nothing on the Corso Dante's sideboard this time. The crunch came in the Sassi-Superga hill-climb, held on FIAT's back doorstep, and still a favourite haunt of works testers. The gradient proved far too much for the *dodici cavalli*'s plumbing, and Enrico found himself confronted with a sizzling *padrone* as well as a sizzling radiator. He refused to take fright, and rolled a cigarette while he waited for the storm. 'If you can design cars as fast as you can roll fags', Agnelli commented after a pause, 'you have a future with us'.

The immediate future called for the adoption of the Mercédès honeycomb radiator, which Agnelli had recognised as the most efficient system on the market. It was to be standard equipment on all FIATs from 1902 onward, though in its original trapezoidal form it resembled a Panhard or Gladiator rather than a Mercédès. Enrico had wasted no time, for photographs of the Duke of Abruzzi's big 7.4-litre 'match' car, which was on the road in November, show that it has the new type of cooler.

The celebrated match took place on 24 November, and was FIAT's first serious try at international competition, since it pitted Enrico's latest creation against the fastest touring car Panhard could make. The Cavaliere Coltelletti's machine had belonged to the great René de Knyff, and was known to be capable of 50 m.p.h. The wager was one of 5,000 lire, and the two cars would race each other from Turin to Bologna, a distance of 190-odd miles. Agnelli and Lancia were to accompany the Duke in his new 28 h.p. car.

The FIAT took the lead and held it for the first thirty miles before the Duke clouted a kerb in Alessandria. All seemed set for a Panhard walkover, but the wily Agnelli had another shot in his locker—Felice Nazzaro, who was following in a standard 12 h.p. model, and set up a faster average than the formidable Panhard. The Duke paid up, but honour was satisfied.

One may suspect that this FIAT would have confronted the French had the Nice-Abbazia Race been held in the early spring of 1902, but what *The Motor Car Journal* called 'a wanton piece of irritation on the part of the Italian authorities' led to a last-minute cancellation. The national calendar was likewise curtailed, and Italy was left with a handful of sprints and hill-climbs. Within these narrow confines, FIAT reigned supreme. At Superga Lancia made no mistakes, defeating Biglia on the first Mercédès to be sold in Italy, while Storero's 12 h.p. collected the light-car honours. At Padua there were

class wins again for the same two drivers, though overall
f.t.d. went to Vincenzo Florio's Panhard, driven for him by
FIAT's 'V.I.P. expert', Nazzaro. (It was said that the Sicilian
magnate was piqued at having to wait too long for the latest
FIAT!) There were two more class victories at the Conegliano
meeting for cars running on the fashionable alcohol fuel and
the season was rounded out by a win for the Duke of Porto,
King Manoel's brother, in Portugal's first race, from Figueras
to Lisbon. Contemporary reports are confusing, for the car is
credited with a 24 h.p. and even a 28 h.p. engine, but it was in
fact a standard 12 h.p. tonneau of the type that Italians could
buy for 13,500 lire. If this first foreign victory resulted from
the disqualification of Tavares de Melo's faster Darracq, it
marked the competition début of another great name in FIAT
history, Pietro Bordino, who shared the wheel of the car with
the exuberant Don Afonso. This latter was nicknamed *arreda*
('Press On') because of his lead-footed driving technique and his
penchant for yelling at carters and pedestrians who blocked his
path!

The press paid little heed to Don Afonso, concentrating their
interest on the Susa-Moncenisio hill-climb, a 23-kilometre
ascent involving gradients of up to 1-in-6. Here the FIATS
were matched against the big French cars on level terms.
Lancia's 24 h.p. model made f.t.d., and set up a new record of
30 min. 10 sec., though Gaul had her revenge when a Rochet-
Schneider beat the Italian cars in the touring category.

The 1902 FIAT range embraced the existing 8 h.p. and 12 h.p.
types with Megevet-made radiators in the Mercédès idiom,
plus a new four-speed 24 h.p. four-cylinder of 120 × 160 mm
(7,238 c.c.) though this was scarcely a production model, only
three being made. For competition work Enrico devised something far more advanced, a *corsa* version with oversquare
6.4-litre unit developing a respectable 40 b.h.p. at 1,200 r.p.m.
The mechanically-operated side valves in a T-head anticipated
1903 practice.

Only four-cylinder cars were offered in 1903, the 16–20 h.p.
having 'square' dimensions of 110 × 110 mm (4,181 c.c.) and

the 24–32 h.p. being slightly oversquare at 130 × 120 mm (6,902 c.c.). They wore radiators in the true Mercédès idiom. Leather cone clutches soon gave way to the Mercédès scroll type, but gate change and pressed steel frames were not standardised until 1904. Already Agnelli had come to terms with the Daimler management at Stuttgart, after some 'lively discussions', and a licence agreement, exclusive to FIAT, was duly signed. Until the outbreak of World War I royalties were paid to the German concern.

The new T-head FIATs were brisk performers; a 16 h.p. tonneau weighing 17½ cwt turned in 40.72 m.p.h. at Bexhill in 1903 faster than any of the comparable tourers in its price class with the exception of the Panhard-based M.M.C. With modern fuels 50 m.p.h. would be within range. The car's showing in the second Thousand Miles' Trial of 1903 was generally good, hills of the calibre of Westerham and Bury presenting no problems. At the Southport Speed Trials in October, Nesbitt and Miller fielded a brace of 24 h.p. models, the former defeating Charles Jarrott's similarly-rated de Dietrich, a fast car with a known 60 m.p.h. on tap.

Italian motor sport was even more restricted in 1903, but FIAT were setting their sights higher. They let it be known that they were behind Italy's challenge for the 1904 Gordon Bennett Cup and there was talk of a private *eliminatoire* in which three 65 h.p. light racers were tried against some 'heavies' rated at 105 h.p. Needless to say no further details were forthcoming, but the *tipo leggero da corsa* was in existence in 1903, though it was not to be seen in public for some considerable time. It was the first FIAT to have a pressed steel chassis, and also the first to use Momo's multi-plate clutch. Cylinder dimensions were 150 × 150 mm for a capacity of 10.6 litres, and output was 61 b.h.p.—not really enough for the Gordon Bennett.

Curiously, FIAT chose to run in the *voiture legère* class of the 1903 Paris–Madrid Race, no doubt because the competition was less fierce. The cars driven by Lancia and Storero in the *marque's* first major international event were developments of the 1902 24 *corsa*, retaining armoured wood chassis. For all the carnage of the 'Race to Death', the FIATs had no crashes or even phenomenal avoidances: Lancia retired, and Storero arrived at Bordeaux, lying seventeenth in his class. His average speed was 31.8 m.p.h., a miserable showing beside Louis Renault's 62.3 m.p.h. on his new 6.3-litre single-camshaft car. Cagno took one of these 'light' FIATs to Belgium for the Circuit des Ardennes, and fared somewhat better, taking third place in his category at 44.3 m.p.h., not far behind Baras's victorious Darracq. Possibly the FIAT's gearing was happier on the hilly Belgian course, but this time there were no Renaults, *le patron* having abdicated from racing as a mark of respect for his brother Marcel, killed at Couhé-Vérac in the holocaust of Paris–Madrid.

For 1904 the touring models received another face-lift. Along with the flitch-plate frames, the quadrant change and the sub-frame for the engine were scrapped, and instead there was three-point suspension for the gearbox. Outputs were increased, and the 24 h.p. was enlarged to 6.9 litres. *The Car Illustrated*, Britain's upper-crust motoring weekly, opined that 'they took a very high place among modern automobiles', and a 16–20 h.p. cost $6,700 in America with '*Roi des Belges*, Leopold or Princess Letizia body', though weather protection could add as much as 300 dollars to the price. At the top of the range was Turin's answer to the Mercédès Sixty, a 10.6-litre four-cylinder monster with detuned *tipo leggero di corsa* engine and Mercédès scroll clutch, available in three wheelbase lengths. This very large vehicle would top the 60 mark, and just under 200 were made in three seasons, most of these going to Hollander and Tangeman in New York. 1905 models had undersquare engines, and at the same time the Momo clutch was standardised on the '16–20' and '24–32'. Frames were narrowed at the front to give the taxi-like lock that became almost a FIAT tradition, and the bigger cars had water-cooled transmission brakes. London prices ranged from £735 for a complete 16–20 h.p. up to £1,440 for a '60' chassis.

Enrico elected to field his 'heavies' for the 1904 Gordon Bennett Cup, and the FIATs driven by Lancia, Cagno and Storero were real monsters, their brutal lines emphasised by the black paint (Red was still reserved for the United States). Rumour hinted at overhead inlet valves *à la* Mercédès, but rumour was wrong, these being the last T-head racing cars from the Corso Dante. if one excepts the stripped tourers used in the first Targa Florio in 1906. Cylinder dimensions were 'square' at 165×165 mm (14,112 c.c.), and like their lighter sisters the Homburg cars had multi-disc clutches. Pre-race reports spoke of 75 b.h.p., though paddock gossip inflated this to a three-figure output which would have made the FIATs a match for the fancied Brasiers and Mercédès. The official betting odds were, however, more realistic at 10–1 against, even the British Napiers and Wolseleys being considered a better proposition at 6–1. The bookies were well-informed, for at Homburg the cars were delivering an unsatisfactory 65 b.h.p. In spite of this handicap Cagno had worked up to fourth place on his second round, and might have finished higher than tenth, but for a burst tyre on the final circuit. Storero retired, and Lancia, who was never in the running, took eighth place at 43.5 m.p.h., way behind Théry's winning Richard-Brasier. In September the *tipi leggeri* were given an outing in the Coppa Florio (presumably because the 14-litre cars were in America) and on the fast Brescia course Lancia won impressively at 72 m.p.h., after Cagno had given up. The moral victor was, however, Teste on the immense 15.4-litre Panhard, whose official average of 71.7 m.p.h. covered a penalty incurred for refuelling in a control.

FIAT's hill-climb showing was exemplary, Lancia beating his old record at Sassi-Superga, and making f.t.d. at Susa-Moncenisio, though once again the Panhard outstripped him at Consuma. It ran conveniently in a different category, giving the FIAT a class win. The *marque* was a match for anything in the touring classes and in India Gropelli's 16 h.p. competed in the Delhi-Bombay Trials, collecting an award for 'absence of noise, absence of vibration, and ease of manipulation'. The 'fours' of the period, indeed, were cars of some refinement, for the 24–40 h.p. owned by the Beale family in America is remembered as 'a quiet, smooth-running automobile', even

if the dusty roads of Pennsylvania discouraged bursts of speed,
and third gear was used more frequently than top.

1904 also saw the first race for the Vanderbilt Cup on Long
Island, and this event soon became a fitting tailpiece to the
European season, used by the less successful Continental
équipes to salve prestige and boost American sales. Hollander
and Tangeman persuaded FIAT to ship a couple of the 14-litre
racers to New York. Clutch trouble, alas! eliminated both
Sartori and Wallace, though the former was in fact disqualified
when he essayed a flying start to circumvent these disorders.
FIATS also ran at Readville, Boston, New York's Empire City
track, and the Eagle Rock hill-climb. At Readville Fogolin's
mount was a stripped '60', while in New York Sartori won a
ten-mile race at 169.37 kilometres an hour, or well over the
'ton'. This was never claimed as a world's record, but it certainly suggests that the Gordon Bennett cars had at long last
found their form. Eagle Rock was, however, claimed as a
1–2–3 victory, but published results told a different story, all
the Italian cars being at least two seconds slower than Bernin
on Gould Brokaw's Vanderbilt Cup Renault. The American
importers also campaigned racing boats during the year, scoring a second place at Manhasset, and beating both W. K.
Vanderbilt's *Hard Boiled Egg* and the Lozier *Shooting Star*
on the Hudson River. Lancia was reported to have entered a
FIAT boat for the proposed Atlantic Race, but fortunately this
suicidal event was cancelled.

The new 16.3-litre overhead-valve FIATS duly appeared in
1905, and this time the advertised one hundred brake horses
were a conservative estimate, actual output being closer to
110 b.h.p. This would give the cars a theoretical edge over all
their Gordon Bennett rivals save Duray's immense de Dietrich
and the tyre-hungry Mercédès *équipe*. The prediction was ful-
filled: only the German cars outran the FIATS over the measured
kilometre near the start-line, and the de Dietrich showed its
form when Duray tried to recover from a disastrous third
lap. This year the Italian cars were entrusted to Cagno, Nazzaro
and Lancia, who set the pace from the beginning, completing,

his first lap in record time a good six minutes ahead of 'Chronometer' Théry on the Brasier. Behind 1904's winner came, not a French car, nor even a Mercédès, but the other two FIATS. The French winced: they continued to wince throughout a second lap on which Théry managed to narrow the gap a little: but nemesis lay in wait for Lancia, and on the third circuit his FIAT expired. 'Overcome by the bitterness of defeat,' said *The Autocar*, 'the burly Italian buried his face in his hands and wept like a child'. Some people said he had overdriven his car and burnt a valve; the official version said that a stone had gone through the radiator; but that shrewd observer W. F. Bradley opined that the FIAT had made violent contact with an eagle on the circuit.

But there was still Nazzaro, and though he was unable to catch Théry, he was none the less a very good second, with Cagno two minutes behind in third place. France had won again: but it was Italy's day, and back at the factory King Victor Emmanuel and Queen Elena shook hands with the three drivers.

The same team turned out for the Coppa Florio, reinforced by a brace of '100 h.p.' cars (actually 1904 Gordon Bennett machines) for Gandini and Weillschot. The pace was hot, and three FIATs were out by the end of the second lap, but Lancia came in third at 62.7 m.p.h., behind Raggio on one of Matteo Ceirano's Italas and Duray's de Dietrich.

For the Vanderbilt Cup Hollander and Tangeman went to town, bringing over two o.h.v. cars for Lancia and Sartori, these being supported by the Swiss driver Louis Chevrolet and Emanuele Cedrino on 1904 *tipi leggeri*, though in the event Chevrolet drove a privately-owned FIAT belonging to a Major Miller who was leaving on a tour of Europe.

As at Clermont–Ferrand, Lancia set a cracking pace, with three very fast laps in less than 24 minutes apiece, or an average the right side of 70. He then eased off a little, but he was still leading when he pulled out of the pits on his eighth circuit and rammed Walter Christie on one of his front-wheel-drive confections. The unlucky Italian managed to nurse his car to the finish, but his average of 56.5 m.p.h. was a humiliation. Worse still, his was the only FIAT to complete the course. Chevrolet had an argument with a telegraph pole, and Sartori retired on the ninth lap without making much impression. Otherwise the American season was not without its splendours, for in May Chevrolet had covered a flying mile in 52.8 seconds, beating a previous record set at Los Angeles in the winter of 1904 by Barney Oldfield. At the Daytona Speed Week a 50-mile handicap fell to Sartori, and there were other wins at Pittsburgh, Cape May, Hartford, Elkwood Park, and in a New York town by the name of Poughkeepsie which was to be closely associated with FIAT in subsequent years.

Hill-climbs were still a rewarding field. There were the usual class victories at Susa-Moncenisio, while touring-car awards at Château-Thierry and Gaillon indicated that French amateurs were becoming FIAT-minded. At Mont Ventoux, where a sticking valve had prevented Lancia from showing his best form in 1904, Cagno rocketed up in 19 min. 18.5 sec., beating the previous year's winner, Henri Rougier on a Turcat-Méry. Mathis did not deign to support Germany's Herkomer Trophy Trials, an absence remarked upon by *The Car Illustrated*, though he turned up in person for the Bleichröder sprint which formed part of the official programme. The boats did well at Monaco, *Fiat X* winning the cruiser race at 20 m.p.h. and 'putting many of the racers to shame'. Nearer home, on Lake Garda, the FIATs had to give best to the French Delahayes, but *Fiat X* had another moment of glory when she took the lead in the ambitious Algiers-Toulon Race. Alas! her crew deemed it advisable to abandon ship, but unlike many of her rivals the Torinese craft was salved, and turned up that December in D'Arcy Baker's Long Acre showrooms. FIAT, incidentally, would supply complete boats to customer's orders, the hulls being built by such firms as their associate FIAT-Muggiano, or Gallinari of Leghorn.

There were few major changes in the 1906 programme, the three four-cylinder types being continued, though prices were lowered, a 60 h.p. chassis now retailing at £1,150. Americans paid a whopping $12,000 for the same thing, and connoisseurs of formal coachwork could specify a long-wheelbase, 11 ft 2 in version. Agnelli and his new chief engineer Fornaca had, however, two new models in the pipe-line though neither was to receive much publicity until 1907.

A six-cylinder FIAT was inevitable. Multi-cylinder engines were now in fashion, and not a few factories apparently forgot the original objectives of smoothness and flexibility in the cause of long and impressive bonnets. The 50–60 h.p. FIAT was universally disliked, albeit its following included Kaiser Wilhelm II and that great English enthusiast, Lionel de Rothschild. In an era when crankshaft whip was endemic to 'sixes', the FIAT was one of the worst offenders, the late Henry Knox recalling an elephantine and tooth-shaking 'period'. In layout it conformed to the Enrico or Mercédès idiom, with cylinders cast in pairs, low-tension magneto ignition, four forward speeds, chain drive, and twin water-cooled transmission brakes. Capacity was 11,044 c.c., making it the biggest road-going FIAT of all time, and 65 b.h.p. were developed at 1,100 r.p.m., though Horace Beale was told that the true output was in the region of 95 b.h.p. This brute came in two wheelbase lengths, the greater of which ran to 11 ft 7½ in. Some cars boasted an ingenious compressed-air starter, operated by a small compressor at the front of the engine, which pumped air at a pressure of 180 p.s.i. into a steel cylinder on the side of the frame. Pulling a lever on the dashboard released this supply of air into the cylinders. These devices were never wholly satis-factory, and FIAT, like Delaunay–Belleville, soon abandoned the idea. Horace Beale recalls it as an essential adjunct to the family '50–60', however, since there was no half-compression lever and no stand-by coil. This particular 'six' was immensely powerful, and for many years after its departure the family coach-house bore the scars of studded tyres that had dug into the floor when an over-exuberant chauffeur had let in the clutch with a bang! The engine was, understandably, rough, but this was blamed on 'uneven mixture distribution'; bal-anced cranks were scarcely comprehended in 1907. The ever-optimistic Baker claimed a 6–71 m.p.h. top-gear range, and conveyed a party of journalists down to Brighton on his demonstrator which, we are told, 'behaved in an exemplary manner throughout'. In 1908 the monster was joined by a small sister, the 35–45 h.p. *Tipo* 4 with 7.4-litre N.A.6 engine and high-tension ignition, but in three years six-cylinder production amounted to a mere 233 units, and all the *Tipo* 4s went to the U.S.A. or Australia. Thereafter FIAT steered clear of 'sixes' for many years—if one excepts the obscure and short-lived *Tipo* 7—and have never allowed them to obtrude overmuch into their range. Maybe they were too honest to match the bravado of S. F. Edge, who could (and did) make a virtue of denture-breaking vibration.

The T-headed 'sixes' were probably no worse than cars like the 50 h.p. Darracq and the 15–20 h.p. Lorraine-Dietrich, but the *'Brevetti'* of 1905–6 was a clear indication of future policy. By this time, of course, the luxury image bulked so large that FIAT decided to introduce their new small model *via* the back door, much as S. F. Edge disguised his 1908 four-cylinder competition Napiers as Huttons. The designer was Cesare Momo, and though in due course the company alluded to the new Via Cuneo works as 'extensions', the first 'Brevettis' were neither true FIATs nor financed in their entirety by Agnelli. They were FIAT–Ansaldis built by Michele Ansaldi, a prosperous manufacturer of ordnance and machine tools. His holding in the new company was 55 per cent, and he did not relinquish his interest until the spring of 1906, when he joined forces with Matteo Ceirano to found S.P.A. As we shall see, this latest Ceirano creation fell to FIAT in 1926, while in later years the Via Cuneo plant served as FIAT's *grandi motori* division until this branch of the organisation was transferred to Trieste in 1971.

The first Ansaldi-built 'Brevettis' were little more than scaled-down editions of the regular product, with 3,053 c.c. four-cylinder T-head engines, mounted in a short wheelbase recommended for hire-car or hotel 'bus use. They also shared the side-chain drive of their step-sisters, though bevel drive was

adopted at the beginning of 1906, when the 'Brevetti' acquired
a three-speed box as well. It had a long run, surviving until
1912 with relatively few changes. Latterly it was called the
15–25 h.p., or *Tipo* 2, designations which invite confusion with
the L-head monobloc *Tipo Due* used by the Allied Forces in
World War I. This, however, did not appear in its definitive
form until 1911. The 'Brevetti' was never specifically offered as
a taxicab, but it often served as such, and helped to forge the
close link that has existed ever since between FIAT and Italian
cab operators, who have received early examples of many a
model, and have suggested not a few improvements. Surprisingly FIAT themselves have never entered the taxi business,
though some concessionaires (including D'Arcy Baker) explored this field. Its shaft drive and modest proportions apart,
the 'Brevetti' was the first FIAT to be marketed in Italy as a
complete car rather than as a chassis.

1906's competition season got off to a good start with Salmson's win in the Swedish Winter Cup rally staged between
Gothenburg and Stockholm. By contrast, the Daytona Speed
Meeting was a Darracq benefit despite Victor Hémery's
histrionics, though Lancia recorded four wins and Cedrino
one, the big FIATs proving more than a match for a later adver-
sary, the six-cylinder L48 Napier driven on this occasion by
W. T. Clifford-Earp. C. V. Tangeman took a leaf out of Emile
Mathis's book by personally conducting a 16–20 h.p. tourer
in the A.C.A.'s Efficiency Trial, and at home the newspaper
Corriere della Sera fell into fashion with British and German
practice by staging a touring-car event, the Coppa d'Oro. The
course was 2,485 miles long, and was run over eight stages,
starting and finishing in Milan, and taking in Verona, Padua,
Bologna, Rome, Naples, Florence, Genoa and Turin. The
entire Italian industry turned out in force, plus Mercédès
and Benz from Germany, Martini from Switzerland, Peugeot,
Ariès and de Dion from France, plus a curious assortment of
'Italian' makes which were in fact foreigners assembled or made
under licence in Italy. The De Luca, Diatto, Fides, Florentia,
San Giorgio and Wolsit were known in their respective

home lands as the Daimler, Clément, Brasier, Rochet–Schneider, Napier and Wolseley. There were also some Darracqs put together in Naples, which were not, as yet A.L.F.A.s. Of this motley crew, the Napiers driven by Macdonald and Glentworth were certainly built in Acton rather than Genoa, and one may doubt whether the Milanese Legnano concern was responsible for many parts of their Wolsit.

Nor was there anything touring about the *Coppa d'Oro* save the cars. It soon resolved itself into a sort of Edwardian Mille Miglia. One may take the parallel a step further, for like the post-war classic on the majority of occasions, it was a triumph for the home team, led by Lancia on a 24–40 h.p. FIAT, who received £1,000 for his pains. Macdonald's Napier in fact proved slightly faster, but on formula Maggioni took second place for Züst, Cagno's Itala was third, and the FIATs of Nazzaro and Boschis were fourth and fifth. The best Isotta Fraschini was Fraschini's, in eighth position behind the two Napiers. In the Herkomer Trophy Mathis won a gold medal on a '28–40' (presumably an advance 1907 model) and Otto Fritsch made f.t.d. in the Güber–Krosse sprint despite a broken piston.

The first big race of the year was staged in Cuba, whither Lancia and Cedrino went for a 217-mile affair at Havana, graced by the presence of President Palma, and guarded by his army. But once again Lancia's luck was out; on the Atlantic crossing he slipped and cut his hand, and in the event his mechanic was thrown out of the car, breaking a leg. A crash also eliminated Cedrino. That year's Targa Florio rules specified standard touring chassis retailing for less than 20,000 lire, so FIAT sent only Lancia, who put up his usual spirited performance before a leaking tank slowed him: he finally went out with a cracked cylinder, leaving Cagno to win for Itala. The positions of Italy's two great names were, however, reversed in the first Grand Prix, held at Le Mans on the 26th and 27th of June. Gone were the Gordon Bennett's tiresome 'national' rules, and works teams of FIATs and Italas fought it out against the full might of France (Brasier, Clément-Bayard,

Darracq, Gobron-Brillié, Grégoire, Hotchkiss, Lorraine-Dietrich, Panhard and Renault) and the inevitable Mercédès from Germany. The British and Americans stayed away. FIAT were using their 1905 o.h.v. cars, and the Italian challenge got away to a poor start when both Nazzaro and Weillschot stalled on the line, forcing their mechanics to scramble for it—outside assistance was forbidden. Lancia made his usual meteoric getaway, but more remarkable was the showing of the relatively inexperienced Weillschot, who had taken fifth place by lap 3, circulating at 62 m p.h., and all but keeping pace with such experts as Szisz and Baras. By the sixth lap the strain was telling, and he ran out of road at Vibraye. Lancia also found life hard, vainly attempting to secure a substitute for the second day's sport; hence his appearance on the morning of the 27th in an ordinary suit. His fifth place was only fair, but it at least broke a long run of ill-luck. Renault's quick-detachable rims gave Szisz such an advantage that not even Nazzaro could catch him, but the Italian fought a protracted duel with young Albert Clément on the Clément–Bayard to take second place. The Italas failed to distinguish themselves, none of the cars surviving into the second day.

The same cars and drivers turned out for the Vanderbilt Cup, though Weillschot, as a director of Hollander and Tangeman, was the official entrant. The race will always be remembered for its complete lack of spectator-control; though Weillschot's excursion into the crowd had no ill-effects save to his FIAT, Shepard's Hotchkiss killed a bystander, and Tracy injured another with his Locomobile. Nazzaro was unplaced, but for once Lancia had a trouble-free drive and actually crossed the line first, though the winner on time proved to be Wagner's Darracq. Wagner was soon to be recruited into the FIAT *équipe*. Unlike FIAT or Lorraine–Dietrich, Darracq was not a 'happy ship', as *le patron* blamed every misfortune on pilot-error, and during 1906 and 1907 relations between management and drivers were strained to the limit. Wagner's change of allegiance was accompanied by plenty of mud-slinging. Alexandre Darracq let go with both barrels, accusing

FIAT of 'seducing one of our principal drivers'. Agnelli retorted by reminding Darracq that Wagner himself had made the first approach, though he cannot have disbelieved all the French industrialist's allegations, since he told his new driver that 'we have no use for car breakers here.' However, he paid twice as well as Darracq, and went on paying Wagner's retainer during World War I, even after he had driven for Mercédès at Lyons in 1914.

So 1906 passed. Shaft-driven 'Brevettis' appeared at the international shows, and the ailing Enrico stepped down in favour of Guido Fornaca, moving to a less strenuous job with Fides. Italian factories were working round the clock, and Italian cars bulked large wherever the *grandes voitures* raced. In two seasons alone FIAT had scored two seconds, three thirds and a fourth, and their annual output had reached the four-figure mark. Nobody could have anticipated the Agadir Crisis, or the effect it would have on the over-extended and under-capitalised empires of Milan and Turin. Nobody, that is, except perhaps Giovanni Agnelli.

Italy was still stony soil for commercial-vehicle sales: her early 'post coaches' were imported from Germany or Belgium, but when Agnelli decided to explore the lorry market he was not content to do so with slightly beefed-up private-car chassis, or to fill his truck catalogues with superannuated tourers such as the old rear-engined Peugeots, which soldiered on in van form until 1904. His first lorry was a forward-control four-cylinder four-tonner with iron tyres introduced in 1903, in which year the Italian Post Office bought their first FIATs. They had a fleet of vans in service by 1905. In 1906 the company offered a double-decker 'bus using the 24–40 h.p. car engine and solid rubber tyres, as well as a smaller 16 h.p. normal-control model, and a car-based shooting-brake with felt-lined gun-cases and a 'fortified' chassis. Those who imagine that lorry-racing is strictly a Russian sport will be horrified to hear that the 1906 Blackpool Speed Trials included a class for motor-'buses, in which one of D'Arcy Baker's FIATs did battle against a Ryknield, a Darracq–Serpollet steamer, and a Crossley–Leyland.

Nor was this the only exercise in diversification, for visitors to the 1903 Paris Salon—FIAT's second—had been confronted by a vast 240 × 270 mm four-cylinder engine with hot-spot and cartridge starter, destined for the Italian Navy's new submarines. In 1906 Fornaca designed a 300 h.p. stationary engine for industrial use.

When the periods vanished at the end of 1906, this was more than a trifling typographic gesture. FIAT now stood for FIAT—and nothing else.

3 Annus Mirabilis

When maximum bore rules, FIAT *and Nazzaro win, when cylinder capacity controls the constructor,* FIAT *and Nazzaro are again first: and when fuel consumption is the limiting condition, there again in the van is the Italian with his Italian car. Now this is not luck—luck does not hold in such infinite variety. It is sheer merit—merit in man and machine—which has got home. In all these three big events, the best car won, though how much its victory is ascribable to the gallant helmsman cannot be stated in percentage*

The Autocar, 1907

In the Italian motor industry, 1907 was a year of contrasts. On the circuits, every major European race save one fell to an Italian driver at the wheel of an Italian car. The unbeatable combination of FIAT and Nazzaro annexed the Targa Florio, the Kaiserpreis and the Grand Prix, the Coppa Florio went to Nando Minoia's Isotta Fraschini, and Cagno won the Coppa della Velocita for Itala. Only in the Ardennes did the rest of Europe have a look in, because no Italian cars started. In any case the 8-litre FIATs had already shown themselves superior to the victorious Minervas in the Kaiserpreis. Inevitably FIAT profited from this bonanza, 1,365 cars finding buyers in 1907 as against 1,087 in 1906, while early in the year D'Arcy Baker was able to tell the press that he had orders for 200 in Britain alone.

But while the red of Italy triumphed over the blue of France and Germany's white, the Agadir Crisis had sparked off a recession which all but undermined the tenuous roots of Europe's motor industry. Companies collapsed overnight. In France Decauville retreated into narrow-gauge locomotives, La Buire had to be reorganised, and Mors went into a decline from which they were rescued only by the dynamic André Citroën. Lesser concerns like Prosper-Lambert and Prunel disappeared altogether. What is more, the economic crisis struck at the source of Italian ascendancy—the Grand Prix itself.

It has been fashionable to ascribe the hiatus of 1909–11 in part to Gallic pique. True, Nazzaro's 1907 victory at Dieppe had been a humiliation, while 1908 saw an even less palatable state of affairs; six out of the first seven cars to cross the line were German, and no red-blooded Frenchman enjoys the strains of *Deutschland über Alles*. But it is equally true to say that in the arid climate of 1909 precious few factories could view with equanimity the construction of giant racers far removed in concept from any catalogued model: not since Jenatzy's victory at Athy in 1903 had a 'stock' machine won a *grande épreuve*. The decision not to hold a Grande Prix was as welcome in Unter-türkheim and Turin as it was in the boardrooms of Lunéville and Ivry-Port. Unquestionably the French exploited the situation by focusing interest on *voiturette* races; these sparked off a generation of high-efficiency four-cylinder machines which were to sound the death-knell of such brutish, chain-driven devices as the FIAT and the Mercédès. One cannot blame them for choosing a field which neither Germany nor Italy had seen fit to explore. Not even Agadir would kill the Italian addiction to the grandiose, and as late as 1914 designers like Fornaca of FIAT, Santoni of Bianchi, and Balloco of Itala considered two litres about the minimum for a touring car. But for the War, the 1,244 c.c. S-type Bianchi would have created far more of a sensation than it did.

The events of 1907 had more far-reaching effects in Italy than anywhere else. Halfbreeds of the stamp of the Fides and the San Giorgio went to the wall, and a project to make Serpollet steamers in Milan was stillborn. Florentia abandoned cars in favour of motor-boats, A.L.F.A.'s crypto-Darracqs were supplanted by all-Italian four-cylinder machines, and Isotta Fraschini involved themselves in a short-lived association with Lorraine-Dietrich in France, which at least gave them a breathing space. While French exports to Britain and Germany showed a sizable decline, their sales to Italy fell to a trickle.

The slump revealed something long suspected by foreign observers—that the Italian motor industry was a paper tiger. Theoretically, the structure was impressive. Turin was already the Coventry of Italy, claiming twenty manufacturers to Milan's fifteen, even if some of these were probably mere stock-promotion schemes. Also within the city's boundaries were five builders of motor boats, six coachbuilders, six garages, five tyre factories, four companies making lamps, three devoted to lubricating oils, two to chassis frames, one to wheels, and one to magnetos. FIAT alone employed some 3,000 hands, and about 124 million lire were tied up in sundry aspects of the automobile business.

The Autocar was disinclined to take this parade of statistics at its face value, commenting on 'the recklessness with which Italian concerns have been increasing their general expenses by building huge and palatial palaces in the guise of offices and showrooms, apparently with the idea of impressing the public with a sense of their prosperity'. The industry had little substance: not only did it have to import its special steels, it also differed from competitors in Britain, France and Germany in that it lacked the support of a network of component suppliers. Even small Italian factories made their own nuts and bolts. Managements were inefficient. Commented *The Autocar*: 'As the productive capacity of each man is very much smaller, it follows that the wage bill presents a much bigger item in the cost of manufacture'. The cars that left Milan and Turin were large, fast, expensive, and aimed at the export market, even if surviving statistics suggest that rather less than the publicised 80 per cent went abroad.

The first signs of trouble manifested themselves in March, when a series of strikes swept Turin. One cannot blame the workers, since hours were long, with a twelve-hour day and sometimes a seven-day week as well. Soon, however, alarming rumours were circulating. Lorraine-Dietrich, having digested Isotta Fraschini, were now said, erroneously, to have taken over FIAT's Milan depot. No wonder D'Arcy Baker's publicity machine was working overtime in London, promoting his new service station at Wembley, his fleet of smart yellow-and-black taxicabs, and the exploits of Nazzaro and 'Mephistopheles' at Brooklands. Fortunately all this paid dividends, and Mr Baker's list of illustrious clients now included the Duke of Rutland, Lord Ancaster, Miss Ellaline Terriss, and the Maharajah of Gwalior, who commissioned a monstrous State Coach on an elongated 20–25 h.p. chassis. This one had a wheelbase of 12 ft $9\frac{1}{2}$ in and measured eighteen feet from stem to stern.

Even if Baron de Turckheim's grasping hands were never close to FIAT, all was not well in the Corso Dante. In the growing prosperity of 1905 the company had declared a dividend of 20 per cent, but a year later a prevailing euphoria had persuaded them to raise this to an unrealistic 80 per cent. The value of shares shot up to a crazy level, and more finance had to be found. Several members of the board found it prudent to resign, and only Agnelli emerged with any credit from this unhappy adventure. Even without these manoeuvres, the price of supremacy was high, with three separate racing formulae in force in 1907.

Once again, Agnelli's foresight was paying off. Those who considered his earlier diversifications an extravagance now recognised the wisdom behind them.

Of the outside activities motor-boat racing was on the wane, and the abandonment of the Grand Prix was to deprive the sport of its principal *raison d'être*. 1907, however, had seen a second place for *Fiat XV* at Monaco, and as late as 1911 Andreas Castro won Argentina's Rosario-Buenos Aires-Rosario race on a Gallinari-built fifty-footer laid down at Leghorn in 1908. This one had a five-ton displacement and was powered by two 200 h.p. six-cylinder FIAT engines.

Now, however, FIAT's maritime interests took a more substantial guise. The company provided the petrol engines for the Swedish submarine *Hvalen* which distinguished herself by sailing the 4,000 miles from La Spezia to Stockholm under her own power. In the realm of *grandi motori* a six-cylinder four-stroke oil engine was tested in 1906, the first two-stroke appeared a couple of years later, and FIAT marine diesels were in full production by 1909. An 800 h.p. engine won a German naval competition, and by the outbreak of War marine motors had been sold to Britain, Denmark, Portugal and Brazil. From 1906 to 1919 FIAT had a financial interest in the San Giorgio shipyard and were directly concerned in the construction of complete merchant ships.

Aero-engines were added to the company's repertoire in 1908, the first of these being a small 3-litre air-cooled vee-eight on Wright lines which weighed a mere 177 lbs. and developed 50 b.h.p. at 2,000 r.p.m. This one was not made in series, and the new department's most significant pre-war products were the big water-cooled o.h.c. units intended for airship use. They were rather heavy, but were to distinguish themselves in two famous record cars, the S76 of 1910–11, and 'Mephistopheles' in his final, 1924 form.

FIAT continued to manufacture trucks, though domestic sales were negligible, a state of affairs brought about by the poor quality of Italian roads, and by the same concentration on 'fast pleasure cars' that had aggravated the crisis of 1907. That year Fornaca himself visited England to explore the situation, and as a consequence the North Eastern Railway build up a fleet of FIAT omnibuses between 1908 and 1910. A FIAT won the Danish Army's Commercial Vehicle Trials in 1908, but no further orders resulted, though in 1910 a three-tonner was working in Patagonia, and a fleet of 24 h.p. touring cars were running a stage service between the railhead and the famous Jenolan Caves in New South Wales. D'Arcy Baker sold four five-ton lorries to the Sudan Government, who planned to use them for the carriage of railway stores, but a mechanic sent out with the FIATs found no roads, 'excepting the tracks that have been made by natives, donkeys, etc. . . .'! Along with J. W. Stocks of de Dion-Bouton Baker picked up

6. (top) For motor-minded royalty: Queen Mother Margherita of Italy with her Sala-bodied 24-40 h.p. landaulette, 1906.

7. FIAT's biggest (centre). The chassis of the 11-litre six-cylinder '50-60', 1907.
(National Motor Museum)

8. (below) Winter laurels. Salmson's 24 h.p., winner of the Gothenburg–Stockholm Rally, 1907.

9. (top) Early racer: Vincenzo Lancia kicks up the dust with his *Tipo* Gordon Bennett on the way to victory in the *Settimano di Brescia*, August 1904.

(FIAT)

10. (centre) Cab-over-engine (literally). A 24–40 h.p. double-decker bus in south Wales, 1907.

11. Fiat Under the Sea. The FIAT-powered Italian submarine *Foca*, 1908.

(National Motor Museum)

some useful publicity when a battalion of the Guards was transported by road from London to Hastings in 1909. Three of the lorries used for carrying stores were FIATS, albeit anyone who read the small print would have been shocked to hear that one of these succumbed to steering disorders and another ran a big-end. Though Italian commercial-vehicle exports rose sharply between 1906 and 1909, FIAT's truck department was still operating on a modest scale. A mere 338 units were delivered in the company's first eight years of lorry manufacture.

The Italian Army's own motor vehicle competition of 1909 led to an early exercise in rationalisation, when a committee was set up under the chairmanship of General Morone to select a new medium-capacity truck for the fighting services. This committee placed an order for 450 chassis (*Tipo Consorzio*), production of which was shared out between FIAT, Isotta Fraschini, Itala, S.P.A., and Züst. The vehicles were duly handed over to the Army when Italy mobilised on 1 August, 1914, but there was some delay in putting them to work, since no bodies had been ordered—only bare chassis. Thereafter the members of this consortium went their several ways.

A less-well-known consequence of Agadir was the FIAT bicycle, offered in touring, racing, and military guises, and manufactured in the Villar Perosa works, though the machines were brought to Turin for assembly and completion. It survived for only four seasons (1909–12 inclusive), but production was on a fairly substantial scale: 25,000 were made in 1910 alone.

Not that any of these alarums and excursions were allowed to slow the rate of technical progress in the Corso Dante. 1908 saw the advent of a modern light car, *Tipo* 1, and the first overhead-camshaft FIAT was running in 1909, these being the work of Guido Fornaca, who had taken over from Enrico.

The thirty-six-year-old Piedmontese had trained as a railway engineer in Rumania before working on hydro-electric projects for the Savigliano concern. A lonely and austere bachelor, he was also an administrator of the first rank; one of his initial tasks at FIAT was to reorganise the drawing-office into individual groups, each responsible for a different part of the car. A more approachable personality was his assistant Carlo Cavalli, who had joined the firm as a draughtsman in 1905. Cavalli's first major solo effort was to be the legendary 501 of 1919, known to Italians as 'the lawyer's FIAT' by virtue of its creator's original calling. What everyone forgot was that Cavalli had been pitchforked into the profession by his parents, and had thankfully hung his wig up many years ago.

In 1907, of course, T-head engines and low-tension ignition still reigned supreme. At the bottom of the range was the 'Brevetti', which sold in England as the 14–16 h.p. on a 9 ft 4 in wheelbase, for £660. The 4½-litre '18–24' was a direct descendant of the old 16 h.p. of 1903, and was available with a choice of three wheelbase lengths—9 ft 3½ in, 10 ft 3¼ in, and 10 ft 11 in. A *roi des belges* retailed at £730, a FIAT compressed-air starter could be fitted for an extra £60, and the same model sold in New York for $7,500. The 7,340 c.c. '28–40' was called a '30–40' by Britons, who paid £890 for a complete car: an example used for long-distance trials with Kempshall tyres averaged 50 m.p.h. for 3,000 miles, presumably at Brooklands. For captains of industry there was the huge 50–60 h.p. six-cylinder at £1,370, £75 more than was asked for a similarly-bodied 60 h.p. Napier.

If such a range was typical of an upper-crust maker's offerings, it did not cater for the three racing formulae in force during the season. In fact, only the Targa Florio regulations were tailor-made for stripped tourers, stipulating as they did a minimum weight of 1,000 kilograms (19¼ cwt), and a cylinder bore of 120–130 mm in the case of four-cylinder engines. The A.C.F. were running their Grand Prix under a fuel-consumption formula, with no capacity limit, while the requisite 9.4 m.p.g. was considered too easy to constitute an effective restriction. M. Charles Faroux, in fact, openly preferred the German club's Kaiserpreis formula—a maximum capacity of eight litres and a minimum weight of 1,175 kilograms. In the circumstances it is scarcely surprising that only four makers tried their hands at all three events: FIAT, Lorraine-Dietrich, Darracq and Gobron-Brillié. Moreover, the Grand Prix Gobron was not a serious contender, Rigolly's car having been around since 1903. It had actually contested the 1904 French Gordon Bennett Eliminating Trials at Mazagran.

The FIAT entries for the Targa Florio were basically stock 28–40 h.p. models, though Fornaca had breathed on their engines to good effect, boosting power from an average 40 b.h.p. to a creditable 60. A top speed of around the 60 mark was, in any case, sufficient for the world's most tortuous circuit. The Targa was both Weillschot's swansong for FIAT and Wagner's last drive for Darracq, and the Italian makers turned out in force, the usual Italas and Isottas being supported by three Züsts (Maggioni, Conti, and Capuggi), three Rapids (the ubiquitous Giovanni Battista Ceirano, Cariolato, and Gallina), and three Juniors, sponsored by the other Giovanni Ceirano, and driven by Gremo, de Martino, and Tolotti. Buzio's Diatto-Clément was at least half-Italian, whereas the Daimlers of Le Blon and Ison did not pretend to be De Lucas.

FIAT had an easy time of it, Nazzaro leading for most of the race to average 33.5 m.p.h., while Lancia took second place, followed by Fabry (Itala), Duray (Lorraine-Dietrich) and Cagno (Itala). Wagner's Darracq harassed the FIATS until a half-shaft went, giving Agnelli both his first big victory of the season and a new driver at one fell swoop!

Next on the agenda was the Kaiserpreis, which drew a huge entry list even if this was predominantly German, and padded with makes such as N.A.G. and Horch, seldom encountered on a circuit. This unprecedented turn-out forced the organisers to run the event in two heats and a final, and once again the FIATs dominated the situation. The cars were straightforward chain-driven chassis powered by oversquare (140 × 130 mm) pushrod engines, and handled by Nazzaro, Lancia and Wagner. The two Italian veterans won their respective heats, and Nazzaro was victorious in the final, his average speed being 52.5 m.p.h. Wagner was fifth and Lancia sixth, while the best French performance was Rougier's thirteenth place on a Lorraine-Dietrich.

For the Grand Prix FIAT's cars were little changed from 1906, though the supporting cast included a fine sprinkling of eccentricities, among them Walter Christie on the front-wheel-drive V-4 which had spoilt Lancia's chances in the previous year's Vanderbilt Cup. Also present were three straight-eights—the British Weigel, the French Porthos and the Dufaux from Switzerland. As it transpired, none of these three studies in crankshaft whip made any impression, while the fuel-consumption rule had little effect on the proceedings, though it was noted that most drivers dispensed with the warming-up period.

Lancia and Wagner set the pace until the latter crashed, Lancia fighting a personal duel with Duray's Lorraine-Dietrich. By the fourth lap the French car was getting the better of the fiery Italian, and on the seventh only three of the FIAT's cylinders were pulling their weight. Lancia finally succumbed to clutch trouble, but not before he had worn down Duray's resistance, the Lorraine expiring on the course with a seized gearbox. This left Nazzaro to take the lead and pull off his 'triple' at 70.5 m.p.h.

'Never', proclaimed *The Morning Post*, 'in the history of the motoring movement has French industry suffered such humiliation as the defeat it suffered yesterday'. *The Financial News* gloated unashamedly over this 'setback to the Gauls and their make-believe superior cars'. Both sentiments made it clear that Edward VII's pro-French sympathies were not shared by his subjects; they were also exaggerated, for French cars filled the next nine places after Nazzaro. Szisz, the 1906 winner, was less than seven minutes behind the Italian on time, and Rigal's Darracq, which finished fifth, recorded the best m.p.g. figures of the race, and was therefore the moral victor—as if anyone cared. Probably the worst sufferers were Lorraine-Dietrich. They might be empire-building in Italy, but they lost an important sale in 1908. Sorel, one of their works drivers, shattered the Paris–Madrid record with an average of 33.3 m.p.h., *en route* for the Spanish Motor Show. He was duly presented to King Alfonso. But that monarch did not buy a Lorraine-Dietrich. Instead he chose one of the monstrous six-cylinder FIATs.

There was no Vanderbilt Cup in 1907, the Italians left the Circuit des Ardennes alone, and FIAT could afford to ignore the Brescia meeting, though Vincenzo Florio tried to enter something called a Panormitan. This was supposedly the product of a mysterious Fabbrica Siciliana d'Automobili, but turned out to be Nazzaro's 8-litre Kaiserpreis FIAT. Understandably the organisers refused the entry.

Some notable minor successes rounded out FIAT's *annus mirabilis*. Salmson scored a second successive win in the Swedish Winter Cup, and Fokin's 'Brevetti' won its class in the tough St Petersburg–Moscow marathon. The *marque* also did well in India, where the season's score included a first prize in a *concours d'elegance* at Bombay for a 40 h.p. limousine entered by the local agents. There were placings in the Platrière and Gaillon hill-climbs, and the cars were doing well in English sprints. At Bottledown one of the winners was Sir Charles Locock's 1905 16–24 h.p.; its owner was later to furnish D'Arcy Baker with a glowing testimonial:

> The car has now gone over 7,000 miles on all sorts of roads and in all weathers, and I have always found her thoroughly reliable and efficient, while the management of the car is so simple that I am able to dispense with a chauffeur altogether.

Though Baker was soon to turn up his nose at Brooklands, he considered the inaugural meeting important enough to import Wagner and a Grand Prix FIAT, the combination taking part unsuccessfully in both the Marcel Renault and Byfleet Memorial Plates. FIAT's best showing was a second in the Montagu Cup for K. Okura, whose '120 h.p.' was one of a stud of three, not to mention a six-cylinder tourer he had shipped home to his father in Japan.

1908 opened with a hat-trick for Salmson and his 24 h.p. in Sweden, while Cedrino was going great guns in America with 'Cyclone', his personal racer. The exact origins of this car are nebulous, and FIAT's own publication *Trent'Anni da Corsa* has hinted that it was built up in the United States. It may have started life as a Kaiserpreis car, in which case it could just have won the Morris Park 24-hour 'grind' the previous September; FIAT thoughtfully catalogued a 'Taunus' model with overhead-valve engine in 1908 and 1909.

Be that as it may, the Italian dominated the Ormonde-Daytona speed meeting. He started by winning a hundred-mile race in spite of losing a tyre before half-distance, at the same time winning a wager for Mr Hollander, who had bet that the FIAT could trounce any American competitor. Also to 'Cyclone's' credit were a couple of longer events—the America and Vanderbilt Cups—while the meeting witnessed the debut of an eighteen-year-old college boy, 'David B. Brown'. This young man talked himself into the cockpit of Cedrino's car, and set a new mile record for amateurs at 92.3 m.p.h. David Bruce-Brown was to die at the wheel of a FIAT in October, 1912, but not before he had made his name as one of the most talented drivers of the era.

In April two '60 h.p. stock chassis' of Kaiserpreis type turned out for the Briarcliff Trophy, driven by Cedrino and Ed. Parker. The former's was entered, as on past occasions, by Hollander, but Parker's FIAT was nominated by a new personality, J. S. Josephs. By contrast, Mr Tangeman's entry was not a FIAT at all, but a 'Hol-Tan-Shawmut', which may or may not have been made by Moon of St Louis. Sadly, Cedrino's second place was destined to be his last major success: a month later he was dead, the victim of a practice crash at Baltimore.

Once again FIAT's Targa Florio entries were conventional 7.4-litre chain-driven cars, but their engines now boasted pushrod-operated overhead valves and high-tension ignition. They were less fortunate than in 1907, Nazzaro being eliminated by steering failure while 'an unnecessary tyre change', lost Lancia the race to Trucco's Isotta Fraschini. For the Grand Prix, run this year under a bore limit of 155 mm for four-cylinder engines, FIAT fielded a team of overhead-valve SB4s, giving 100 b.h.p. from just over twelve litres. The drivers (Nazzaro, Lancia and Wagner) were the same as in 1907, but unfortunately Fornaca had skimped things in the engine department, and all three cars succumbed to mechanical trouble. It was said that 'many production parts' had been incorporated, which may explain why Lancia lasted only a lap before retiring with a broken piston. The other two FIATS showed a considerable turn of speed while they were going, Nazzaro was fastest on the second lap, and on the third circuit Wagner took the lead. For all the talk of 'steering failure', it is almost certain that both were eliminated by broken crankshafts.

There was, however, some consolation for Wagner, since he took third place in St Petersburg-Moscow on a 24 h.p. touring model, while once again Fokin's 'Brevetti' won its class. The SB4s had obviously received some under-bonnet attention before they reappeared in the Coppa Florio at Brescia, for on this very fast circuit Lancia set a new lap record of 82.3 m.p.h., and Nazzaro dominated most of the race to win at 74.1 m.p.h. Wagner's departure was spectacular, and this and subsequent incidents seem to lend force to Agnelli's known misgivings. His front axle gave way, 'the breakage being so clean that it looked as though the axle had been sawn through'. If the big FIATS needed any further vindication, this was forthcoming in the first American Grand Prize at Savannah, where Wagner won at 65.2 m.p.h., and Nazzaro (who would undoubtedly have beaten his team-mate but for a burst tyre) was third. The young Italian–American Ralph de Palma justified his inclusion in the *équipe* by making the fastest lap at 69.8 m.p.h., as well as fighting his way up from sixteenth to ninth after a series of punctures and lubrication troubles had delayed him. C. T. Croker drove a four-cylinder FIAT of unspecified type from New York to San Mateo, California, in 18 days' running time, the best solo trans-Continental performance at a time when the absolute record stood to five stalwarts who had taken a Franklin across in twenty-hour shifts at the wheel. Finally, a 40 h.p. FIAT made f.t.d. at the Bedfordshire Automobile Club's Luton Hoo hill-climb; its driver was James Radley, later to be famous as an aviator and a driver of Rolls-Royces in the Austrian Alpine Trials.

The next three seasons were spent by Europe recovering

from the alarms of Agadir. FIAT after, a slight drop in sales to 1,213 in 1908, came back with a record 1,807 in 1909, but racing was now virtually confined to America, with 'Taunus' models distinguishing themselves in stock-car events. There were, however, a few pickings to be gained in Europe: Florio himself came second in the Targa Florio, and Emile Mathis won sprints at Brussels and Nancy.

The season's big fixture was, of course the Vanderbilt Cup, and this marked Hollander's last appearance in the FIAT pit. Three cars were entered, the drivers being Strang, Hearne and Parker: their identity is, however, in dispute. Some reports give the bore and stroke of all the engines as 5.1 × 5.6 inches (130 × 140 mm), which suggests that they could have been of 1908 Targa Florio type. FIAT records cite Parker's car as of 130 h.p., a rating associated with the 1908 SB4, while according to Peter Helck the Parker car had a 7.4-litre engine, and the other two were 8-litres, and therefore either 1907 Kaiser-preis machines or production 'Taunus' models running stripped. Either way, neither Strang nor Hearne lasted the course, though Parker drove well to finish second at 61.58 m.p.h. behind Grant on a six-cylinder Alco.

If 1909 was a lean year, 1910 was even leaner—in Europe, that is. Nazzaro emerged briefly from an enforced retirement to win the big-car class of the Modena speed trials at 84.6 m.p.h., Mathis won the Bollinger Cup hill-climb in Switzerland, and there were odd successes in such far-off places as Mar del Plata and San Sebastian. Schudt was third in the big-car class at Semmering in Austria. But though FIAT ignored the Vanderbilt Cup, they not only entered their big guns— Nazzaro, Wagner and de Palma—for the Grand Prize; they also made this the occasion to unveil their first overhead-camshaft engine.

It is a matter of opinion whether the 10-litre S61 was a true racer, or just a super-sports machine designed for the keen private owner. FIAT have never committed themselves on this point, any more than they have commented on the late Laurence Pomeroy's belief that Ettore Bugatti had a hand in the design.

2. Pensioner and Novice. Taken in Turin in 1916, this picture shows the 28·3-litre S76 record car of 1911, and a production model of the *Tipo* 70, ancestor of the 501.

3. *Annus mirabilis*. Felice Nazzaro exercises his *Kaiserpreis* winner in the paddock at Homburg, 1907.

(FIAT)

14. Golden Boy. David Bruce-Brown behind 14·1 litres of S74 engine, Dieppe, 1912.

(National Motor Museum)

15. The one he didn't win. Felice Nazzaro before the 1908 French Grand Prix with the SB4-155, basis of the famous 'Mephistopheles'.

(National Motor Museum)

It was certainly catalogued, at £1,330 for an open tourer in England, and about fifty seem to have been made between 1911 and 1913, some with the rare rounded-vee radiator fitted to contemporary 5s and 6s, and a few even with a bevel-driven rear axle in place of the side chains of the racing models. The chassis was straightforward FIAT, with four-speed separate gearbox and multi-plate clutch, but under the bonnet was a 130 × 190 mm (10,087 c.c.) sixteen-valve engine, its overhead camshaft driven by a vertical shaft from the front, while the full-pressure lubrication was inherited from Fornaca's *Tipo* 1 of 1908. There were two plugs per cylinder, ignition was by low-tension magneto, and the water pump was assisted by a vaned flywheel. Output in standard form was 115 b.h.p. at 1,500 r.p.m., which gave road-going versions a top speed of about 95 m.p.h. on a 1.7:1 top gear. Bottom, at 6.25:1, was equivalent to the highest ratio on not a few small family saloons of the early 1930s! Perhaps the best-known of all the S61s was the '100–120 h.p. Mathis' which Emile Mathis sold to Sir Frederick Richmond in 1913. This had a long and distinguished career at Brooklands in the 1920s, driven by Duff, Rampon, Eldridge, Warde and Cobb, before being retired in 1929. Even then its useful life was not over, for it was acquired by Anthony Heal in 1937, and proceeded to enliven the Edwardian classes at Prescott, Brighton, and the Crystal Palace. It is still, happily, with us, though of recent years its appearances have been infrequent.

At Savannah the FIATs gave the Benz of Hémery and Bruce-Brown an excellent run for their money. Both Nazzaro and Wagner ran out of road in the early stages, and were called in for scrutiny, which revealed a damaged front axle on Nazzaro's car. Though he struggled on, changing his chains twice, he was soon out of the running. The inspection of Wagner's S61 revealed a broken spring clip on the front axle, but Wagner dismissed this with a shrug, and put his foot hard down. On the seventh lap the inevitable happened: the FIAT inverted itself, happily without damage to either driver or mechanic, though once again an axle had snapped. It was now up to de

Palma, and he drove flat out in an attempt to stave off the two Benz. It was all to no avail, for a cracked cylinder put him out while he was still in the lead, two laps from the end.

It was therefore poetic justice that the S61's one major European victory should fall to Victory Hémery's lot. The 1911 Grand Prix de France at Le Mans was nicknamed *le grand prix des vieux tacots*, and the winning FIAT was no works entry. It was a sports chassis refused by its client, a Paris café proprietor, 'on grounds of late delivery', and Hémery proceeded to defeat a motley opposition at an average speed of 56.71 m.p.h.

Not that the era of the giants was over, for FIAT saw the dying epoch out with a thunderous white elephant, the S74 of 1911. This one ran to over fourteen litres, but during the interregnum the company had already excelled themselves with two (or possibly three) track cars of even more heroic proportions, none of which ever contested a major race. The SB4-190 ('Mephistopheles') disposed of 18,146 c.c., and the S76 of 1910–11 was truly a 'four to end all fours' with a swept volume of 28,352 c.c.

'Mephistopheles' is probably the most controversial racing car of all time. It is a matter of opinion just how rapidly he circulated at Brooklands in 1908. His later years are clouded with mysteries such as the improvised reverse gear used by Eldridge in 1924. When the car took the World's Land Speed Record, certain authorities (notably the late W. F. Bradley) declined to accept that 'Mephistopheles' was still a FIAT, whatever he may have been in 1908. A corpus of detective work worthy of Sir Arthur Conan Doyle has been published to prove (or disprove) that there was more than one 'Mephistopheles', the chief protagonists being William Boddy of *Motor Sport* and Dr Augusto Costantino of FIAT's own *Centro Storico*.

It is certain, however, that on 8 June, 1908 Felice Nazzaro drove the car in a challenge match against Frank Newton on the veteran six-cylinder Napier, 'Samson'. The Napier first saw the light of day in 1904, and had done battle against FIATS on two previous occasions, at Clermont-Ferrand in 1905, and at Ormonde-Daytona in 1906. At Brooklands, it broke its crankshaft, giving Nazzaro a walkover at 94.75 m.p.h. The rest of the story is open to debate.

According to hand timing, Nazzaro's best lap was at 107.98 m.p.h., but the B.A.R.C.'s electrical timing apparatus gave the remarkable figure of 121.64 m.p.h. Newton later opined that the FIAT's maximum speed was not far in excess of 100 m.p.h., which seems to give the lie to 120 m.p.h. laps. FIAT, however, say that they designed the car for a speed of 193 kilometres an hour, or roughly 120.

On paper, the story starts when Sir George Abercromby ordered a special FIAT from D'Arcy Baker, with the express purpose of winning the Montagu Cup at Brooklands, and succeeding where Okura had failed in 1907. He agreed to pay £2,500 for such a car, but later—after the FIAT/Napier match— he changed his mind, with the result that he and Baker fought an inconclusive lawsuit in 1909. The crux of Abercromby's plea was that FIAT had insisted, before accepting his order, that they should be permitted to build a second, identical car. It was not the strongest of pleas, which is perhaps why the dispute ended in a compromise solution whereby Abercromby agreed to buy 'Mephistopheles' for £1,250, while both parties were responsible for their own costs.

It seems probable, however, that FIAT had decided to build the car before Abercromby entered the picture. The story goes back to the *annus mirabilis* of 1907, when the FIAT-Nazzaro combination seemed invincible. Among those who subscribed to this thesis was, as we have seen, the editor of *The Autocar*, but such sentiments were anathema to that publicist extraordinary, Selwyn Francis Edge. Edge and his propaganda machine had been synonymous with Napier cars since 1900: he had won Britain her first international victory on a Napier in 1902: and if he had not invented the six-cylinder engine he had certainly done more than anyone else to popularise it. Brooklands' first season had been dominated by Edge's stud of Napiers: in addition to his own 24-Hour Record, the *marque* had twelve first places, four seconds and four thirds to its credit. He was no man to accept defeat at the hands of a paid works driver—he therefore wrote personally to Felice Nazzaro, challenging him to a trial of speed.

This was surely a sprat to catch a mackerel. An old hand of Edge's calibre must have known that as an employee of FIAT Nazzaro could only accept if Agnelli gave permission. And Agnelli, faced with a recession on his front doorstep, wanted no skirmishes with flag-waving *inglesi*. He refused permission, and local legend says that Nazzaro scribbled his negative on a postcard and sent it back to Edge.

Agnelli's attitude gave Edge the opening he wanted, and he took up the cudgels directly, stating his terms: £500 to the winning driver, and the winner to buy the loser's car.

As yet, of course, FIAT had nothing capable of beating the big Napier. It would, in fact, be interesting to know which reached Agnelli's desk first—Edge's challenge, or Abercromby's request for a track car. Fornaca went to work on the fastest car he had—the 155 × 160 mm, 12-litre SB4-155 evolved under the 1908 Grand Prix rules. Already the company contemplated the issue of a small batch of these machines to American private owners—hence those 'production parts' that were to prove the car's downfall at Dieppe. A car was assigned to Nazzaro, who put it through its paces on the highway at Bruino, not far from to-day's Rivalta plant. The results were discouraging: 105–110 m.p.h. was about the limit, and if Edge and Napier were to be put in their place Fornaca had to aim for 200 kilometres an hour (124 m.p.h.). His eventual solution was to redesign the existing pushrod unit with a bore of 190 mm. which gave him 180 b.h.p. One of the more delightful factory legends says that owing to a misunderstanding of the geography of Brooklands, the car was originally assembled with left-hand steering, this being changed over on arrival at the Track. This triggered off charges of 'substitution' from suspicious Britons; hence the name 'Mephistopheles'. Alas! it is one of the less credible parts of the 'Mephistopheles' story, for the SB4-190 has, and always has had, a right-hand brake pedal, and a last-minute conversion would have posed some most interesting problems. In match trim, the FIAT weighed 29 cwt. 66 lbs, and Fornaca's team had done their work well, the only hitch concerned a personal quirk of Nazzaro's. He insisted on driving in black kid gloves. Baker's anxious helpers combed eight or nine shops in the neighbourhood of Weybridge before coming up with an acceptable pair! In addition to his agreed £500, the Italian champion received another £200 from Baker.

As far as is known, 'Mephistopheles' was based on Britain for the rest of his working life, and did not return to Italy until 1970, when he was acquired by FIAT for display in their *Centro Storico*. Before World War I various drivers—Abercromby himself, Mrs Noel Macklin of Invicta fame, and C. R. Engley—tried their luck with him at Brooklands, but he was a handful. Abercromby, however, lapped the Track at 106.38 m.p.h. in 1910, which makes one wonder why he had been so reluctant to accept his purchase.

But what of the 'second identical car'? Did it exist? Nazzaro brought a 180 h.p. FIAT with wire wheels to Brooklands on 30 June, 1909, the entrant being a Mr A. Baker White. The footwear apart, it was hard to distinguish from 'Mephistopheles', and on this occasion the Italian driver was billed to attack the world's flying-start kilometre and mile records.

This, alas! was not to be. In Mr Boddy's words:

The back axle was bent going over a bump . . . and the cylinders lost compression. On the morning of his appearance a blow-hole was discovered in no. 4 cylinder. At first Nazzaro decided not to appear, but, in order not to disappoint the spectators, the offending block was removed, a little plate two inches square supported by eight screws was used as a patch, and the run took place.

Nazzaro might have saved his time. No doubt he deemed it advisable to placate Baker, who had laid on a champagne luncheon for his guests, not to mention the famous taxi race won by his friend Harvey du Cros, Jr. Nazzaro's best lap was, however, a miserable 102.01 m.p.h., and his best speed over the kilometre came out at 105.5 m.p.h., a figure which approximates to Newton's estimate of the FIAT's potential. As to the car's identity, Mr Boddy insists that it was a duplicate of the original 'Mephistopheles', while Dr Costantino asserts that it was the 1908 car suitably modified. So far the facts seem to support Mr Boddy, but the question is largely one of words and language. FIAT insist that there was only one 'Mephistopheles', but they admit the possibility of there having been more than one SB4-190, in other words a car built to 'Mephistopheles' specification.

It is also almost certain that this second car ended up in the U.S.A. At Atlanta Speedway that November, Louis Strang drove a '200 h.p. FIAT' entered by W. E. C. Arnold. It was extremely hard on tyres, though very fast. There remains that mysterious projectile 'Jay-Eye-See', used by the J. I. Case Company of Racine, Wisconsin, as a promotional device for their agricultural machinery and cars, and barnstormed round the country by Louis Disbrow. Its chain-driven chassis and large o.h.v. pushrod engine were unmistakably FIAT, and though all manner of cylinder dimensions have been quoted for the car, these are invariably oversquare as were those of the SB4-190. Suggestions that 'Jay-Eye-See' used a FIAT airship motor must be rejected, as these units wore their camshafts upstairs, and the '290 horse-power' claimed by Case's racer in its latter years smack more of mid-Western hyperbole than of fact.

Late in 1910, of course, FIAT did instal one of their airship motors in a car, with a view to an attack on the World's Land Speed Record. They also found a sponsor for this venture in the shape of the Russian prince Boris Soukhanoff.

The S76 was one of the most terrifying creations to emanate from any factory. The light, almost flimsy chassis, side-chain drive, four-speed gearbox and wire wheels carried on the SB4 story from 1909. Power, however, was furnished by one of the largest four-cylinder engines ever built, a 190×250 mm (28,353 c.c.) overhead-camshaft affair intended for the Forlanini airship, and developing no less than 290 b.h.p. at 1,900 r.p.m. Unlike 'Mephistopheles', the car was quite well streamlined, with an airship tail, a full undertray, and a curvaceous pearshaped radiator which anticipated the regular style used on touring FIATs from 1913 onward. The filler cap was recessed into the shell in the manner of Vintage Beardmore cars, but in spite of this neat little touch the cap stood a clear five feet off the ground. The crew, of necessity, sat high: had the mechanic tried to look 'round' and not 'over', he would have been fried alive by the crude stub exhausts on the near side of the engine. The S76 turned the scales at close on 38 cwt, and Nazzaro considered it 'uncontrollable', after testing it on the streets of Turin with the Englishman Jack Scales in the mechanic's seat. A contemporary report describes the big FIAT as 'shooting flames in the faces of innocent pedestrians, and deafening them'. The necessary urge was, however, present, 115 m.p.h. coming up in second gear, though not, one hopes, on the Via Roma or the Corso Dante.

It was left to Pietro Bordino to bring this monster to Brooklands in 1911, though he declined to lap above 90, and one circuit in the 'hot seat' was enough for Soukhanoff. The FIAT was next tried at Saltburn Sands, where a timed speed of 116 m.p.h. was reached before the brute bogged down, and only just escaped being caught by the tide.

By this time Bordino had had enough, and Soukhanoff hired the Belgian–American Arthur Duray. Duray was willing: the problem was to find a level stretch long enough to allow the FIAT to display its undoubted talents. The A.C.F.'s *Commission Sportive* would not authorise the use of Arles-Salon, and no suitable Italian venue was forthcoming—one imagines that the Piedmontese, at any rate, had had their fill of the S76's private smog! Eventually Soukhanoff and Duray went to Ostend, a traditional home of world's records since Louis Rigolly had first topped the 'ton' in his Gobron–Brillié. In December, 1913, the car recorded a one-way kilometre at 132.37 m.p.h., faster than Barney Oldfield's existing figure of 131.72 m.p.h. on the 'Blitzen' Benz.

But that was as far as matters went. Since the end of 1910 a 'mean' time based on two runs had been mandatory, and Duray was never destined to complete his second one. He waited six weeks, but was ultimately defeated, not only by the weather, but also by Ostend's motorphobiac tramway superintendent, who telephoned the police every time the FIAT ventured out of its garage. Even then he did not abandon hope: though the car went back to Turin, the spares remained in Belgium, only to be 'liberated' by the advancing Germans in 1914. Soukhanoff, one must assume, became a casualty of the Russian Revolution. As for the S76, it languished at the factory for several years, being trotted out in 1916 to pose with Cavalli's *Tipo*-70 prototype. It was eventually sold to a Mexican enthusiast in 1920, and was last heard of in Tampico some eight years later. Only the one car was made, though a second engine was built. It proved too heavy for use in airships and was eventually scrapped.

'Mephistopheles' and the S76 were 'one-off specials', but FIAT's last giant, the 14.1-litre S74 of 1911, was a regular Grand Prix machine. It may seem an improbable step for the company at a time when Europe's nearest approach to a *grande épreuve* was Le Mans's perambulating motor museum, an event which a stripped sports model proved capable of winning. It would have been more logical for FIAT to try their luck with 3-litre high-efficiency *voiturettes*, along with Delage, Hispano–Suiza, Sunbeam and Vauxhall. These developments were to seduce even Sizaire–Naudin away from their legendary 'singles', and 1912 was to see the first of Ernest Henry's twin-cam Peugeots. But while Louis Coatalen was extracting seventy-five brake horses from a straightforward side-valve unit, Fornaca was living in the past; and to discover why we must explore the fortunes of FIAT on the other side of the Atlantic.

The golden years of FIAT in America, of course, *followed* the racing exploits of Cedrino, Strang and Bruce–Brown, and they were based, not on the big pushrod cars or even the S61, but on the luxury machines with L-head monobloc units built under licence by the FIAT Motor Company at Poughkeepsie. This venture gave FIAT a continuity of sales in the United States unrivalled by any contemporary foreign *marque* with the exceptions of Mercédès and Rolls-Royce. FIATs were catalogued virtually without a break from the end of 1902 until 1924, even if their attempts to sell the 501 as a 'luxury compact' were fore-doomed to failure. Agadir ended the first wave of the foreign-import boom, sweeping away such ephemera as the American-built C.G.V., Mors and Napier; but Hollander and Tangeman raced their FIATS as energetically as ever, and the cars were kept before the public eye. 1908 was actually a better sales year than 1907. Around 1913 the luxurious foreigners finally bowed out, under pressure from a new generation of native quality cars (Packard, Pierce-Arrow, Simplex and Locomobile) which were as well-appointed as anything from the Old World, and often blessed with flexible six-cylinder engines at a time when Europe's super-cars relied on four massive 'pots' and audible power impulses. By this time, of course, FIAT of America were making 200–400 cars a year, and were thus unaffected either by the new trend or by the War.

The Poughkeepsie venture was a necessary step. In 1907 and 1908 alike Hollander and Tangeman exhibited at the New York and Boston Shows, and in the latter year they opened a big repair depot in New York, with Cedrino as manager. Meanwhile FIAT had moved up to second place in the imported-car stakes, with 181 units sold to Renault's 266. Mercédès (94) was a bad third, and Panhard came fourth with 69. In October there arrived at New York Docks the largest individual shipment of chassis ever to be imported from Europe—thirty-one FIATS. This makes an interesting comparison with the 1960s and 1970s when Jaguars came over in batches of three hundred. Hollander and Tangeman had reason to congratulate themselves if they sold seven cars at a show: but when the E-type was unveiled at New York in 1961 six found buyers in the first thirty minutes, and when the doors finally closed Sir William Lyons's order-books were richer to the tune of eleven million dollars! By 1910 Americans had the choice of five different FIAT models, from a *Tipo* 1 chassis at $2,750 up to the S61 at $7,500, and the *marque* was to be seen as far afield as Chicago and Kansas City. Before the year was out, the first all-American FIAT, a 5.7-litre four-cylinder *Tipo* 54, was on the road.

The FIAT Motor Company was an American corporation,

backed by Ben J. Eichberg, a New York diamond importer, and directed by J. S. Josephs. Laurie Treas, the treasurer, had a financial interest in *Horseless Age* magazine, and Pough-keepsie's licence agreement with Turin permitted them to manufacture any current FIAT model, as well as importing types of which the sales-volume did not warrant local production. This in practice meant anything of less than four litres' capacity.

Poughkeepsie was entirely self-contained: all it imported from Italy were the RIV bearings (made by a FIAT subsidiary in Agnelli's home town of Villar Perosa) and axle casings, while the works had their own foundry and body shops. Though one American model—the six-cylinder Type 56—was exclusive to Poughkeepsie, basic design remained the responsibility of Turin, and a consulting engineer, Ing. Maraini, paid annual visits to the American plant to see that Agnelli's exacting standards were maintained. The senior management of FIAT Motor Company had been recruited from such illustrious firms as Pope-Toledo, Lozier and Thomas. In the words of A. L. Warmington, a former executive at Poughkeepsie:

> The automobile had everything: prestige, distinction, and *éclat*. If you owned, rode in, or drove a FIAT you really were in top place. In society circles it was the correct car to use, and at the opera or other society gatherings the chauffeur-driven FIAT limousine or landaulet was most prominent.

Mr Warmington recalls a lady client who sent the body department a pink stocking as a colour match for her new limousine. No wonder most American FIATs were sold complete by the factory, whereas in Hollander and Tangeman days the *marque* had drawn heavily on such specialist coachbuilders as Quinby of Newark, New Jersey.

Poughkeepsie was not, of course, the first foreign factory to build FIATs under licence. In 1907 the Austro-FIAT company of Vienna came into being, and this concern manufactured both cars and chain-driven lorries, the latter being widely used by the Imperial army and the postal authorities. Most of the passenger models were the smaller Types 1 and 2. Despite

Italy's change of alliance in 1915, the association survived the War, though all connections between Turin and Vienna were finally severed in 1921. Thereafter Austro-FIAT marketed a 2½-litre four-cylinder 9/32 PS of their own design, which wore a rounded-vee radiator in the N.A.G. or Delaunay-Belleville idiom, and gave way to a light car with swing-axle rear suspension in 1928. From the early 'thirties onward only trucks were made, and these are still in production under the name of Ö.A.F. (Österreichisches Automobil Fabrik).

Undoubtedly a desire to boost American sales was behind the team of new cars fielded for the 1911 Grand Prize Race at Savannah. These S74s were descendants of the S61, their overhead-camshaft four-cylinder engines being enlargements of the earlier type, with a bore and stroke of 150 × 200 mm for a capacity of 14.1 litres. They retained the low-tension ignition and side-chain drive of earlier racing FIATs, and their power units towered above the surrounding scenery in the manner of the S76 record machine. The new car was, however, appreciably less powerful, with 190 b.h.p. on tap, and far lighter, at 3,322 lb. It was, alas! obsolete before it ever turned a wheel, and the team were destined to race only once in Europe, in the revived Grand Prix at Dieppe in 1912. It is significant that this event was run concurrently with the *Coupe de l'Auto* for 3-litre cars, the latter attracting a bigger and more interesting field.

At Savannah in 1911 the three S74s were assigned to Wagner, Caleb Bragg and David Bruce-Brown, and the two American drivers led the field in close formation for the first fifty miles, circulating at an 80 m.p.h. which was a good 2 m.p.h. faster than the native products could manage. This advantage was, however, offset by an appalling appetite for tyres, which helped Ralph Mulford on the Lozier to remain within striking distance. Curiously, though, the towering FIATs cornered quite well—it was later noted at Dieppe that Bruce-Brown negotiated the bends with 'gyroscopic steadiness'. Whatever their limitations, they were not lacking in speed, and Wagner managed a record lap at 80.3 m.p.h., only to overdo things shortly afterward, running out of road and damaging his rear axle and steering-gear. His departure resolved the race into a battle between the two surviving FIATs, the Lozier, and Eddie Hearne's Benz.

It was now Mulford's turn to over-reach himself. He omitted to slow down for the streetcar tracks, and the Lozier became airborne, with disastrous consequences to the propeller shaft. Hearne maintained the pressure until he suffered a puncture with only twenty-five miles to go, and Bruce-Brown went through to win at 74.45 m.p.h., a tribute to his mastery of a big and brutal machine. Hearne was second, followed by de Palma's Mercédès and Bragg on the third FIAT.

While the monsters of the Enrico era progressed towards their final phase, FIAT were already turning towards more compact designs. Not that as yet they aspired towards the small and inexpensive family car. As late as 1913 Baker could create a minor sensation with the headline 'A FIAT for £375!' when the first Zero tourers went on sale in London. An American journalist who reviewed Italian industry in 1910 found that S.P.A. were actually undercutting FIAT in the up to 30 h.p. category, as well as offering effective competition for Fornaca's large, but inexpensive 35–50 h.p. *Tipo* 4. But FIAT were going modern: T-head engines vanished with the last of the 'Brevettis' in 1912, and though a few large chain-drive cars were made as late as 1914, the vast majority of vehicles made after 1909 had shaft drive. Even in 1908 the catalogue contained a new live-axle model, *Tipo* 1, which owed nothing to Untertürkheim save the honeycomb radiator and its *brevetti Daimler* plate. It was introduced almost apologetically to Britons as a 'cab chassis', though the original Italian (*tipo fiacre*) implies the world of the jobmaster rather than of the jarvey.

Tipo 1 is one of the great landmarks in FIAT history, along with Enrico's 12 h.p. of 1901, Cavalli's 501 of 1919, Fessia's 1936 *topolino*, and Giacosa's 600. Its general layout was perpetuated on the vast majority of FIATs made up to 1918, not to mention the light and medium commercials of the period, and it typifies a new generation of thinking that was to rescue Europe from the Agadir doldrums.

The engine was a neat little side-valve monobloc unit with integral head, single camshaft, three-beating crankshaft, full-pressure lubrication by gear-type pump, and high-tension magneto ignition. The spray-jet carburetter was a FIAT product, and cooling was by pump, assisted by vanes on the flywheel. In its original guise *Tipo* 1 had a bore of 80 mm and a stroke of 100 mm, for a capacity of just over two litres, and output was a satisfactory 16 b.h.p. at 1,400 r.p.m., though these '50-series' engines could withstand much higher rates of rotation. In service they proved incredibly tough: a 1913 *Tipo* Zero two-seater now living in retirement in the National Motor Museum at Beaulieu saw forty years of active service, collecting a string of premier awards in British trials in the early 'thirties, and serving as a garage tow-car in World War II. The clutch was the sweet and well-liked FIAT multi-disc, but though the 'Brevetti's' three forward speeds were retained, the gearbox was now mounted in unit with the engine. The simple chassis frame was sharply inswept at the front to give a turning circle of only 25 feet, and suspension was semi-elliptic all round. With a wheelbase of 8 ft 4 in, the body space measured no less than 7 ft 8½ in, while fuel consumption was of the order of 26–30 m.p.g. The *Tipo* 1 was a lot cheaper than the 'Brevetti'— London prices were £395 for a tourer, £410 for a fully-equipped taxicab, and £435 for a landaulette. From 1909 onwards a four-speed gearbox was available, though this was not standardised until *Tipo* 1 gave way to the *Ibis* during 1911.

The new model was vigorously promoted. Despite a factory strike in the last few weeks of 1907, the first twenty-five chassis were ready for shipment on time, and *Tipo* 1 reached England the following spring, to do battle against some two dozen-odd rival breeds of taxicab. One wonders, in passing, whether anyone opted for some of the eccentricities then on the market, such as the old-school opposed-piston Arrol-Johnston, the friction-drive Certus, or the front-wheel drive Pullcar. Baker, of course, was ready: he had registered his FIAT Motor Cab Company way back in August, 1907, before any FIAT cabs existed, and by the end of 1908 he had a fleet of over two hundred taxis on the streets of London. A year later there were close on 300, not to mention a number of *Tipo* 1s and '*Brevetti*' reserved for contract hire at £60–£75 a month. In 1911 the venture made a profit of £37,359, but Baker had sold out by mid-1913, and though a few of the post-War *Tipo* 1 cabs were used in London, FIAT taxis were never again a common sight in the metropolis. *Tipo* 1 was also seen in the United States, thanks to the efforts of Ralph de Palma, who won a ten-mile economy test sponsored by the New York Automobile Trade Association. An operator in Portland, Oregon, ordered a dozen cabs finished in 'havana brown with yellow frame and running gear, dark calf and havana brown upholstery, imported lace trimming, and silk curtains'.

At the 1908 London Show it was noted that no chain-driven FIATs were on display, and indeed only one of the season's other two models retained the old transmission. This was the six-cylinder *Tipo* 4 of 35–45 h.p., but a live rear axle was found on the first of the *Tipo* 3s, a 4.9-litre T-head 'four' with high-tension magneto ignition, which Britons knew as the '28–35'. 1909 saw the advent of *Tipo* 5, outwardly an 8-litre edition of *Tipo* 3 on a 10 ft 7½ in wheelbase, which cost £895 in London or $5,250 in New York. Chain drive was still available to order, but of greater interest were the side valves in a L-head. Some 300 of this transitional type were sold: one was submitted to the R.A.C. for trial, and was timed at 63.98 m.p.h., though an average fuel consumption of 9.9 m.p.g. reveals that not all those slow-revving Edwardian tourers were frugal in their habits.

1910, of course, was to see the general adoption of the monobloc engine on a new 'six' (*Tipo* 7) and two largish 'fours' (the 3 and the 4). While FIAT were not yet deserting the elephantine—a 9-litre model was catalogued as late as 1916—the first steps towards mass production had been taken.

4 Fifties and Fighting Vehicles

*I have just returned from America where I wanted to see
for myself the danger which is threatening, not only
Italian industry, but that of France and Germany too. It
would be ridiculous to deny it. Our own costs have increased
steadily of late because of the rise in iron and steel prices, and
the increase in wages. Competition is becoming more and more
difficult every day.*

Giovanni Agnelli, 1912

The second decade of the twentieth century saw the world
plunged into a cataclysm of unprecedented violence. 'The
lamps', said Lord Grey of Falloden, 'are going out all over
Europe', but in their place would come the harsher glare of
universal mechanisation. The War introduced Everyman to
the internal combustion engine; it also quadrupled the demand
for motor vehicles. In 1914 FIAT had been the leader of the
Italian industry; in 1919 they were about to become general
providers to world markets, and once embarked upon this path
Giovanni Agnelli and his successors never turned back. Hence-
forward it was a matter of fulfilling a demand; it did not matter
whether this demand was for ten thousand 501s a year, or for
seventeen hundred 128s a day, as in 1972.

Once the War was over, the world would clamour for motor
cars. The despatch rider with his Douglas, Indian or N.S.U., or
the private who coaxed his overloaded 18BL FIAT over the cruel
roads of the Isonzo would be questing personal transportation
once he was demobilised. And these cars would have to be
cheap, simple and easy to service. The chauffeur-driven carriage
would assume a minority role.

Not that such a happy state of affairs could be expected in Italy. The inbalance between rich and poor was endemic to that country, and it would survive the unrest of 1920, the corporative state created by Benito Mussolini, and the chaos which supervened after Marshal Badoglio surrendered in 1943, dividing the nation in two. The great gulf still exists, which is why there is still a satisfactory home market for the exotic vee-twelves of Ferrari and Lamborghini. The average Italian could certainly not afford any kind of new car in 1920, and such a luxury was also to be denied to his son.

Agnelli, however, saw further afield. Since 1901 he had been thinking in terms of global sales, and FIAT's racing successes had given him the *entrée* to every viable market by 1910. As late as 1912 a manufacturer still measured success in terms of his quota of crowned heads and titles, and on this score FIAT could match the rest of the First Division—the entire Italian Royal Family, Wilhelm II of Germany, Alfonso XIII of Spain, and Wilhelmina of Holland, not to mention twenty-two members of the British peerage, seventeen Indian princes, and five Austrian archdukes. In America the Vanderbilts and the Whitneys were driven in FIATS. Even at the outbreak of War D'Arcy Baker was promoting a line of Grosvenor-bodied field ambulances on the Zero and *Due* chassis as 'supplied to Millicent, Duchess of Sutherland, Miss Maxine Elliott, the London Panel Practitioners, the Oakley Hunt, the Ulster Field Force, and other well-known ambulance organisers'. Not that FIAT's 'absolute reliability and strength' went unrecognised in less class-conscious circles, for by 1917 the straight-frame *Tipo Due* commercial chassis had become the French Army's standard ambulance.

1910 saw FIAT heading the Italian motor industry, with a capital of 2,400,000 lire and a payroll of 3,500: their assets were treble those of their closest competitor, Isotta Fraschini, and six times those of the respected Bianchi concern. In the same year FIAT's output was 1,698 cars to Bianchi's 450 and Itala's 320, while in 1911 they were responsible for nearly half Italy's new motor vehicles. In the 1912–14 period FIAT production

16, 17, 18. '50' variations: the standard Zero torpedo of 1912 (top) was one of the first FIATS to feature series-manufactured coachwork. The detachable wheels are probably a later addition. The Type 56 tourer (centre) has very similar styling but was made only at Poughkeepsie. By 1914 the *Tipo* 5 (bottom) could be had with wire wheels and a rounded-vee radiator suggestive of a La Buire. Note the early example of a wrap-round windscreen.

(Carrozzeria Pininfarina
Herbert A. Schoenfeld)

19. Aeronautical beginnings. FIAT-Farman 5A pusher biplane with FIAT A-10 motor, 1914.

(FIAT)

20. FIATs for the Army. A line-up of 3As (left) and 2Bs (right), 1915. Clearly visible is the early type of pear-shaped radiator.

(FIAT)

21. Italy's first tank. Civilian and military officials superintend the trials of the Carro 2000, 1917.

(FIAT)

almost exactly equalled the nation's annual exports. 3,236 FIATS were made in 1914, when Italy shipped 3,291 cars abroad. Demand was steady, and sometimes there were not enough FIATS to go round: the relatively poor profit of Baker's company in 1911 was blamed on slow deliveries. In Switzerland, where the War had boosted the native industry and given the ailing house of Martini a much-needed if temporary shot in the arm, FIAT was still the most popular foreign *marque* in 1918. Though Swiss cars (1,653) outnumbered the 1,375 vehicles of French origin and the 763 German machines, there were 283 FIATS registered to 221 Renaults, 220 Peugeots, 175 part-Swiss Zedels, and a mere 143 Fords. Nor was this degree of penetration confined to Europe: Australian statistics for 1912 show 239 FIATS in use, and though these were small beer beside the 899 Fords, or even the 699 Talbots (popularised, no doubt, by the trans-continental adventures of Dutton and Brasier), they compared favourably with Overland (220) or Hupmobile (200). As yet FIAT offered nothing small or cheap, which explains why de Dion-Bouton (607) and Renault (534) were more popular in the Common-wealth. A fairer comparison would be Napier, also a manufac-turer who mixed fast tourers with taxicabs: they accounted for a mere 119 units, in spite of Imperial Preference. By 1914, inci-dentally, New South Wales alone registered 219 FIATS—a figure surpassed only by the ubiquitous Ford and the well-loved Talbot. A surprising number of FIATs from the 1911–15 era—mainly *Tipo* 2s—are still to be found in Australia.

In America FIAT had settled comfortably into a small niche in the carriage trade, and with prices in the $4,500–6,500 bracket they could operate profitably on an annual sale of less than five hundred cars. Distribution was nationwide, and the 1915 census shows that the *marque* topped the foreign league in Massachu-setts (which registered 182) and Rhode Island (77). Not much could be expected of Colorado (5) or Minnesota (25), while Michigan, as the 'automobile state', had little use for European cars, and registered a mere 23 foreigners in all, of which nine were Renaults.

Agnelli, however, was taking a broader look at the situation, as his statement on America shows. FIAT were still a big fish in a small pond, and it was not lost on their chief that America's own expensive behemoths were outselling the giants from Poughkeepsie. Massachusetts, for instance registered 1,794 Pierce-Arrows and no fewer than 3,102 Packards in 1915, and the latter firm's Twin-Six would soon raise their sales even higher. What is more, he was well aware that Detroit was fast replacing Paris as the world's general provider.

Italy was immune against any American invasion, war or no war. Foreign exchange was always in short supply, and the national requirements—first-class brakes and outstanding climbing ability—ruled out the woolly and inefficient motorcars at which the U.S.A. excelled. The danger was, however, only too evident in Britain and even more so in the British Empire, where the American car was tailor-made for local conditions. Agnelli's fears were to be realised in 1915, when Coventry and Birmingham switched to munitions, and the demand for cars was maintained by the 'business as usual' attitude which prevailed on the home front. Ford had been assembling in Manchester since 1911, and by 1913 it was the best-selling 'British' *marque*, with 6,139 units delivered to Wolseley's 3,000. Suddenly British industry awoke to the presence of a full-scale invasion. Fords apart, 5,152 American cars were imported in 1913, and 6,799 in 1914, but by 1915 imports were running at 3,000–4,000 a month, or more vehicles than FIAT could make in a whole year.

On his return from the U.S.A., Agnelli reminded Italians that the average price of a new American car was two-and-a-half times less than Turin was currently charging. Accurate comparisons are difficult, but the list price of a contemporary 1.8-litre *Tipo* Zero tourer in dollars was about $1,625, and it was not a lot of car by contrast with the big Buicks and Hudsons that sum would buy in the New World. Quantities alone made for a lower cost per copy. In 1912 FIAT sold 2,799 cars: by contrast Buick delivered 19,812, Cadillac 12,547 and even Packard accounted for 4,059 at a time when their cheapest model listed at $3,200. By American standards, FIAT no longer ranked in the top fifteen by 1914, when second-line makers of the calibre of Metz, Chalmers and Oakland were turning out more than 6,000 vehicles a year.

Thus a movement towards volume production became inevitable. 800 examples of an individual model were the exception in FIAT's first decade: between 1908 and 1911 they delivered 1,623 of their first inexpensive car, *Tipo* 1. Its successors, the 1,847 c.c. Zero and 1 series, ran from late 1911 to 1915, and accounted for 4,569 units. The War was to accentuate this process, for the demands of the Allied fighting services were insatiable, and at peak (during 1917) FIAT set a new record, with 1,898 motor vehicles made in a single month—more, in fact, than they had manufactured in the banner year of 1909. In 1918 the FIAT complex in Turin embraced a million square yards of ground, 30,000 workers (including 5,000 women), eleven railway junctions, 10,000 yards of goods sidings, and a fleet of two hundred lorries employed on inter-factory liaison. Already a new multi-story plant was being erected at Lingotto, though this was not to be opened until 1920.

Agnelli's policy of diversification had paid off in 1907: it was to pay off again after the Armistice. As an empire-builder, he had the edge on all his American rivals, and it is worth noting that only three of America's Top Ten in 1914 (Willys-Overland, Studebaker and Jeffery) had serious truck interests, while none of them were involved in railways, aviation or marine engines. The Piedmontese colossus never ventured timidly down any avenue, and consequently the reconversion period of 1919–21 held no terrors for FIAT. In England, Talbot's war was profitless, and the aftermath would drive them into the arms of Darracq. Nearer home, Itala's infelicitous efforts to produce Hispano-Suiza aero-engines led them to a lingering death. By contrast, FIAT inherited a fair share of the depleted aircraft market of the early 1920s, and this department was destined to play a major role in the build-up of Mussolini's Regia Aeronautica.

In the private-car field, standardisation was the keynote of FIAT policy between 1911 and 1918. This may seem an inept term to apply to a range which amounted in 1914 to eight chassis models and five types of engine, not to mention a ninth species made exclusively by Poughkeepsie for North American consumption. All these models have, however, certain characteristics in common—side-valve monobloc engines, full-pressure lubrication, high tension magneto ignition, four-speed unit gearboxes, multi-plate clutches, and bevel drive, though there was one exception to this last feature, the rare chain-driven *Tipo* 6 made between 1912 and 1914. True, the so-called '50' models differed in certain details, but these were minor ones such as the water-cooled transmission brakes of the bigger cars, the dual ignition offered by Poughkeepsie, and the Italian 'disease' of the period—a passion for experimenting with radiator shapes.

By contrast with the cars they replaced—the vast T-head 'sixes' and the race-bred o.h.v. *Tipo* Taunus—the 50s were, of course, tame. But then, as Mr Anthony Bird has sagaciously pointed out, performance was not a valid yardstick in those days, and the FIATs would do all that was expected of them, which implied a comfortable cruising speed of 35–40 m.p.h., and a genuine maximum of around the 50 mark, even in the case of the modest 1.8-litre versions. They were well-made and had few vices.

The most irritating aspect of the '50' family is FIAT's own notation. While the advent of monobloc engines brought with it a standard system of numbering, the method has been obscured by the habit (of which the present writer has been guilty) of using prefixes in the 50-series to designate *cars*. The factory used single digits, from 0 to 7, for their chassis models, *engines* using the 50 prefixes. Thus a *Tipo* 1 will have a *Tipo* 51 engine. So will a *Tipo* 0, since the difference between the two species lies in the chassis alone.

The Italian-built models of the period are:

Tipo 0	12–15 h.p.	4-cylinder	*Tipo* 51 or 51A engine
Tipo 1	12–15 h.p.	4-cylinder	*Tipo* 51 or 51A engine
Tipo 2	15–20 h.p.	4-cylinder	*Tipo* 52, 52A or 52B engine
Tipo 3	20–30 h.p.	4-cylinder	*Tipo* 53 or 53A engine

Tipo 4	35–50 h.p.	4-cylinder	*Tipo* 54A engine
Tipo 5	50–60 h.p.	4-cylinder	*Tipo* 55A engine
Tipo 6	50–60 h.p.	4-cylinder	*Tipo* 55A engine
Tipo 7	20–30 h.p.	6-cylinder	*Tipo* 57 engine

To make life even more complicated, the 52 and 53 engines were enlarged at the end of 1911, while Poughkeepsie used a notation of its own, assigning 50 prefixes to chassis. Thus American versions of the 3TER, 4 and 5 are known as the 53, 54 and 55 respectively, and the American Type 56 was a large shaft-driven 'six' unrelated to the Italian *Tipo* 6. There is also no connection, other than approximate size, between the later 4s and 5s, and the models of like designation marketed in 1908–9. Models 2, 3, 4 and 7 were introduced in 1910: the improved 1 and Zero followed in 1911; and the range was rounded out in 1912 with the addition of the nine-litre 5 and 6.

The Zero, which could be bought in London for £375 at the eve of War, was the simplest model on a wheelbase of 8 ft 4 in. The engine derived directly from the original *Tipo* 1 of 1908, but dimensions were now 70 × 120 mm (1,847 c.c.), output was up from 16 to 19 b.h.p., and a four-speed gearbox was standard. Rear suspension was three-quarter elliptic. and these cars would do about 50 m.p.h., with a useful 30 available on third gear. The Zero came with a factory-built four-seater tourer body, and wheels were of wood, with Michelin detachable rims.

Alongside the standard Zero the company made a few *Tipo* Brooklands cars. These featured pretty, flush-sided torpedo bodies which anticipated the 501S of 1921. The radiator was a miniature of the pear-shaped affair which had graced the S76 record car, and quick-detachable artillery of wire wheels were standard equipment. The engine was tuned to give 21 b.h.p. and the works driver Boschis managed 70 m.p.h. on test. Only 78 were produced. *Tipo Ibis*, also new in 1911, used the Zero's mechanics in a longer chassis with wider track, and this model frequently carried hire-car bodywork.

A step further up the range, the 15–20 h.p. *Tipo* 2 was a copy-book middle-class family car which fell into the British 'fifteen point nine' category. Output was around 26 b.h.p. and the original 80 × 130 mm (2.6-litre) power unit grew into a 2.8-litre with 140 mm piston stroke by 1912. This one, unlike the smaller cars, had a flywheel fan. *Tipo* 3 started life in 1910 as a 95 × 140 mm (3,969 c.c.) machine, enlarged two years later to 4.4. litres. This was a big car with a wheelbase of 10 ft 3⅞ in, boasted a water-cooled transmission brake, and cost £725 in London at the outbreak of War. Fifty chassis from the first series were fitted with 3.9-litre six-cylinder engines and sent to America and Australia under the designation *Tipo* 7. The standard 3s and 3As were only average performers on 40 b.h.p., but FIAT still had an eye on the sporting market, and in 1912 they added a short-chassis *spinto* version, *Tipo* 3TER. In sports guise the 3 wore semi-elliptic rear springs and (usually) wire wheels: clad in sports tourer bodywork it was quite handsome and good for an honest 60 m.p.h. A very few examples were given the S53A engine, a pushrod unit intended for competition work.

Even in landaulette form, a 3A could still be bought for under £1,000, but Croesus was not forgotten, and *Tipo* 4 was quite a lot of car, though it shared a wheelbase with the more modest 3 and 7. Its 5.7-litre engine developed 53 b.h.p., and this FIAT was a favourite with the King, who kept a brace of tourers, one for civil occasions and the other for his visits to front-line troops. An early 4 saloon with wrap-round windscreen was exhibited at the 1911 Paris Salon. At the top of the range were a pair of real giants, the 5 and the 6, with elephantine 9-litre engines and a high bonnet line commensurate with a piston stroke of 170 mm. The extra length of the power unit called for a wheelbase of 10 ft 7½ in and the 6 was the only chain-driven model to be offered after the disappearance of the S61 in 1913. It was not very popular: Italians with hairy tastes could shop better elsewhere, as witness the big o.h.v. 42–70 h.p. Bianchi and the even more brutal 100 h.p. KM-type Isotta Fraschini. This latter ran to an overhead camshaft, chain drive, four-wheel brakes, a *spitzkuhler* more aggressive than that of any Mercédès, and a top speed of about 90 m.p.h.

to the FIAT's 69. Admittedly the chassis price of £1,200 represented more than one would pay for a complete *Tipo* 6, but the 5 and 6 were not sports cars by any standards. The American magazine *Motor Age* laid it on the line in their advice to an amateur tuner who hoped to adapt his 5 for beach racing. 'We believe', they opined, 'that you have set yourself a thankless, hopeless task', and expressed surprise that their correspondent had attained 68 m.p.h. on a 2.33:1 back axle.

It is only fair to add that the American-built Type 55 version was a heavier car, especially in its later manifestations, while not everyone considered its going lethargic. Horace Beale, who was nurtured on the sporting T-headers, recalls 'being soundly beaten by a "55" when driving a Hudson "Super Six" at night. I mistook the open approaching exhaust for a four-cylinder Stutz, and thought I had a fighting chance. I was quite thoroughly mistaken'. Be that as it may, image and market alike were changing, and FIAT sold only 86 *Tipo* 6s as against 457 of the bevel-driven *Tipo* 5s.

The '50' family underwent little modification. Pressed-steel artillery wheels became a regular option in 1913, and electric lighting and starting were available on all models save the Zero a year later. 1915 versions of the 3, 4 and 5 came with full electrics as standard.

More complicated is the question of radiator shape: there seem to be few rules to this game. The situation was, however, general throughout the Italian industry. On Isottas, no holds were barred, for the rare 100 h.p. was seen with three styles— a pear shape as found on contemporary FIATS and Züsts, a Germanic vee, and a gentler, squatter rounded-vee reminiscent of the Standard 6½-litre Bentley. So it was with FIAT. Though the S76's streamline shape was confined to Brooklands versions of the Zero, two other configurations were in common use. The earlier, squared-corner version derived from the first *Tipo* 1 of 1908, and was found on most cars until 1913, when it gave way to the pear shape, which in its turn evolved into the taller variant used on the 501 and his relatives until 1925–6. To make life more difficult, some later 5s and 6s (not to mention a few

of the last S61s) used a rounded vee not unlike that of contemporary La Buires. The two basic species existed side by
side during 1914, when the English catalogue offered buyers
a free choice: I have never, incidentally, seen the pear shape on
a Zero. Curiously the first prototypes of Cavalli's transitional
Tipo 70, which took the road in 1915, reverted to the old
configuration.

Poughkeepsie followed its own path. Initially their staple
was *Tipo* 4, at $4,000 for a touring car and $4,500 for a limousine, but during 1912 an American version of *Tipo* 5 joined the
range. Alongside this they offered Type 56, a vast 110 × 150 mm
(8,553 c.c.) 'six' on classic FIAT lines. Wheelbase was 11 ft 3 in,
and like Poughkeepsie's big 'fours', it came with dual ignition
and all brakes on the rear wheels. At $5,000 for a seven-seater
tourer it was the most expensive model in the range, and
owners compared its flexibility with that of a Rolls-Royce.
Certainly it could creep majestically along in top with the
huge engine scarcely rotating, but it lacked the 55's urge, being
flat out at around 50. By 1914 the 54 was on its way out, while
55s and 56s came with a clock and electric lights as standard,
though a starter was still $150 extra. During the season the
firm tried its luck with a compact, the Tipo 53, or 'Light
Thirty', which was merely the short-wheelbase Italian 3TER,
complete with foot transmission brake and full electrics. A
tourer cost $3,600, but it was too small for the carriage trade
and was dropped during 1916. All 1915 American FIATs had
electric starters and streamlined dashes, though the old-school
radiator with its Mercédès look did not disappear altogether
until 1916. During this period McLaughlin of Oshawa handled
Poughkeepsie's products in Canada as a second string to their
regular Buick business.

The 1916 American FIAT was a handsome and well-pro-
portioned car, especially with the 'Riviera' touring body which
cost $4,850 on a 55 chassis and $5,350 on the six-cylinder 56.
The pear-shaped radiator was becoming fashionable in the
United States: too much so for FIAT, who instituted legal
proceedings against Oldsmobile for copying it too closely on

22. Stillborn Infant. A plan view of the 500 two-seater which appeared in FIAT's first post-war catalogue, 1918.
(FIAT)

23. Vintage Best-Seller. A first series 501 torpedo, 1919. Note the taller and less rounded radiator, the unusual side-lamp location and the angular wings used until 1922.

(FIAT)

24. Anglo-Italian. A 510 with special all-weather bodywork by Lanchester, 1920. Though detachable wheels were standard, at least one owner seems to have preferred the old fixed wheels and detachable rims. **25.** (below) Greek Taxi. A 502 for service in Athens, 1925. The combination of balloon tyres and brakeless front axle is interesting, as is the transliteration on the outside radiator badge.

(National Motor Museum)

their new, inexpensive vee-eight. For 1917 only a revised Type 55 (the E-17) was offered on a longer, 11 ft 8 in wheelbase. It was made in small numbers until February, 1918, when the factory was sold to Duesenberg Motors Corporation for aero-engine manufacture. Josephs had not apparently given up, though, for *Automotive Industries* noted:

> The FIAT company will continue to occupy a part of the building, and the production and assembly of FIAT cars will go on much as usual.

This was wishful thinking. When FIAT cars reappeared in the United States early in 1920, an advertisement in *Motor Age* stated that 'every FIAT product is completely made at the Turin factories'. Poughkeepsie's days were over, despite a rumour current in 1928 to the effect that Vincenzo Lancia was buying the plant for the production of 'Dilambdas' for the American market. Undoubtedly the vee-eight Lancia was designed for the New World, but when last heard of FIAT's erstwhile U.S. branch was making refrigerators.

Back in Turin, the commercial vehicle programme was closely related to Fornaca's private car designs. Though delivery van versions of *Tipo* 1 were offered, FIAT, as we have seen, never made the mistake of basing their trucks too slavishly on touring chassis of inadequate strength. Their standard one-tonner used the mechanical elements of *Tipo* 2 in a reinforced straight frame with heavy-duty rear axle. It rode on pneumatic tyres, and cost £385 in England. The bigger *Tipo* 15 was built round *Tipo* 3's 4.4-litre unit, and served in Tripolitania during the Italo-Turkish War of 1912–13, in which an armoured-car version was also tried. This carried a single machine-gun in a revolving turret. Heaviest of the lorry range was *Tipo* 18, a hefty, solid-tyred affair with separate four-speed box and side-chain drive. Payload was three tons, the engine was a long-stroke (95 × 180 mm) development of the regular '50' theme, and in 1914 it could be bought in London for £766. All these models retained the squared-corner radiator until well after the War. During 1912 FIAT also went into the bus business with the establishment of the S.I.T.A. company in Tuscany. It is still active to this day, and I well remember the aplomb with which its drivers conducted their big 626N diesel coaches through dried-up river beds on the Siena-Volterra-Livorno route in 1947, when the road system was still very makeshift, and burnt-out *Wehrmacht* transport lay in the ditches.

FIAT's image might take a utilitarian turn after 1910, but the firm duly supported the revival of the Grand Prix in 1912 with a team of three S74s, driven by Wagner, de Palma and Bruce-Brown. The stars of this race were the new twin-cam 7.6-litre Peugeots, and the 3-litre Sunbeams and Vauxhalls entered for the concurrently-run *Coupe de l'Auto*, but on the first lap Bruce-Brown led from the Peugeot of Georges Boillot and Hémery's 15-litre chain-driven Lorraine-Dietrich, a dinosaur even bigger than the FIATs. Mechanical troubles eliminated the Lorraines on the second circuit, at a quarter distance Bruce-Brown, Boillot and Wagner were the leaders, with Hancock's Vauxhall in fourth place. The second day's racing saw the defeat of the monsters: had the FIATs retained the Rudge-Whitworth wire wheels which they wore in practice sessions, they might still have triumphed, but rumour said that the wires had a dangerous effect on handling, with the consequence that the cars had been sent back to Paris to have them swapped for the older fixed wood type with detachable rims. Henceforward the FIATs were dogged by slow tyre changes, and Boillot was able to edge past Bruce-Brown to take the lead. On Lap 14 the big Italian car sprang a fuel leak, and the unhappy Bruce-Brown was disqualified for refuelling away from the pits, a fate which also befell de Palma. The young American carried on to the end, his mastery of the unwieldy giant making him the hero of the race: he also made the fastest lap, at 76.8 m.p.h. Boillot's Peugeot won, and Wagner had to be content with second place, his average speed being 67.32 m.p.h. to the visitor's 68.45. A sign of the times was the ability of Rigal's 3-litre Sunbeam to lap a mere 2 m.p.h. slower than Bruce-Brown on the top of his form.

The 1912 Targa Florio was a fairly tame event, and FIATs finished third and fifth—the winner was Cyril Snipe (SCAT);

Garetto's Lancia came second. This was, of course, a private entry: Lancia himself might be too busy as a manufacturer to drive for FIAT any more, but he never fielded a works team anywhere. Tenth place in the race went to a Florio: by this time the Cavaliere, too, made his own cars, having progressed beyond camouflaged FIATs. His works manager was a young man named Vittorio Valletta, whom we will encounter again.

In America, 1912 was destined to be the *marque*'s last great season, though several S74s were sold to private owners in that country. At Santa Monica in May, Teddy Tetzlaff led for most of the race in spite of ramming a barricade and bursting a tyre. He won by a hairsbreadth from Caleb Bragg on a sister car. At Tacoma in July 'Terrible Teddy' used his S61 to score a couple of wins, while he reverted to the big 14-litre machine for Indianapolis, where he finished second. This year's Grand Prize was run at Milwaukee, and J. S. Josephs entered a team of three S74s (Tetlaff, Bragg, and Bruce-Brown). Three days before the race, Bruce-Brown was killed in a practice crash, and Bragg was only just persuaded not to scratch. In Bruce-Brown's place was nominated the great Barney Oldfield, driving, incredibly, in his first major road race.

Peter Helck has compared Tetzlaff's scorching style with Lancia's at his zenith. He charged straight into the lead, pursued by Bragg, who was only a few seconds behind, and took over when his team-mate came in for a tyre change. The internecine strife continued, with Tetzlaff lapping at 77.03 m.p.h. But brutality will out: after 244 miles a radius rod broke, leaving de Palma's Mercédès to continue the battle with Bragg. He nearly made it, too, but as he swung out to overtake, wheel touched wheel, and the Mercédès overturned, throwing the crew clear. Bragg won at 68.4 m.p.h., and Oldfield did well to take fourth place. The Vanderbilt Cup was something of an anti-climax for the sole FIAT representative was Tetzlaff on one of the smaller S61s, and his transmission broke. Characteristically he was in the lead at the time, and had maintained an average of 73 m.p.h. He had also, as in the Grand Prize, been responsible for the fastest lap.

This was the end. There was no works team, even from Poughkeepsie, in 1913, the S74s were showing their age, and the only big win of the year went to Frank Verbeck, who won the Los Angeles-Sacramento road race on an elderly stripped touring car, probably a 1909 *Tipo* 4. Giordano's fifth place in the 1913 Targa Florio, was followed by a third place for Lopez in 1914. A photograph of the latter's car suggests that it was a stripped 3TER, perhaps with the o.h.v. engine.

With two exceptions, 1914 was just as lean. A *Tipo* 3 won a hill-climb in Moscow, and Brambeck's *Tipo* 4 was the first car to finish the Swedish Winter Trial, though on formula he was only fifth, behind a Minerva, two Horchs, and a Hupmobile. There was a fifth place, too, for McNeill in Australia's Melbourne-Sydney Trial, but in America the scene was but a pale echo of the golden age of Cedrino and Bruce-Brown. The Grand Prize and the Vanderbilt Cup had moved again, this time to a fast 9½-mile circuit at Santa Monica, California. For the former race Tetzlaff and Lewis entered S74s, and Verbeck an S61. Only Tetzlaff was in the running—until a connecting-rod broke in the early stages. Verbeck also ran in the Vanderbilt, but retired without making any impression. Ironically, the cream of Europe's racing cars were just about to descend on America once more, but this time Peugeot would be the leaders, not FIAT. The chain of events that was to inspire Harry Miller's twin-cam 'eights' and thus pave the way for the Type 51 Bugatti, had nothing to do with Turin. 1915 passed without a single victory for FIAT, though *Motor Age* published a touching tribute to 'Cyclone', once the pride of Emmanuele Cedrino, and later campaigned by Barney Oldfield. 'Undoubtedly the oldest racing car now in active service', commented the magazine, 'it has a displacement of 600 cubic inches and in its day was very speedy. It is now in the hands of a Richmond, Virginia, motorist and is for sale, it is understood, for $500'. If this really was 'Cyclone', it was much too big to have been any kind of Kaiserpreis FIAT—but it was not, in any case, destined to survive much longer in original guise. A few months later it was announced that the doughty old engine had blown up during a meeting at Phoenix, Arizona, and was to be replaced by a Mercer unit. A vehicle purporting to be 'Cyclone' was around in Southern California in the 1950s, but there was precious little FIAT about it.

The two spots on the European horizon were the Austrian Alpine Trial and the Grand Prix. The former was a tough rally now established as a worthy successor to the Herkomer and Prince Henry events, though it was too remote for many a manufacturer, and Britons might have ignored it altogether had not a privately-owned Rolls-Royce baulked at the Katschberg in 1912. Such an unheard-of defeat called for massive retribution, in the form of a works team from Derby. By 1914, of course, Rolls-Royce had made their point, and the *marque* was represented only by the amateur, James Radley.

Among those firms, however, who were still interested were FIAT, or rather their Viennese associates. Three cars were entered, and three clean sheets were won. The exact identity of these cars remains an enigma. Contemporary reports quote the unlikely cylinder dimensions of 85×150 mm, whereas FIAT say that the Trial models were standard *Tipo Dues* of 80×140 mm. Interestingly enough, the eminent German historian Hans Heinrich von Fersen has shown me photographs of a special o.h.v. Austro-FIAT engine made in 1912, and it is possible that developments of this unit were used in 1914.

The 1914 Grand Prix at Lyons was run under a 4½-litre formula. Not only did it mark the beginning of modern racing— it was also something of a send-off to the old Europe, the safe, secure continent that Sarajevo would shatter, and the October Revolution reduce to ashes. A large and interesting field included three Italian teams, Aguila-Italiana and Nazzaro entering as well as FIAT. Itala, still reeling from Guido Bigio's untimely death, had given up racing, which meant that Cagno was back with his old employers, though Nazzaro drove one of his own products and Wagner had transferred to Mercédès.

FIAT's S57 racer had inherited its monobloc engine from the 50 series, and its single overhead camshaft from the S61 and S74. Lubrication was by gear-type pump, and the 100×143 mm four-cylinder unit was supposed to give 135 b.h.p. at 3,000 r.p.m.: as the much faster Mercédès was credited with a mere 115 b.h.p. one wonders if the FIATS came up to form on race day. The four-speed gearbox and multi-disc clutch were regular practice, though mounting these in unit with the engine was not. Chain drive had at last been abandoned, and after the misfortunes of Dieppe in 1912 FIAT were once again reconciled to Rudge-Whitworth wheels. But most interesting of all were the four-wheel brakes—not, it would seem, an original part of the design, but an afterthought. FIAT were not alone in taking this advanced step, for the Delages, Peugeots and Piccard Pictets were also so equipped. The French and Swiss, however, favoured the uncoupled arrangement which had already defeated Crossley and was to render the management of early Austin Sevens a slightly hazardous business: the S57's system boasted simultaneous actuation. In view of contemporary driving techniques, it is not, perhaps, surprising to find that the lever acted as the service brake, the pedal working on the rear wheels only. The cars were capable of a little over 90 m.p.h. and were therefore no match for the rapid Peugeots and Mercédès. Hence the advanced anchors were irrelevant, and in any case both Cagno and Scales (now promoted from a mechanic's seat) retired. Fagnano kept station almost from start to finish, taking eleventh place, but the lap speeds tell their own story. The best Mercédès performance was 69.65 m.p.h., the Peugeots were good for 68.65, and the Sunbeams for 67.82 m.p.h., but the quickest FIAT managed a mere 65.21 m.p.h. The S57 was to redeem itself after the Armistice, and is of interest as the last 'works' FIAT model to be sold into private service after the factory had finished with it. All subsequent Grand Prix and *voiturette* racers have disappeared without trace, probably into some Mussolinian scrap drive.

This was not quite the end of the story, however. During the War Sunbeams contrived to build a new six-cylinder racer and send it to Indianapolis, and FIAT proposed to follow suit in 1917. What is more, they had put in a lot of work on the original 1913–14 design, boring the engine out to 4,859 c.c. An extra magneto and some modifications to the valve gear had boosted output to 150 b.h.p., while the original airship tail with its side-mounted spare wheels had given way to a simple, unstreamlined back end incorporating a bolster tank and twin vertical spares. Handling was said to be vastly improved, thanks to slight increases in both wheelbase and track, and Scales and Fagnano were retained as drivers. Though 'all speed tests have had to have been made on the open road under everyday conditions', the cars had done as much as 112 m.p.h. They were waiting in Genoa Docks, with Giovanni Agnelli himself in attendance, when the 1917 '500' was cancelled. Racegoers would not see the revised S57/14B until 1919, and then its appearance would also mark the début of the great Antonio Ascari.

In fact, Ascari's S57 was in neither Lyons nor Indianapolis trim. True, the body bore a superficial resemblance to the 1917 car, but a closer look revealed a lower bonnet line, the absence of bulges on the bonnet sides (betokening but a single magneto), and a larger fuel tank, capacity being increased from 130 to 160 litres. What is more, both Ascari's car and the one used by Masetti to win the 1921 Targa Florio had 4½-litre engines.

The War did not put an immediate stop to private-car production, for the Italian Army adopted *Tipo Due* as its standard staff vehicle, as well as taking a number of 3s and 4s. The wartime edition of the 2B incorporated a number of improvements, among them a streamlined dash, full electrics, and quick-detachable wheels, which were usually FIAT-made five-stud discs. The standard body was a seven-seater tourer, which called for a longer wheelbase. At the other end of the scale the company evolved an elephantine artillery tractor, which for sheer brute force can only have been surpassed by the 150 h.p. Austro-Daimler *C-Zug* used by the Central Powers. At eleven tons, the FIAT was a great deal heavier than that nightmarish product of Anglo-French ingenuity, the Daimler-Renard tractive unit of 1908. It was powered by an immense four-cylinder petrol/paraffin unit developing 70 b.h.p., could attain a tarmac-pulverising 7 m.p.h. on the level, and in similar conditions could haul 100 tons, not to mention a payload of another three-and-a-half tons behind the cab. Even on a 1-in-7 gradient it could cope with 25 tons. The rear wheels were chain-driven, caterpillar tracks could be added to give extra traction, and the specification included a lockable differential, first tried on FIAT trucks in 1911.

Armoured car development continued, the French and Russians using some ponderous affairs based on Poughkeepsie-built Type 55 chassis. These wore twin rear wheels, the tyres were stuffed with 'special filler', and an auxiliary steerman's position was provided at the rear, as on the British Army's Austins and Peerlesses, 'the advantage being that the armoured car can run up as close to the firing line as desired, use the turret guns, and immediately back straight away without having to turn around and subject the car to broadside firing from the opposite line'. Alas! the average armoured fighting vehicle of the period had the aerodynamics of a haystack, and carried more boiler plate than engines of limited power could bear, hence movement was seldom 'immediate'. The later history of these chassis was to be curious, as we shall hear. Italian tank development had hardly got off the ground when the Armistice was signed, but in 1918 FIAT built two prototypes of 'Carro 2000', Italy's first track-laying vehicle. It had a higher centre of gravity than its British or German contemporaries, and the 240 h.p. six-cylinder engine was offset in the hull to allow the crew to move freely down the vehicle's full length. Its 65 mm cannon was the largest piece of ordnance to have been installed in a revolving tank turret at the time of construction.

More important, the War added the aeroplane to FIAT's repertoire. Italy boasted only 57 service aircraft of all types in 1914, and the first product of the company's new division, the S.I.A. 5B, was a pusher biplane on Farman lines. S.I.A., of course, stood for Societa Italiana Aeronautica, though it was also an interlingual pun, being an Italian translation of *'fiat'*. During the period of hostilities the two companies were to be responsible for 1,336 aeroplanes and 15,830 aero engines, these latter deriving from the 9½-litre o.h.c. six-cylinder A10. The next step was the A12, a 24-valve 'six' with alloy pistons and I-section connecting-rods which was persuaded to give as much 320 b.h.p., and attracted the attention of Britain and America alike when their own development programmes lagged behind. No FIAT engines were ever fitted to American-built aircraft, though the U.S. Army used FIAT-built S.I.A. 7s as well as French Brégust XIVs with FIAT motors. British service types tested with the A12 included the Vickers 'Vimy' twin-engined bomber and the de Havilland 4 and 9 biplanes. Alas! FIAT also had their hands full, and the R.F.C. and R.A.F. received only 611 of the one thousand A12s for which they had contracted. This engine was also used on some interesting long-distance flights which were somehow organised during the War. These included Turin-Naples-Turin non-stop, and Turin to London in under seven hours. By 1918 examples of the 700 h.p. A14, the War's most powerful operational engine, were going into service.

FIAT motors were used in Italian-built Aviatiks as well as by such important firms as Caproni, Macchi, Pomilio and Savoia-Marchetti, but S.I.A. themselves soon progressed beyond Farman-type pushers. Not, however, before examples of these had been persuaded to haul a 25 mm cannon into the air, and to raise the World's Altitude Record to 6,453 metres in April, 1917. Later FIATs included the SP4, a single engined bomber used to drop agents behind the enemy lines, and the 7 reconnaissance biplane with A12-bis engine, designed by Torretta and Lerici. The *Tipo* 7 evolved into the 9B with A14 engine and twin guns for the observer, but though this did 127 m.p.h., it had an unhappy service record. Last of the wartime S.I.A.s was the R2 with 300 h.p. A12bis engine, designed by a new name, Celestino Rosatelli: this was an exemplary machine which remained in service until 1925. Rosatelli, a graduate of Rome University, played as important a part on the aircraft side of the business as did Fornaca and Giacosa in the history of the cars. He came to FIAT from S.V.A. (Savoia-Verduzio), and stayed with them until his death in 1945. Among his best-known creations were the famous 'CR' series of unequal-span fighter biplanes culminating in the CR42 of 1939, and the BR20, Italy's standard medium bomber in World War II. During the First World War the company opened a flying-field at Mirafiori, though another twenty years were to elapse before they were to start building cars 'out of town'.

On paper FIAT had a good war. In terms of capital growth, the results were astounding. A company whose assets at the turn of the century had been a mere 800,000 lire, increased to 25 million by 1914, emerged from the conflict with its capital quadrupled. Already Agnelli was thinking in terms of 12,000 cars a year, and he was reaching for markets far wider than those embraced by Fornaca's Zero; in fact Cavalli had shown part of the company's hand with the *Tipo* 70, a 2-litre car which had begun its trials in 1915. The Italian authorities obligingly placed a sizable order, and just over a thousand were eventually made. In the pipeline was something even more promising, a miniature four-cylinder which anticipated both Peugeot's 'Quadrilette' and Herbert Austin's Seven. A 5-litre luxury model was also promised, and rumour said it would be a 'six', FIAT's first since the end of *Tipo* 7's brief run in 1911.

One of these objectives Agnelli was soon to attain. Deliveries passed the ten thousand mark in 1922, thanks to a patchy racing programme which Kent Karslake has summarised delightfully as 'FIAT *lux et tenebrae*'. But the public had to wait until 1925 for a an 'Everyman's FIAT', and even then it was not everyone's cup of tea. Italy was about to enter on her darkest years, and to reap the whirlwind of a young nation ruled by oligarchs who had cared more for national prestige than for the well-being of the people.

5 Ministry of all the Talents

*From the very start the car immediately suggests to the driver
that sense of goodness—it is hard to describe it otherwise—
which characterises any high-class automobile. The manner of
engagement of the gears . . . and the sound of the engine all
combine to assure the experienced driver that the car is a
thoroughbred.*

501 Road Test, *The Autocar*, April 1921

FIAT's performance in the early 1920s was a remarkable one.

The erstwhile purveyors of luxury carriages finally crossed
their Rubicon with an inexpensive 1½-litre model offering new
standards of durability and refinement. On the circuits Giulio
Cesare Cappa's two-litre 'sixes' won the 1922 French and
Italian Grands Prix, while the company's first racing *voiturettes*
the 802 and 803, got away to a promising start. Round the
corner lay a formidable 'double', the first successful use of
forced induction in a major race, and the World's Land Speed
Record. In the air, the name was becoming known in Schneider
Trophy circles, and the breadth of Agnelli's thinking was
reflected in three more 'firsts': the first Italian agricultural
tractor (1919), the Regia Aeronautica's first all-Italian single-
seater fighter (1924), and Italy's first really big reinforced
concrete edifice, the five-storey Lingotto plant completed in
1922, at the end of a rebuilding programme which involved new
blast furnaces and a large research laboratory.

FIAT, of course, were already self-contained, and could claim
in 1921 that 'all power required by the factory, including the
current for heating the furnaces, is produced at FIAT's own
generating station in the Alps'.

Lingotto was a further step forward. It incorporated a test-
track on the roof, and was to spearhead an astonishing spurt

in production which even the industrial disputes of 1919–20 and the uneven tenor of the Italian political scene under Giolitti and Facta could not stem. Only 1,973 private cars were delivered in 1919, but 1920, incredibly, saw a record 6,584, climbing to 8,988 in 1921. The 10,000 mark was passed in 1922, and in 1923 13,629 of Italy's 22,820 new cars were FIATS. Exports followed the same upward swing, from a modest 3,000 in 1920 to more than 8,000, or sixty per cent of all production, by 1923. But the clearest indication of recovery was the firm's balance-sheet. In 1921, as Italy settled down to an uneasy industrial peace, FIAT made a marginal profit of 20,000 lire: a year later, with 501s pouring out of Lingotto at an ever-quickening tempo, the company was in the black to the tune of a resounding nineteen million!

One might argue that this was no miracle. Meteoric arrivals in the First Division were not unknown, and the same period alone had seen such cases as Dodge and Chevrolet in the United States, and Morris in Britain. Morris's performance, indeed, appears more meritorious than FIAT's. In 1907, when Agnelli's cars were sweeping the board, William Morris was still selling and servicing the motorcycles of Oxonians. In 1913, as *Tipo Zero* heralded Agnelli's first assault on middle-class markets, the Morris-Oxford was strictly an assembled car, albeit an excellent one. Yet in 1935, when Lord Nuffield's Series I 8 h.p. was pushing Cowley's output to six-figure levels, FIAT's private-car deliveries were less than a third of this amount. As for Chevrolet, who could have foretold that a world's best-seller could stem from a stolid six-cylinder tourer aping the fashionable Belgian Métallurgique, and sponsored by a young Swiss who had made his name at the wheel of Enrico's huge chain-driven FIATS?

Such bald comparisons must, however, ignore more than one major factor. Both Britain and America possessed healthy home markets capable of assimilating the right kind of car in steadily increasing quantities—Morris and Chevrolet alike rode to success on this solid clientele. FIAT, with ninety per cent of Italian motorists among their customers, could not make a living out of these alone. All it gave them was responsibility: they dared not make a bad car. It is also salutary to remember that America's entry into World War I did not mean the end of private-car production: in 1917 and 1918, while Morris made shells at Cowley and Agnelli's factories churned out trucks, aircraft, and aero-engines, the roads of the United States were richer to the tune of nearly 200,000 more Chevrolets.

Italy may have emerged from the conflict on the winning side, but she was not a winner. True, she had been spared the carnage that had robbed France of a generation, or the trench warfare that had devastated much of Belgium; but she inherited unrest on a scale rivalled only by Germany. In 1920 a series of strikes had weakened Britain's economy, with trouble spreading to the pits and the railways, but this was nothing by contrast with Italy's record: 1,881 major stoppages and a million-and-a-half man-hours lost in 1920 alone. An obsessional fear of 'Bolshies' permeated right-wing British circles, but no factory in Coventry or Birmingham suffered the fate of FIAT, where a workers' soviet took over, barring the doors against Agnelli and Fornaca. Slump or no slump, the Italian home market was weakly: even in 1928 FIAT could easily have satisfied the entire national demand for cars, buses, trucks and farm tractors without working a second's overtime. Nor was this state of affairs alleviated by a system of graduated taxation beside which Whitehall's iniquitous 1921 formula pales into insignificance. A '25 *cavalli*' paid £104 a year and a 50CV like Isotta Fraschini's new straight-eight contributed a swingeing £600 to the national exchequer. Italian *cavalli* were more mettlesome than their British counterparts. The 501, which was a 10CV in Paris and an Eleven in London, emerged as a Sixteen in Rome. The Roman bureaucrats went to town on FIAT's big 'sixes', the 4.8-litre 519 of 1922 growing into a 41CV, whilst even the modest 510 concealed thirty-three expensive horses under its bonnet. By the 1930s Italian industry was resigned to the fact that a long-wheelbase 3-litre limousine was the limit, even for kings, ambassadors, and the Fascist Grand Council. Isottas were common in Los Angeles, New York and London, but hardly ever seen in Rome or Milan.

As we shall see, both FIAT and Lancia explored the super-car market in the immediate post-Armistice years but neither company's V-12 even reached the general public. Italy was to wait another twenty-seven years for its first production Twelve —and when this arrived it was aimed at a very different kind of V.I.P.

These were the outward and visible signs of malaise. Beneath the surface, however, Italy was reaping the whirlwind of cavalier treatment meted out by remote and aristocratic 'liberal' governments. Undoubtedly their misdeeds were exacerbated by a lack of *rapport* between Rome and Piedmont, and one wonders whether the workers of Turin were much worse off than their opposite numbers in Lancashire. The facts are nevertheless depressing. FIAT was an enlightened and left-inclined company, yet their standard daily rate of pay in 1919 amounted to fourteen lire (eleven shillings) for an unskilled worker, and 25 lire (just under a pound) for skilled grade. A ten-hour day was the norm, and despite FIAT's good labour record and the social welfare programme instituted by Giovanni Agnelli there had already been two bad strikes, one at the end of 1907 and the second in 1913.

The 'land fit for heroes' promised by Lloyd George in 1918 did not exist in the United Kingdom: but in Italy it was a joke in the worst possible taste. Returning soldiers found neither jobs nor prospects. The War had decimated the chances of emigration, while the price of swapping sides in 1915 was isolation from two of the country's best export markets—Germany and Austria. Once again the shortage of raw materials made itself felt, and Italy's merchant marine had suffered badly from enemy action. Many young Italians had been junior clerks in 1914; by 1918 they held commissioned rank in Victor Emmanuel's army, and there is no more effective malcontent than a *tenente* in a demob suit, armed with a copper handshake. As early as 1919 Gabriele d'Annunzio attempted a *putsch* in Fiume, and though Benito Mussolini's newborn Fascist Party as yet lacked a sense of direction, it was strongly nationalist. This streak was of course to triumph over Mussolini's other dislikes (the Church, 'official' socialism, and the Roman Establishment). In September, 1920, the future Duce was still sitting firmly to the left of centre, and had this to say of the Occupation of the Factories:

> I not only accept that unprecedented control of the factories, but their social and co-operative management as well. . . . I demand that the factories increase their output. If this is guaranteed to me by the workers in place of the industrialists, I shall declare without hesitation that the former have the right to substitute themselves for the latter.

By the end of the year he knew better. He must have been aware that the soviet which had dislodged Agnelli and Fornaca soon begged them to return to the helm, and at Bologna the following April he protested that his *Fascisti* did not 'worship violence for violence's sake'. Once his nineteen-year dictatorship was under way, the *volte face* was complete, for much of his support came from the big industrialists (though not from Agnelli), and expediency demanded an alignment with capitalism. Mussolini even advocated the liquidation of unprofitable state industries, and this realistic attitude was to encompass the slow death of Itala, whose illness was beyond even the curative powers of the state-financed I.R.I., or Reconstruction Finance Corporation. Thereafter Mussolini confined his efforts to meddling—classic instances are the spanners thrown into the Ford-Isotta negotiations of 1930, and the abrupt termination of O.M.'s private car line a year later.

Mussolini gave Italy efficient government. His role as the saviour of the Italian motor industry has, however, been overstated. Though he was a keen driver and pilot, and understood motor cars, his contribution, except as a road-builder, cannot rival that of Adolf Hitler in Germany. He may have advocated the eight-hour day in *Il Popolo* as early as 1919, but concerted strike action made it a reality two years before he came to power. As for the ninety per cent export target with which the carmakers were saddled, this was certainly dear to Mussolinian economic policy, but its architects were the last of the old-line Liberals Giolitti and Facta.

Mussolini's main contribution to industrial recovery was rearmament. Other governments might retrench and preach universal peace, but *Il Duce* wanted an efficient air force. In 1923 he merged the naval and military air arms to form the Regia Aeronautica, and two years later he could boast of sixty-four operational squadrons and a thousand aircraft. This was good business for car firms with a finger in the aeronautical pie, and this meant Ansaldo, Isotta Fraschini and s.p.a. as well as FIAT, whose *sezione aeronautica* enjoyed a boom, aircraft deliveries jumping from 117 in 1922 to 516 in 1924. Also salutary was the motorisation of the army, for FIAT's lorry business had suffered a disastrous slump, now that the market was flooded with war-surplus trucks. During the War, with the factories working twenty-four hour shifts, 20,000 *Tipo* 18 three-tonners alone had been made, and even in 1919 the impetus had not been wholly lost, for FIAT had turned out another 10,618 commercial vehicles. By 1920 this was down to 7,730 units, but in 1921 a mere 1,328 were made. There was, after all, no point in an operator's parting with £550 for a new 15TER when the surplus-merchants offered the same thing, fully equipped, for a paltry £190. Not even a successful 4,000-mile exploratory tour of the Sahara, accomplished by a squadron of FIAT lorries, could drum up business that just was not there, and the only new commercial model introduced in the immediate post-War period was the 1T, a taxicab version of the 1915 *Tipo* 1 private car.

In spite of this, FIAT architected their own revival, by making the right cars at the right time, and resisting the temptation to explore the carriage trade too deeply. Though the 2B and 3A were still catalogued as late as 1920–21, these antiques were reserved for the home market. The remaining post-Armistice models were entirely new, and a brochure issued while Italy was still at war indicates that the company was prepared to cover every sector, from the baby car to the semi-luxury sector previously represented by the 4.4-litre *Tipo* 3 and the 5.7-litre *Tipo* 4.

Students of the technical press already had a shrewd idea of Cavalli's plans, for his interim 2-litre *Tipo* 70 had been on the road since 1915, and had been built in limited series. *Motor Age* considered that the most significant departure was the standardisation of a five-seater tourer body, but then Americans were unaware that this had also been done with the old *Tipo Zero* since 1912. In fact the main differences between the 70 and 1914 50-series cars were the use of Sankey steel detachable wheels and full electrics, though a closer investigation would have revealed that both brakes now worked in separate shoes on the rear wheels. The transmission brake was not to reappear until the adoption of hydraulics at the end of 1930.

The 'streamline' body was a direct heritage from the 2B, and the Zero-type radiator used in 1915 soon gave way to a modern version of the pear shape, identical with the post-War style as found on the 501, 505 and 510. Other distinguishing features of the experimental 70s were tubular radiator cores, two-bearing crankshafts, and fixed cylinder heads, but production models used a three-bearing detachable-head unit developing 21 b.h.p. at 2,400 r.p.m., sufficient to propel the car at 45 m.p.h. Wheelbase, at 8 ft 2½ in, was slightly shorter than that of the definitive 501.

The 70, incidentally, was the last FIAT to use the old type-notation that had been in force since 1908. For most of the inter-War period a new, standardised system of nomenclature came into force, with three-digit type serials assigned to all vehicles. The 500 group was reserved for private cars. 600s went to commercials, 700s to tractors, and 800s to racers. As in pre-War days, engine designations were closely related, with 100 units in cars and 400s in racing machinery: units specifically intended for truck use carried 300 serials. There were, of course, some inconsistencies. All members of the 514 family, including the very similar 515, used the 114 engine, but there were two distinct commercial variants. The regular 8-cwt light van on the car chassis was marketed as the 514F, but the one-ton lorry, a different design conceived around 514/114 mechanical elements, became the 614. After World War II, of course, confusion set in, for when a new generation of FIATs started to appear, the factory reverted to the 100s for their 'chassis' types, the designation 101 being assigned to the 1400 of 1950. As no separate series of motor prefixes was issued, a 101 engine can be either a 65× 100 side-valve or an 82 ×66 mm pushrod unit of much the same capacity.

The 501 formed the spearhead of Agnelli's new economy-car programme, but it was not the smallest FIAT depicted in the company's 1918 catalogue. Already Fornaca and Cavalli were toying with a true baby, the first model to bear the designation 500. This diminutive and boxy device had a four-cylinder, side-valve monobloc engine, four forward speeds, and a worm-drive back axle, while another startling departure was the 6-volt coil ignition. According to British sources, cylinder dimensions anticipated those of one of 1946's most revolutionary lightweights, the Renault 4CV, at 55 ×80 mm (760 c.c.), but Dr Costantino thinks it may actually have been a '500', in which case its designed maximum speed of 37–40 m.p.h. appears even more remarkable than the 50 m.p.h. attained by the 569 c.c. *topolino* in 1936. Its looks were comical, especially when clad in Mathis-like coupé coachwork with 'military fenders', and remind one of that other Italian miniature, the air-cooled Temperino. The FIAT press office was charmingly unspecific when it came to detailed information, but their objectives were made clear in the English-language edition of their catalogue:

> This is a small car, seating two people: it is recommended to the business man, the travelling salesman, the doctor, the colonist, for its light weight, strong construction, high speed, and low cost of upkeep.

Prototypes were undoubtedly built, but in February, 1919, *The Light Car*, which had already alarmed Britons by predicting a list price in the region of £160, announced that owing to industrial unrest and the heavy demand for the 1½-litre 501 FIAT had shelved their smallest model. Undoubtedly it would be some time before there were enough FIATs to go round, but Agnelli's rethinking was far more basic. He recognised that the market was not yet ripe for such a miniature, and if the *topolino*'s incredulous reception years later is any yardstick, he was right.

As for the 'colonists', their answer already existed in the shape of Cavalli's 501, which was to sell close on 80,000 in seven seasons, and to make its mark as sports car, taxicab, and even light van. The large number still to be found in Australia and New Zealand is excellent proof of the soundness of the design, and FIAT's Antipodean sales took a tumble when it gave way to the 503 (an insufficient improvement on the original 1919 theme) and the 509 (too small and fussy for conditions 'down under').

Cavalli's masterpiece is unremarkable when viewed in cold print. It was heavy (17–19 cwt for a tourer), congenitally over-cooled and undergeared, and not particularly fast: 53 m.p.h. was about par for open models, and a saloon tested by *The Autocar* was flat out at 46. The brakes evoked mixed reactions, and standard models were ugly, especially the rectangular two-door *berline*. The 501's merits lay, not in what it did, but in how it did it—and went on doing it, over astronomical mileages. In September, 1956, *The Motor* ventured a generous tribute, rating it alongside the 'Silver Ghost' Rolls-Royce, the flat-twin Jowett, and the Austin Twelve in the 'dependability stakes'. *The Autocar* considered its suspension 'quite wonderful for so small a vehicle'. *The Automotor Journal*, while critical on certain aspects of the design, felt that it was 'absolutely on a par for quality and workmanship with the finest Italian cars of 1910 and 1912, and a great deal more efficient'. The gearbox was 'so easy that it can hardly be imagined that the veriest novice could make a bad change'; and *The Motor*, after praising the sewing-machine sweetness of the three-bearing, side-valve power unit, added a kind word for the luxurious appointments of the saloon, which included spring-mounted silk blinds to each window, and 'a handsome little nickel-plate vanity case' to attract the distaff side.

The engine had dimensions of 65×110 mm (1,460 c.c.) and was a direct descendant of the 70. Other details included magneto ignition, pump and fan cooling, gravity feed from a nine-gallon dash tank, the regulation FIAT multi-plate clutch and the four-speed unit box with right-hand change. New were the underslung semi-elliptic rear springs and the spiral bevel back axle. The brakes were also inherited from the 70, which did not altogether please *The Autocar*'s testers. 'They are quite adequate', it was admitted, 'for ordinary purposes, but their control by wires hardly appeals to the expert, and the foot-applied rear brakes are not the equal of the propeller-shaft brake on the Zero model'. (Reading between the lines, one gathers that one of the side-effects of the labour disputes in Italy was a shortage of suitable brake-lining material, for after 1922 the 501's anchors usually passed muster with press and owners alike.) The gear ratios (5, 11, 10, 14, and 25 to 1) were a classic Aunt Sally of the period, coming in for the same harsh treatment as Jaguar's boxes before they acquired synchro-mesh on bottom. Not everyone was as rude as *The Automotor Journal*'s Edgar N. Duffield:

> The third is unnecessarily low, the second is strictly a starting gear, and first is a joke, and would be even if one crammed the car with professional fat men.

—but the 501 lost a lot of urge in the cause of flexibility. As an illustration of what could be done, a New Zealand magazine tested one of the lightly-tuned 'S' (*sport*) versions with the optional 4.6:1 axle ratio, and found it capable of an easy 62 m.p.h., as well as cruising at 45 instead of the 38–40 m.p.h. of the standard article.

The car's merit was reflected in its second-hand value, rivalled in Britain only by the stolid inlet-over-exhaust Humbers of the pre-Rootes era. British industry took the 501 far more seriously than anything to come out of Italy since the big shaft-driven Italas of 1906–7. Arrol-Johnston cribbed it shamelessly for their 10.5 h.p. Galloway light car of 1921, Harvey du Cros's known affection for the model (D'Arcy Baker was both a close friend and near neighbour) may well have influenced Herbert Austin when he came to design his Twelve, and the Harper Bean consortium, already teetering on the edge of the abyss, acquired a 501 for comparative tests against their Swift Ten. Mr W. McKerrow, then a Swift engineer, recalls the FIAT as 'the best of the foreign opposition'.

He disliked the integral exhaust manifolds of early 501s, but felt that the Swift's non-adjustable chain drive for the cam-shaft compared most unfavourably with Cavalli's gear drive, 'with its automatic take-up for back-lash'.

Initially, bodies were the main problem. It was obvious common sense to ship bare chassis to countries as far afield as Australia, but the body shortage was also reflected in Denmark, where some pretty sports and cloverleaf styles were made; and even more so in Britain. Early Italian tourer bodies were crude and uncomfortable by British standards, and did not measure up to the high standards set by engine and chassis. For a while a motley assortment of coachwork found its way on to chassis sold on the British market, causing the querulous Edgar Duffield to wish that he could get A.C.s to fit one of their '11.9' two-seaters to a 501—one wonders what S. F. Edge thought of this suggestion! A temporary solution was found to the problem when Harper Bean Ltd finally failed, for surplus 11.9 h.p. Bean bodies fitted like a glove, thanks in part to the similar styling of bonnets and radiators. Eventually D'Arcy Baker imported only the saloons complete, the open models coming from Shorts' aircraft factory at Rochester, while Page and Hunt of Farnham contributed a pretty three-quarter coupé which figured in FIAT's 1924 and 1925 English catalogues. The model's popularity with ladies and professional men encouraged the specialists, firms like Marshalsea, Mann Egerton and Maddox producing a number of coupés and all-weathers on the chassis between 1923 and 1925.

Few major changes were made to the 501 during its long career, which did not end until February 1926. In the late summer of 1922 the angular 'military fenders' gave way to the 'crown' type, and in 1923 FIAT introduced a *tipo coloniale* (501C) with 220 lbs less chassis weight and a slightly wider track. Four-wheel brakes and balloon tyres were to become factory options during 1924.

The 501 was not a cheap car—except in relation to previous small FIATs. While it was the least expensive full-size machine that an Italian could buy (most of the home-market competition came from the early overhead-camshaft 4C Ansaldo), it competed in Britain, not against Morris, Citroën and Clyno, but against the bigger and heavier Austin Twelve. A 501 tourer cost £670 in 1920, £550 in 1922, and £495 at the beginning of 1923, when a fully-equipped 1,548 c.c. Morris-Cowley retailed for less than £350. In America, of course, it was a lot more expensive—$2,575 for a tourer and $3,275 for a saloon in 1921. At this time Buick's big 29.4 h.p. Six could be bought for less than $1,800, even the sedans undercutting the FIAT at $2,895.

Parallel with the 501 were two bigger sisters, the 505 and the 510. These were more luxuriously equipped, but the only basic difference in specification was the use of exhaust pressure to lift the fuel from a rear-mounted tank to an auxiliary reservoir on the scuttle. In each case the cylinder dimensions were 75×130 mm, giving a capacity of 2,297 c.c. for the four-cylinder 505, and 3,446 c.c. in the case of the 510, a four-bearing 'six'. The 505 did 48–50 m.p.h. on a 4.8:1 top gear, while its ten-foot wheelbase rendered it ideal for formal coachwork, a favourite style on the Continent being the *coupé de ville* used for hire work. The English list price of a tourer was £800 in 1922, but the 505 never enjoyed anything like the 501's popularity, and total production was around 30,000 units. Curiously enough, it outsold the 1½-litre models in Australia for a while, several Melbourne department stores operating fleets of 505 vans. The 510 had a wheelbase of 11 ft 2 in, and was usually seen in England with semi-open drive landaulette coachwork by Hooper, Maythorn or Arthur Mulliner. The factory's claim of a 3–60 m.p.h. range in direct drive was substantiated by owners, one of whom wrote of a surprising 72 m.p.h. on 46 b.h.p., though he took exception to a third gear on which 30 was the limit. The 510 was strictly a luxury item for all its lack of frills, and production ran at a steady 1,500–2,000 a year throughout its currency, which terminated late in 1925.

With Rome breathing down Turin's neck, FIAT's exports expanded apace, and by 1924 the company could claim six major foreign 'affiliates' (Argentina, Germany, Great Britain, Poland, Spain and Switzerland), and three minor ones (Rumania, Turkey and Yugoslavia), albeit not all these were factory-controlled. Favourable reports came in from Turkey and even Manchuria: an owner in Harbin had nothing but praise for FIAT service, though his balloon-tyred 1925 model was too light for the 'roads' of Henry Pu-Yi's domains, and he found cruising speeds of 15 m.p.h. tedious. Japan, too, was taking 501s: not, be it said, her first FIATs, even if Mr Okura's personal imports are excluded. Between 1917 and 1921 the Mitsubishi company had built a small series of prototype four-cylinder cars (Type-A) based on the pre-War *Tipo Due*. Mitsubishi's contemporary light lorry bore the designation F-15, which is even more suggestive.

In these early post-War years FIAT's best markets were France and Great Britain, and this tallies in part with official Italian statistics. These reveal that in the first half of 1921 the industry shipped 1,301 cars to the United Kingdom, as against 599 to Switzerland, 485 to Spain, 353 to Belgium, and 343 to Australia—France is not yet mentioned. In Denmark, FIAT ran third behind Citroën and Renault, but as the country registered only 15,435 private cars, penetration was of necessity limited. An even smaller market was Portugal, where the 501's popularity was relative, since it took FIAT thirty years to sell a mere 2,039 units. Nevertheless there was comfort for Lingotto in the realisation that up to 1931 their cars were outsold only by Ford, Chevrolet and the ubiquitous Citroën.

All these were success stories. Alas! the same could not be said of FIAT's final effort to sell in America, or her even briefer re-invasion of Canada in 1920. The consequences might perhaps have been different had FIAT, like Sunbeam and Peugeot, tried their luck again at Indianapolis, instead of leaving their exploration of the race-tracks until 1925, when it was too late. This, however, is doubtful: the tide had turned against foreign imports in 1913, and the War had closed the gap between domestic and European super-cars. If the early 'twenties saw Locomobile survive only as a prestige division of William C.

Durant's last empire, and Mercer, Stevens-Duryea and Daniels on their last legs, others were flourishing, among them Lincoln, Packard, Peerless and Pierce-Arrow. Cadillac sold 15,000 cars in 1923. The surviving foreigners were few and far between— the Springfield-built Rolls-Royce, the straight-eight Isottas energetically promoted by V. V. d'Annunzio, the poet's son, the monstrous 40CV Renault, and the brutal six-cylinder Mercédès.

After Poughkeepsie's demise, there was nothing to take Type 55's place. True, FIAT's 1918 catalogue had mentioned a '*Tipo* 503', but this stillborn species was merely a 'stretched' 510, and no match for 'Silver Ghosts' and Twin-Six Packards. FIAT's own V-12, the 520, was to be a victim of the company's slow retreat from America, and though the 519 was shown in New York in 1924, it was too late to save the situation. In any case, Americans no longer wanted foreign cars—total imports amounted to 522 units in 1922, but only 483 a year later. Mr Josephs might slash the 501's price to $1,955, and plug it as 'a car for shopping, theater-going, and trips between town and country', but its 'speed for pick-up' demanded more shifting than Americans would tolerate. Even with Fleetwood limousine bodywork and a $7,400 price-tag, the 510 was still too ordinary, and by 1923 FIAT's New York operations, though still directed by Josephs, were down to a care-and-maintenance basis, dependent on conservative dowagers who motored to the opera in their outmoded 55s and 56s. A few 510s were sold, and one of these reappeared in the 1940s in several Hollywood films with an 'occupied Europe' background. This actual town car was still in existence in 1972.

FIAT were not to stage another major attack on North America until the 1950s, but while the U.S.A. waxed apathetic, Britons could not get enough 501s. In 1922 Edgar Duffield complained that he had had to cancel his order owing to the continuing body shortage, while Baker was reduced to concocting publicity out of any small pickings that came his way. With the Roads Act of 1921 came a tax rebate on cars more than nine years old, and he seized this straw with both hands. 'We at Albemarle

Street', he trumpeted, 'have been flooded out with requests for certificates of age of FIAT cars delivered nine, ten, twelve, fourteen and sixteen years ago. The fact remains, however that none but cars of the finest quality could have stood the test of time in such numbers'.

His independence now stood him in good stead. Already in 1920 he had done something that Agnelli would never have sanctioned. While the workers manned the barricades of Turin, Baker cast around for something to sell, and finally unearthed fifty of those Poughkeepsie-built 9-litre 55 chassis destined for Russia, and stranded in England after the fall of Kerensky's Provisional Government. They had already been earmarked for use against the Irish rebels, but the War Office had second thoughts, and chose Lancias and Crossleys instead. The aged monsters were snapped up and rebodied, emerging in Baker's showrooms as 'new' 40–50 h.p. FIATs at £1,500 apiece with tourer coachwork. The result was a real bargain, retailing for less than the price of a bare chassis in Italy. In those days journalists were not historians, and the model was actually tried by *The Motor*, whose testers took kindly to its immense, lazy, Edwardian engine:

> At slow speeds it pulls commendably smoothly for a four-cylinder unit, and accelerates well without any signs of distress. It is, however, at over 20 m.p.h. that it really gets into its gait, and from this speed the finger of the speedometer rapidly mounts up to over 60 m.p.h., as the throttle is depressed. The FIAT is obviously a fast touring car, and it easily makes 40 m.p.h. up really steep hills in top gear, the engine pulling grandly when the throttle is opened.

The Bakers themselves owned a landaulette, which was still on the strength at Hedsor in 1923, but the project boomer-anged. The 55s were nominally new, and thus subject, from 1921 onwards, to tax at the rate of £1 per unit of horse-power. Four cylinders of 130 mm bore mean an R.A.C. rating of 41.9 h.p., which explains why one will search British buyers' guides in vain for a mention of the model.

We shall encounter the overhead-valve 520 and 519 later

in the story, but if Agnelli's approach to the carriage trade was warier than Baker's, he did not forget the sporting enthusiasts who had bought Brooklands-type Zeros and short-chassis 3TERs. By 1921 there were 'S' versions of the 501 and 510 in the catalogue.

The 501 was 'tweaked' but mildly. The compression was raised from the standard 4.3 to 5.5:1, which gave 26 b.h.p. at 3,000 r.p.m., where touring units were content with 20–21. The standard factory body was a bulbous-tailed *torpedo sport* not unlike that fitted to the 12–50 h.p. Alvis, and top speed was quoted as 57 m.p.h., albeit quite a lot more was on tap for those willing to add all the recognised options—a lightened flywheel, a high-compression head, slipper-type pistons, a 4.6:1 back axle, and Rudge wheels. In later years New Zealanders were to achieve astonishing results with modified Austin A40 pistons, but contemporary Italian tuners went a degree further. The celebrated Silvani devised an o.h.v. conversion (which Antonio Lago sold in London for £33), and claimed 89 m.p.h. from his hottest *trasformazioni*. The 501S attracted some unusual coachwork, notably a staggered two-seater with cowled radiator which bears an uncanny resemblance to the 1925 M.G. Kimber Special (FC 7900). The latter *marque*'s historian, Wilson McComb, has suggested that this variant may have inspired Cecil Kimber. 1922 was to see the even more ferocious 501SS, though this was really a racing car.

If the 501S was the true ancestor of to-day's Abarthised 850 coupés and spyders, the 510S was strictly a fast tourer. It was an ugly brute with an aggressive vee-radiator on an abbreviated, 10 ft 2 in wheelbase. Its artillery wheels apart, it bore a superficial resemblance to the contemporary 22–90 h.p. 'RLSS' Alfa Romeo, but on 53 b.h.p. its performance was scarcely Alfa-like, and 70 m.p.h. was hard work. Less than five hundred were made, of which the few survivors are limited to the Antipodes. The Queen of Siam took delivery of a hideous saloon version with vee-screen and 'military fenders' in 1922. In that year a four-seater sold in London for £1,045, or £65 more than was asked for a standard 510. Most Britons would, however, have preferred Sir Herbert Austin's indestructible four-cylinder Twenty at £695.

Workers might strike, governments might clamour for bigger export quotas, and commercial-vehicle sales might be frustrated by the interminable flow of reconditioned ex-army 15TERs, but FIAT had no intention of letting these headaches affect their racing programme. The early 1920s, indeed, were to see the final flowering of the competition department, under a splendid team which reads like a Who's Who of European automobile design—Fornaca, Cavalli, Becchia, Bertarione, Cappa Jano and Zerbi.

Tranquillo Zerbi's greatest achievement was, of course, his double-twelve aircraft engine of 1931, and in the minds of car enthusiasts he is indelibly associated with the stillborn two-stroke racing unit of 1925, He was, however, a designer of immense versatility who had worked on diesels at Sulzer before joining FIAT in 1919. He took over the car programme from Cavalli when ill-health curtailed the ex-lawyer's activities, and before his untimely death in 1938 he masterminded the development of the 508 light-car family.

The story of Giulio Cesare Cappa emphasises the importance of FIAT in Italian engineering history: almost every automobile engineer worthy of his salt inevitably turns up in one or other of their drawing-offices. Cappa's first major design had been the Aquila-Italiana of 1906, which pioneered the use of aluminium pistons seven years before W. O. Bentley put them on the map. He moved on when Matteo Ceirano started to buy into the company, and gravitated to FIAT, where he was largely responsible for the 803 and 804 before transferring his allegiance to Itala. Here he designed the o.h.v. *Tipo* 61 (which might have succeeded with sounder financial backing), and a lilliputian 1,100 c.c. twelve-cylinder racer which was a predestined Lost Cause. By 1933 he had returned to FIAT's orbit *via* the newly-acquired O.M. company, for whom he created the *autocarretta*, an ingenious lightweight 4×4 widely used by the Italian Army.

The four leaders were impressive enough, but the entire team could fairly be called a Ministry of All The Talents. Under Cappa was Vittorio Jano, who had started as a draughtsman with Giovanni Ceirano's Rapid concern before moving to FIAT in 1911. His stay was brief, for in 1923 he and his friend Luigi Bazzi quarrelled with the management, and entered the service of Alfa Romeo, there to create the P2, the immortal twin-cam 1750, and its straight-eight derivatives. The circle was completed in 1938, when Jano went to Lancia: the consequences of the transfer are too numerous to give in detail, but they included the splendid V-6 'Aurelia', perhaps the greatest *gran turismo* of its decade.

Also in the cast was Bertarione, renowned for his later work with the Sunbeam-Talbot-Darracq combine and for Hotchkiss. Finally there was Walter Becchia, who succeeded Bertarione at Suresnes, and created the magnificent cross-pushrod Lago-Talbots, the finest all-rounders of the immediate post-1945 era. No wonder that some cross-pollination ensued: the early eight-cylinder racing Alfas looked uncommonly like FIATs, and the 2-litre Sunbeam's ancestry was so patent that unkind journalists dubbed it 'a FIAT in green paint'.

Not that all this massing of talent was apparent in 1919, when Italy was the only European country to stage a major race. FIAT, of course, had nothing more modern to offer than the old S57s in reworked 4.8-litre Indianapolis form, though insistent rumours suggested that the company had actually built a team of 2½-litre racers for the cancelled 1914 *Coupe de l'Auto*. This remains an insoluble mystery: for though Peugeot's *voiturettes* duly turned out for the 1919 Targa Florio, and one of the Mors light cars came to England in 1920, the FIATs, if they ever existed, vanished without trace.

In 1919, be it said, S57s existed in both original and modified guises, for at the Parma-Poggio di Berceto hill-climb that October Antonio Ascari fielded a slab-tank 4½-litre with single magneto, and the same car carried off the honours at Consuma. At Denmark's Fanoë speed trials in August, f.t.d. went to Minoia on a car credited with a capacity of 4,682 c.c. No doubts, however, exist as to the nature of the Targa Florio FIATs, which had 4.8-litre engines and airship tails. They were matched against two of their erstwhile rivals from Lyons, Nazzaro and Aquilia-Italiana, while the two 2½-litre Peugeots were 1914 *Coupe de l'Auto* models, and the Italas 1913 *avalve* racing machines. Only one new car put in an appearance: this was Réné Thomas's 4.9-litre Indianapolis-type straight-eight Ballot with four-wheel brakes. Ascari and Masetti handled the two S57s: the former took fourth place, but Ascari's first and only lap ended thirty yards down a ravine, where he remained, unhurt and undiscovered, until after the race!

The following year saw only the S57s in circulation again: they dealt easily with limited opposition at Parma-Poggio di Berceto and Consuma, even if the *marque*'s best showing in Sicily was once again a fourth place for Piro, nearly an hour behind the victorious Nazzaro of Meregalli. Not that this benefited FIAT's star driver, who had sold out of his unprofitable business venture in 1916, and was now back with his old employers. Interestingly enough, the Nazzaro was followed home by the ES-type Alfa Romeo of an unknown by the name of Enzo Ferrari.

While the 1914 Grand Prix cars ruled a rather arid roost, there were also some stirrings at Brooklands, where J. F. Duff made a number of appearances in an old friend, the ex-Mathis, ex-Richmond S61, now with racing body. This veteran was in poor shape: the block was porous, and it was so seldom firing on all four cylinders that on these auspicious occasions Duff would raise his arm, giving his friends time to lay their bets! The spokes of the wooden wheels were loose, calling for frequent douches of cold water, but these maladies notwith-standing the FIAT scored two firsts and two thirds during its first post-War season, and latterly Duff was able to buy a spare power unit which he proceeded to cannibalise. Under-standably, 1921 was a better year; the FIAT now ran with a cowled radiator, and at the Summer Meeting Duff lapped at 102.66 m.p.h., as well as taking the car to Fanoë, where he swept the board with a kilometre in 21.69 seconds, and a mile in 34.15. The S61's showing was creditable, for the opposition included Kordewan's works-entered 11.1-litre Stoewer D7 (for which spares were actually flown in from Stettin during the meeting!) Joerns's vast Opel, and von Thune with a very fast '28–95' Mercédès. A good year's sport was rounded out by another f.t.d. at Westcliff Speed Trials, where Duff capped his triumph by beating the fastest motorcycle (Bert LeVack's Indian) in an impromptu runoff.

Towards the end of 1921 the S61 was passed on to Philip Rampon, for Duff had acquired an even more exciting monster —none other than 'Mephistopheles', who was found dormant in a Fulham mews and purchased for £100. (The used-car boom of 1919–21 might inflate the value of Rolls-Royces to Sotherby levels, but king-sized FIATs were clearly immune). Age had not wearied the devil of the Corso Dante, for he proceeded to lap Brooklands at 106.88 m.p.h., and even turned a standing lap at 91.52 m.p.h. at the August Meeting, though a second place (behind one of the 1912 15–litre Grand Prix Lorraine-Dietrichs) was his final effort in 1921, thanks to cracked pistons. D'Arcy Baker, still questing publicity, enshrined the ancient's exploits in his advertisements, which described 'Mephistopheles' as 'an unaltered 1910 model'! Both veterans were seen at the Track during 1922, Rampon adding a win in a Private Competitors' Handicap to the S61's ever-growing laurels, though Duff was less lucky. 'Mephistopheles' duly emerged at Whitsun, complete with brand-new alloy pistons by Ricardo, and lapped at 107.01 m.p.h., but too new a wine had gone into those old bottles, and he exploded. In the ensuing disintegration, both rear cylinders emerged from the bonnet before dropping out of sight again. The SB4-190 engine had made its last rotation.

Anyone who equated all privately-entered FIATs with museum pieces was quite wrong, as 1922's score proved. But G. M. Giles of Bugatti Owners' Club fame was collecting a string of British trials awards with his 501, and these cars also distinguished themselves in Paris-Nice (three clean sheets), in the Victorian Alpine Trial (a second place for Maurice Shmith), in a standing-kilometre sprint at Lisbon (where de Heredia's 501S was beaten only by a Mercédès and a Delage), and in the Paris-Copenhagen marathon, in which Caspersen's stark 501S two-seater came second behind Frits's Essex. There were also victories in fuel-consumption events as far afield as Stockholm and Brisbane: in the latter case the winner made a gallon of fuel last for an astounding 66.8 miles.

1921 had seen the S57s in action once more at home. They were now concentrating on hill-climbs and sprints—firsts at Brescia, at Parma-Poggio di Berceto, and in the *chilometro lanciato di Toscana*, as well as a second at Rocca di Papa— but that spring saw the model's gallant swansong in big-league racing. Masetti won the Targa Florio at 36.2 m.p.h. to give FIAT their first big European triumph since the *annus mirabilis* of 1907. Second place went to another seasoned combination, Max Sailer in a 28/95 six Mercédès, but in eleventh was Bergese on a standard 501S. His average speed was 33 m.p.h., and he won the 2-litre category as well. Though amateurs such as Niccolini and Brilli-Peri were still campaigning their S57s in 1923, the great days were over.

Better things were on the way. The Ministry of All the Talents had put their first post-war racer, the Tipo 801, on the road in 1920, though it was not seen in public till 8 May, 1921, when Minoia won the 3-litre class at Parma-Poggio di Berceto.

In its original guise Tipo 801 was a transitional motor car, for FIAT's intention was to produce a 3-litre straight-eight for the current Grand Prix Formula, and this unit was not ready until fairly later in the season. The chassis specification featured four-wheel internal-expanding brakes, which were pedal-operated, unlike those on the S57s, while the radiator was neatly cowled, and the body was a marked improvement on the *Indianapolis* style, with flat sides and a tail which tapered to a knife-edge. Curiously, there seem to have been delays in the body shop as well, for the Parma car closely resembled the original S57s in outline.

To this chassis was fitted an interim engine, in the shape of a twin-overhead camshaft 16-valve four-cylinder of 85 × 131 mm, developing 112 b.h.p. at 4,000 r.p.m. Lubrication was on dry-sump principles with twin oil pumps, sparks were provided by twin Marelli magnetos, and this version of the 801 made only two subsequent appearances: at Consuma, and in the 1921 Targa Florio, when Minoia finished well down the list in eighth place.

Cappa's 402 engine arrived too late for the French Grand Prix, but it set the tone for subsequent FIAT racing units. The 'eight' had a bore of 65 mm, and a stroke of 112 mm, and its gear-driven camshafts and dry-sump lubrication derived from the superseded 401. The twin blocks were of forged steel with welded-on sheet steel water jackets as used on FIAT aero-engines (and the 1917 engine for Indianapolis), and the crank-shaft ran in nine roller bearings. Output was 115 b.h.p. at 4,600 r.p.m., and there was a four-speed unit gearbox. While the four-cylinder 3-litres would do only 90–95 m.p.h., the 'ton' was said to be possible with the new motor.

With Le Mans over, there was only one possible venue for the FIATs, and that was the Italian Grand Prix at Brescia. Here three 801s (Bordino, Sivocci, and Wagner) were pitted against the similarly-dimensioned eight-cylinder Ballots of de Palma, Goux, and Chassagne.

A battle royal ensued. This was Bordino's first Grand Prix, and he leapt into the lead, setting a record lap at 96.3 m.p.h., and averaging 93 m.p.h. for the first 140 miles. Such speeds sufficed to stave off the Ballots, though Sivocci crashed his FIAT on the first lap, and the two surviving cars were dogged by tyre trouble, Bordino's ultimately succumbing to a fractured oil pipe. As for Wagner, the crowd misinterpreted his frequent tyre changes as excessive caution, and he found himself bar-racked by a pocket Mussolini who balanced himself on an oil-drum, haranguing all and sundry on the sins of 'foreigners' who threw away races when the honour of Italy was at stake. This tub-thumper was only silenced when the veteran driver came in with a tyre in shreds, but the remaining 801 simply could not make up for lost time, and Wagner did well to take third place, at 86.9 m.p.h., behind Goux and Chassagne.

26. (top) Pietro Bordino with the 3-litre 801 on road trials. The picture was taken in 1920, so it may still have had the interim four-cylinder engine.

27. (left) Glorious Swansong. Count Masetti's starkly bodied S.57/14B after winning the Targa Florio, 1921.   (Cyril Posthumus)

28. Sport in the Soviets. Alessandro Cagno with his prize-winning 510; All-Russian Reliability Trials, October 1923.

Utilitarian Aspects. **29.** The 501F van was one of a fleet operated by Harrods in 1924. **30.** The formidable diesel-electric locomotive below disposed of 440 horsepower and went into service in Calabria in 1926.

(Harrods' Ltd. and FIAT)

No Piedmontese, however, takes a defeat lying down, and in 1922 the firm were back with two strings to their bow: a Grand Prix car for the new 2-litre formula, and a 1,500 c.c. *voiturette*, their first exploration of this class.

The Cappa-designed 2-litre 'six' (*Tipo* 804) was a logical development of the eight-cylinder 801. Its cylinders were cast in threes, and the construction was identical to that of the 1921 unit, save that now only a single magneto was used, driven by skew gears off the camshaft. Twin carburetters were envisaged, but never used, and in normally aspirated form output was steadily increased from 92 to 112 b.h.p. Cylinder dimensions were classic, at 65 × 100 mm, a point that did not go unnoticed by S. F. Edge once the FIAT started to win races. His A.C.s, he reminded readers of the weekly press, had been using this bore and stroke since 1919! Bench tests revealed that the engine would run happily for five hours at maximum revs of 5,000, though Felice Nazzaro averred that he seldom found more than 4,500 necessary on a circuit.

The chassis followed the established formula, with torque-tube drive, four-speed unit gearbox, multi-plate clutch, semi-elliptic springs (the front ones passed through the axle), and Hartford friction dampers. The four-wheel brakes had acquired servo assistance, and the excellent aerodynamics of 1921 had been still further refined. The exhaust system was contained in a metal tunnel for much of its length, the radiator cowling enclosed the filler cap, and there was a full undertray. The car turned the scales at 13.4 cwt, or $4\frac{1}{2}$ cwt less than the 1921 3-litre Ballot.

For his *voiturettes* Cappa used four-cylinder 65 × 112 mm (1,486 c.c.) monobloc engines on very similar lines. Output of these 403 units varied from 55 to 63 b.h.p. according to tune, and the racing department fitted them to two different chassis. The 802 was something of a propaganda device, with near-sports two-seater bodywork, and a 501 radiator and bonnet. It also shared the touring model's 8 ft $8\frac{1}{2}$ in wheelbase frame, though its front-wheel brakes were something not to be seen on any sort of 501 until the summer of 1924. It ran in races under the designation 501SS, and a very few were sold to amateurs. The 803 was, by contrast, an 804 in miniature with the pointed-tail racing shell, cowled radiator, and front springs passing through the axle. The wheelbase was 7 ft 8$\frac{1}{2}$ in, and these cars were strictly for works use.

For the Targa Florio, FIAT made a big effort. Biagio Nazzaro, Felice's nephew, was given one of the 1921 3-litre straight-eights. He was supported by two 802s (Bergese and Giaccone), and Lampiano on a car variously described as a 501S or 501SS (*alias* 802). These FIATs were to do battle against a full team representing Mercédès' first major foreign sortie since 1914. Lautenschlager, Salzer and Masetti drove rebuilt pre-War 4$\frac{1}{2}$-litres, Scheef and Minoia had a brace of the new twin o.h.c. blown 1,500s, and Sailer and Christian Werner super-charged six-cylinder '28-95's. Goux and Foresti handled the new four-cylinder Ballots, while from Austria came some 1,100 c.c. 'Sascha' Austro-Daimlers, one of which was en-trusted to the future *rennleiter*, Alfred Neubauer.

Like Ascari in 1919, the young Nazzaro was soon eliminated by a spectacular crash, leaving the small FIATs to fight it out against the Mercédès. The latters' chassis were their Achilles' Heel, and though Bergese succumbed to engine trouble, Giac-cone drove brilliantly, staying up with the leaders, and com-pleting his third lap a mere four minutes behind Goux' Gallot. He took fifth place, by far the fastest of the 1$\frac{1}{2}$-litre brigade. Lampiano was twelfth, Neubauer's Austro-Daimler 19th, and Scheef's small supercharged Mercédès 20th.

The 804s turned out for the French Grand Prix at Strasbourg, in the hands of the two Nazzaros and Pietro Bordino. Opposi-tion came from four eight-cylinder Bugattis (de Vizcaya, Friderich, Marco and Maury), three Ballots with four-cylinder engines but a similar cigar shape (Foresti, Goux and Masetti), three straight-eight *desmodromique* Rolland-Pilains with hyd-raulic front brakes (Guyot, Hémery and Wagner) three four-cylinder Sunbeams (Chassagne, Kenelm Lee Guinness and Segrave), and two twin-cam 1$\frac{1}{2}$-litre Aston Martins (Gallop and Zborowski).

It rained for the whole night before the race, and in tricky conditions it was soon apparent that Felice Nazzaro had lost none of his old skill. A standing lap at 70.5 m.p.h. put the spectators in mind of 1907, and in the early stages the Italian led from Friderich's Bugatti and Guyot's Rolland-Pilain. Alas! much of the fire went out of the race when Friderich retired, while the first ten laps also saw the elimination of the entire Sunbeam *équipe* with valve trouble.

It looked like a rapid FIAT procession, assisted by careful planning and good pit-work. The company had thoughtfully adopted quick-detachable fuel tanks, and when Biagio Nazzaro damaged his the substitution was made in fourteen-and-a-half minutes.

Suddenly, tragedy struck. Biagio Nazzaro's FIAT shed a wheel and left the course, killing the driver. Then the same fate struck Bordino, though he was going slowly at the time and was able to stop without injury to himself. Unaware of his nephew's death, Felice Nazzaro lapped steadily on, to win at 79.2 m.p.h., well ahead of the second placeman, de Vizcaya on a Bugatti, whose speed was 69.2 m.p.h. Investigation showed that the cause of the disasters had been creeping cracks in the rear axles; however, contrary to general belief, no damage was discovered on the victorious car.

This year's Italian Grand Prix was staged at the new Monza Autodrome, but by race-day an impressive entry had dwindled to two German Heims and the Diattos of Meregalli and Alfieri Maserati. The result was an incredibly dull procession led by Bordino's 804 at 86.89 m.p.h., while the supporting *voiturette* event was almost as discouraging. On this occasion FIAT brought along four full-house 803s (Bordino, Giaccone, Lampiano, and Salamano) which were supposed to do battle with O.M.s, Talbot-Darracqs, Bugattis and Mercédès. None of these materialised, though the race was not entirely empty of interest. thanks to the presence of the new twin o.h.c. Chiribiris and the little Austro-Daimlers already encountered in Sicily. The Chiribiris, more powerful on paper, with 70 b.h.p., were quite a good match for the FIATs, and in the early stages they fought

hard. In the end, however, the spectators were treated to a
FIAT procession, with Bordino scoring his double at 83.4 m.p.h.,
followed in line ahead by Giaccone, Lampiano, and Salamano.
The slowest of the four averaged a consistent 81.3 m.p.h.

The outside activities continued. Indeed, there was a new
departure in August, 1918, when Italy's first farm tractor was
demonstrated to Valenzano, the Italian Under-Secretary for
Agriculture. This machine, the *Tipo* 702 FIAT, had a 6.2-litre
side-valve four-cylinder engine based on the larger lorry units,
and could run on petrol or paraffin. As deliveries got under way,
a demonstrator was sent round the country, carried on an
18BL truck which towed a trailer full of display material.
992 FIAT tractors were delivered in 1920, the first full year of
production, and the model's advent had a beneficial effect, in
that it enabled Italy to supply 70 per cent of her agricultural
machinery requirements by 1926, as against a puny 15 per cent
in 1915.

Aircraft, as we have seen, were good business. Even before
Mussolini's March on Rome, the Italian Government had
gone into the 'instant air force' trade, sending air missions to
less advanced countries. The object of the exercise was to establish a nucleus of Italian instructional personnel, and to secure
orders for the Italian aircraft industry. By 1920 such missions
were active in Czechoslovakia, Finland, Japan, Peru, Poland,
Turkey, and Yugoslavia, and running expenses of each group
were said to be £3,900 a month. This venture, incidentally,
paid dividends; in 1922 the Argentinian and Ecuadorean
air forces were said to be under Italian 'management', and
over the next twenty years FIAT were to export aircraft to
22 countries.

Engine development continued apace, albeit the firm's
first air-cooled radial, the 300 h.p. A18 of 1920, did not go
into production. Far more successful were the big V-12s, the
18,696 c.c. A20 and the 27½-litre A22, which had considerable
affinity with the Cappa-designed racing car units. Notable
were the welded-steel water jackets, the bevel-driven overhead camshafts, and the four-valve-per-cylinder layout.

Originally rated at 400 h.p., the A20 in later guise gave as much as 550 b.h.p. for short periods, and found its way into a number of service aircraft, among them Rosatelli's CR20 fighter which entered squadron service in 1927.

Rosatelli's characteristic unequal-span biplanes with Warren girder bracing were under development, and in 1919 he produced his first BR bomber, powered by a 650 h.p. FIAT A14 engine. Structural failures delayed quantity production until 1924, but in the meantime the first CR fighter had put in an appearance.

These neat little biplanes were to become synonymous with formation aerobatics at international meetings in the late 1920s, but in its original guise the CR was a sesquiplane with a lower wing of greater span than the upper, a fuselage with metal-tube framework, and an armament of two fixed synchronised 7.7 mm machine-guns firing through the airscrew. The prototype's 300 h.p. Hispano-Suiza engine was replaced on subsequent models by an air-cooled Isotta Fraschini 'Asso' unit, and later by FIAT's own A20. Also new in 1923 was the firm's first commercial aircraft, the A1 four-passenger biplane with a four-wheel undercarriage.

1920 had seen FIAT's first interest in the Schneider Trophy— de Briganti's unsuccessful Macchi M-12 flying-boat was powered by a 680 h.p. engine of their manufacture. In 1921 another FIAT-powered Macchi, the M-19, won the Italian Eliminating Trials and was certainly the nation's fastest and most seaworthy craft of the period. In the race itself Arturo Zanetti was unlucky, for his machine caught fire and he retired.

The transitional phase was nearly over. While the racing *équipe* had yet to reach its technical zenith, FIAT were to abandon competitions for good in 1927, and the successful 501 would be followed by an even more successful, if less dependable 1-litre lightweight, the 509. But to explore this part of the story, we must return once more to the motor shows of 1921.

6 Ecco la Bambina!

*A silent, vibrationless engine with plenty of power, snappy
without being harsh, simple and perfectly accessible: a good
clutch and a deliciously sweet gearbox: well-sprung and sturdy
at speed: possessing good four-wheel brakes: it was hard to
find any points to criticise.*

509 Road Test, *The Autocar*, November, 1925.

Malheureusement, le moteur n'était pas assez puissant,
et ne résistait guère a une pression soutenue et
prolonguée de l'accélérateur. Il est regrettable que FIAT
n'ait pas dôté cette voiture d'un moteur plus puissant,
évitant dans doute les ennuis de bielles coulées
qu'evoque inévitablement la 509.

Albert Peuvergne, *L'Automobiliste*, March 1969

1925 was a key year in the FIAT story. It marked the effective
end of the racing team, and it marked the début of a new and
sophisticated baby car, the company's first 1-litre offering.
Thenceforward the 'Cars of International Reputation' were
within reach of the humblest customer, and more than 90,000
509s would be sold. Italy felt the effects of the Great Depression
in 1927, three years ahead of everyone else, but despite occasional lay-offs, FIAT sales went steadily up. 37,053 units were
delivered in 1925, but by 1928 the figure was 44,404, or 88 per
cent of the national total.

With the 509 came S.A.V.A., a hire purchase firm aimed at
boosting the home sales of Italy's first universal car, and a
cheap insurance scheme which was in operation by 1928.

The model's overhead-camshaft engine represented advanced practice at a time when the majority of cheap family cars, especially the smaller ones, were wedded to side-by-side valves. Of the new generation, Singer's 'Junior' was first seen at the 1926 London Show, and the Morris 'Minor' did not put in an appearance until two years later. In America only Buick, Chevrolet and Nash among the major producers preferred pushrods. German design was still ossified by financial stringency, and had yet to emerge from a diet of 1912 themes. The French might be in the midst of what Tim Nicholson has termed an 'ebullient decade', but there was nothing ebullient about the products of the nation's 'Big Four'—Renault, Citroën, Peugeot and Mathis. Only Peugeot deviated appreciably from the norm, and in the 1920s they could not match FIAT in terms of volume production. Their 1927 deliveries were a mere 21,276 cars. They were not to score a major hit until 1930, with their undergeared but indestructible 201. As for Britain, she might have pioneered low-priced o.h.c. machinery like the 10.5 h.p. Wolseley and the Rhode, but neither was produced in really large numbers, and Wolseley's technical enterprise had brought that once-proud company to its knees by 1926.

FIAT, of course, had raced overhead-valve engines as long ago as 1905. Between 1908 and 1913 the favoured few had been able to buy the ferocious 'Taunus' and S61 models. Why, then, did the company wait until 1925 before releasing an o.h.v. model in any quantity?

To explore the motives one has to follow the evolutionary path back to 1912 and *Tipo* Zero. When Fornaca elected to give Europe an inexpensive middle-class tourer, he swapped the role of bespoke tailor for that of a department store selling suits off the peg. And for a general provider there is only one viable path—onward and upward. Mistakes can be catastrophic and a new FIAT model had to be assured of a good sale from Athens to Aberdeen.

Even the shrewd Agnelli, however, could not resist a final fling at the maharajah market in the fool's paradise of 1919, and the

1921 Shows saw the appearance of his super-car, Tipo 520—the first Italian-built V-12 to take the road, and the first strictly touring FIAT model to be marketed with overhead valves. Historically, it went the way of the Ensign Six, the Gnome-Rhône, and the Réné Fonck. Impoverished Italians could not afford more than one behemoth, and this they already had in the shape of Cattaneo's *Tipo* 8 Isotta Fraschini.

The Isotta's influence is usually assessed in terms of eight cylinders in line, four-wheel brakes and a movie background ranging from Rudolph Valentino to *Sunset Boulevard*. But to an Italian, it is remembered chiefly because it sparked off one of those waves of imitative styling which are as endemic to Milan and Turin as they are to Detroit.

If Italian makers aped the Mercédès in the early years of the twentieth century, this was surely because the German car was the exemplar of luxury, speed and elegance. But by 1910 an Italian style of radiator had crept in: the standard wear was crypto-Mercédès with squared corners, and the front end of a FIAT was not readily distinguishable from that of a Lancia, S.P.A., Bianchi, or A.L.F.A. If FIAT themselves originated the pear shape on their S76 of 1910, everybody else, as we have seen, followed suit, and in the immediate post-War period this configuration was found on O.M.s, Bianchis, and the latest of Giovanni Ceirano's creations.

By 1925 the old idiom had departed, vestiges of the 1914 shape being detectable only on the ageing *Tipo* 501 FIAT and its big sisters. The rest of the Italians—and this meant the milder Alfa Romeos, Bianchi, Ceirano, Chiribiri, Diatto, Lancia and O.M. as well as the rising generation of FIATs—now affected an angular, Rolls-Royce style of bonnet and radiator.

Sometimes these imitative tendencies assumed extreme forms. By 1927 it was hard to distinguish a 503 FIAT from an S4 Bianchi without opening bonnets, especially as certain bodies (notably the cabriolet-spyder and tourer) appeared identical in every detail. When trans-Atlantic influences crossed the Alps in the later 1920s, a further extraordinary session of follow-my-leader ensued, with ribbon radiator shells on the '667' O.M. and

31. The One That Got Away. Some 50% of SuperFIAT production, clothed and unclothed, shares the company's Paris Salon stand with a 501 and a 510S, 1921.

(FIAT)

32. *Cabriolet Ministeriale.* A 4·8-litre 519, 1924.

(FIAT)

Utility. Elegance and Sport.
33. The original 509 *berlina* of
1925 (top) was painfully
functional and it took a
William Lyons to inject a
touch of beauty with his
Swallow saloon (**34,** centre)
on the 1929 509A chassis.
Wire wheels were also
available on the 509S *bateau*
(**35,** bottom), which looked
faster than it was. This one
took part in the *Coppa
Agnelli*, July 1927.
    (FIAT: Jaguar Cars Ltd: FIAT)

the 514 and 522 FIATS. The same Chrysler-Terraplane idiom expressed itself on the grilles of FIAT's 'Ardita', Lancia's 'Augusta', Alfa Romeo's 6C-2300, O.M.'s 'Alcyone', and Bianchi's original S9. 1936 editions of this latter 1½-litre saloon had short, beetling bonnets in the latest aerodynamic pattern: so had the *mille cinque* FIAT. Even had Italy possessed as many independent makers as Britain or France, one has a feeling that the master touch of a Pininfarina or a Giovanni Bertone would still have been needed.

It has often been asserted that Lancia's unitary-construction 'Lambda' set the pseudo-Rolls-Royce fashion in Italy. This is not so. The definitive 'Lambda' was not on sale until 1922, and a year earlier both O.M.'s *Tipo*-465 and the 6.8-litre twelve-cylinder FIAT had been in evidence. The true begetter of the fashion was surely Cattaneo's Isotta, which was certainly running in 1916. Interestingly, the adoption of the new 'Grecian' line by FIAT coincided with a new radiator emblem in the shape of a round badge, surrounded by a laurel wreath to commemorate a distinguished racing record. It was supplanted in 1932 by a stylised rectangle, but reintroduced on 1965 models of the 1600S cabriolet, since when it has been reserved for FIAT's sporting products.

Why, though, did Agnelli, the realist, the student of American mass-production, take a sudden plunge into cloud-cuckoo land in 1921 ? It could have been the temptation of Poughkeepsie's faithful following in the Eastern United States, or even those maharajahs who had progressed from chain-driven '28–40's' to *Tipo* 5s. His first post-War catalogue offered nothing bigger than a 5-litre side-valve 'six', provisionally designated *Tipo* 503: this, like the worm-driven 500, was stillborn. The 520 was cast in a totally different mould.

It must rank as Italy's first complete V-12, since only parts of Lancia's abortive 6-litre of 1919 seem to have been made. It may even be Europe's first touring Twelve, for the existence of the Lorraine-Dietrich, another of the 1919 crop, is problematic, and Gabriel Voisin's first piece of 'science fiction' was unveiled, along with the big 'Superfiat', at the 1921 Paris Salon. Be that as it may, the 520 was a preview of FIAT technical thinking for the next few years. The overhead valves would reappear on the 519 of 1922, along with the servo-assisted four-wheel brakes, while the 'Rolls-Royce' radiator and bonnet were common to all FIATs of the 1926–28 period. The car was enormous, with a wheelbase of 12 ft 8 in, and a track of 4 ft 11 in. A bare chassis turned the scales at $33\frac{1}{2}$ cwt, which made complete examples genuine two-and-a-half tonners. Despite its stolid Sankey artillery wheels, the vehicle was elegant, and when the bonnet was lifted one was greeted with a vision of Bugatti-like cleanness.

The two blocks were set at an angle of sixty degrees, the heads were detachable, and there was the usual full-pressure lubrication. The dual coil ignition reflected the 32CV Hispano-Suiza, then Europe's luxury carriage *par excellence*. Water pump, generator, and FIAT-made carburetter were all tucked away behind cover plates, while an interesting feature was the air-pressure fuel feed, 'automatically put into operation by the electric starting motor', some six years before the Autopulse electric pump became fashionable in the U.S.A. All this was, of course, admirable sculpture, but with it came pyromaniac tendencies, as owners of the later 519 discovered. The enclosed carburetter was liable to empty its contents into the surrounding cavity. In nine cases out of ten it would then evaporate without further ado, but given the wrong combination of road camber and parking angle, a commutator flash from the starter could provoke an interesting little conflagration.

Retained were the multi-plate clutch (now Ferodo-faced), and the unit gearbox, though an American-style central ball change was adopted, and three forward speeds were deemed sufficient. Advanced for its period was the silent second gear, the spiral bevel back axle was a 501 heritage, and suspension was by semi-elliptics at the front and by long cantilevers at the rear, assisted by friction dampers all round. The four-wheel brakes were actuated by a hydro-mechanical servo fed from two pumps in the base of the gearbox—of which more anon. Other refinements included an engine-driven tyre pump, a thermostat in the cooling system, a telescopic steering-column, and a well-stocked instrument panel complete with clock, rev counter, and altimeter as well as the usual gauges. The car was displayed at Olympia in 1921, and a chassis price of £1,800 was quoted. This was less than was asked for any of Britain's three leading luxury models (the 'Silver Ghost', the Lanchester Forty, and the 40–50 h.p. Napier). Admittedly the 40CV Renault cost only £1,250, but this was a rustic contrivance by Lanchester or FIAT standards. A fairer comparison (and probably the reason for the 520's abrupt disappearance) was Packard's well-established Twin Six, now in its penultimate season, and available with tourer bodywork at £1,550 all on.

FIAT had some rapid second thoughts. A handsome boat-tailed torpedo turned up at the Grand Palais in 1922, but that was the last that was heard of the 520, and it is unlikely that more than three were built. It is significant that even the type-number was re-used, on the company's first inexpensive seven-bearing 'six': a clear indication that top management preferred to forget the whole episode.

The V-12's uncluttered cylinder blocks did not form the only parallel with Ettore Bugatti. After Ettore created the white elephant to end all white elephants in 1927, he scaled down his 'Royale' into the Type 46, a vehicle which inherited the giant's splendours as well as its oft-cited maintenance nightmares. Agnelli, robbed of his super-car by the economic situation, came back with something more manageable, the 4.8-litre *Tipo* 519 unveiled at the 1922 shows. What is more, he sold it to at least one Crowned Head, Christian of Denmark.

On paper the 519 was just as attractive as the 520, with the added merits of more compact proportions and a list price on the right side of £1,300. But while Bugatti duplicated his 12.8-litre straight-eight in miniature, FIAT took the 'twelve's' essential features and incorporated them in an in-line 'six' of 85 × 140 mm (4,766 c.c.). This time a magneto was preferred, though its drive was in line with those of the water pump and generator, all concealed behind the same familiar cover plates. The more modest engine also called for an extra forward ratio, but everything else, from the alloy pistons to the complicated

servo brakes, derived from the original monster. The model
was made in two wheelbase lengths: 11 ft 9½ in for the standard
519, and 10 ft 10 in for the 'S' version, usually seen as a five-
seater torpedo with wire wheels, and sometimes with a vee
radiator in the 510S idiom.

This time it seemed that FIAT's comeback would be effective.
Already the four-wheel brakes had proved their worth on the
circuits, even with the regulation artillery wheels the car was
not lacking in looks, and a chassis weight of less than 22 cwt
meant that formal-bodied versions turned the scales at just over
two tons. The advertised output of 77 b.h.p. was only a little
less than that of the Twelve despite its two additional litres.
Gear ratios (4.08, 6.9, 9.7, and 15.3 to 1) were well spaced for a
luxury tourer of the period, and standard versions would top
the 70 mark, 80 being well within the compass of a 519S. A
maximum of 45–48 m.p.h. on third was entirely adequate, and
even a landaulette tested by *The Autocar* turned in a fuel
consumption of 17 m.p.g. At 78,000 lire in Italy, of course, it
was far too expensive for the vast majority, but in the export
markets at which it was aimed the car was fairly priced—£1,175
for a limousine in England in 1925. By the end of the model's
run complete cars retailed for as little as £850. Factory-built
bodies were beautifully appointed—the 1923 catalogue spoke
of 'cabinet work in rare woods to match the colour of the upholstery, companions, silk curtains, assist straps, flower vases,
ash trays, electric lamps in the running boards', intercom
systems on chauffeur-driven versions, and rear-seat windscreens
on tourers. Some splendid bespoke bodies were created by
firms of the calibre of Pininfarina, D'Ieteren *Frères* in Belgium,
and Maythorn in England.

The 519 got a good press. It had everything: top-gear starts
were viable, its Alpine background made it a superb hill-
climber, and the springing, with its 'extended anti-rolling leaf'
at the rear, encouraged the sort of exuberant driving that
limousines seldom got, even in Italy. *The Autocar* might find it
'a little unwieldy, especially on wet roads', but *The Motor*'s
comments were more enthusiastic:

Considering that the coupé de ville body is not exactly what one
would regard as ideal for fast cornering, the car held the road on
bends with the ease of an out-and-out racing car.

An Indian owner found the all-enclosed power unit proof
against the worst a monsoon could bring, while another un-
expected 519 fan was an undertaker in the East Riding of
Yorkshire, who had owned no fewer than thirty-three examples
by the time he finally hung up his top hat in 1956.

Alas! occasional pyrotechnic displays were not the 519's
only failing. One need not pay undue heed to *The Autocar*'s
comment that 'many people would prefer right-hand change',
but a vibration period in the middle 'thirties' was an undesirable
characteristic on a town carriage, and the process repeated itself
at mile-a-minute speeds. One chauffeur, indeed, opined that
50–55 m.p.h. was a wise limit for any 519. Only *The Motor*
seems to have found the clutch action rough, but the brakes
were disconcerting, to put it mildly. As *The Autocar*'s tester
confessed:

> The servo brake is liable to be a little puzzling, because, in
> common with most such mechanisms it is extremely difficult to
> feel the shoes when the pedal is depressed, with the result that
> the brake is likely to be applied over strongly. Once accustomed
> to the action of the pedal, the operation is smooth, the brakes
> being applied without the slightest suggestion of unequal action,
> and with a most decided effect, in addition to which rapid
> application of the brakes in case of emergency result in a very
> powerful action without any violence.

—all of which adds up to a straight-line stop from 40 m.p.h.
in 103 feet with two tons of motor-car. Unlike the early Hispano-
Suiza servo, the FIAT system was not apparently prone to lose
interest at speeds below 15 m.p.h., but by 1922 Birkigt had
eliminated these teething troubles, whereas the 519's unhappy
reputation pursued it to the grave. The car also took an un-
conscionable time to get into production, only forty being
delivered in 1923. Peak year was 1925, with 1,133 units delivered; at the same time the original design was supplanted by
the B-series, distinguishable by their semi-elliptic rear spring-

ing and some extra avoirdupois. Later cars were also more expensive in Italy, at 93,000 lire for a standard torpedo. The 519 was rallied and raced, competing in the 1925 All-Russian Reliability Trials and the first Mille Miglia of 1927: it even essayed the Targa Florio, for which it must have been about as suitable as André Dubonnet's renowned tulip-wood 'Monza' Hispano-Suiza, but it was phased out in 1927, after 2,411 had been made. The fact that it remained current for another twelvemonth in such prosperous export markets as Britain and Switzerland shows that it must have been hard to sell in its declining years. Its successor was the foursquare 3.7-litre 525, a worthy piece of crypto-Detroit based on the inexpensive 520 and 521. But the 519 has its place in history as the last FIAT aimed at the chauffeur-driven luxury market. Subsequent prestige models were of a different stamp altogether. The 2800 of 1938 was a ministerial device which looked wrong without a flagstaff or a two-tone syren, and since World War II the costliest FIATS, from the 8V to the 'Dino 2400', have been the preserve of the wealthy enthusiast. Only in 1971 was there a reversion to luxury themes with the 3.2-litre 130, designed to rival Rover, Jaguar and Mercédès-Benz in the executive sector.

The 519 was a beautifully-made mistake, but its unhappy career did not disturb the even progress of the well-established 501 family. During 1924 the faithful 1½-litre became available with front-wheel brakes and 730 × 130 balloon tyres, a similar treatment being applied to the 505 and 510. Concessionaires and *filiali* were authorised to convert existing vehicles to this new 'B' specification for the equivalent of £25. In some markets, notably France, only B-types were sold: by April, 1925, all 510s shipped to Britain came with f.w.b., but as far as Lingotto were concerned this refinement was always an optional extra. To the end in 1926 501s were still being delivered with brakeless front axles, though the last 505s and 510s, as we shall see, were transitional types based on their 1926 successors. In 1923, incidentally, the range had been further extended by the announcement of the 502, a long-chassis 501 aimed at the taxi and private-hire market. It was made in modest quantities—only 1,598 in 1924 as against over 16,000 of the basic species—and was available with the usual 'B' modifications.

The middle 'twenties saw FIAT's first diesel-electric railcar, as well as the opening of a new engineering test laboratory, not to mention drastic expansion of the S.I.T.A. 'bus network, which had extended its tentacles into Tripolitania. By 1927 the company's routes had a mileage of 37,300. At the same time FIAT went empire-building again, acquiring the Ansaldo aircraft business in 1925.

This purchase has led many a writer to assert that Ansaldo's car factories were swallowed by FIAT, and this would seem a logical step in view of Ansaldo's attempts to tap the mass market with their early overhead-camshaft 4C, an austere, cut-price offering which combined Soria's advanced power unit with the appearance of a Chevrolet. This is not so: though Soria's resignation in 1927 brought any serious technical development to a halt, Ansaldo struggled on as an independent until 1932, when the firm was acquired by C.E.V.A. This concern continued to dispose of unsold stocks, and was building straight-eights from parts on hand as late as 1936. By contrast, the aircraft side was absorbed into FIAT under the name *Aeronautica d'Italia*, and continued the manufacture of the A120 reconnaissance monoplane, which had been accepted by the Regia Aeronautica before the change of ownership. A120s remained in service until the Ethiopian War, and were always regarded by the Service as Ansaldos rather than FIATs.

Next on the list were S.P.A. This company had been founded in 1906 by two old friends, Matteo Ceirano and Michele Ansaldi. Like Agnelli, the S.P.A. directors had been quick to diversify after Agadir, and in 1910 they won an Army competition for light lorries in the face of FIAT opposition. Though their first aero-engines, the work of Aristide Faccioli, had been unsuccessful, by 1918 this side of the business was prospering. By this time S.P.A. were as truck-minded as Delahaye in France, albeit they continued to make quality cars in limited numbers. These included an advanced 30–40 h.p. twin o.h.c. six, which had front-wheel brakes in 1922. Unfortunately the failure of Turin's Banco di Sconto upset the S.P.A. applecart, and in October, 1926, FIAT came to the rescue by acquiring the firm's share capital. This spelt the end of the private cars, but commercial vehicles continued under the S.P.A. name, though from 1928 onwards these were marketed by *Consortium FIAT*, a sales and hire-purchase organisation on the lines of the German industrial consortia of the early 1920s. In later years S.P.A. were to be renowned for their fire-engines and specialist military types, notably the TL37 4×4 artillery tractor widely used in World War II. The firm was finally integrated into FIAT as a division in February, 1947, but to this day the truck factory at Stura has a sturdy independence of its own. This is reflected on the grille of every FIAT diesel truck made to-day, for under the emblem are to be seen the words *costruzione S.P.A.*

This purchase helped FIAT to cash in on the revival of commercial-vehicle business, delayed by the flood of war surplus machinery, which took years to unload: it is salutary to remember that Leyland were still advertising works-reconditioned R.A.F.-types as late as 1926, and stocks of American Peerlesses lasted still longer. In 1923 the FIAT commercials offered in Britain had an Edwardian flavour. There was the 12-cwt *Tipo* 1 at £350 for a van or £675 for a taxicab, the one-ton *Tipo Due* at £425, the 30-cwt 15TER as a 'pay-as-you-enter' light omnibus (£725), and even the hoary old three-ton 18BL at £775, albeit production had ceased in 1921. None the less, these FIATs had quite a vogue: London's first pneumatic-tyred P.S.V. to be licenced under Scotland Yard regulations was a 15TER, while Harrods acquired forty-odd FIAT vans between 1920 and 1922, keeping some on charge until 1934. By this time, however, commercial versions of the 501 and 505 were available, *The Commercial Motor* commenting on the 'noiseless running' of these new models at the 1926 Bath and West Show. There were other new types: the 603 was a worm-driven two-tonner utilising the 2.3-litre 107 engine. It was also available in 23-seater 'bus form, in which case a 3,446 c.c. six-cylinder

110/112 unit was specified. At the top of the range was the 605, designed for a payload of 50 cwt, and coming complete with Rolls-Royce-style radiator, pneumatic tyres and four-wheel brakes, though the six-cylinder car engine was retained. Another novelty was a 6-cwt van based on the 509, but deliveries were on a modest scale. In 1927 FIAT–S.P.A. were responsible for 84 per cent of Italian truck and 'bus production, but the national output of 3,086 units represented a drop in the bucket beside France's contribution of 31,667, or even a resurgent Germany's 12,000.

Exports continued to bulk large, and the exhortations of Giolitti and Mussolini took effect with a vengeance. In 1927 Italy exported 62.1 per cent of all her cars, nearly double the 36.1 per cent of Canada, whose industry was used by Detroit as an ingenious way round British preferential tariffs. By contrast France's quota was 28.4 per cent, Britain's 18.3, and the U.S.A.'s a paltry 7.2 per cent, even if this added up to an alarming quantity of Fords, Chevrolets, Overlands and Essexes.

FIAT's share was affected by the change in emphasis from 501 to 509. This worked against Lingotto in markets such as Australia, where the demand was for toughness and simplicity, as well as in countries like Denmark, where the 509's fussy behaviour and rod-throwing habits were a disappointment after the 501's quiet, lazy and inexorable manner of going. Against this, the new baby scored in territories afflicted with fiscal problems or enthusiastic driving habits. Belgians took to the 509, and so did Frenchmen, the 509 being the first FIAT model to make a major impact in Gaul. This is highlighted by import statistics. In 1925 only 999 of France's 16,376 imported cars came from Italy, this despite the fact that the 501 was not impossibly expensive at 22,800 fr for a chassis. It undoubtedly offered more refinement than a Citroën (22,230 fr complete) or a 6CV Renault (17,450 fr). But in the first six months alone of 1926 France took 971 Italian cars, a locally-made four-speed gearbox was devised to circumvent one of the 509's worst failings, and the model's exploits in the Monte Carlo Rally assured it a staunch following for the rest of its career.

The outlook was even rosier in Great Britain, where four cylinders and a bore of 57 mm added up to an Eight paying the same annual tax as an Austin Seven. Further, the leisurely driving habits of the average Briton were tailor-made for a gearbox with low overall ratios, and the 509 family outsold any inter-War FIAT model with the exception of the *topolino*. The presence of the *marque* on six stands at the 1927 Glasgow Show indicated that this popularity extended north of the Border as well, and 1928 was to see an attempt to assemble the little cars at the Vickers works. FIATS were seen in Latvia, Poland, and Yugoslavia, while the Bucharest *filiale* was doing good business. If American operations had ground to a halt, and the Australian attitude to the 509 was reflected in meagre sales (346 units in 1928), FIAT had no major worries. After all, in that most classic of 'free' markets, Switzerland, their share of total registrations was over ten per cent (2,854 cars), and this was nearly double the number of Citroëns in circulation.

Meanwhile Agnelli was looking eastward to Russia. FIAT postal vans had been used before the War in Moscow and St Petersburg, and licence-production of 15TERs had just got under way before the Revolution: indeed, these formed the basis of the State-made Amo F-15 lorry of the 1924–30 period. What is more, the U.S.S.R. was tackling the problem of mechanisation from scratch. Having as yet no industry of its own, the Soviet Government decided to stage two enormous long-distance trials to select the vehicles best suited to national requirements.

The first of these was staged in October, 1923, over a 2,300-kilometre circular route starting and finishing in Moscow, and taking in Smolensk, Vitebsk, Pskov, Leningrad, Novgorod and Tver, a shorter course being used for commercial-vehicle entries. FIAT did well in both categories, Alessandro Cagno's 510 being awarded the Grand Challenge Cup of the Organising Committee.

The second *concosso panrusso* of 1925 was a far bigger affair run between Leningrad and Tiflis, a distance of close on 5,400 kilometres. The 250 competing machines were said to include 'sports, touring, industrial, agricultural, and special purpose vehicles,' and according to *Auto Italiana* 11 per cent of the route was made up of 'zones innocent of any road, or rough mountain paths'. This time the authorities announced their intention of placing big orders with the victorious firms, and almost everybody (with the exception of the British motor industry) turned out. The FIATs were the sole Italian represent-atives, but they were opposed by Citroën, Hotchkiss, Suère and Talbot-Darracq from France, Praga and Tatra from Czechoslovakia: Adler, Aga, Benz, Horch, Mercédès, N.A.G. and Stoewer from Germany: Austro-Daimler and Steyr from Austria: and Buick, Cadillac, Chrysler, Dodge, Hudson, Lincoln, Moon, Nash, Packard, Pierce-Arrow, and Studebaker from America. FIAT's contribution amounted to two 519s (one entrusted to Cagno), two 510s, and two 505F lorries with Russian drivers.

The carnage was considerable. 92 cars succumbed to broken suspensions, five went out with gearbox disorders, 20 with expensive underbonnet noises, and 30 from 'miscellaneous breakages'. Cagno had things his own way in the big-car class after Zeidler's Mercédès ran out of road near Novgorod and the much-fancied Packard and Studebaker opposition faded away. He collected the trophy for the best individual per-formance as well as the fuel-consumption award. It was his swansong—and also the 519's only major competition success. Alas! for FIAT—the top brass of the Kremlin opted for Lincolns and Packards instead of 519 tourers, Ford were behind the vast Gorki complex of 1930, and it was not until forty-one years later that the Soviet colossus joined forces with FIAT to build the industrial town of Togliattigrad.

Meanwhile the racing programme went ahead. For 1923 some new 2-litre straight-eights (*Tipo* 805) replaced the six-cylinder 804s. This change of direction was waspishly ascribed by *Motor Italia* to Bertarione's departure to 'among the aborigines of England', and certainly the FIATs were to face a team of green cars from Wolverhampton which were almost Chinese copies of the 804. In the circumstances it was hardly tactful of Prince Nicholas of Rumania (even in 1926) to turn up for a state visit to the Bucharest *filiale* at the wheel of a 3-litre Sunbeam tourer!

The 1923 Grand Prix FIATs had 60×87.5 mm bi-block engines on classic lines, the main change being the use of a spur-gear drive for the twin overhead camshafts. These units were said to weigh 22 lbs less than the old 404s, but they differed from all previous Grand Prix engines in having Wittig vane-type superchargers driven off the nose of the crankshaft, 'compressed air being delivered *via* a passage cast in the engine base chamber to a sealed carburetter, in Mercédès style, but a hinged flap, operated by the mechanic, could be opened when running at moderate speeds, when normal aspiration was reverted to'. This unit was credited with 130 b.h.p. at 5,500 r.p.m., sufficient to propel the 805s at 124 m.p.h. Chassis design was little changed, the successful quick-detachable tanks of 1922 racers being retained, though the 519's complex servo anchors were adopted. At the same time a supercharged version of the 803 *voiturette* was prepared, forced induction boosting output from 63 b.h.p. to 80 b.h.p., a promising recipe in a vehicle turning the scales at less than 11 cwt.

The new cars were not ready for the Targa Florio, and FIAT's best showing was De Seta's sixth place on a nearly-stock 501S. At the Parma-Poggio di Berceto hill-climb the aged S57s of Brilli-Peri and Niccolini once again made the two fastest times, and it was not until 29 June that the public had a sight of a supercharged FIAT in the *Gran Premio Vetturette* at Brescia. On this fast, easy circuit Cagno's 803 had no difficulty in disposing of an assorted field of Chiribiris, Bugattis, O.M.s and Bianchis. His winning average speed was 80.3 m.p.h.

Four days later it was the 805s' turn, in the French Grand Prix over the Tours course, with open bends that could be taken flat out. Opposed to the works machines of Giaccone, Salamano and Bordino were the Sunbeam-built six-cylinder 'FIATs in green paint', Réné Thomas's complex and untried V-12 Delage, three locally-made Rolland-Pilains (no longer *desmodromiques*, as in 1922, but still with hydraulic front brakes), some ultra-short-wheelbase eight-cylinder 'tanks' from Bugatti, and Gabriel Voisin's bizarre six-cylinder 'flat irons', which had barely an outside chance on 75 b.h.p., for all their sophisticated aerodynamics.

FIAT were taking things seriously albeit with confidence, opining that they could match the opposition, even without blowers. This view was based on two months of practising on the 1922 cars. The straight-eights duly arrived from Turin under their own power, and observers noted the 'harsh, healthy crackle' of their exhausts.

A FIAT benefit seemed almost a certainty, especially after Bordino turned in a practice lap at 85.6 m.p.h., whereas Segrave's best for Sunbeam was 81 m.p.h. In Segrave's own words: 'I estimated my chances of winning, and soon realised that there was no probability of this'. For the first seven laps of the race the Briton felt the same way, while FIAT's no. 1 driver circulated at a cracking 87 m.p.h. But soon after that Bordino had retired, 'with a stone through his engine base chamber'.

On the sixteenth circuit a hesitant note was detectable in Giaccone's engine, and he brought his car in for a plug change. All to no avail: a lap later the second FIAT was out, reputedly with a broken exhaust valve.

That left Salamano, and Salamano was in the lead, circulating briskly, whereas Lee Guinness's Sunbeam was fighting clutch trouble—his mechanic Perkins first organised some manual assistance *via* a wire wound round the pedal, and then had recourse to his necktie when the wire bit into his wrist. Nemesis, however, was at hand, for the FIAT ran out of petrol on the course, and that was that. '*C'est le quatorze*', observed Segrave's mechanic Paul Dutoit, '*qui est en panne*'. Henry Segrave and Sunbeam had snatched what was to be Britain's last international Grand Prix win for 32 years, with the exception of the blown Sunbeam's performance at San Sebastian in 1924.

It soon transpired that FIAT's superchargers were at fault. In Salamano's case the tip of a compressor blade had broken off, wedging the throttle open, and forcing the Italian to do twelve laps at full throttle, using the ignition cut-out on corners to the detriment of the engine's thirst. The loose, dusty surface of Tours had played havoc with the blowers, and engines that had stood the strain of tough tests on the easy, clean concrete of Monza had proved unequal to this new challenge.

In theory, therefore, the Wittigs should have been trouble-free in the European Grand Prix at the Monza Autodrome, but FIAT had learnt their lesson, and on this, the 805's second appearance, it emerged with a Roots-type supercharger which boosted output to 146 b.h.p. and gave the cars an extra 12 m.p.h. of straight-line speed. There had been other, more grievous troubles, for during fuel-consumption tests two racers had suffered stub-axle failures. Giaccone was killed, and Bordino sustained serious injuries to his shoulder, which did not prevent his taking his place in the team. Replacing Giaccone was the veteran Felice Nazzaro.

The FIATs no longer had to face the Sunbeams, though the Rolland-Pilains and Voisins put in another appearance, along with three straight-eight Millers from America and three Rumpler-designed rear-engined six-cylinder Benz which represented Germany's first serious post-War bid for Grand Prix honours. Among the non-starters were the six-cylinder P.1 Alfa Romeos (withdrawn after a fatal accident to Ugo Sivocci) and some twin overhead camshaft sixteen-valve four-cylinder Bianchis, that firm's only attempt at a G.P. car. One suspects that their advertised 90 b.h.p. would have been no match for the FIATs, anyway.

In the event, only the Millers approached the speed of the 805s, and though Bordino's injured arm forced him to give up at half-distance, Salamano stormed through to win at 91 m.p.h. from Nazzaro and Murphy (Miller). To Agnelli's existing laurels could be added the first Grand Prix to be won by a supercharged car.

The *voiturette* event advertised as part of the Monza programme had been cancelled owing to lack of support, so the next appearance of the supercharged 803s was at Brooklands, where Salamano and Malcolm Campbell were down to drive in the Junior Car Club's 200-Mile Race. The choice of Campbell was the consequence of Bordino's injuries and Cagno's absence in the Soviet Union. British journalists welcomed this chance to see how the FIATS would fare against the unblown, but so far invincible 1½-litre Talbot-Darracqs. Louis Coatalen was, however, taking no risks, and he scratched his entries, giving FIAT another potential walkover, even if Salamano's best practice lap (at 103 m.p.h.) was not so very much faster than those of the quickest British cars, the A.C.s and Aston Martins.

It was Tours all over again. Though Cushman's Bugatti led away from the start, the race soon settled down to a Salamano-Campbell duel, with the rest of the field well behind. The Briton's superior knowledge of the Track told on the bends, though Salamano, as a works tester, was familiar with Brooklands and the two cars were pretty evenly matched.

But not for long. On the thirteenth lap Salamano's car blew up, and soon afterwards Campbell's followed suit, leaving C. M. Harvey's Alvis to take the chequered flag, and, incidentally, to rescue the *marque* from a parlous financial situation.

What had gone wrong? Piston failure was suspected; it was even hinted that the FIAT drivers had disregarded instructions and indulged in an internecine dice. This was untrue; they kept to a steady 4,500 r.p.m., and were prepared to throttle back to 4,000 once the race was in the bag. It has even been suggested that the old Wittig blowers (certainly used at Brescia) had been retained on the *voiturettes*, since this particular installation had never given any trouble, unlike that on the 805s. It seems certain, however, that the Brooklands 803s wore Roots superchargers, and the only clue to a possible (and hitherto unexplored) solution is to be found in the 1924 Targa Florio, the model's last race.

On this occasion Salamano found his car a handful in practice, and crashed it, fortunately without serious damage. It was then handed to Felice Nazzaro, who said that it was 'almost undrivable', and refused to use it in the race. The second 803 was entrusted to Bordino, who is described in a contemporary report as 'having a terrible time aboard his lightweight, high-powered FIAT, which, with short springs and shock absorbers screwed up as tight as they would go, was most uncomfortable to ride in and exceptionally difficult to hold on such a road'. Now there is no comparing the tortuous mountain passes of Sicily with the oval concrete of Brooklands, but the Track's bumpy surface accentuated handling defects, and the notoriously tricky 1924 straight-eight Grand Prix Mercédès defeated at least one driver on the banking. Could it be that the 803 was 'too fast for chassis', and just pounded itself out of business?

There were the usual minor Italian wins in 1923, in which several ancients and hybrids were still in circulation. The S61 was going strong at Brooklands, and Moraes' aero-engined device recorded fourth fastest time at La Turbie as well as a third place in the s.s kilometre at Nice. At Fanoë Dynesen ran a mysterious 6,809 c.c. six-cylinder FIAT with cowled radiator, and the irrepressible Ernest Eldridge acquired the disembowelled remains of 'Mephistopheles' for £25. As early as February, *The Autocar* reported that 'the frame was sawn in half, and lengthened, and an aeroplane engine is being installed'.

This was common enough practice in the era of Louis Zborowski and A. G. Miller, but Eldridge was keeping things in the family, so to speak, for his new engine (acquired from a war-surplus store in the Vauxhall Bridge Road) was a vast 21.7-litre six-cylinder o.h.c. FIAT A12 dirigible motor disposing of some 300 brake horses. The chassis was extended by seventeen inches, and a special sub-frame made to take the new power unit, although the original 1908 gearbox was retained. Eldridge's clutch, incidentally, had plates fabricated from ordinary sheet steel. As first seen at Brooklands that summer it was still a bare chassis, with two seats perched well over the rear axle. It was also less than reliable, 'shedding bits as it went' on one of its first appearances. By November, though, the big FIAT had taken the world's standing-start half-mile record at 77.68 m.p.h.

The rejuvenated 'Mephistopheles' was a terrifying brute. W. G. S. Wike, a subsequent owner, has left this record of him as a road car, published in *Motor Sport* during World War II:

36. American Tour: Pietro Bordino in action in Argentina with a *Tipo* 805, 1925. Note the liberal protection accorded to the radiator.

(FIAT)

37. The last Grand Prix. Bordino sits in the *monoposto* 806 with which he won the 1927 Milan G.P., while Nazzaro and Salamano (left) look on.

The Detroit influence. **38.** The basic 520 of 1927 (top) was American under the skin: without, it was hard to distinguish from the four-cylinder 503, its left-hand steering apart.

(FIAT)

39. The 525SS (centre) of 1930 was a classic Italian beauty with knock-on wheels and offset instrument panel, but by 1932 the 522C 'cabriolet Royal' (**40**) was a convertible victoria in the best 1930 U.S. idiom, down to its ribbon radiator shell and five-stud disc wheels.

The car was magnificent to drive: there was a huge ignition lever, as big as a Bugatti gear lever, and one did not advance it under 800 r.p.m. as the whole show caught fire, but when one did shove it forward (at above 75 in top) the acceleration was pleasing. Yet I drove it around the streets of Birkdale even using top gear—about 50 r.p.m., I should think.

Eldridge had set his sights on the World's Land Speed Record, and this he achieved in 1924, though preliminary trials at Southport brought defeat at the hands of another famous record car, Campbell's 1920 350 h.p. V-12 Sunbeam. In July Eldridge recorded 146.8 m.p.h. over the kilometre on the narrow, treelined course at Arpajon in France, only to be confronted with a protest from his French rival, Réné Thomas, then after the title with the 10½-litre twelve-cylinder Delage. The FIAT had no reverse gear: in fact it had never had one, from the days of Nazzaro and Abercromby. Nothing daunted, Eldridge enlisted the aid of a works mechanic attached to Jacques Loste's workshops in Paris, and returned to Arpajon, where Thomas had raised the Record to 143.7 m.p.h.

The Delage's record was, however, destined to remain on the books for a mere six days. Eldridge could now (according to A.I.A.C.R. rules, at any rate) go backwards, and he now went forward to good purpose, achieving a mean speed of 146.01 m.p.h. on a road that was not even officially closed. Gedge and Ames, both of whom rode with him, must have been brave as well as tough, for the mechanic had to manipulate both a hand pump for the petrol and an oxygen injection apparatus, while a return run on treadless tyres held no terrors for Eldridge, and 'Mephistopheles' had a well-substantiated reputation for throwing covers! Both Delage and FIAT duly turned up in the appropriate Champs-Elysées showrooms, and D'Arcy Baker made considerable capital out of Eldridge's new Record in his weekly advertisements.

The question of the reverse gear has never been resolved, and unfortunately the mechanic responsible is now dead. William Boddy has propounded the three alternatives open to Eldridge —changing the crown wheel over to the other side of the pinion, fitting a third shaft above the gearbox, its gears mating with the input and output shaft gears, or crossing the driving chains. Whichever method was used, the improvisation was deleted immediately after the successful run. No traces now remain—beyond some 'unexplained holes in the vicinity of the gearbox' remarked by Dr Costantino.

As for FIAT's views on the record, these seem to have been ambivalent. Unquestionably the official attitude squared with that of the late W. F. Bradley, who always maintained that 'Mephistopheles' in his 1924 guise was not a FIAT, but a 'special' incorporating a large proportion of FIAT parts. It is also true that the company rejected an appeal for help from Duff in 1922, on the grounds that the original SB4-190 design had long since passed the limit of logical development. In company publications the car has always been termed a 'FIAT-Eldridge' rather than a FIAT, but while Turin refused to back the venture in any way, the record was duly acknowledged in the August, 1924 issue of the house journal *Rivista FIAT*.

'Mephistopheles' was raced again on both sides of the Channel during 1924, turning in an unofficial record lap of Brooklands at 124.33 m.p.h., and failing in a match against Parry Thomas's Leyland-Thomas at Montlhéry because it could not keep its tyres on. This weakness frustrated further record attempts, as well as enlivening subsequent match events at Brooklands and Montlhéry alike. William Boddy has described the Thomas-Eldridge battle at the Track in 1925 as 'one of the most exciting ever seen, and devastatingly dangerous', with Eldridge spurning either goggles or helmet. The two giants fought it out lap by lap, both shedding treads as they went. The Leyland-Thomas lapped the faster, at 123.23 m.p.h. to the FIAT's 121.19 m.p.h., though unofficially 'Mephistopheles' improved on this to the tune of a sizzling 125.45 m.p.h. He then passed into the hands of L. C. G. Le Champion, and gradually faded from the Brooklands scene.

Lesser FIATs were, of course, still much in evidence. Three 501S cars turned out for the Swedish Winter Races on the ice, Barnard's 501 took second place in Australia's Sydney-Mount

Kosciuscko Trial, and there were other victories as far afield as India and Malaya, as well as a class win in Germany's Eifel Tourist Races. Dynesen's FIAT-Special reappeared at Fanoë, now with a ten-litre Mercédès aero engine under its bonnet, doing 125 m.p.h., and beating Kordewan's vast works-entered Stoewer in the process. The factory racing programme continued, but the brilliant design team of 1921 was steadily breaking up, and now Jano moved on to create Alfa Romeo's P2 straight-eights, which were probably the best 'FIATS' in circulation during 1924.

The Targa Florio was an inauspicious beginning to the season, for the enormous entry initially promised by FIAT boiled down to a pair of supercharged 803s for Bordino and Salamano, and a 519S for Pastore. The *voiturettes* gave their drivers a punishing time on the Sicilian course, and the four laps of the Targa were quite enough for the FIAT crews, though competitors in that year's Coppa Florio had to cover a fifth circuit. Bordino, still affected by his accident at Monza, fought his way through to fourth place in the Targa, only to collapse at the pits, whereupon Nazzaro took over, with the intention of qualifying for the Coppa. A hole in the sump (which Bordino had been too exhausted to mention) was bad enough, but the old maestro could not cope with the appalling handling, and the car overturned. Pastore's clutch gave up at the end of his Targa stint, eliminating the big sports model. By this time FIAT's superchargers were certainly of Roots type, and they seem to have given no trouble even on the dusty Sicilian roads.

As for the European Grand Prix at Lyons, this was anyone's guess. The 805s were little changed apart from the substitution of mechanical servo brakes for the untrustworthy hydraulic arrangements, but rumour spoke of a fantastic supercharged two-stroke 'six'. Rumour was wrong, however, and the cars with which Nazzaro, Bordino and Salamano practised were the 1923 straight-eights, though their engines were now delivering 150 b.h.p. This, on paper, should have made them a match for the supercharged six-cylinder Sunbeams, Jano's blown straight-eight Alfa Romeos, and the V-12 Delages. There were also five unsupercharged Bugattis, the Rolland-Pilains had acquired cuff-valve engines and were now called Schmids, and Louis Zborowski had entered a Miller. When the practice period closed, FIAT had four cars at Lyons, and in the race these were handled by Nazzaro, Bordino, Marchesio and Pastore.

It was not Turin's day. Bordino drove brilliantly despite his physical handicap, giving the Sunbeams and Alfas an excellent run for their money. Alas! the latest anchors were not an improvement, and the Italian had to use all his skill when he overran a corner—he accomplished the scarcely credible feat of spinning round the *commissaire*'s table, and continuing flat out. After ten laps he was still in second place, but the entire FIAT team eventually retired, leaving Campari's Alfa Romeo to win from Divo's Delage. The *équipe* scratched from the Italian Grand Prix, and for the next six months FIAT's competition prospects kept the gossips busy. In January, 1925, W. F. Bradley summarised the situation for readers of *The Autocar*:

> It is quite unlikely that FIAT will be seen in the year's big races. This regrettable abdication does not mean that the famous Italian firm is withdrawing from racing, but that internal re-organisation, factory extensions, and the necessity for increasing production make it difficult to give attention to a racing pro-gramme. As a proof of FIAT's interest in speed contests, the rac-ing department has been reorganised, and Felice Nazzaro has been placed at its head.

—which, being interpreted, meant that Nazzaro was the non-playing captain of a team which did not quite know where it was going!

Bradley was correct in his surmise, however, for the works programme in 1925 amounted solely to Cagno's Soviet ad-venture and a brief American safari for Bordino, who took a *Tipo* 805 across the Atlantic and tried his luck on the Cali-fornian board tracks. He also entered for the Indianapolis 500-Mile Race, in which he took 12th place, not to mention

18th in the year's American Drivers' Championship. Thereafter European G.P. cars and drivers stayed away from the United States until the George Vanderbilt Cup of 1936.

At home 501s annexed the touring-car class of the Stelvio hill-climb, as well as the 1,500 c.c. section of the Monza Fuel Economy Trials. Silvani took one of his tuned 501S models to the Autodrome in November, and collected a whole string of records, running non-stop for 144 hours to average close on 49 m.p.h., and a month later the Garda Winter Trials saw the competition début of the little 990 c.c. 509. Pagni won the 1,100 c.c. section at 29.54 m.p.h., followed by a whole string of sister cars, with only a Derby to break the sequence in fourth place. The 501Ss beat the *Tipo-469* O.M.s in the 1½-litre category. In France Soreau took a second place in the 1,500 c.c. class of Paris-Nice.

But the big news of 1925 was, of course, FIAT's first true baby, the overhead camshaft 509 unveiled at the Paris Salon in October, 1924. FIAT celebrated its birth with the establishment of their own hire-purchase organisation, but in Italy the *bambina's* arrival was regarded as a national event. When W. F. Bradley collected his road-test tourer from the Milan depot the following autumn, he found a group of taxi-drivers poking about under the bonnet, while another bystander had crawled beneath and was scrutinising the rear-axle casing. Britons, who did not see production 509's until early 1926, were not a little anxious: the sophisticated FIAT with its powerful semi-servo four-wheel brakes and comfortable accommodation for four people was streets ahead of the Austin Seven and the rustic, if dependable, 'Long Four' Jowett. The powers that be at Longbridge and Idle must have breathed again when they discovered that the 509 was no bargain-basement item. A two-seater cost £225, and the saloons £90 more.

The heart of the new infant was a 57×97 mm (990 c.c.) two-bearing overhead-camshaft engine developing 20 b.h.p. at a high 3,800 r.p.m. Cooling was by thermo-syphon with fan assistance, and the dynamo was driven off the nose of the crankshaft. Both the magneto ignition and the gravity feed were, of course, recognised period practice, but 12-volt electrics were remarkable on a cheap lightweight. At long last FIAT had forsaken their traditional multi-disc clutch for a single dry plate, and the three-speed gearbox had central change. Final drive was by torque tube to a spiral bevel back end, and the chassis rode on semi-elliptic springs all round. The effective four-wheel brakes were supplemented by a rear-wheel handbrake. A tourer was fairly heavy at 16 cwt 51 lbs, necessitating low and wide gear ratios—6.01, 12.6, and 21.2 to 1. A generous wheelbase of 8 ft 4 in left plenty of room for four-seater coachwork, and by 1927 two four-door styles—a tourer and a Weymann fabric saloon—had been added to the range.

The little FIAT had many virtues. The camshaft drive was quiet, and if driven in a sedate manner the car was not rev-happy. It could stand up to mountain work without over-heating, and was blessed with a sweet clutch and an easy gear-change, not to mention such ingenious refinements as warning lights for dynamo charge and oil pressure, and tool boxes tucked away behind the valances. The brakes were well up to the car's performance even if the pedal was uncomfortably close to the steering-column, and *The Light Car* enthused over the 509's handling. 'Locking over sharply round a right-angle bend at a very high speed', commented their tester, 'results only in producing a shriek of protest from the tyres, the car showing no tendency to roll'. There were compensations for a 6:1 axle ratio in a top-gear range of 10–52 m.p.h., second-gear starts were possible, and the FIAT could be persuaded up to 30 m.p.h. in this gear. More remarkable was an easy cruising gait of 40–45, and not everyone shared Albert Peuvergne's misgivings as to bottom-end weakness. S. C. H. Davis, who disliked the 509, 'felt that it would go on for ever'. Fuel consumption was 34 m.p.g. in normal conditions, though some owners, like Leonard Potter, got as much as 45. Writing in *Motor Sport* of his very second-hand tourer, Potter recalled it as 'a really marvellous car. Easy starting, perfect brakes, lovely steering, gear-change like butter, and excellent hill-climbing'.

Most of the 509's sterner critics, in fact, belonged to a later era of rebels against the low gearing favoured from the end of the Vintage period. By contrast with its 1925 opposition, it was an outstanding car. The 6CV Renault was agricultural and noisy, and its transverse rear suspension gave a bouncy ride. The C-type Citroën, still selling briskly, had rear-wheel and transmission brakes of uncertain quality which made a virtue of its 38 m.p.h. top speed, while the German Opel 'Laubfrosch' was a Citroën in all but name. The handy little Peugeots of the 172 family were narrow and cramped even if they no longer had staggered seating, and in four-seater form they were afflicted with axle ratios even more abysmal than the FIAT's. As for the Austin Seven—its 'spit and hope' lubrication might be far more reliable than it had any right to be, but its sudden death clutch and uncoupled brakes were barbarous by comparison with the 509's arrangements. Only the Renault had proper anchors on all four wheels in 1925; the Citroën was dropped early in 1926, retaining its brakeless front axle to the end.

Perhaps the finest tribute paid to the FIAT—albeit an indirect one—came from H. K. Whitehorn of Tilling-Stevens, who used a 509 two-seater as a test-bed for his company's petrol-electric transmissions. The result was simple one-pedal control, and Whitehorn taught himself to drive on it. It is, however, a matter of opinion whether the car really could serve as a 'mobile power station', for the 'automatic' FIAT weighed 23 cwt, altogether too much for the twenty brake horses. It was painfully sluggish on hills, and getting out of Maidstone was sometimes a problem. Amusingly enough, in 1934 Tilling-Stevens almost succeeded in selling a new design of petrol-electric trolleybus to the Municipality of Milan, which would have involved them in a licence agreement with FIAT. Needless to say, the Fascists soon put a stop to this deal!

Stories of bearing failure were undoubtedly exaggerated, but by mid-1926 FIAT were extremely worried. This led them to take the unprecedented step of major modifications without any publicity at all. In fact the 509A replaced the 509 during the autumn. In its new guise the engine incorporated a re-designed oil pump, an improved induction manifold, and a new-type updraught Zenith or Solex carburetter in place of the 109 unit's FIAT instrument. An easy way of distinguishing a 109A unit from a 109 is the location of the 'gas-works', which are on the right-hand side on early engines, but on the left on 109As. At the same time British prices were reduced, to £215 for open models and £273 for the coupé and saloon. A year later a tourer could be bought for a mere £200, saloons listed at £250, and a wide range of styles embraced a fixed-head coupé *royal*, a *camionnette normande*, and even a baby taxicab. The 509A was to be the mainstay of the FIAT range until 1929, and even in its last year more than 24,000 were produced.

Give an Italian a cheap family car, and he will strip and race it. This had been true of the 501, and it was to be truer still of the 509, albeit the factory was quicker off the mark than the amateurs, since the 509S was displayed at the 1926 Milan Show. During the year the cars recorded at least a dozen 1,100 c.c. class wins in Italy alone. It is well to remember, too, that these were not the empty victories which characterised the later years of the 'Balilla' and the *millecento* at a time when FIATS and FIAT derivatives dominated this category, and Italians were cut off from foreign imports. 1926 was the heyday of French '1,100's' such as the Salmson, Amilcar, and B.N.C., and Amilcars were actually being assembled at Verona by the S.I.L.V.A. concern. Not a few of Italy's great drivers cut their teeth on these *voiturettes*, Luigi Fagioli and Baconin Borzac-chini favouring Salmsons and Antonio Brivio a Derby. Thus Benigni's 509S did well to win the 1,100 c.c. category of the Targa Abruzzo, and in other events (including a kilometre sprint in Poland) the FIATS beat the Amilcars, though they had to give best to the twin-cam Salmsons in a touring-car race staged at Monza in April. By contrast, attempts to race the standard article were tragi-comic, as witness Eric Longden's entry of a stripped two-seater in the J.C.C.'s '200' at Brooklands. The poor little creature got off on the wrong foot by baulking Harvey's Alvis and forcing it into the railings, while it was

41. Made in England – or nearly so. 520 chassis in the erecting-shop at Crayford, 1928.

(Martin Walter Ltd.)

42. Downhill plunge. Demonstrating an early 514 at Urbino, 1929. The flowery script on the radiator was regular home-market equipment, though omitted from the English specification.

(FIAT)

43. Torinese Cadillac ? The first prototype of the straight-eight 530, 1929.

44. Rearming Italy. A CR32 fighter biplane in the colours of the *Aviación del Tercio*, Mussolini's contribution to the Spanish Civil War.

twenty-three laps behind the leaders when second gear stripped and put it out of its misery.

Longden was unlucky: the S models did not reach England until a year later, and only two dozen were imported, thanks to a list price of £290 which made it more expensive than either Amilcar or Salmson. In its standard form, it was sporty rather than sporting. The bodies were pretty little two-seater *bateaux*, originally panelled in wood (which proved allergic to the English climate!) but later in fabric or metal, with flared wings and vee screens. By raising the compression to 6.15/1 FIAT managed to squeeze an extra 7 b.h.p. out of the engine, but the retention of the 6-to-1 back end restricted speed to a screaming 57 m.p.h. which was a positive invitation to light-seeking con-rods. Most S-models had wire wheels. For those in quest of more urge there was the 509SM (*sport Monza*) with a 30 b.h.p. engine and a 5.1:1 top gear. Very rare indeed was the 509SC, with 36 b.h.p. Roots-blown unit, staggered two-seater coachwork, and cowled radiator *à l'*Amilcar. This one would top the 80 mark, but the 109 unit, like later supercharged editions of the famous 4ED Meadows, had been developed beyond logical limits, and reliability was lost. S-types were made in relatively small numbers: a complete breakdown is not available, but in 1927 and 1928 deliveries amounted to 368 cars as against 42,000-odd of the regular 509A.

Not all specialist tuners were Italians. In England V. H. Tuson bought a 509S and went to work on it, emerging with the 'SM's' 5.1:1 back end, 8:1 pistons, tulip-shaped inlet valves, and bronze exhaust valve guides, in which form the car would put nearly sixty-five miles into the hour at Brooklands, and lapped at 76 m.p.h. during a Light Car Club Relay Race. Tuson used his car in trials and sprints as well, retaining it until 1934. He recalls it affectionately as 'a fine, sturdy little car capable of taking a tremendous amount of punishment'.

1927 was another good season for the 509, Molla and Ferrari collecting the class honours in the first Mille Miglia at 41.77 m.p.h., a speed which compares interestingly with the 48.27 m.p.h. of overall winners Minoia and Morandi on a 2-litre

O.M., not to mention the 40.89 m.p.h. of the fastest 5-litre, the Silvani/Minozzi 519S. The best of the traditionally 'unwieldy' eight-cylinder Isottas, incidentally, averaged close on 46 m.p.h.! A 509 won the 2,300-mile Agnelli Cup Rally in Italy, and Carignano's 509 was one of six unpenalised competitors in a tough marathon staged in Rumania, though a Hupmobile was adjudged the outright winner. In the Freiburg hill-climb, the FIATs had to give best to a Pluto (German-built Amilcar), and though Valpreda's 509S set a class lap record in a 224-mile reliability race run in a thunderstorm at Modena, he was beaten by Guidelli's Derby. One of the keenest exponents of the little FIATs was the Spaniard Juan Zanelli, who won the 1,100 c.c. class of the Targa Abruzzo.

Meanwhile at the beginning of 1926 the 501 at long last gave way to an improved, flat-radiator model, the 503. Four-wheel brakes and balloon tyres were now standard, as were a new, Ricardo-type cylinder head and split-skirt alloy pistons, which boosted output to 27 b.h.p. Even saloons were capable of 50 m.p.h., though weight was up, to close on 21 cwt in the case of a tourer. *The Motor* credited it with the best springing of all the popular 1,500 c.c. models, and none of the 501's silence or flexibility had been lost. Some 42,000 were delivered in two seasons, and there was even a sports model, the 503S, with a cowled radiator suggestive of William Lyons's Austin Swallow, not to mention wheel discs in polished aluminium. Though the veteran alpine motorist Douglas Fawcett loved his 503 ('We came, we saw, and it conquered', he told readers of *The Motor*) the car attracted the same modified rapture as did Morris's contemporary flatnose range. It was not a case of deterioration: the 503 was old hat alongside the sophisticated 509.

Inevitably the 505 and 510 received the same treatment, emerging as the 507 and 512 respectively. Though the new designations were not announced until 1926, the up-rating came into effect in the last few months of 1925, resulting in a race of half-breeds which were more 507 than 505. Rising taxation frustrated the home sales of both these types, and only 3,701 507s were made. The 512, which survived into 1928 as an insurance against teething troubles with the new, American-style 520, was even rarer.

FIAT abstained from racing altogether in 1926, though rumours were rife, and that April a mysterious low-built *monoposto* was reported as circulating at indecently high speeds at the Monza Autodrome. The company's increasing interest in the Schneider Trophy was blamed for this abdication, while people continued to discuss the mysterious two-stroke which had engaged the attention of the wiseacres during 1925. This actually did exist, being a Zerbi design with six vertical cylinders of 52 × 58.5 mm, two geared crankshafts, and twelve opposed pistons, each sharing a common combustion chamber. Ignition was by twin magnetos, and the Roots-type blower was fed by a single carburetter. For months on end it screamed its guts out in the factory test-house, rendering the experimental staff dumb as well as deaf, and burning pistons at a terrifying rate. It was eventually persuaded to give 152 b.h.p., but as by 1927 Delage were extracting 170 brake horses from their orthodox, if complicated, straight-eight, Zerbi was probably wise to drop the 451 and concentrate on that other mechanical headache, the AS3 aero-motor. Though the two-stroke 'six' never went into a car, it was a brave essay into a hitherto untried formula.

Not that Zerbi and his team had finished with the 1½-litre Grand Prix formula, though both *The Autocar* and *The Light Car* expressed justified doubts as to their appearance in the French G.P. None the less, there was a *Tipo* 806, and it was quite as complicated as the stillborn two-stroke.

The final abandonment of riding mechanics had allowed FIAT to combine a new low, narrow frame and a neat stream-lined body: even the top and bottom of the steering-wheel had flat segments to reduce drag. But the engine, offset in its frame, was a fantastic affair in the shape of a twin-six with twin side-by-side crankshafts running in plain bearings, and triple overhead camshafts: the central one coped with the inlets, and the two outer ones were for the exhausts. A front-mounted Roots blower completed a specification which could beat the Delages and Talbot-Darracqs with a rousing 175 b.h.p. In fact Zerbi extracted 187 b.h.p. from the unit during its brief currency.

The first trials were conducted by Bordino at Monza on 24 July, 1927, and on 4 September he proceeded to win the Milan Grand Prix in pouring rain at 94.57 m.p.h., though the opposition amounted to an assortment of Bugattis and Campari's 2-litre Alfa Romeo. Robert Benoist, who had just won the G.P. of Europe at Monza with his works Delage, and was eligible to compete, decided to avoid a confrontation.

It was a masterly exit. The 806 was entered for the British Grand Prix at Brooklands, but the pressing problems of the Schneider Trophy furnished a convenient pretext for a last-minute withdrawal, which was to be unavailing. By ducking a Franco-Italian battle on English soil, all FIAT achieved was defeat by the British in a home match at Venice. The company was never to race again officially though rumours of a renaissance persisted as late as 1933, and sports cars like the 525SS were certainly works-prepared, as well as serving as test-beds for FIAT hydraulic brakes.

If the shadows of a creaky economy haunted the private-car scene, the *sezione aeronautica* continued to benefit from Mussolini's nationalism. There was no political capital to be made out of motor-racing in the *formule libre* which succeeded two seasons of blown 1,500s, but the Regia Aeronautica was an excellent instrument of propaganda, especially when its crack pilots undertook long-distance formation flights or laid on aerobatic displays at international flying meetings. FIAT's contribution to Italian front-line strength included the BR1 and BR2 single engined bomber biplanes, and Ansaldo A120, the CR fighters, and the R22 reconnaisance biplane, another Rosatelli design which had much in common with the single-seaters. The BR2 was probably the most powerful single-engined service aircraft of the later 1920s, its 54½-litre A25 liquid-cooled unit disposing of 1,090 h.p., while the CR20 with 410 h.p. A20 engine would do 169 m.p.h. at sea level, and had a ceiling of 27,880 ft. It remained in squadron service until the Abyssinian adventure of 1935, and survived almost until

World War II as a fighter trainer in dual-control guise. A seaplane version, developed by FIAT's associate company C.M.A.S.A., was used for instructional purposes by the Schneider Trophy pilots at Desenzano. FIAT V-12 engines were found in many Italian aircraft of the period, notably the bizarre Savoia-Marchetti SM55 twin-hull flying-boat immortalised by Italo Balbo's globe-circling exploits of the early 'thirties; in its original 924 form, however, it used a pair of 'broad-arrow' Twelves made by FIAT's erstwhile racing rivals, Lorraine-Dietrich. With the purchase of C.M.A.S.A. in 1929, FIAT acquired an interest in another famous flying-boat, the German Dornier 'Wal', for which the Pisa firm held a manufacturing licence. Mussolini's propaganda methods were sometimes less than scrupulous; when a C.M.A.S.A.-Dornier collected a string of international records in 1925, *Flight* observed maliciously that 'it is somewhat humorous to reflect that, although the records are recognised as Italian, the machine was virtually German, the engines British, and one of the pilots a German'. Soon afterwards FIAT engines supplanted Bristol 'Jupiter' radials as standard equipment on Italian-made 'Wals'!

The Schneider Trophy was of course to Mussolini what the 750-kilogram Grand Prix formula was to become to Adolf Hitler, and vast sums of money were expended on the attainment of Italian supremacy. Macchi remained obstinately loyal to flying-boats in 1925, and for lack of a suitable Italian engine their entries used the American Curtiss D-12, probably the best liquid-cooled motor of its time. Alas! the Schneider engines had been tested almost to destruction by FIAT technicians in search of enlightenment, and this was America's year.

This meant that the venue for the 1926 Race was Hampton Roads. The Italians had good reason for optimism, with a new low-drag V-12, the AS2, from FIAT, and some slim, elegant, twin-float low-wing monoplane seaplanes from Macchi. FIAT bought their crankshafts from Vickers of England, and the three M-39s were assigned to Mario de Bernardi, Arturo Ferrarin, and Adriano Bacula.

By aeronautical standards, the tempo of preparation for a

car race was incredibly lethargic. The new Macchi did not make its first high-speed flight at home until 17 September, and the race date was set for 13 November, which meant only ten days of practice over the course. Faulty carburation and piston failures bedevilled the Italian *équipe*. Already the only spare engine had been cannibalised, and a worse disaster was only just averted when Ferrarin force-landed on a practice flight. He was still drifting (without radio or navigation lights, of course) when dusk fell, and was rescued just in time. Encouraged by a string of hortatory telegrams from Rome, the technicians contrived to build one good engine out of two defective units.

In the race it fell to Bacula to play a waiting game, circulating at a modest 200 m.p.h. to ensure that there should be at least one Italian finisher, while his team-mates flew flat out. In fact only Ferrarin failed to stay the course, succumbing to a broken oil pipe. De Bernardi won at 246.442 m.p.h. from Schilt's American Curtiss, and Bacula. Two days later the victor set a new World's Seaplane Speed Record at 258.873 m.p.h.

Mussolini was jubilant, and the Italians put on a splendid show at Venice in 1927, albeit Al Williams's promised American challenger did not materialise, leaving Britain to oppose the Italians with a Short 'Crusader', two of Reginald Mitchell's sleek Supermarine S5s, and a pair of Gloster IV biplanes. Macchi came up with an improved M-52, and FIAT produced the AS3, this time with a German Krupp crankshaft, since Vickers could hardly be expected to work for the opposition! On paper the AS3 was a masterpiece, combining lower weight and a reduced frontal area with a promised output of 1,000 b.h.p. as against the 880 of the 1926 racing engines. Alas! it never developed its full power, and a last-ditch experiment with magnesium-alloy pistons proved unavailing.

In the end it was decided to fit the AS2 unit to Guazzetti's Macchi, to give Italy her necessary 'long-stop', while de Bernardi and Ferrarin took their chances with the AS3s. Neither aircraft distinguished itself: de Bernardi was eliminated by lubrication troubles, and Ferrarin also retired early.

Guazzetti fought gamely until a fuel line fractured. Blinded by a stream of petrol the Italian pilot almost charged into the Excelsior Palace Hotel before recovering in time for a good landing. The Trophy went to Webster's Supermarine S5, though de Bernardi subsequently had his revenge by lifting the Seaplane Speed Record to 296.82 m.p.h., a good 15 m.p.h. beyond the British aircraft's capabilities. He was timed downwind at 313.4 m.p.h., and has his place in history as the first human being known to have exceeded 300 m.p.h. A month later the Italian Altitude Record fell to Renato Donati in an Ansaldo AC3, so FIAT had every reason to congratulate themselves on the season's showing.

But the Depression already threatened, and the latter half of 1927 had seen drastic cut-backs at FIAT where production fell from 200 cars a day to a mere fifty. True, the situation was sound, with the 509A (at 20,299 units) accounting for a good fifty per cent of the company's output. The time had, however, come to abandon things other than the competition department. The 519 had also gone, while there seemed little future even for the 512, which cost 65,000 lire as a tourer in Italy, and 48,000 francs in France.

The American idiom was taking over, and in November FIAT unveiled their contribution to the new cult of the cheap 'six', the 2¼-litre *Tipo* 520. The ensuing years were to see a new trend, and one which FIAT has pursued ever since— coverage of all aspects of the popular and middle-class markets, to the exclusion of unprofitable side-issues.

7 A Touch of Detroit

Acceleration that makes all the difference in traffic.
Speed that leaves all behind on the open road.
Finger-light, finger-tip control that makes driving a real
joy. The looks and the luxury of a thousand-pound car.
Handsome, distinguished, graceful. Yet its price is only £525.

525 advertisement, February 1930

The depression hit Italy in 1927.

Its effect was not immediately apparent at Lingotto, where 1928's sales were 42,694 cars, rising fractionally to 42,780 in 1929 despite the Wall Street crash. If 1930 statistics showed a nose-dive, this was due more to internal miscalculation than to any fall in the demand for vehicles.

The Italians were quick to take alarm. In 1929 the R.A.C.I. demanded that members owning foreign cars should publicly state the reasons for their unpatriotic behaviour, and in August, 1930, Rome reacted violently by raising the import duty on private cars from 110 to 130 per cent.

Not that imports were a real problem. By 1931 they were pegged to three-figure levels which were not to be exceeded until 1952, while firms like Ford and Citroën who set up Italian assembly plants found an unco-operative Government ready for them. All Henry Ford's cash and attorneys could not buy him Isotta Fraschini in 1930, though there is good reason to believe that Isotta themselves were not averse to the deal. Those of us who regard to-day's Turin Show as the clearing-house of international stylists would have found the Milan Shows of the 1930s dreary, nationalist affairs. Impoverished British and French makers would exhibit in Prague (despite the Czechoslovak

Government's nervous protectionism, which inflated the price of a Ford V8 to £900) and in Belgrade (Yugoslavia was still almost roadless), but they left Milan alone. Only four foreign makers bothered to send cars in 1932.

A hortatory cut of 10 per cent in FIAT's wage bill, made in February, 1932, emphasised the prevailing gloom, though as early as 1923 Mussolini had faced squarely up to the problem of unemployment, and one of the results had been the *autostrada* network. The first stretch, between Milan and Varese, had actually been opened in September, 1924, and in 1932 the opening of the Milan-Turin link coincided happily with the tenth aniversary of the Duce's accession to power. In fact Mussolini's road-building operations were as important to Italian car design as Hitler's were to be. The Duce would happily meddle with industry, edging Isotta Fraschini, O.M. and Bianchi out of the private-car business, but he and his Party had a healthy respect for Italian technology, and it is more than probable that this keen conductor of an 'RLSS' Alfa Romeo realised what his motorways would achieve. By 1925 the average Italian car combined excellent handling with superb climbing ability—even the dullest six-cylinder FIATs of the late 'twenties were a pleasure to drive. With the motorway era came short-stroke engines which throve on revs, and the engineers of Milan and Turin started to think in terms of the *autostrada* rather than the sharp ascent to Superga. The 509, in fact, was almost obsolete when the first one rolled out of Lingotto.

If anyone could afford a mistake, it was of course FIAT. The 514 of 1929 was undoubtedly the wrong car at the wrong time, and it did not help a situation already aggravated by a world-wide slump, with the consequence that private-car production plummeted to an all-time low of 16,319 in 1931. But what FIAT lost on the swings, they gained on the roundabouts. Mussolini's demands for front-line aircraft were insatiable—first a thousand, then 1,500. When he reclaimed the Pontine Marshes, heavy tractors were needed and these were FIAT-built Pavesis. His army was kept busy suppressing unappreciative Arabs in Libya, which meant more and bigger trucks,

most of which came from FIAT or S.P.A.: a six-and-a-half
tonner was in full production by 1932. Lingotto took its
place as one of the tourist attractions of Italy. Said *The Light Car*
admiringly in June, 1928:

> When a party of sixty members of a London institution recently
> visited the factory they were able to travel in motor coaches
> down the long line of machine-shops, passing from floor to floor
> by means of elevators until they emerged at the famous race-
> track on the roof. The party returned to earth by way of one of
> the spiral roadways in this unique factory.

Already Agnelli's empire was poised for unlimited expansion
when required. A brochure issued in 1930 took the form of a
statistical bombardment more alarming than anything Fascism
could offer. FIAT employed 35,000 people, and her installations
in Turin alone occupied $7\frac{3}{4}$ square miles. The building of
Lingotto had required 40,000 tons of cement, 20,000 tons of
iron, 22 acres of window-glass, 69 miles of assorted piping, fifty
miles apiece of belting and electric cable, and eleven miles of
shafting. Every day $2\frac{1}{4}$ million gallons of water and 140,000
kilowatt/hours of electricity were required to keep the wheels
turning, and the head office's clerical staff were kept busy every
day to the tune of 250 telegrams, 2,000 phone calls, and 2,500
letters. Feeding this giant were two foundries and three iron and
steel works; and though Fornaca had died in 1928, the company
had acquired a brilliant general manager in the shape of Vittorio
Valletta, who was to serve FIAT until his death in 1967, with only
a short break during the hysterical anti-Fascist reaction of 1945.

Apart from the introduction of a line of crawler tractors in
1932, FIAT halted their expansion in the dark years, if one
excepts the consortium formed in 1929 to provide a common
marketing organisation for FIAT, S.P.A. and Ceirano commercial
vehicles. It had its own depots in twelve provincial capitals, and
its existence has mislead later writers into the belief that the
S.A. Giovanni Ceirano was added to Agnelli's empire. This is not
strictly true: after 1927 Ceirano kept going on Government
contracts for lorries, and their last car design, the S150 with
Parisi independent front suspension, was made only in penny

numbers. Giovanni himself wisely wound up this last offshoot of his family's complicated automobile adventures in 1931, and S.P.A. acquired the assets. The Ceirano factory ultimately passed into the hands of the Army, and to this day it is a maintenance depot for Service vehicles.

Having established themselves as general providers, first with the 501 and then with the 509, FIAT were now following the tide of fashion, branching out into cheap 'sixes' with the 'second' 520 in November, 1927. This will go down to history as the first model on which left-hand drive and cellulose finish were standard, and it also marked the first generation of a fiendishly complicated family of inter-related types which survived until 1936.

The American writer Jan P. Norbye has denounced the biggest of the clan, the 525, as 'a sort of dour mirror-image of Detroit's conglomerate styling theme of the mid-twenties', while even *The Motor*, whose testers liked the model, confessed that it was 'an example of how Americanised cars of well-known European makes are becoming', adding that 'the body might have been turned out by the Fisher Corporation'. If the original 520 could be likened to a scaled-down 512 or an elongated 503, the 521 and 525 were trans-Atlantic in mien, and the little 514 resembled nothing so much as last year's K-type De Soto after a visit to the head-shrinker. By 1931 one had actually to drive a 522 to realise that it had nothing to do with the Chrysler Corporation: the stylised dash with its unergonomic instruments, and the dreary interior trim accentuated the American overtones.

In fact this was what the public wanted in the immediate pre-Depression years. Multi-cylinderism was not confined to America. In some ways Europe went even further overboard, for in 1928 the cheapest Ford, Chrysler, General Motors and Willys-Overland products were all 'fours', and the Ford and Plymouth persisted into 1932, which time no self-respecting Continental maker would have risked a four-cylinder unit of more than two litres' capacity. By 1927 small 'sixes' were all the rage: Peugeot had their Type 183, Mercédès-Benz their

'Stuttgart', Austin their Sixteen, and Wolseley their '16–45', forerunner of Morris's 18 h.p. overhead-camshaft model. Renault progressed from an American-aligned 3.2-litre 'Viva' to the doleful little 1,400 c.c. 'Monasix', and in 1929 Citroën were to join battle with Emile Mathis by introducing their 2½-litre C6. Even the upper-middle class High Tories fell victims to the new trend: Sunbeam's '14–40' gave way to a 'Six', and Crossley of Manchester supplanted their doughty old Fourteen with a pushrod 2-litre. The Crossley, be it said, was not for the masses at £495, but Austin, Morris, Peugeot, Renault and FIAT were aiming at the family man with £350 to spend: in other words, a customer who would otherwise opt for a Whippet Six, one of the cheaper Chryslers, a Pontiac or an Oldsmobile. Inevitably they took the basic American theme: side valves, coil ignition, mechanical pump or Autovac feed, a three-speed gearbox, a single-plate clutch, semi-elliptic suspension, four-wheel brakes and all-steel saloon coachwork— and adapted it to local conditions. Some of them even fell for the blandishments of eight cylinders in line, which meant a longer bonnet, if nothing else. This was predominantly a Franco-German disease, however. The Italian fiscal system discouraged straight-eights.

The *Tipo* 520 FIAT—originally promoted as *modello* 20 to avoid confusion with 1921's enormous V-12—was typical of its era, as well as fathering a long generation of blood relations. Basic features embraced a straightforward seven-bearing s.v. unit with vibration damper, and chain-driven camshaft, cooled by pump and fan. The 12-volt coil ignition was fed from a distributor mounted centrally on top of the block (from personal experience I can testify that this arrangement was proof against two feet of flood water!) and there was an automatic advance-and-retard with manual override. The carburetter was a Solex, with Autovac feed. The unit gearbox, single dry plate clutch, and central ball change were heritages from the 509 and 519, though the *marque*'s Alpine background dictated both a low, 5.5:1 top and four forward speeds. The chassis had friction-type shock absorbers at front and rear, and the compact wheelbase of 9 ft 6 in could take full five-seater bodies, the saloons and tourers closely resembling the earlier 503s and 507s, while artillery wheels were retained. Cylinder dimensions were 68 × 103 mm for a capacity of 2,244 c.c., and technical progress was reflected in the output of 46 b.h.p.—identical with that of the old 3,446 c.c. 510 introduced in 1919.

Italians regarded the 520 as a status symbol, and it was quite cheap at 27,000 lire. Performance was adequate rather than spectacular: 55–60 m.p.h. on top, 38 on third, and 29 on second, with a comfortable cruising gait of 35–40 m.p.h. The 10–30 m.p.h. acceleration time in third was 8.8 seconds, second gear would cope with a gradient of 1-in-7½, and the car would stop from 50 m.p.h. in 120 feet. A tourer cost £340 in England, later reduced to £315 in 1929, when the range embraced a fabric sportsman's coupé at £395—Weymanns were, however, never very popular in Italy. About 20,000 520s were made in two seasons, two interesting variants being a detachable-top *berlina* in the old Lancia 'Lambda' idiom and a taxicab version with a small-bore, 35 b.h.p. engine. This emasculatory process called for a top-gear ratio of 5.9:1 but, the 520T outlived the parent model, remaining in the range until 1930. Though Silvani offered a tuning kit, the 520 was seldom seen in competitions.

More successful were its two 1928 developments, the 521 and 525. These were truly 'the mixture as before', even if a narrower radiator shell was used on all 521s, as well as on the 525 from mid-1929. At the same time bodies were further Americanised, the touring cars and roadsters being quite handsome. The 521, sold as the 18–55 h.p. in England, had a 2,516 c.c. unit developing 51 b.h.p. at 3,400 r.p.m.: disc wheels usually replaced the 520's Sankeys, from the summer of 1929 bright parts were chromium-plated, and by 1930 the cars had acquired mechanical fuel pumps and Delco-Lovejoy hydraulic dampers. The first examples were built on a wheelbase of 10 ft 3½ in, but subsequently this was reserved for seven-seater coachwork (Tipo 521L), a short-chassis 'C' version being added to the range. A higher, 5.1:1 top gear gave a 65 m.p.h. performance, without detriment to flexibility: *The Motor* found that West End traffic could be negotiated without a downward change. The turning circle was well up to FIAT standards at 37 ft 10 in, and I remember the 521 as a well-handling and quiet vehicle which belied its Chryslerish looks. It remained in production until May, 1931, and sold better than the 520, with a respectable 22,000 units in spite of the Depression. Jacques Bignan used a 521 to finish fifth in the 1930 Monte Carlo Rally in spite of his choice of the nightmarish Athens route.

The 525 was an attempt to combine prestige and rationalisation, and used a bigger 82 × 118 mm (3,740 c.c.) version of the basic 120/121 theme. A longer wheelbase of 10 ft 8⅜ in made it a natural for limousine coachwork, and it was a far better all-rounder than the ambitious 519. Initially it had the 521's ordinary cable-operated brakes, but a Marelli vacuum servo was standardised in 1930, and the last series of 1931 had dual-circuit Lockheed hydraulics. FIAT's first. In the summer of 1929 chromium plating and the 521's uniform styling made their appearance. At the same time the cars were redesignated 525N, and a short (9 ft 10 in) wheelbase version was introduced for owner-drivers.

This 525S was an admirable family saloon weighing just over 33 cwt. Gear ratios were 4.36, 5.73, 8.96 and 14.49 to 1, and it would top the 70 mark, with a useful 54 coming up on the close-ratio third. 'As soon as the car is on the road', commented *The Motor*, 'one knows that it is of high-grade European design. The steering, road-holding and braking are all that can be desired.' The English price of £525 would have made it an attractive proposition had the annual tax not been a swingeing £25.

If Mussolini continued to favour Alfa Romeo, a 525N limousine entered Vatican service during 1929 as the personal gift of Giovanni Agnelli. This was upholstered in amaranth and cerise trim, and journeyed from the FIAT depot in Rome's Via Calabria as part of a cavalcade of twelve cars. Felice Nazzaro was at the wheel. '*Ecco la* FIAT', exclaimed Agnelli on arrival, but Nazzaro was so overawed that he appeared not to understand Pius XI's request to see the engine, and his chief had to step hurriedly into the breach! Not to be outdone, the Milan Automobile Club weighed in with a present of an 8A Isotta Fraschini, and both cars were still on the strength in 1935, along with a Graham-Paige, a 'Nurburg' Mercédès-Benz and an ornate C6 limousine donated by Citroën-Italiana.

Not that the 525 was a mere town carriage, for it led to a partial breach of FIAT's anti-competition rule. The occasion of this was the 1929 Alpine Trial, an event which bid fair to rival the status of its illustrious pre-1914 forebear. It was to attract support from British, French and German makers, becoming a happy hunting-ground for unsporting firms like Vauxhall and Armstrong Siddeley as well as the more familiar Invictas and Roesch Talbots. William Lyons chose the 'Alpine' for the s.s.i.'s competition début in 1933.

The 1929 event saw a formidable field headed by the blown Mercédès-Benz of Caracciola and Werner, and they were matched against Turin's big guns—three special 525s entrusted to Nazzaro, Salamano and Pastore. These 'SS' cars were short-chassis versions with British-looking two-four-seater bodies, and special high-compression engines with dual-choke carburetters pushing out 88 b.h.p. Rudge-Whitworth wire wheels were used, but the cars' real function was to test FIAT's own version of the Lockheed hydraulic brake.

They romped up the Katschberg, but in a narrow village street near Bolzano Nazzaro had to choose between a wall and a farm-cart. As the rules specified that all repairs had to be done by the driver and mechanic, precious time was wasted changing the front axle and springs. Salameno retrieved FIAT's honour by making the fastest time on the Stelvio Pass, but alas for Nazzaro, history repeated itself almost down to the last detail in Bergamo, and the 525s were eliminated from the team event.

There were other successes. In 1929 the veteran racing driver Paul Bablot won his class at Mont Ventoux—he was to repeat the process in 1930 with a 521—and Massacurati had quite a good season with a 525 in North Africa, finishing fifth at Oran against such opposition as Type 43 Bugattis, 3½-litre Lorraines, and Chenard-Walcker 'tanks'. In the Moroccan G.P. for sports cars he was beaten by another tuned crypto-American, Renault's new small 'Nerva' straight-eight.

FIAT built a few touring 'SS' cars in 1931, these wearing Viotti 2–4-seater bodies and the hydraulic brakes and Carello headlamps of the last-series 525s, while a few short-chassis saloons were also fitted with the sports engine. But even the 525 was too expensive for a falling market, and it was decided to rationalise the six-cylinder range round the new 2½-litre 122 engine and the 522 chassis. The model's swansong was in the 1931 Monte Carlo Rally, when Jacques Bignan once again elected to start from Athens, only to be disqualified on a technicality.

Meanwhile, however, there had been a final bid for the carriage trade with the 530 straight-eight. Like the 500 of 1918–19, this was a case of advance publicity followed by sudden silence: visitors to the 1929 Olympia Show had expected to see the new '30–90 h.p.' FIAT, but they did not. It took thirty-seven years for FIAT to disgorge any details, and even then these came without comment.

As originally tested, the 530 was basically a 525 with two extra cylinders and a capacity of five litres. In styling it closely resembled the contemporary 'Master' Buick, with seven-seater body and a high waistline, though the 'hood doors' were an interesting anticipation of Detroit's 1932 fashions. Output of the nine-bearing engine paralleled that of the 1929 Cadillac, at 95 b.h.p., though the 6-volt electrics were unusual for a FIAT. Wheelbase was 12 ft 1½ in, and it turned the scales at about 44 cwt. One may suspect that the factory considered this first prototype underpowered, for a new version was prepared in December, 1929, and took the road the following year. In its final guise the 530 was an elephantine motor car with cylinder dimensions of 90 × 130 mm (6,616 c.c.) a lowered 4.4:1 compression gave an even 100 b.h.p., and weight was up to 46½ cwt. From all accounts the second-series 530 was an excellent specimen of a formal carriage: unfortunately it catered for a dying market, as the last days of Minerva were to prove. *Ergo*, it went the way of O.M.'s contemporary straight-eight; Ansaldo and Bianchi, who persevered with their eights-in-line, did themselves no good thereby.

The 'sixes', however, paid for themselves. 1929's deliveries amounted to 9,031 521s and 2,974 525s as well as two thousand-odd 520s. Nevertheless the bread-and-butter line was still the 509A, which marched happily on. The veteran British journalist H. Massac Buist called it 'the biggest thing in small cars', and FIAT's list of illustrious clients read like something from 1908— Crown Prince Umberto, the Princess Giovanna (later Boris of Bulgaria's consort), the Queen of Yugoslavia, the Sultan of Morocco, Prince Nicholas of Rumania (making amends, perhaps, for the Sunbeam 'episode' of 1926), 'H.R.H. the Princess of Servia', and such exotic worthies as 'Ras Aylu, Provincial Governor of the Goggiam', and 'H. E. Jomet Pacha, President of the Turkish Great National Assembly'. During 1928 a standard tourer turned up at the Sanctuary of the Madonna of Monticino, having surmounted a 1-in-4½ gradient considered impassable to motor cars. No wonder the 'reverend Rector' witnessed with great surprise 'the invasion of his sacred grounds'. A 20-to-1 bottom gear has its compensations.

The 509A also won FIAT their first and only Monte Carlo Rally in 1928, when Jacques Bignan made it from Bucharest in a standard saloon. With four passengers and their baggage aboard the car weighed in at 30 cwt, but he won, in spite of six ditchings in Rumania and Hungary alone, and an opening crawl of 600 miles (much of it in bottom gear) at an average of 15 m.p.h. Malaret clinched matters by taking second place, while Bon was 11th and Murray's British-entered 503 18th. Miss Wilson's 509S won its class in the Bournemouth Rally, and Bignan was the outright winner in the 1929 Le Touquet event beating Malaret, who chose to start from Archangel (of all places) in a Voisin and failed to qualify. Reporters covering the rally were shocked to encounter an aged 501 *berlina* in Le Touquet, dressed up as a thatched cottage and serving as a mobile canteen!

The S-types still raced, winning the Italian class championship in 1928, and the Swiss sports championships in 1928 and
1929. 1928 saw class victories in Tunis-Tripoli, in the Targa
Florio (where the Salmson opposition expired), and in the Mille
Miglia, where Tamburi and Ricceri repeated the process the
following year at an average speed of 55.69 m.p.h. Not even
the supercharged 'SC' could beat a good Salmson when it was
running right, and in the Tripoli Grand Prix Riccoli's FIAT had to
trail behind two famous drivers, Borzacchini and Biondetti.
Nevertheless the successes persisted into 1930, when FIAT
announced that in future they concentrate on tuning 514s and
would therefore no longer provide factory service for racing 509s.

In England a rising young coachbuilder named William
Lyons fitted a curvaceous two-toned sports saloon body to the
509A chassis, and this FIAT-Swallow figured in D'Arcy Baker's
1929 catalogue at £260 (wire wheels £5 extra). About a hundred
Britons considered it better value than the foursquare four-door
Weymann saloon at £240, and its demise was probably due to
the basic model's discontinuation. More ambitious was a pretty
little two-door saloon by Pininfarina intended to show what
could be done with a light car. This wore twin horns, wheel
discs, twin rear-mounted spare wheels, and enlarged radiator
with stoneguard, Lucidus headlamps, plush upholstery, and
blinds to all the windows, but like all 'Christmas trees' it could
scarcely drag itself along, and when the late David Manning
exhumed it from a Bournemouth garage in 1957 it had done
only 16,000 miles.

The 509 had served its purpose, but in choosing a replacement FIAT were to make a serious tactical error. They had fallen
victims, like many another firm, to the wave of euphoria that
preceded the Wall Street collapse of 1929. In this they were not
alone, for Sir William Morris still relied too heavily on a solid
1½-litre car, the 'Cowley', and not a few of 1929's new models
were bigger still. Of France's 'big four', only Peugeot offered
anything really small in the shape of the archaic Type 190, and
Renault had just discontinued the 951 c.c. 6CV after a nine-
year run. Flushed by the success of their new 'sixes', FIAT

came to the conclusion that the mass market wanted nothing smaller than a 1½-litre. They also made it look like a De Soto. *The Autocar* proclaimed the new 514 as 'the legitimate successor to the 10–15 h.p.' (the 501), though Angelo Tito Anselmi came nearer the truth when he called it 'a pause in the success story of FIAT'. Not a gleam of heterodoxy penetrated its typical early-30s specification. The 67 × 102 mm (1,438 c.c.) four-cylinder engine was really a 121 unit in miniature, 6-volt electrics were deemed sufficient, and the horizontal Solex carburetter was fed by gravity from an eight-gallon dash tank, which, like the power unit, was rubber-mounted. The low and wide ratios (5.6, 8.29, 13.05 and 21.22 to 1) of the four-speed box were commensurate with a saloon weighing a level ton. Unusually the four-wheel cable-operated brakes were actuated by both pedal and lever. Six-stud disc wheels were standard, but *lusso* versions came with bolt-on wires, chromium-plated bumpers, a side-mounted spare with cover, a clock, a stop-lamp, and safety glass all round: from 1931 hydraulic dampers replaced the friction type of early 514s. There was a wide range of body styles: two- and four-door saloons, roadster, tourer, *coupé royal*, and *coupé-spyder*, while Britons fared even better, for Mulliners produced a four-door fabric saloon with sun roof, and Martin Walter a two-seater cabriolet with dickey which they called the 'Rome' model. This one, unlike the Mulliner, was not produced for stock. Like their bigger sisters, the roadsters were pleasant-looking cars. The 514 would do a stolid 55 m.p.h., and if a fuel consumption of 28 m.p.g. was a disappointment to former 509 owners, press and customers alike found the new car's smooth progress worthy of the standard set by the 501. Said *The Light Car*:

> The outstanding characteristic of the FIAT is its silky smoothness and silence: a faint hiss from the engine and a slight tremor at certain speeds alone betrays the working of the 1,438 c.c. engine. The gearbox is quiet, the body is dead silent, and the brakes smooth and powerful.

It is easy to dismiss the 514 as an outsize lemon. Its looks, performance and design were all mediocre. Germans disliked it, during its currency Australian sales fell to a trickle, and in France *La Vie Automobile's* road-test report was so crammed with *clichés* as to be damnatory. (True, Amédee Gordini's first competition car was a 514, but *le sorcier* achieved nothing with it). Sales, at 37,000 in three seasons, were barely a third of the 509's. But in fact it proved a versatile work-horse. The sports versions had a fair competition record: what is more, the uncomplaining little engine did much more than power 8-cwt *furgoncini*; it was adapted to a one-ton lorry, the 614, even if this extra weight demanded an 8:1 back axle. In 1931 the Army was testing the 1014, a curious articulated 6×4 'mechanical mule' which proved capable of surmounting a 1-in-1½ gradient.

Nor was the 514 any worse than such contemporaries as Austin's Twelve-Six, the 1,300 c.c. 7CV Renault, the first Hillman 'Minx', the Peugeot 201, the side-valve Singer Ten, the Swift, and the worm-driven 10–25 h.p. Rover. Of these, only Singer and Swift shared FIAT's four-speed box, though Rover, Austin and Hillman were to adopt such a layout during 1932. The FIAT's ratios were reasonable, and infinitely preferable to Peugeot's standard gearset (6.25, 11.75 and 21.95 to 1). Equally average was the weight, while its 10–30 m.p.h. acceleration time (which counted far more in the eyes of contemporary drivers than any standing-start figures) were quite good, at 8.4 seconds. By contrast the Peugeot took 10 seconds, the Singer 10.6, and the Swift and River 11 seconds.

The 514's 1931 sales of 10,600 units were dismal, but nobody else did much better. The Renault lasted one season only (1932), and sold about 10,000 cars, while Swift's demise in May, 1931 makes a fair comparison difficult: suffice it to say that in 1929 and 1930 the Coventry factory was making Tens at the modest rate of 1,800 a year. The Singer (800 units in two years) was even less successful, and in 1931 the FIAT outsold Austin (9,519), Peugeot (9,565) and Rover (8,500). Even on the English market the 514 was fairly competitive, at £225 for a saloon, as against £189 for the Rover, £198 for the Austin, £210 for the Peugeot, and £259 for the Swift. In export markets, only the Peugeot approached FIAT's record: though

Austin had an efficient overseas agency network, less than twelve per cent of all Twelve-Sixes were exported.

FIAT tried hard with sports versions of the 514, which retailed on the home market for the equivalent of £240. The original 514S of 1930 was a pretty little two-seater using a tuned 34 b.h.p. engine in the lengthened 'F' light van frame. These were not ready for the 1930 Mille Miglia, in which standard 514s dominated the 'utility' class. In July, however, Italy staged her own Alpine rally, the *Coppa delle Tre Venezie*, a curious mixture of speed and regularity in which FIAT hedged their bets by entering 525SS models as well as sports 514s. Nazzaro's big 'six' put up some remarkable averages, but on this occasion the 1½-litre FIATs dominated the proceedings. Costa's 514S was the outright winner, both 1,500 c.c. team prizes went to similar models, and stock 514s collected the 'utility' honours. Nazzaro had to be content with fourth place in the big-car class behind an O.M. and two Lancias.

Later sports models (the 514CA and 514MM) reverted to the saloon chassis, with 37 b.h.p. engines and higher-ratio axles, which boosted speed to around the 70 mark. Radiators now had a rearward rake reminiscent of the supercharged 'works' O.M.s, then at their zenith. W. F. Bradley was diverted by 'bonnets long enough to cover eight cylinders, mudguards which covered very little of the wheels, and quite a turn of speed', while for the 1931 Mille Miglia the factory offered free preparation and pit service to amateurs using 514s. 'FIAT', averred *The Autocar*, 'hope to crush all other makes by an enormous entry', and according to gossip their effort was to be spearheaded by three supercharged 514s in the hands of Salamano, Pastore, and the great Nazzaro.

Again rumour was wrong. The 98 starters included a police team of three 1½-litre Bianchis, but no supercharged FIATs, while not even a massive turn-out of works supported machinery could give the *marque* anything better than 18th and 19th places, plus the usual class wins. These no longer included the 1,100 c.c. category, where the aged 509s had to be content with fourth, behind Tufanelli's straight-eight Maserati, Charles

Goodacre's Austin Seven, and Carnevali's Rally (*alias* Salmson).

The 514 was not selling, and Zerbi's 508 was not yet ready. Thus a stop-gap was sorely needed, and this made its appearance at the 1931 Milan Show. The recipe was inexpensive: take the essential ingredients of the 514, bring it up to date with the cruciform-braced frame and hydraulic brakes of the latest 2½-litre versions, and market it in one body style only, a four-door saloon. Two colour choices were available, and at 22,000 lire the 515 cost little more than the original 514 of 1929.

FIAT had 'simplicated', but they had not lightened. The 515 was heavier, thirstier and lower-geared, and nobody wanted it, even as a taxi or as a four-door sports saloon with fabric top, both of which were soon added to the range. No attempt was made to market the car in Britain or Germany, and the Portuguese took precisely three. It was retained in the catalogue until 1934, and then quietly dropped, after 3,405 had been sold.

Also in 1931 the six-cylinder range had been tidied up, and was now based on a revised version of the 2½-litre unit with mechanical pump feed. Other features were a four-speed silent-third gearbox, a cruciform-braced frame, hydraulic dampers, and dual-circuit hydraulic brakes, with which came FIAT's celebrated sudden-death transmission hand-brake, an excellent emergency device if used with due respect for the drive-line! The 522, with its ribbon radiator shell, resembled an enlarged 514 with wire wheels, and it was both more austere and more compact than the superseded 521. A saloon cost £335 in England, though for an extra £90 sybarites could treat themselves to a *cabriolet royal* with blind rear quarters and dual sidemounts. There was also a short lived 'L' version on a 10 ft 1 in wheelbase, which soon acquired larger-section tyres, more luxurious trim, and thermostatically-controlled radiator shutters, in which guise it was redesignated the 524C. The parallel 524L was a full seven-seater. The 522C was a good, average family car, even if one cannot agree with *The Autocar* ('the four-door body has very nice lines'), or with *La Vie Automobile*, whose testers rated it '*une remarquable voiture de grande tourisme*'.

Attempts were made to inject some individuality into 522 and 524 alike. The former emerged with a lowered waistline in 1933, when free wheels and internal locks for the sidemounts were introduced, whilst the last 524Ls were unhappy dissonances using the body shape of the 'Ardita' (Tipo 518) and a Terraplane-like grille. It was all to no avail: 1933's deliveries (460 522s and 326 524s) told their own story.

By contrast the rare 522S was a pretty and pleasant car, if its only claim to fame is as the first sports model to be fitted with a free wheel as standard. First seen at the 1931 London Show, it was supplied either as a Viotti 2/4-seater in the 525SS idiom or as a four-door pillarless sports saloon, while changes involved a dropped frame and a tuned engine with revised inlet manifold and twin horizontal Solex carburetters. The 7.2:1 compression made for a slightly finicky palate. Double-acting friction dampers were used in place of the 522's hydraulics, and the three upper ratios of the four-speed box were high and close at 4.09, 5.65, and 7.75 to 1.

Italian writers have waxed scathing over the 522S, and it was a little naughty of FIAT to advertise 'safety at 90 m.p.h.' for a car that was flat out at 85: indeed, *Motor Sport* found 75 the limit when they tested an open model in April, 1933. They did, however, rate chassis, brakes and suspension 'above suspicion', and praised the car's brisk performance in town traffic. The dual-circuit brakes could bring the FIAT to a halt in 57 feet from 40 m.p.h., but at £585 it was just too expensive for Britons. It was also too expensive for Italians, and only 732 found buyers.

Export business continued, and in 1931 FIAT maintained branches as far afield as Sofia, Cairo, São Paulo, Montevideo, Santa Fé, and Bahia Blanca. There was even an 'inspector' in Moscow, albeit it was not made clear what he was supposed to inspect. In some markets, notably Switzerland, the company remained strong, and as late as 1930 FIAT topped the list of new registrations, though Ford pipped them in 1931. In France the 522C, at 52,500 fr, was hardly competition for the C6G Citroën (32,000 fr) or even the big Renault 'Vivastella' at

35,500 fr. Things were even less happy in Australia: neither 509 nor 514 could take the place of the 501 and 505. Agents tried hard with the 'sixes': in 1929 the South Australian concessionaire was plugging the 521 as 'a roomy car of ample power with unsurpassed acceleration in getaway and top-gear climbing performance'. All of which it undoubtedly was, but it still cost £A399 as a tourer and was thus inferior value to a Nash '400' (£A385). Anyone who wanted six cylinders on the cheap would, in any case, opt for an Essex (£A270) or Whippet (£A275).

Hard times pointed towards foreign manufacture or assembly. Traditionally this phase in FIAT history is associated with the 'Balilla', which sold under the names Polski-FIAT, N.S.U.-FIAT, Walter 'Junior' and 6CV Simca, but in fact the first model to be built in series outside Italy was the 521, put into production during 1930 at N.S.U.'s Heilbronn works, in Germany. Under the FIAT-N.S.U. deal the German firm gave up cars in favour of motorcycles, and the erstwhile car plant turned to something which it called the 'Standard'. In effect it was a 521 on the 522's 9 ft 10 in wheelbase, but operations were on a modest scale. 1932 deliveries amounted to 548 cars (plus another 990 imported complete from Turin). By contrast Germany's best-selling make, Opel, registered 16,200 units, and even the costly Horch sold 1,043. It took the 'Balilla' to make a commercial success of Heilbronn.

In 1931 a factory in Barcelona started to assemble 514s for the Spanish market, while in Czechoslovakia Walter of Prague-Jinonice decided to extend their own range of high-quality six-and twelve-cylinder machinery with an assortment of licence-produced FIATs. These included the 'Bijou' (514), 'Prinz' (521C) and 'Lord' (521L), but the company's principal interest was always aeroengines, and in 1933 their total production of FIATs and Walters amounted to a mere 517 vehicles. Revised grilles and locally-made bodies characterised many of the 2½-litre versions.

French assembly dated from 'Balilla' days, of course, but there were two attempts to start English factories. As D'Arcy

Baker seldom bothered to keep Turin posted on his doings, documentation is scarce, but the first venture was launched in 1928. It involved the use of part of the Vickers ordnance works at Crayford (where, incidentally, Wolseley had once made their Stellite light car). Components came from Turin 'in milk or meat vans', and the British content was said to include Dunlop tyres and wheels, instruments, bodies and even springs. Contemporary photographs show 520s moving down a rather bare assembly line, and this model seems to have been Crayford's principal concern, although a few 509As were also 'processed'. Baker tried again in 1930, assembling 514s at Acton. Delaney Gallay Ltd supplied the radiators, but it is a matter of opinion how much of the rest of the car was British. By this time, however, FIAT's United Kingdom sales were falling to token proportions, and England was one of the few countries where the 'Balilla' failed to redress the balance.

In the commercial-vehicle sector FIAT and their associates still held some seven-eighths of the home market, though a total production of 21,098 units between 1921 and 1930 shows that business was anything but brisk. In 1929 they could claim that they had sold four times more lorries in Turkey than had anyone else, but what were a hundred trucks? Italy's 1931 exports of commercial vehicles were 1,251 units, less than half Germany's contribution, and about a quarter of the United Kingdom's figures. Already in 1929 a chronic petrol shortage was leading to experiments with substitute fuels, and by 1934 *gazogènes* were going into production. In 1931 FIAT built some electric refuse collectors for the municipal authorities in Milan.

As late as 1930 heavier vehicles still bore the s.p.a. label, FIAT's own standard medium model being the 35-cwt 621, using the 2,516 c.c. six-cylinder 121 car engine, replaced in 1931 by the 122 type. Six-wheeler and 17-seater 'bus versions were also offered, and the 621 was still around in 1939, though by this time a four-cylinder diesel engine was standard, and the angular 1929 cab had given way to a streamlined American-style affair.

Heavier vehicles were on the way, among them the 640, a forward-control double-decker 'bus chassis with 7-litre side-valve engine, some of which went into service in Rome during 1930. A FIAT subsidiary also made the curious Pavesi tractor with its all-wheel drive and articulated backbone.

In 1931 Italy went diesel, Alfa Romeo taking out a Deutz licence, while Isotta Fraschini preferred the M.A.N. system, and O.M. used Saurer-type units. FIAT made their own, launching the 632/634 range of heavy-duty normal-control trucks for payloads of six-and-a-half tons, with four- and six-cylinder engines.

Aircraft development continued apace, and at the 1928 Berlin Aero Show a CR20 appeared in the new guise of a 'postal biplane', a role which *The Aeroplane* found amusing. Said the inimitable C. G. Grey of the Italian exhibit:

> Not only is it a comprehensive if small exhibition of fighting machines in a show which is strictly limited to civil aircraft, but every Italian machine flaunts the fasces and axe which form the official badge of the Fascisti, thus providing an effective counterblast to the sickle and hammer which is blatantly displayed on the Bolshevik stand on the other side of the gangway.

According to Grey FIAT did not bother to cover up the channels for the two synchronised machine guns in the fuselage sides! What he omitted to mention was that the aircraft was exhibited as a fighter trainer, while the 'fasces and axe' were standard wear on all Italian aeroplanes, civil and military. 1931 saw a development programme for giant bombers, to which Caproni and Breda contributed as well as FIAT. Their 'BRG' was an enormous three-engined high-wing braced mono-plane with two 700 h.p. A24s in the wings and a slightly more powerful A24R in the nose, but neither this nor Caproni's even vaster six-engined effort was adopted. More successful was Rosatelli's 1932 single-seater fighter, the CR30. This was a development of the CR20 theme powered by the 550 h.p. A30 engine, did 230 m.p.h., and was used for the *Regia Aeronautica*'s formation tour of Europe in 1934. In spite of this home orders were modest, the Air Ministry preferring to wait for the improved CR32, but CR30s were sold to Austria, China and Paraguay.

The late 1920s had seen the genesis of the light aeroplane movement in Britain, thanks to Geoffrey de Havilland's 'Moth' and the Avro 'Avian', and the Depression had little effect on the well-to-do private-flying community, with fly-ins and rallies throughout the summer. Inevitably FIAT were interested, and 1929 saw their contribution, the A.S.I., a neat little high-wing monoplane with folding wings, tandem open cockpits and dual control, powered by an 85 h.p. air-cooled radial engine of their own manufacture. A cabin development, the T.R.I., followed in 1930. Renato Donati flew one of these latter into second place in the Circuit of Italy, ahead of the rival Romeo Ro5s which were also FIAT-powered, while the A.S.I. distinguished itself in long-range flights. Donati and Campannini used one to set up a new closed-circuit record for light aeroplanes, and Francis Lombardi, later to make his name as a specialist coachbuilder, flew from Rome to Mogadishu in Italian Somaliland in February, 1930. Soon afterwards he added an even more impressive performance to his score; Rome-Tokio in 9 day 7 hours, thanks to Soviet officialdom, which permitted him, incredibly, to go by way of Siberia. By 1933 the civil range embraced two low-wing monoplanes from the drawing board of Gabrielli. The G.2 was a three-engined six seater 'executive transport' powered by FIAT's new in-line air-cooled inverted engines, while the single-engined G.5 was a three-seater personal type. Gabrielli was also responsible for the G.8, a tourer or trainer biplane on Warren-girder principles powered by an A54 radial of 140 h.p.

Quite a wide range of modestly-rated FIAT radials was available by 1931, and in that year Donati successfully test-flew a diesel conversion of the old A12, though this line of development was not pursued in Italy. One of the most intriguing FIAT-engined craft of 1930 was d'Ascanio's helicopter with blown A50 radial unit, which hopped and hovered about Rome's Ciampino airport, and took several 'chopper' records. In these days when rotating-wing aircraft are a commonplace it is interesting to note that d'Ascanio collected an altitude record by ascending to 59 feet, while his best duration was 8 min 45.2 seconds.

Some more interesting records fell to the Savoia-Marchetti SM64, a big FIAT-powered monoplane which collected the world's distance and duration records in 1929. In 1930 Maddalena and Cecconi improved on the previous figures, staying in the air for 67 hr 15 min, and flying 8,200 miles in a straight line. FIAT V-12s were also fitted to the twin-hull SM55 flying-boats of Marshal Italo Balbo's first 'air armada', which flew by stages from Rome to Rio de Janeiro in December, 1930. But perhaps the most interesting contract won by the aero-engine division concerned the world's then largest aircraft, Dornier's Do.X twelve engined flying boat. The Italian Government, not content with its outsize landplanes, became enamoured of this monster, and ordered two of them from Germany. This meant two dozen twelve-cylinder A22s, but alas! the Italian Dorniers (like the prototype, which did not use FIATs) turned out to be white elephants, with poor handling characteristics and a low ceiling. One of them was destroyed by a storm while lying at anchor on Lake Garda.

Not all Italy's aircraft were ponderous failures, and Mussolini was determined to avenge his defeat at Venice in 1927. The Trophy was not contested in 1928 (nobody was ready), but the struggle was resumed at Calshot in 1929, with Britain's Glosters and Supermarines opposed by everything that Italy could throw into the battle. This year Macchi and his chief designer Castoldi went to Isotta Fraschini for their engines, as did Savoia-Marchetti, who fielded an astonishing tractor/pusher affair with twin tail booms, but for the first time FIAT contributed a complete seaplane, the C-29 with 1,000 h.p. AS5 engine. Compared with the Macchis, this was a compact little craft with a wing span of less than 22 ft and a length of 17 ft 7 in. Its career was brief and catastrophic. On its second test flight at Desenzano it caught fire, and though Francesco Agello was able to descend safely before irretrievable damage had been done, he landed heavily on a further attempt, and the machine sank. After this it is hardly surprising that nothing was done with the second C-29, though it came to Calshot along with the Savoia, and was wheeled out of its hangar for the delectation of the photographers. It never flew then or at any other time, though there was some consolation for FIAT in the fact that the only Italian finisher in the race was Tenente dal Molin on a 1927–type Macchi with AS3 engine.

But Britain had won, and in 1931 the British were not willing to wait while Macchi came up with an answer to Reginald Mitchell's Supermarine S-6B. Thus the race became a fly-over, and the Schneider Trophy became the permanent property of the Royal Aero Club.

Castoldi had, however, built three new aircraft, the Macchi MC72s, and in addition Tranquillo Zerbi had designed an engine which for sheer complexity is probably unrivalled in the history of piston-powered aeroplanes. FIAT's AS6 can best be described as two V12s mounted one behind the other on a common crankcase, with two counter-rotating crankshafts driving contra-rotating airscrews. There were two overhead camshafts per block, 96 valves and 48 sparking plugs, in spite of which it weighed only 2,045 lbs, and was eventually persuaded to give 3,100 b.h.p. from over fifty litres.

But not immediately. The aircraft made its first flight in July, 1931 in the hands of Schneider Trophy pilot Monti, attaining 375 m.p.h., in spite of carburetter trouble and propellers that declined to rotate in phase. Repairs were effected, but soon afterwards Monti crashed into the lake and was drowned.

The second machine's life was equally brief, though it managed 390 m.p.h. before blowing up in the air and killing another of the hand-picked pilots, Bellini. Thanks to technical assistance from Rodwell Banks of Castrol, all the countless headaches were sorted out in April, 1933, when Agello, still intact after his adventure with the C-29, set a new World's Seaplane Speed Record at 423.76 m.p.h. Cassinelli subsequently added a 100-kilometre record at 391 m.p.h., setting the seal on the AS6's hard-won reliability. Nor was this the end, for on

23 October, 1934, Agello brought the MC72 out for the last time, with wooden floats replacing the original metal ones. This time the absolute record went up to a cracking 440.67 m.p.h., which comfortably beat the landplane figure as well. What is more, it was not beaten again until 1939, when the German Dieterle flew a Heinkel He 100V-8 at 464 m.p.h. To this day no piston-engined marine aircraft has attempted to improve on Agello's figure.

The aeronautical scene was healthy, and likely to stay that way, since in 1934 Mussolini told the world that Italy was investing a thousand million lire in rearmament. Car production was also on the upturn, with 31,507 units delivered, and better things were in store despite the exigencies of Mussolini's Abyssinian and Spanish adventures.

For in the meantime FIAT had once again landed themselves with a best-seller, and the magic designation 508 had arrived. More than twenty years were to elapse before it disappeared for good, and in the intervening period it was to assume six nationalities, dominate 1,100 c.c. sports-car racing, and take Italy's dictator on the last, short drive of his life.

8 Plucky Little One

The engine of the 'Balilla' has much of the big-car feeling which characterises the chassis, and carries out its task with a pleasant absence of fuss, and has a useful reserve of power low down. It runs smoothly throughout its range, and is mechanically quiet, but the exhaust note is rather hearty, and care has to be used when accelerating in towns in second gear.

508S Road Test, *Motor Sport*, January, 1935

Italy's recovery from the Depression was not assisted by Mussolini's imperialist adventures. These demanded foreign exchange, which meant a consistently high percentage of exports. They also demanded more petrol than Italy could afford, and prices rose steeply from the outbreak of the Abyssinian War. A gallon cost 2s. 10d. in January, 1935, but 5s. 4d. by December. Substitute fuels became a matter of urgency, and that autumn the French, Belgian, and Italian automobile clubs collaborated in a long-distance trial for commercial vehicles burning sundry solids and liquids. Gold-medal winners were Berliet, FIAT, Panhard and Saurer. Among the competitors in the 1936 Mille Miglia were two Alfa Romeos and three FIATs with Ferraguti coal-gas producers, but these ponderous devices were really no worse than the appalling alcohol fuel with which Italian motorists had to contend until 1938. By then the price of petrol was down to 3s. 3d. per gallon, but this was still twice as much as Britons paid, and gas-producer 'buses were in frequent use in 1939.

Another symptom of rearmament was a sharp drop in commercial-vehicle exports. Italy's 1931 figure of 1,251 units was anything but impressive, but though FIAT, Lancia and O.M.

were making some excellent 'heavies' in the early 'thirties, there was a drastic fall to 317 in 1932, and even in 1934 only 575 were sent abroad. By contrast Great Britain's exports were 13,742 units, and the Germans, who were also rearming in earnest, sold 2,250 trucks to foreign customers.

The slow recovery of FIAT's private-car business is a classic rebuttal of the socialist argument that an export trade can prosper without a healthy home market. One need only draw yet another comparison with Morris. At any time between the Wars Italy's entire demand for private cars could have been supplied by FIAT alone: even in the nation's best 'buying year', 1938, there were a mere 38,675 new registrations. For all Morris's catchy 1926 slogan, *British Made for Empire Trade*, Cowley never exported more than 17–18 per cent of their annual output between 1925 and 1933, whereas 50 per cent was about the norm at Lingotto. Yet the British firm overtook FIAT for the first time in 1923, with 20,024 units to the 13,629 of the Italian colossus, and they stayed ahead until 1939. 1935 was a good season for both factories, with 'Balillas' coming off the lines at the rate of 25,000 a year, and a much-needed Morris best-seller in the shape of the 918 c.c. Eight, yet new Morrises outnumbered new FIATS three-to-one. Admittedly one was unlikely to encounter any kind of Morris in Tallinn or Sofia, and there was no comparing M. Pigozzi's Simca-FIAT venture at Nanterre with Morris's disastrous earlier attempts to make anglicised Léon Bollées at Le Mans.

Even empire-building slowed down, though already work was going ahead on a new factory at Mirafiori, where Agnelli had wanted to build in 1899. FIAT's only significant purchase in the immediate post-Depression period was, in fact, the result of a step taken by Vittorio Valletta in 1928—though the Officine Mecchaniche did not become a part of FIAT's domains until 1933.

It was an attractive buy. O.M. were an old-established firm of streetcar and locomotive builders with roots going back to 1849, and they had added motor-cars to their interests when they acquired Züst in 1918.

Throughout the 1920s they built up a solid reputation on the

Detroit, Phase II.
45. The four-speed 'Balilla' (top) of 1934–7 was a restrained effort repeated on a larger scale with (**46**) the 'Ardita 2000' (centre). This Buhne-bodied cabriolet once owned by the author offered precious little vision in any direction. It is hard to believe that **47**, Pininfarina's 1935 aerodynamic limousine (bottom), is also a 2-litre Ardita under the skin.

48. Sorcerer's Song. Amedée Gordini on his way to victory in the Circuit d'Orléans, 1935. Its curious grille apart, this 508S looks very stock, even down to wings and running-boards.

(FIAT)

49. 'Balillas' in Britain. A. C. Westwood (left) and R. M. Sanford with the stripped 508S cars they drove in the Light Car Club's Relay Race at Brooklands, 1936.

(author's collection)

strength of a solitary, conventional side-valve design, made initially as a modest 'four', but subsequently evolved into a 65 × 100 mm, two-litre 'six' which was almost indecently fast, endeared itself to the British public, and won the very first Mille Miglia of 1927. Unfortunately for O.M.'s prospects, Barratouché, their chief was a 'one-speech Hamilton'. Though they tried a 1½-litre Grand Prix car in 1926, and tried to expand the 1921 theme into a 3-litre straight-eight, they found themselves facing the Depression with nothing better than a bored-out edition of their *Tipo-665*. Not that they were broke: in 1928 they had extended their Brescia works to allow of increased private-car production, and even in 1931 the supercharged works 2.3-litres won the *Giro di Sicilia* as well as taking second place in the Mille Miglia. Some people, however, wondered whether some of O.M.'s continuing prosperity was not due to the fifty per cent share in the undertaking that Valletta had bought for FIAT as part of Agnelli's policy of bolstering up Italian industry.

By 1931 their own technical stagnation (plus governmental pressure) was driving O.M. inexorably in the direction of trucks, and their new Saurer-based diesels were doing well. Under FIAT control the cars disappeared altogether, though two former O.M. executives, Coletta and Magnano, set up a new company, the Officine Esperia of Milan, and continued to develop them in a half-hearted way, toying with Wilson preselective gearboxes and introducing a new 2.3-litre 'six', the 'Alcyone', with synchromesh and overhead exhaust valves. This turned up at the 1934 Milan and London Shows—though not, it would seem, anywhere else. Coletta was actually planning a 1½-litre four-cylinder as late as 1936, but this one did not even get off the drawing-board. O.M. were finally integrated into FIAT as a *sezione* in 1968, and their current products include tractors and fork-lift trucks as well as their traditional range of medium- and heavy-duty diesel lorries and 'buses.

Meanwhile FIAT pinned their hopes on a 'car for Europe'. This *Tipo* 508, the original 'Balilla', was allegedly named after a Fascist Youth group equivalent to the Wolf Cubs: in fact, however, it commemorated a Genoese boy-hero of the revolt against the Austrians in the late eighteenth century. Unveiled at the 1932 Milan Show, it represented a big step forward in more senses than the purely economic. Here was the 509A theme brought up to date: a true compact with a wheelbase of 7 ft 4½ in, and a turning circle of 29 ft 6 in, it was appreciably lighter than the 509 family at 13¼ cwt for a two-door saloon. It could match and surpass the 509A's performance without the complexities of an upstairs camshaft; the simple three-bearing side valve engine had a capacity almost identical with that of the earlier type, at 995 c.c., yet was actually more powerful, developing 22 b.h.p. at 3,400 r.p.m. What is more, it signified a move into the *autostrada* age in that the almost-square (65×75 mm) dimensions allowed of sustained revs without expensive noises. FIAT claimed that at a steady 55 m.p.h. the new 108 unit was turning at a mere 3,500 r.p.m.; it would be kinder not to think of such velocities in terms of the 109A! Finally, the 'Balilla' was eminently tunable, and in overhead-valve form over 50 b.h.p. were eventually obtained without recourse to supercharging. Crankshafts *did* break: but V. H. Tuson found that the critical point was 6,300 r.p.m.

The new car inherited both the splendours and the miseries of contemporary FIAT thinking. Its 12-volt electrics would have been considered a luxury in France or Germany. Its strong cruciform-braced frame and hydraulic brakes were inherited from the unfortunate 515; the latter, be it said, were not seen on another mass-produced model from Continental Europe until the introduction of Citroën's *traction* in 1934, though by that time all Morrises wore Lockheeds. Other refinements were the hydraulic dampers and the optional free wheel. Styling, of course, reflected the 514 and 522, and the scaling-down process was as infelicitous as it always is. Not everyone liked the plunger-type ignition key, which one pushed in for sparks and rotated for the various combinations of lights: the switch was neither fool-proof nor cheap to replace. The transmission handbrake was an excellent last-ditch defence, and no more. But FIATS of this era—and indeed all their successors until the middle 'sixties—were blessed with hand-throttles which could be used to give ultra-sensitive control in dense traffic; the one on my 1934 'Ardita' worked admirably in this unintended context. In the interests of economy a three-speed box was deemed sufficient, and this was innocent of synchromesh, but in 1932 nobody missed either the extra cog or the painless shifting. At that time the only cheap baby car with four forward speeds was the Austin Seven, and this had been 'up-rated' by the addition of an unhelpful 23.3:1 underdrive. If the 'Balilla's' chosen ratios (5.2, 9.5 and 14.9 to 1) were agricultural, they were no worse than anyone else's, and they gave maxima of 58, 28, and 14 m.p.h. respectively. Further, different axle ratios were supplied for different functions—4.89:1 on the lighter roadsters, 5:1 for the Army's two-seaters, and 5.375:1 for light vans.

The 'Balilla' really was cheap—£135 for a roadster and £162 for the two-door saloon on the home market, though Britons paid about £40 more. A recognised option was a *spinto* engine giving 28 b.h.p. on a 6.3/1 compression, and a tourer was available as well as the saloon and roadster, not to mention the Service version with raised ground clearance and box-back two-seater coachwork. Late in 1933 downdraught carburation was standardised, and a four-door pillarless saloon with integral boot was added to the range, though few of these were made on the original three-speed chassis.

The 508 arrived too late to contest the 1932 Mille Miglia, in which the 514s cleaned up the 'utility' class. Neither the old nor the new type was seen in the Alpine Trial, although Dr Lettich's 522 won a Glacier Cup, but 1933 saw the 'Balilla' make a real impact upon the competition scene. In January Prince Narischkine took eighth place (and third in the light-car category) in the Monte Carlo Rally, despite running out of road on more than one occasion. Then came the Mille Miglia, which matched the FIATS against some really formidable opposition from the Maseratis and the new six-cylinder super-charged M.G. 'Magnettes', road-equipped racers with well over 100 b.h.p. under their bonnets, and costing more than four times the price of a 508. Admittedly the M.G.s were beset by plug trouble, but while the British contingent made mince-meat of the much-fancied Maseratis, there was a moral in the comparative average speeds. The class-winning 'Magnette' of Eyston/Lurani turned in 56.89 m.p.h. to the 54.67 m.p.h. of the Ambrosini/Menchetti 'Balilla'.

FIAT, of course, were quick to remind the world that Ambrosini's car was 'one of the standard 508 type chassis fitted with a special cylinder head and a fourth-speed attachment, the rear axle ratio being raised to 4 to 1', which sounded innocuous enough. But Count 'Johnny' Lurani has described the hotter Mille Miglia 'Balillas' as 'very non-standard'; the 'special head' was an o.h.v. conversion by SIATA of Turin, and even with this alone output was up to 38 b.h.p. A supercharged *monoposto* SIATA used for sprints would approach 100 m.p.h. on 48 b.h.p. For those who wanted to see what a standard 508 would do over a thousand miles, there was still the Ricci/Maggi machine, winner of the 'utility' class. This averaged 53.85 m.p.h., and had been doctored only in respect of a *spinto* engine and the high-ratio back end.

The rest of the season was unspectacular. FIAT supported neither the Targa Florio nor the French *Bol d'Or*, while the standard 'Balilla's' three-speed box was a hopeless handicap in the Alpine Trial. Narischkine's team was soundly beaten by the M.G.s and Singers. At Monte Ceneri Ambrosini's blown o.h.v. projectile was timed over the kilometre at 94.83 m.p.h., in spite of which he had to give best to an Amilcar and a Maserati, and the Coppa Acerbo was too short a race to give the FIATs a chance against either M.G. or Maserati. Knap's Walter-built sports 'Balilla' won its class in the Czechoslovak '1000', but in Britain the S-variants had yet to be seen, and FIAT participation in the sport was restricted to sundry antiques. Tuson's 509S was still active, as was E. A. Prime's 1913 *Tipo* Zero, 'chuffing and chugging' up trials hills and drawing indignant protests from its owner, who considered *The Motor*'s comments almost libellous. FIAT (England) Ltd duly entered their 1903 16 h.p. tonneau for the Brighton Run, though by this time the S61 and 'Mephistopheles' were regrettably dormant.

During the season the factory came up with their own idea of a sports model. At 14,900 lire it was appreciably more expensive than the saloon, and it was only lightly tuned, output being 30 b.h.p. on a 7:1 compression with the aid of a downdraught Zenith carburetter. Other changes included a 4.3:1 back axle, a rear tank with mechanical pump feed, and friction-type shock absorbers; its 68 m.p.h. top speed was well within the reach of a good J2 M.G. or Singer Nine Sports. What singled the 'Balilla' out was, however, its lovely two-seater spyder body in the Zagato Alfa idiom, with vestigial tail fin, flared wings, and topless screen.

In 1934 the touring 'Balilla' theme crystallised into its final form, the *4 porte 4 marce* version taking its bow at the Milan Show; the original three-speeder was phased out during the summer. The principal changes were a lengthened wheelbase to accommodate a four-door pillarless saloon body of the type already seen on late three-speed models, a sloping grille derived from the 2-litre 518, and instruments grouped in a single dial. A higher-compression 24 b.h.p. engine kept pace with growing weight (up by 2 cwt in the case of saloons), and buyers still had the choice of disc or wire wheels. *The Autocar* found the new 'Balilla' 'notable for the way in which it can be driven long distances at speeds fairly close to the maximum', and it accelerated through the gears to 50 m.p.h. in 35.2 seconds. A wide range of sub-types included military and commercial species, while an attractive addition to the catalogue was a little cabriolet made in limited numbers by Garavini. The four-speeder also acquired a notoriety of its own. The first publicity posters distributed in Italy showed a lady clad in the *haute couture* of 1934 beside her *berlina*, but the Vatican took exception to the length of her skirt, and some hasty sartorial amendments became necessary! The four-speed gearbox had synchromesh on its two upper ratios, and was also applied to the 508S, which acquired a new pushrod engine with cast-iron head developing 36 b.h.p. at 4,400 r.p.m. This model came in three different body styles. These were the spyder *Sport* with flared wings: the spyder *corsa* ('*Coppa d'Oro*') with narrow competition body, cycle-type wings, and no running-boards; and the *berlinetta aerodinamica*, a pretty fast-back coupé introduced in 1935, with offset instruments and a large boot entirely dedicated to the fuel tank and spare wheel. 508S models sold in England used locally-built replicas of the *Sport* which came out rather heavier than the native article. The wings alone weighed 120 lbs, which explains why most of them soon became artificial '*Coppa d'Oro*'s, though Tuson, who liked the standard style, used to strip his for racing, a process which took only thirty minutes.

No two 508S models seem to be identical, and all manner of variations appeared. Detailed production figures have never been released, but from surviving engine serials it is reasonable to assume that 1,600 were made between 1933 and 1937. Along-side the genuine 'S' cars FIAT had a halfway house, in the shape of a four-door saloon with the o.h.v. engine, friction dampers, and a 4.875:1 back axle. About a thousand of these found buyers, and they were actually quieter than their side-valve counterparts, thanks to the outsize air cleaner fitted to the 108CS unit. One was used by Kozma and Martinek to win the light-car class of the 1936 Monte Carlo Rally.

More important, the 508S represented a new idiom in small sports cars. It was reasonably priced (15,900 lire in Italy or £248 in England), but it possessed the manners of a thoroughbred. Ratios of the four-speed box (4.3, 5.7, 8.6, and 14.4 to 1) were ideal for fast road work, and were thus more conducive to dura-bility than those of contemporary English models, which had trials-oriented spacing. The 1936 PB-type M.G. had ratios of 5.375, 7.31, 11.5, and 19.24 to 1, and the 'Le Mans' Singer was even lower-geared. Inevitably the M.G. scored on standing-start acceleration, with an 0–50 m.p.h. time of 16.4 seconds to the FIAT's 18.6, but the Italian car would cruise at 68, close to the maximum speed of 72 m.p.h. *The Autocar* spoke of 'readiness to get off the mark rapidly, coupled with a gear change that enabled lightning movements to be made between gear and gear, freedom from fuss and stress when travelling at speed, and sturdiness and fine road-holding in conjunction with accurate and light steering'. Rodney Walkerley, writing in *The Motor*, called it 'one of those cars you drive for the fun of it', recording a timed quarter-mile at 75. *The Light Car*'s Dennis May was left with a feeling of 'acceleration', and of steering that was low-geared, 'but with no trace of that faint waywardness which so often makes itself felt with that kind of guiding apparatus'. He considered the exhaust note 'nice, but decidedly naughty', the weather protection reminded some testers of an aircraft's blind-flying hood, and the pedals were uncomfortably close together. (This last is only too true: my own size-twelve feet can cope with all the M.G.s I have driven, but the 'Balilla' defeats me utterly!) No wonder the amateur and professional tuners went to work with a will.

Among the Italians who tried their luck was Piero Dusio, later the *padrone* of Cisitalia. In the 1935 Mille Miglia he fielded a *berlinetta aerodinamica* with 62 b.h.p. supercharged engine and streamlined nose suggestive of the later *millecento*, which the press singled out as 'the noisiest of the pack'. In Germany Reichenwallner and Brendel, leaders of the local FIAT fraternity, did their own tuning and achieved some success with Derbuel-blown versions. Blowers, curiously enough, were little used in the British Isles, though one of the 'Six Counties' FIATs was running supercharged in 1936. The principal English expert was V. H. Tuson, who achieved some formidable results and also prepared cars for other owners, with the consequence that almost all the four dozen 508S models imported in 1935 and 1936 ended up in club racing. A Tuson-modified car would have a Hardy Spicer propeller shaft (universal failures were endemic to the 508 family), remetalled con-rods, 2 mm ground out of the inlet ports, tulip-shaped inlet valves, bronze exhaust valve guides, and a copperised head. His own 'Balilla' would see 85 fully equipped, and 95–100 m.p.h. stripped for racing. It lapped the Brooklands Outer Circuit at 92 m.p.h., and went through two seasons with the minimum of trouble. Le Strange Metcalfe's car with Tuson manifold, Martlet pistons, and a lower compression (8.2 to Tuson's 9.6/1) was eventually worked up to 105 m.p.h., and lapped Goodwood at 68.7 m.p.h. in the nineteen-fifties. In Czechoslovakia Walter produced one

'Balilla' to full SIATA specification, as well as mounting sports 'Balilla' bodies, bonnets and grilles on sporting versions of their own six-cylinder 'Regents'.

Undoubtedly the star of the whole 'Balilla' firmament was Amedée Gordini. His cars were nominally Simcas, though in fact Pigozzi's factory never produced any S-types. Gordini's early experiments with alloy blocks were frustrated by porous castings, but in *Autosport*'s words, 'practically every moving component in the engine was changed or modified, probably the only FIAT items left being the bore and stroke'. His 1935 racing engines have 48 b.h.p. at 5,500 r.p.m., but he was adept at weightparing, and though he was still using a standard spyder *corsa* body his version turned the scales at under 10 cwt, instead of just over 11.

First to exploit the new model's potential were FIAT (England) Ltd, who at last had something to sell—the horse-power tax militated against short-stroke engines, and the touring 'Balilla' had flopped in Britain. The company set Jack Wren and Dudley Froy to cover a thousand miles of the Brooklands Mountain Circuit in two one-day spells. The car used was the l.h.d. demonstrator (BHX 91) and it ran stripped, averaging 55.11 m.p.h. in vile November weather. Fuel consumption was 21 m.p.g., and each pint of oil lasted 200 miles. Said *Motor Sport*:

A little thought will emphasise the merit of this very fine performance. On every lap of this 1.17-mile course the car had to be braked heavily once, and the indirect gear ratios used on both corners. This, coupled with the revving of the engine as the car accelerated away from the corners, and the strain on the chassis caused by high-speed cornering, is very definite proof of the toughness and reliability of a remarkable little sports car.

Thirty years later George Liston Young and Ian Smith of the FIAT Register re-enacted the exploit in even worse conditions at Goodwood, on Mrs Elsie Wisdom's 1936 T.T. mount, DPL 998. The attempt started inauspiciously, thanks to dirt in the fuel lines, and towards the end both drivers appeared to be swimming around in the cockpit, but not only was the car faster (56.02 m.p.h. overall), but it used less petrol and oil.

Mickey Mouse in England.
50. (top) The standard 500 cabriolet is competing in the 1937 M.C.C. Torquay Rally, its roll-top bellying characteristically in the wind.
51. (centre) A. C. Westwood is using his 'topless' Smith SIATA Special as a bedroom during the 1939 RAC Rally.
52. The four-seater cabriolet (bottom) was made exclusively for Britain, this being the de luxe model with bumpers and two-tone metallic finish.
(National Motor Museum)

Paris Fashions.
53. Peculiar to France was this handsome fastback coupé version of the 1939 Simca-8, alias FIAT 508C.

(Chrysler France S.A.)

54. Ahead of its time. 508CMM coupé by Savio, 1938. On this very early example the standard FIAT grille is retained.

(FIAT)

O.h.v. cars were, in any case, still few and far between in 1934, and were no match for M.G. or Maserati in major events such as the Mille Miglia or the Coppa Acerbo. There were, however, numerous important class victories: the *Giro d'Italia*, the Belgian Ten Hours, and the Klausen and Harmashatar hill-climbs.

1935 opened with a couple of good rally placings—tenth for Husem's saloon in the 'Monte', and fifth in the Paris-St Raphael *rallye feminin* for Mme Dubac-Taine. Becker's M.G. 'Magnette' defeated the FIATs in the Grand Saconnex hill-climb at Geneva, but Stothert collected a first-class award in the R.A.C. Rally, and in the 1,100 c.c. class of the Mille Miglia the FIAT contingent had to face the Bianco/Bertocchi Maserati and Gazzabini's K3 M.G. At Bologna the British car's average stood at 84.8 m.p.h., faster than Earl Howe's 1933 showing; though Gazzabini eventually retired, Dusio's blown 'Balilla' coupé had to give best to the Maserati. At Château-Thierry a Salmson won the 1,100 c.c. sports class, albeit Mme Roux' 'Balilla' was the best tourer, and the combination of the two smallest categories in Paris-Nice relegated FIAT to a second place. In the Targa Florio, apart from one Maserati which retired, all the 1,100s were FIATs, so Toia's class win was an empty one, but Gordini and Pèle trounced the Singers and Amilcars in the *Circuit d'Orléans*, and Pilloud finished ahead of Lapchin's Singer in the Circuit des Vosges mountain rally. The Alpilles hill-climb went to Salmson: in the Eifelrennen the FIATs came up against new opposition in the shape of the rather heavy f.w.d. 'Trumpf-Junior' Adlers, and defeated them. In the *Bol d'Or* Gordini won the 1,100 c.c. sports class at 48.81 m.p.h., though the outright winner was a K3 M.G. driven by the Frenchman P. Maillard-Brune. In the Marne G.P. for sports cars Gordini carried off the 1½-litre class.

Le Mans saw the Barnes/Langley Singer beat the Mme Itier/Jacob FIAT after Gordini, partnered by Amadeo Nazzaro, a nephew of the great Felice, gave up with cooling troubles, but the Walter-built 'Balilla' of Migno/Buchero had no trouble in the Czechoslovak '1000' despite a field of nineteen 1,100s.

ffrench-Davies was second in the County Down Trophy Race in Northern Ireland—an auspicious beginning for the small band of Irish FIATs which were to enjoy a long and distinguished career. One of them ended up as Desmond Titterington's first competition mount.

In the Grossglöckner hill-climb Luigi Villoresi's 'Balilla' easily disposed of M.G., Austin and D.K.W. opposition, while the cars were at the top of their form in the Targa Abruzzo, FIATs winning the 1100 c.c. class and finishing fourth and fifth overall behind a brace of the new 2.3-litre six-cylinder Alfa Romeos and the 1½-litre Aston Martin of Lurani/Strazza. In the Lorraine Grand Prix the 1,100 c.c. and 1,500 c.c. categories were again combined, but the FIATs of Gordini, Mme Itier and Sarret were 'much too good for the opposition', and easily outstripped the best of the 1½-litre brigade, a Salmson-engined Rally. There were more hill-climb victories— Eymontiers, Stelvio, Feldberg, Mount Gugger, and Harmashatar—while Villoresi was runner-up to Count Lurani's Maserati in the Italian Sports Car Championship, but the season ended on a low note with the Ulster T.T. Here four of Singer's new lightweight o.h.c. Nines (the Barnes brothers, S. C. H. Davis, and A. B. Langley) were matched against three Irish-registered FIATs, and Charlie Manders's 995 c.c. Adlers from Dublin. The German cars presented no serious competition, and a savage Singer-FIAT battle was resolved when 'Sammy' Davis pulled steadily away from Bill Dobson's 'Balilla'. Then a dramatic succession of steering failures eliminated the Singers, one by one—and, incidentally, killed that company's sports-car business stone dead in a few minutes. Dobson's FIAT was the only '1,100' still running at the end, and even he was unplaced. None the less, Turin had every reason for self-congratulation, with fifteen wins to seven each for M.G. and Salmson, and four for Singer. In fairness to France and Britain, though, neither M.G. nor Singer had a continental dealer network to match FIAT's, and Salmson had made no sports cars since 1930.

1936 got away to a good start with the Kozma/Martinek

success in the Monte Carlo Rally, and also with a minor British win—for A. C. Westwood's 'Black Diamonds' team in the Great West Motor Club's Bagshot Trial, of interest in that the FIATs were now venturing into the M.G./Singer domain, as well as making an impact out of all proportion to their limited numbers. Biagini won his class in the Mille Miglia, and there were first-class awards for Westwood and Tett in the R.A.C. Rally. The latter went on to win the Blackpool Rally outright. At La Turbie it was Singer's turn to win, but in the mistral-swept Coupe de Provence on the seldom-used Miramas circuit, Gordini led the 1,100s home at 63.3 m.p.h., followed by Pupil on another FIAT. The Light Car Club's Relay Race at Brooklands must mark the high point in the 'Balilla's' English career, for no fewer than three all-FIAT teams were fielded, one of them a feminine *équipe* (Miss Chaff, and the *Mesdames* Wisdom and Lace). The ladies took fourth place, defeating their male opponents. In the *Bol d'Or* Gordini's cars really found their form, finishing 1–2–3 against Amilcars, M.G.s and Salmsons, and there was a similar procession (Brendel, Soergel and Zinn) in the German Eifelrennen. In the County Down Trophy, however, Sullivan had no luck with his supercharged 508S, while Manders's Adler was actually faster than McGrattan's unblown FIAT which finished tenth.

Industrial unrest in France eliminated Le Mans from the calendar, but Gordini scored his expected class win in the Belgian 24 Hours at Spa, and he tried hard in the French Grand Prix at Montlhéry, a sports-car event this year, because the French were determined to win something! This objective they duly achieved, but by lumping the three smallest classes together they handed this combined category to the T.T.-type $1\frac{1}{2}$-litre Rileys, leaving the Gordini/Querzola Simca (now rebodied *a la* Maserati) to finish 20th, albeit ahead of the Singers. In the Alpine Trial the German FIAT drivers were beaten by the little two-stroke D.K.W.s, and the T.T. resolved itself into an uninspired Singer/FIAT battle in which neither side distinguished itself. Sullivan was 13th and Mrs Wisdom was unplaced in DPL 998, by this time using an experimental

1,089 c.c. unit installed by the British concessionaires at Wembley. In the Targa Florio, watered down that year to two laps of the Madonie, 'Balillas' placed 1–2 in the 1100 c.c. class at 5–6 overall behind four Lancias.

1937 was the breed's last major competition season, though the cars could still challenge the M.G.s in British club events. There were the inevitable class wins in the Mille Miglia and the *Bol d'Or* while the Gordini 'Balillas', which had sprouted *topolino*-like beetle-noses, beat a linered-down Ford Ten at Le Mans, and finished sixth and seventh in the *Coupe de la Commission Sportive* at Montlhéry. M.G., however, won in the Eifelrennen, and though Amedée Gordini dominated the driving tests of Paris-Nice he lost on general classification to Jacques Savoye's Singer. There was some compensation in the Prince Rainier Cup at Monaco: *le sorcier*'s 995 c.c. FIAT was the only light car in the event, in spite of which he finished fifth, behind three 3½-litre Delahayes and Louis Gerard's rapid 3-litre Delage. Three 'Balillas' turned out to challenge the Singers in the T.T. at Donington Park—Mrs Wisdom's faithful DPL 998, and a pair of Gordinis (Amedée himself and Maillard-Brune), making their debut on British soil. Both sides had past failures to avenge, but in the event it was Barnes's Singer that went out in a blaze of glory, with the best British performance in a Franco-German procession. Maillard-Brune's brakes gave out, and Gordini crept in, tenth and last.

Thereafter the FIAT brigade had better fish to fry. Gordini and Tuson alike went to work on the new *millecento* (*Tipo* 508C), and FIAT themselves developed the Savio-bodied 508CMM coupé. Even so, Westwood was still campaigning his sports 'Balilla' in 1939, doing well in the Scottish and Welsh Rallies.

'Balillas' were excellent export sellers. In Portugal they were used for newpaper delivery, on the Danish market the original three-speeders were scarcely more expensive than the Austin Seven, and quite a few examples found their way to India and Malaya. In this context, it is interesting to note that the State of Perak, with average new registrations of three dozen cars a year, took no fewer than four 508S two-seaters in 1934. In Czechoslovakia Walter's output remained modest, though it included 36 assorted S-types, and this model was also assembled by N.S.U. in Germany—the Heilbronn works, incidentally, were still delivering 521-based 'Standards' as late as 1933. The 508 put the German operation firmly on the map, with 1,704 cars sold in 1934 and over 3,000 in 1935, which meant effective competition for the smaller Hanomags and the Cologne-built Model-Y Ford, if not for Opel, D.K.W., or Adler. A new departure was an agreement signed between FIAT and the Polish Government for the licence-production of 'Balillas' in Warsaw.

Already FIAT-built trucks were well established in Marshal Pilsudski's domains. An S.P.A. had won a 3,000-kilometre Army trial in 1924, and since 1929 the Ursus factory had made S.P.A.s under licence. Initially, Polish 'Balillas' were assembled from c.k.d. kits, but by 1938 the Polski-FIAT edition of the 508C was locally-made even down to rough castings, only the instruments being imported from Germany. Production continued right up to the Nazi invasion of September, 1939.

Most important of FIAT's foreign affiliations was, of course, the French *Société Industrielle de Mécanique et de Carrosserie Automobile* (Simca), the creation of a Piedmontese scrap merchant, H. T. Pigozzi. He had settled in Paris in 1926, and when he established his company in 1934 he had had 'five years' experience of manufacturing automobiles without a factory, or even a machine'. In fact full manufacture of French FIATS did not start until the advent of the first three-speed 'Balilla' in 1932, and one wonders if *La Vie Automobile* was correct in stating that this 6CV was *'entièrement construite en France'*. In 1934, however, the earlier hole-and-corner operations gave way to something more serious, based on the run-down works of the defunct Donnet company at Nanterre. By mid-1935 Simcas were appearing in fair numbers, and two types were being made: the 6CV, or four-speed 'Balilla' saloon, and the 11CV, *alias* 'Ardita 2000'. Both species were readily distinguishable from their Italian counterparts by their horizontal bonnet louvres and pressed-steel spoked wheels, while 'Arditas' had handsome French-style bodywork. A cabriolet won a prize at the Auteuil *concours* in 1936.

The 'Ardita', new at the 1933 Milan Show, was FIAT's first car with synchromesh as well as their last new model with beam axles at front and rear. It was also a compromise born of necessity, to use up the excellent and rigid 522 chassis with their dual-circuit brakes. To these traditional components was wedded a short-stroke four-cylinder side-valve unit of 82 × 92 mm (1,944 c.c.) which was virtually scaled-up 'Balilla'. The result was a solid family saloon capable of 65 m.p.h., and better than 20 m.p.g. The standard body was a four-door six-light pillarless *berlina à la* Terraplane, though a traditional torpedo was listed for export, and sports models wore close-coupled saloon bodywork in the 522S idiom.

Many 'Arditas' earned their keep as taxis, and latterly the cars were delivered with seven-seater *berlina ministeriale* bodies of more streamlined shape. Personal experience of an elderly 2-litre confirms the views of contemporary road-testers—the 518 was a car of some charm, with a taxi-like lock and sportscar handling, provided that one made full use of the rather meagre output. *The Motor* was over-generous in suggesting that the 118 engine was indistinguishable from a 'six', but the car would cruise happily all day at 50–55 m.p.h., ignoring the average main-road hill. Gear ratios were typically and infuriatingly Italian. First (16.35 to 1) was painfully low, and second (8.64) too high to start a heavy car from rest. The 6.7:1 third gave a useful 55, while the dual-circuit Lockheeds were without doubt the best drum brakes I have encountered on a cheap family car. If pushed, the engine would run up to well over 4,000 r.p.m. Homemarket prices ranged between £310 and £370, though it was rather more expensive in England.

Once again FIAT shuffled the pack to produce a wide range of 518 derivatives. There were two standard wheelbases: 8 ft 10¾ in for five-seaters, and 9 ft 10 in for limousines. As an alternative to the 2-litre 118A engine there was the smallbore 1,750 c.c. 118, while the rare sports models combined the short chassis with the high-compression 2-litre 118AS unit which disposed of 56 b.h.p. and gave a genuine 70 m.p.h. There were the usual 'colonial' sub-species, plus a commercial cousin, the 25-cwt 618, produced in civilian form with a car-type cab and coil ignition, and for the Army with the older 614's sheet metal and a magneto. The company even offered a further choice in the shape of the 527, which consisted of a lengthened 'Ardita' chassis powered by an up-rated edition of the old $2\frac{1}{2}$-litre 'six', with alloy head and downdraught carburetter. In sports saloon form this 'Ardita 2500' was a handsome car capable of 72 m.p.h. on 60 b.h.p., but it had outlasted its welcome, and only 260 were sold between 1934 and 1936. By contrast, a few 518s were still being turned out, mainly for Roman officialdom, as late as 1938.

On the commercial side even two-tonners were oil-engined by 1935, though petrol units were still available on certain 'heavies'. Most of the novelties had a martial air, and an interesting range embraced some *dovunque* (go-anywhere) six-wheelers and the TL37 artillery tractor with four-wheel-drive and steering, all under the S.P.A. name. New in 1936 was another famous S.P.A. design, the $2\frac{1}{2}$-ton 38R. This vintage-looking normal-control lorry had a 4,053 c.c. four-cylinder petrol engine: it also boasted hydraulic four-wheel brakes and was usually seen with the open-sided cab favoured by the Italian Army. The last ones were not made until 1948.

In 1933 the *sezione grandi motori* pulled off a brilliant coup on the Cosulich Line's M. V. *Vulcania*. This liner had been commissioned in 1927, but her double-acting Burmeister and Wain diesels failed to produce anything better than 18 knots, and the problem was to fit units of adequate power into the existing engine-room. In 1933 FIAT found the answer: the four original motors were replaced by two ten-cylinder two-stroke diesels which more than doubled the total output, so that speed rose to a satisfying 22 knots. On the eve of War plans were afoot to re-engine the battleships *Augustus* and *Roma*: the Navy's goal was 24–26 knots, and prototype units of eight and twelve cylinders were actually built, but both capital ships were sunk by enemy action before FIAT's ideas could be put to the test. In 1939 it was estimated that no fewer than 350 merchantmen and warships were powered by FIAT motors.

Inevitably the *sezione aeronautica* was preoccupied with matters military. The CR30 gave way to the very similar CR32, a superbly manoeuvrable biplane with a 600 h.p. twelve-cylinder FIAT engine, one of the last liquid-cooled types to be made in quantity, since Italian officialdom plumped firmly for radials in 1934, and had to fall back on the German Daimler-Benz when they realised their mistake six years later. The CR32 distinguished itself against the Russian Rata low-wing monoplanes in the Spanish Civil War: an unfortunate triumph this, for it convinced the high-ups in Rome that biplanes were still tactically viable. Some 350 were delivered, and four-gun installations were tried on the model, only to be abandoned on grounds of weight and handling. Rosatelli also tried a variation of his biplane theme with a gull upper wing, and by 1936 he had progressed to the CR41 with 900 h.p. Gnome-Rhône K-14 engine and an armament of two 20 mm cannon or four 12.7 mm machine-guns. This one was, however, passed over in favour of the next generation—Castoldi's Macchi MC200, and two new FIATs, the traditional CR42 and the Gabrielli-designed G.50 low-wing monoplane, all with the 840 h.p. fourteen-cylinder FIAT A.74RC38 engine. Interestingly, Gabrielli's monoplane flew two years before the CR42, in February, 1937.

Mussolini might rattle his sabres, but FIAT had long had a financial interest in the A.L.I. airline, and from 1933 onwards the Douglas DC2 was to set a fashion in modern, multi-engined all-metal low-wing monoplane airliners with retractable undercarriages. FIAT produced two interpretations of the Douglas theme in 1935 and 1936, the twelve-passenger APR2 and the bigger G.18 for eighteen passengers, with a wing span of 82 feet. Both started life with two 700 h.p. A59 radials, though by 1937 the G.18 had been re-engined with 1,000 h.p. A80s. APR2s went into service in 1936 on the Milan-Turin-Paris route, and were said to be the fastest airliners on scheduled work in Europe, with a cruising speed of 217 m.p.h.

Of the same generation was Rosatelli's BR20, a twin-engined all-metal bomber with twin fins and rudders, designed for a bomb load of 1,600 kg. Engines were the 1,000 h.p. A.80RC41s, and it was well armed, with power-operated nose and dorsal gun turrets, something that neither *L'Armée de l'Air* nor the *Luftwaffe* could claim in 1936. Flying weight was 22,266 lbs, and the FIAT would do an impressive 267 m.p.h., with a cruising range of 5½ hours at 217 m.p.h. It was first flown in February, 1936, and deliveries to the squadrons were under way before the year was out. Alas! for Italy's bellicose intentions, things moved more slowly thereafter, and only 582 were delivered all told, of which 162 were on charge when Italy entered the War. The Japanese bought eight BR20s, and development continued well into the 1940s. The later BR20BIS had a streamlined nose in contrast to the angular contours of the first series, and 1,250 h.p. A82 motors. It was also the first Italian aircraft to be flight-tested with a tricycle undercarriage. BR20s were used against England in the winter of 1940: indeed the *Corpo Aereo Italiano* stationed in occupied Belgium was an all-FIAT unit, the escorts being CR42s and G.50s.

By 1936 the picture had changed at Lingotto, and it had changed for good. The last 527 had taken the road, and FIAT no longer raced, though the rumour-mongers never abandoned hope. In 1933 they had predicted a new sports-racer for Tazio Nuvolari to drive: in 1936 there was talk of a Scuderia Ferrari/FIAT alliance to build a World's Land Speed Record challenger round the AS6 engine: in 1937 the 508C's tantalising specification prompted further rumours of a works team. In January, 1938, however, the press office in Turin had the last word. 'We are definitely not intending any kind of re-entry into racing', they said, 'although sports FIATs are likely to race, driven by private owners'.

The raw material was already there. The 'Balilla' had married the best in traditional chassis design to the new short-stroke engine, and in the summer of 1935 FIAT returned to the ranks of the leaders with the 1500, an aerodynamic saloon with independently-sprung front wheels and a backbone frame.

Less than a year later *The Light Car*'s gossip columnist was at it again. On 4 April, 1936, he announced that 'rumours have appeared lately that a new production of the FIAT company will be called "Mickey Mouse".' Quick as lightning came an indignant denial from Wembley.

This time they were wrong, and the press were right. Before the month was out Italians had seen their first *topolino*, *alias* 'Mouse', *alias* Simca-Cinq. The baby car, brainchild of Albert de Dion and Georges Bouton, and publicised by Herbert Austin, was entering upon a new and even more sophisticated phase.

9 Thoroughly Modern *Mille*

The 1100 was an epoch making car through years dense
with technical progress and economic and social changes.
It went through the Second World War. It was born when
the people who rode in it still wore hats, both men and
women: it accompanied steel helmets through air-raids,
and was still in time to carry again lengthened skirts
and hair, and bald pates. It heard the last sighs of
romantic literature between the two World Wars, and,
after the second, the eccentricities of existentionalism.

FIAT brochure, 1953

There were three generations of FIAT on show at London's
Olympia in October, 1935. £375-worth of 527 limousine
represented the Detroit period; the 'Balilla', now at its zenith,
signalised the 'square' engine as well as 'square' looks; and
there was a crowd-gatherer in the shape of a sleek, streamlined
saloon, the 1500. This, too, was competitively priced at £298.

Even the designation was new. It signified 1½ litres of overhead-valve, short-stroke 'six' with a bore of 65 mm, and a
stroke of 75 mm. Here was a leader from FIAT, and one which
had little in common with previous designs.

The chassis was a girder-type backbone on German lines,
forking outward at the front to take the engine, and at the rear
to accommodate the fuel tank. Though conventional semi-
elliptic springs were retained at the back, there was independent
front suspension by Dubonnet coils. The four-door saloon body

was supported on outriggers, and was fully aerodynamic, albeit without the grotesque waterfall grille and clumsy slab sides that had marred Chrysler's 1934 'Airflow' and its more slavish imitators. The only surviving excrescences were the running-boards and the spare wheel, which was mounted on the rear panel. The headlamps were countersunk into the front wings, the 'Balilla's' projecting boot had given way to an internal-access affair, and even door handles were recessed, while a gently sloping alligator bonnet crowned with a stylised grille offered a degree of forward vision sadly lacking on many a previous specimen of 'streamline'. When the pillarless doors were opened, one was greeted with tubular seat frames, a headlamp flasher (yes, in 1935!) and even a built-in radio aerial. Disc wheels were standard. The four-bearing engine followed recognised FIAT practice—the single downdraught carburetter was fed by mechanical pump, cooling was by pump and fan, and the four-speed gearbox had synchromesh on its two upper ratios. A longish wheelbase of 9 ft 2 in left plenty of room for five people, and weight, at 20½ cwt, corresponded closely to the company's last 1½-litre, the 514.

The result was no kind of sports car, though a maximum speed of 70 m.p.h. and an 0–50 m.p.h. acceleration time of 21 seconds were more than adequate at a time when 65 was con-sidered the limit for a European 1½-litre saloon. In *The Autocar*'s opinion, 'it could be treated to some considerable extent as a top-gear car, for the engine will pull down to about 10 m.p.h. on top'. Understandably the all-round vision came in for high praise, while the Dubonnet coils, which were also the basic ingredient of such dreadful systems as the American 'Knee Action', worked exceedingly well on the FIAT. 'The motion is soft, with a fair amount of up and down movement, but not to a pronounced extent, and there is no disagreeable side roll'—the rewards of a low centre of gravity and a wide track. With a heavy load on board, tail float was possible, but the 1500 was un-affected by bad surfaces, and the steering was both light and accurate. The only feature to arouse universal condemnation was the umbrella-handle handbrake, unpleasant in its own right, and rendered worse by its use in conjunction with the customary FIAT transmission arrangements. It was not repeated on either the 500 or the 508C.

The *mille cinque*, was, as Count Lurani has said, 'FIAT's idea of a small luxury family car'. It was never intended to compete with the Lancia 'Aprilia', a driver's machine *par excellence*, and a good 8 m.p.h. faster than the 1500 on both the two upper ratios, though curiously enough acceleration times up to 50 m.p.h. are very similar. Seen through British eyes, of course, the Lancia scored on every count, for it was rated at 12.9 h.p., whereas the FIAT was a Sixteen, and therefore competing against substantial saloons such as the Series II six-cylinder Morris, the Hillman with its perilous transverse-leaf i.f.s., and Austin's stately 'Hertford'. (In passing, though, I recall being informed bitterly in 1947 by a Tuscan enthusiast that there were no *mille cinques* left in Siena Province—'the British requisitioned the lot'!) Sales were steady, reaching their peak in 1937 when 16,707 units were delivered, and there were no major changes to the specification between 1935 and 1944, when Allied bombing and German interference called a temporary halt to production. Some extremely handsome bodies were made on this chassis, chiefly by Ghia, Viotti and Pininfarina, who pioneered the vee-grille standardised on 1940 editions of the 1100 and 1500. A handful of 1500B chassis which reached Britain in the early months of the War were fitted with mock-Pininfarina drophead coachwork by Ranalah, and sold at £365.

The 1500 was seldom seen in competitions, though Luigi Villoresi used one to win the light-car class of the 1937 Monte Carlo Rally, and FIAT (England) Ltd sponsored T. C. Wise's entry in the 1938 event. This ended in disaster when the distributor drive sheared in the tests—a pity, for up to then the car had been penalty-free. Some Adler-like Viotti coupés with panoramic windscreens were, however, prepared for the 1937 season, and these proved more than a match for the early Lancia 'Aprilias'. Lurani, in those days a keen Lancia exponent, was one of their victims, in the Maddalena hill-climb of 1938. 'The FIATs', he recalls, 'were highly tuned and lightened, and driven by first-class men. In my case, it was no less than Giovanni Bracco, later to win the Mille Miglia for Ferrari'.

The Viotti 1500s duly turned out for the 1937 Mille Miglia, one of them in the hands of Vittorio Mussolini, the Duce's son. As yet 'Aprilias' of any kind were few and far between, so the Minio/Castagnaro FIAT duly collected 12th place, and the 1½-litre class, with other 1500s in 13th and 14th positions. In the Littorio Races at Rome Airport Dufour and Mussolini were first and second in their category, while at Susa-Moncenisio Capelli, later to be one of the 8V's most successful conductors, was 33 seconds quicker than the best of the Lancias. This pattern was repeated in the Targa Abruzzo, Capelli's *Scuderia Ambrosiana* car averaging 61.5 m.p.h., with Minio and Mussolini in close attendance. As Rangoni's 'Balilla' was the best '1100' and both the 750 c.c. categories fell to *topolino*, this was a good day for FIAT.

Meanwhile a new team, Dante Giacosa and Franco Fessia, had been hard at work on a baby car that was to break entirely new ground, and establish the first real landmark in utility motoring since Sir Herbert Austin unveiled his first Seven in July, 1922.

'*La Topolino*' ('Mickey Mouse') buzzed his way into the picture on 7 April, 1936, and has never been out of it since. In nineteen years Turin alone were to turn out half a million, irrespective of production at Heilbronn (N.S.U.) or Nanterre (Simca). He was to become the pet of housewives and enthusiasts alike: among racing drivers in Britain who favoured the 500 were 'B. Bira', Charles Brackenbury, Earl Howe, Charles Martin, Dick Seaman and Rob Walker. He was raced to some purpose, notably at Le Mans, and earned his quota of international class records. Joe Lampton's mistress in *Room at the Top* drove a 500. In 1938 and 1939 the *topolino* was the United States's best-selling foreign import, with a total of 434 units. Danes called him *mariehone* (maybug), but to Britons he was always 'The Mouse', except when he succumbed to one of his more infuriating ailments! In middle age his chassis and suspension were the basis of the 500 c.c. Formula III, and as late as 1971 a small engineering works in Wiltshire was making fibreglass replicas of his rolltop convertible body for use in drag racing.

The secret of the 500's success was, of course, Fessia's insistence on a true big car in miniature, with no short cuts. He used a four-cylinder side-valve engine and not a 'twin': he gave his baby a proper four-speed synchromesh box and FIAT's superb hydraulic brakes. Above all, the *topolino* was a two-seater and no more, with room for two children or luggage on the unfurnished rear platform. Not for FIAT the errors perpetrated by Peugeot or Austin, whose infants grew heavier and more gutless with the years, Officially, the first four-seater 500 was the *giardinetta*, a station wagon introduced along with the 16 b.h.p. overhead-valve engine in 1948. The four-seater cabriolet of 1939 was produced exclusively for the British market.

The recipe was at once simple and sophisticated. The straight-forward chassis frame was liberally drilled to save weight, and the front wheels had transverse-leaf i.f.s., quarter-elliptics with torque arms being used at the rear. Brakes derived from the 1500 and the 'Balilla', and the engine was mounted over the front cross-member, with its radiator above and behind—this arrangement not only saved space, but dispensed with the need for an interior heater. The two-bearing engine had dimensions of 52×67 mm for a capacity of 569 c.c., and cooling was by thermo-syphon with fan assistance. The 12-volt coil ignition was a mixed blessing, for the tiny battery lived under a hatch in the rear compartment, and loose metallic articles had a knack of finding their way into violent contact with the ter-minals. Indeed, everything was so small that much of the accessibility conferred by the lift-off bonnet was theoretical! Output of the power unit was 13 b.h.p. at 4,000 r.p.m., and the four-speed gearbox had quite reasonable ratios, rendered possible by a modest weight of $10\frac{1}{2}$ cwt. Third was, however, on the low side at 8.64:1, and over-energetic pursuit of the ultimate (about 45 m.p.h.) in this ratio could lead to a broken crankshaft. Fuel was fed by gravity from a $4\frac{1}{2}$-gallon tank on the dash: a half-gallon reserve was controlled by a three-way tap in the cockpit.

The streamlined nose was a miniature replica of the 1500's front end, though the bonnet was of course far shorter and the combined head and side lamps lived out of doors. The body was a neat two-seater roll-top convertible (available also in fixed-head form): door handles were recessed, and the spare wheel was housed in the sloping tail panel. Direction indicators were an extra, albeit a desirable one—the sliding windows gave greater body width, but rendered hand signals a chore. By contrast there was sufficient legroom for six-footers, despite an overall length of a mere 10 ft 8½ in. The turning circle was a ridiculous 28 feet.

The 500 was a bargain. In 1936 Frenchmen and Italians paid less than £100, though by the outbreak of War it cost as much as £125 in its native land. The English price was £120 at a time when a *de luxe* Austin Seven retailed for £128 and the comparable Series I Morris Eight for £132.50. Only Ford of Dagenham's Model-Y undercut the FIAT, at £100 for a saloon.

The 500 had its weaknesses—cold-starting was one, the cure being an S.U. carburetter in place of the regulation Solex— but it could top the 50 mark, 41, 27 and 16 m.p.h. being safe maxima in the indirect gears. Acceleration, of course, took time, 13.3 seconds being needed to reach 30 (the Morris did it in 11.2 seconds and the Ford in 11.7). A minute's hard work was required to attain maximum speed, but there were the dual compensations of viceless handling (500s did not roll) and extreme frugality. Simca advertising spoke of *l'appetit d'un oiseau*, and the most brutal driving recorded 40–42 m.p.g. One English owner averaged 48 over 11,000 fast miles, and 50–55 was relatively easy. The extremes (obtained in officially-observed tests) are represented by 63.97 m.p.g. over 517 miles in 1939, and a fantastic run from Paris to Madrid on the eve of the Spanish Civil War, which combined an average speed of 26 m.p.h. with a consumption of 78 m.p.g. For a very small car the 500 was most flexible, *The Light Car* managing a

55. Theme and variations, or what happened to the 1500. Pininfarina's 1936 cabriolet merely blends his body to the existing sheet metal, with assistance from some fancy bonnet louvres.

(Carrozzeria Pininfarina)

56. By 1937 he has progressed to a 2 + 2 coupé featuring a vee-grille and four-headlamp clusters which would have looked modern 17 years later.

(Carrozzeria Pininfarina)

57. On his 1938 car (left) the effect is mock-Cord, the exposed lamps apart. Odd man out (**58.**) is FIAT's own 1500, of 1949, (above) but it's not difficult to see the origins of that grille.

(Carrozzeria Pininfarina: B. H. Vanderveen)

59. Thinking aloud in Turin: first series 8V coupé, 1952.

60. Thinking aloud in America: Nash's N.X.I. with FIAT 500 engine, built in 1950 to test customer reactions to a small car.

judder-free getaway in third, something I would never have essayed in my *topolino* days. Said *The Autocar*:

> About 45 m.p.h. is the normal speed on the open road, but it can be driven for miles at a stretch with the throttle pedal hard down and no sign of distress forthcoming. It is surprising and interesting to find how many other vehicles were overtaken by the little FIAT.

The Light Car revelled in gear-changes 'of the racing kind', and *Motor Sport* found that 'fifty can be held all day on suitable roads, and the FIAT corners so well that much time can be made up on winding roads that would not be possible on more conventional baby cars'. William Boddy, whose first reaction had been to treat the car as 'a joke, and not a very clever one at that', waxed enthusiastic:

> The design of the FIAT 500 is so eminently sensible that it was one of the best economy cars the World has ever seen. To enumerate, there are the hollowed-out doors to give elbow room, that radiator-behind-engine layout to achieve extreme accessibility and a low bonnet line: the simple, pullover hood which turns the virtually open body into a snug coupé: the big shelf behind the seats, which acts as luggage platform, a sofa for up to three children, or temporary seat for an adult: the clever i.f.s., that has been proved on far faster cars, and the compact dimensions and 4.00×15 tyres which spell lightweight.

These words, be it said, were penned in July, 1952, when 'W.B.' sampled one of those reconditioned pre-War examples that were still the only FIATs that Britons could buy. Even Mr Boddy, always a staunch opponent of inflation, could not cavil at the £250-odd asked for such cars. *La Vie Automobile*'s summary of the *topolino* was succinct—'*très refroidie, une excellente montagnarde*', while French roads encouraged frugality, for their test car turned in 56.5 m.p.g. at a steady 40.

Topolino-tweaking became an industry. Gordini was, as ever, the master, even though Simca would not let him develop his own o.h.v. conversion. In Italy SIATA marketed such a thing with 19 b.h.p. for £10, though more interesting was their first 'Amica', introduced early in 1939. This was the forerunner of a whole generation of post-War Abarths, Gianninis and Morettis. The car was cloaked with a vee-grille and a handsome little two-seater full cabriolet body resembling a scaled-down 508C by Viotti or Ghia. Victor Derbuel offered supercharged N.S.U. versions in Germany, and most of the British wizards had a go, among them Douglas Hawkes and John Eason Gibson. 60 m.p.h. and a standing quarter mile in 27.5 seconds could be achieved with normal aspiration, but 65–70 demanded a blower, and Arnott's conversion cut the FIAT's 0–50 m.p.h. time from over a minute to 33.6 seconds. In 1939 a garage in Purley offered the Smith SIATA Special, a coupé with the roof cut off and 21 b.h.p. o.h.v. engine. Reports spoke of 6,000 r.p.m.—a frightening thought, though an example tested by *The Motor* achieved 65 m.p.h. driven solo, as well as an easy restart under full load on a 1-in-4 gradient. Similar open bodies, albeit without the engine modifications, were offered by Devon Motors in Melbourne and by N.S.U., who displayed a species of B.M.W. 328 in miniature at the 1939 Berlin Show. Another style peculiar to Heilbronn was a wood-and-fabric version of the standard cabriolet, which looked dreadfully *ersatz*.

Along with the *topolino*-jokes came the *topolino*-exploits. My favourite one, as representing the nadir of masochism, was undertaken in Paris in the autumn of 1936 by MM Gauthier and Delaplace. They logged 50,000 kilometres in fifty days without once passing beyond the *octroi* limits, and making two half-hour stops in every twenty-four hours for driver changes and routine maintenance. An A.C.F. observer was always carried, and rush-hours were spent in the *grands boulevards*. 74,900 gear changes, 84,150 *débrayages* and 82,400 applications of the brakes later, the Simca ground to a final halt, having averaged 27 m.p.h. and 47 m.p.g. Beside this monumental exercise in patience the long-distance exploits of Gordini (who took seven international class records at 64-odd m.p.h. in 1937) or Cecchini (who did an hour at 86.02 m.p.h. in a linered-down 'streamliner' in 1938) pale into insignificance.

Not to be outdone, the British staged a two-lap scratch race for stock 500 coupés at Brooklands in April, 1938. Competitors included Arthur Baron, the Hon. Peter Aitken and Peter Clark. Commented *The Autocar*, with unholy glee:

Overjoyed enthusiasts at Brooklands had looked forward to this for weeks. Pieces of cheese on string had been prepared as bait, and there was talk of releasing a cat behind the runners at the start.

Despite some astronomic revs, and a great deal of 'bumping and boring', not a rod was thrown, not a 'Mouse' inverted itself, and everyone finished. The winner's average speed was 42.45 m.p.h. There were also 'mouse' classes at other British events, notably Poole Speed Trials.

By 1937 the *topolino* was a familiar sight in most European countries. French postmen drove them, and the little car's *chic* had won it *concours* awards at Aix-les-Bains, Deauville, La Baule, and Auteuil. English sales were running at sixty a week. 500s competed in the Monte Carlo and R.A.C. Rallies, as well as in Paris-Nice, in which Louis Coatalen's son Hervé won the 750 c.c. class. Thirty-two 'mice', some of them pretty little sports two-seaters with spatted rear wings, contested the two 750 c.c. categories of the Mille Miglia, the fastest one (Dusio/Bassadonna) averaging nearly 50 m.p.h. Viale drove a Simca version into 9th place in the *Bol d'Or*, and Le Mans, revived in 1937, saw Gordini's idea of a baby sports-racer, with friction dampers supplementing the standard hydraulics, a reinforced frame, downdraught carburation, and a body reminiscent of the successful 3½-litre Delahaye. Running weight was less than 900 lbs, which explains how *le sorcier* managed 75 m.p.h. on 18 b.h.p. Viale and Alin finished 17th and last, but their average speed was a creditable 52.09 m.p.h. In 1938 Horvilleur's speed in the *Bol d'Or* was 52.5 m.p.h. for twenty-four hours, and Aimé's 'stock' model was faster than a 750 c.c. Rémi-Danvignes. At Le Mans Aimé and Plantivaux added the Index of Performance to the score, while by 1939 the 'mice' were really moving, with Baracelli averaging 63.85 m.p.h. over the 980 miles of Tobruk-Tripoli, even if the Alins were not quite so fast on the Sarthe Circuit. For the curtailed Mille Miglia of 1940 the smallest FIATs appeared with new slab-sided bodies rather like those of early sports-racing Ferraris, as well as with the now-mandatory o.h.v., and speeds of 87 m.p.h. were recorded. Venturelli and Ceroni, the class winners, averaged 70.8 m.p.h.

The 500 helped FIAT to set a new production record of 54,931 cars in 1937, and work continued on the Mirafiori plant. Fears of war and fresh economic stringencies were soon to raise prices and lower sales, but exports remained strong. Italy shipped 22,175 private cars in 1939. At the time of her entry into World War II, 83,266 *topolino* had been made.

The design was right from the start, and few modifications were found necessary before 1948. Both brake drums and starter were enlarged in the early part of 1938, and '1939 models' sold in England had gear-type oil pumps in place of the original vane-type. In August 1938 the cars were given semi-elliptic rear suspension, an alteration which called for some reinforcement and lengthening of the frame. The four-seater cabriolets reached our shores in April, 1939. Their 5.1/1 back axles gave a laborious and noisy 52 m.p.h., though acceleration low down was unimpaired, and *The Motor* published a long feature on 'family motoring at 60 m.p.g.', achieved with a load of 34 stone. 45 m.p.g. was possible with more enterprising driving, and the list price was £133.50, or £8 more than the going price of *de luxe* two-seaters, which could now be had with bumpers and two-tone metallic paint. (Early imports had arrived at Wembley 'in the white', and had been farmed out to local body-shops for a 'quick spray'. This tended to be somewhat streaky!)

With the 500 established, the time was ripe to retire the 'Balilla'. Sales had dropped sharply in 1936, and only 8,152 were delivered in 1937, before the introduction of *Tipo* 508C, first of the world-famous *millecento* series. The name—which became official in 1940—was to survive in the company's catalogues for thirty-two years. The original 1937 formula persisted until the end of 1952, and the long-chassis vans survived for several years thereafter. Many people consider it the greatest FIAT of all time, though I have to confess to a personal bias in its favour, having covered 72,000 miles in a 1938 saloon between 1952 and 1957. One of Britain's most discriminating journalists, D. B. Tubbs, has written of his 508C: 'The steering was beautiful, the road-holding extremely good, the car was comfortable to ride, and did 30 to the gallon'.

In appearance the 508C resembled a cross between the 500 and the 1500. The four-door pillarless saloon body was a shorter and more upright edition of the 1500's, while the grille and exposed lamps suggested the *topolino*. The 1100, however, had a bows-down attitude whereas 500s tended to settle by the stern.

The 68 ×75 mm (1,089 c.c.) pushrod engine had much in common with the old sports 'Balilla' unit, apart from the use of an alloy head. Retained were the mechanical pump feed, downdraught carburetter, hand throttle, and manual advance-and-retard, while the inevitable combination of hydraulics and a transmission handbrake was another 'Balilla' heritage. The ratios of the FIAT synchromesh box were controlled by a long and willowy lever which felt less positive than the cranked one on the 1500, and the frame was a heavily-drilled cruciform affair, with coil-and-wishbone i.f.s. at the front and semi-elliptics at the rear. Power was transmitted *via* an open propeller shaft and fabric universals to a spiral bevel back end. The result was an engaging little saloon weighing 17½ cwt, and selling in Italy for 25,000 lire (about £250).The English price was a mere £198, or £10 more with *de luxe* equipment. By 1939 over 52,000 had been sold.

The car was streets ahead of 1937 practice, and could still hold its own in the early 'fifties. In terms of plain statistics, it would do 72 m.p.h. in top, 58 in third, 40 in second, and a rousing and noisy 24 in bottom (17.19 to 1). The 0–30 m.p.h. acceleration time was 7.5 seconds, 60 came up in 39.5 seconds, and under test conditions a gallon of petrol sufficed for 32 miles. Of the British opposition only the Vauxhall Ten and the M-series Morris could match its frugality, while none of these could attain, let alone hold, 70 m.p.h. The respected Austin 'Cambridge', indeed, was barely doing 50 by the time the FIAT rejected mile-a-minute speeds. The tough and lively Ford still had its agricultural transverse suspension, Standard and Hillman remained faithful to the unpredictable Bendix brakes, and the Vauxhall's brand of i.f.s. made the car curtsey-prone when the anchors were forcefully applied.

So much for performance. But performance was not all, and the FIAT represented effective and comfortable transport for four, provided one kept a weather eye on tyre pressures. The road-holding, while not quite as roll-free as the 500's, was excellent, though by British standards the noise level was inacceptable, and conversation ceased to be a pleasure above 55 m.p.h. The engine rocked on its flexible mountings, and the clutch, which *Motor Sport* termed 'fairly decisive', was on the rough side. Bottom gear coped with anything on which the wheels could get a grip, but a British family motorist would have found the FIAT lacking in flexibility. Austin Tens and Hillman 'Minxes' could be trickled along at an easy 10–12 m.p.h. in top, but skilled boot-craft was needed to keep the 508C moving at less than 20 without a downward change. None the less, good examples *cruised* at 70, and very mild tuning allowed of 80. Fuel consumption of my car was 30 in town, 36 m.p.g. on long runs, and as much as 44 with the economy techniques necessitated by the Suez Crisis of 1956. From the maintenance angle the front suspension was the early 1100's Achilles' Heel: it demanded regular greasing which one ignored at one's peril. Worse still, it could freeze in sub-zero weather, producing a ride comparable only to a lodging-house bedstead! The fabric universals seldom lasted more than 12,000 miles, but gave ample warning of impending demise, while even in 1938 journalists were finding the sharp cut-off of FIAT's dipped beam not to their liking—they still do, thirty-four years later. Let *The Motor* sum up:

Not many minutes pass before any driver of experience expresses his pleasure at the way the FIAT handles. It is a delight to drive, involves fairly liberal use of the gearbox to get the best performance, but is intriguing into the bargain.

Also in the 508C range were a *torpedo coloniale*, a special army version with angular bonnet, box back and right-hand steering, a semi-series cabriolet by Viotti, and a roll-top cabriolet-saloon in the German manner. During 1938 a long-chassis six-seater saloon was produced for cabmen and quiverful families. This *Tipo* 508L had a 9 ft wheelbase, in spite of which the turning circle was only 31 feet. On a 5.37:1 rear axle it could not match the standard model's performance, but surprisingly this long, narrow device was just as pleasant to drive. George Liston Young has said of his that it 'handles very well; the only thing you have to remember is that there is quite a lot of motor-car behind you. It is entirely viceless, and the cornering would be even better if there were a bit more power to drive you through'. The 508L was also made in van and lorry forms.

If the *topolino* had appealed to the tuners, the *millecento* was a natural. In England Hanover Motors offered saloons with belt-driven Arnott superchargers for £35 extra, for which fortunate owners got 80 m.p.h., an 0–30 m.p.h. acceleration time of 6.5 seconds, rather more noise and thirst, and, remarkably, the regular FIAT warranty; this in spite of Turin's known dislike of forced induction on touring engines. Tuson replaced his 'Balilla' (DPH 968) with a home-brew of his own, using a new 508C chassis to which he fitted a light racing shell and wire wheels. Gordini, now directly associated with Pigozzi's Simca firm, transferred the mechanical elements of the French-built 8CV to a lightweight chassis clothed in a frameless full-width two-seater body fabricated from alloy. Telescopic and friction dampers were provided, and on an 8:1 compression the engine gave 60–65 b.h.p. This recipe added up to a weight of 1,108 lbs, and in 1939 form speeds of 108 m.p.h. were recorded. FIAT themselves made a road-going coupé, the 508CMM, for which Savio built the body. This was the forerunner of the entire present-day generation of hardtop sports cars and *granturismi*: no wonder *The Motor* headed their road-test report: 'A 1950 model comes to town'. By Tuson or Gordini standards it was anything but light, at 16 cwt dry, and FIAT were content with such minor modifications as lead-bronze bearings and a raised compression which boosted output from 32 to 42 b.h.p. But once again adverse criticism was limited to the harsh exhaust note and to the lack of rearward vision through the divided back window. Low drag produced some astonishing results. 95 on top, 70 on third, and 50 on second were remarkable from a touring 1100 in 1939, but a consumption of 40 m.p.g. at a steady 60–70 m.p.h. was something to which pre-War journalists were unaccustomed. On the road it was an experience to be savoured, and on a level with such standouts as the 328 B.M.W. and the XK120 Jaguar.

> The gateway on the high bottom gear and the steady sweep up into the 70s and 80s is something almost unbelievable for an 1,100 c.c. car. At 50 m.p.h., where most cars of this size are beginning to struggle, it is just getting nicely into its stride, and the steady increase of speed from 60 to 80 m.p.h. is something to excite even the most blasé critics.

Alas! Britons never got their hands on this *avant-garde* gem, though the 1940 list price (£375) was announced. Italians paid 295,000 lire, or just under £300, and immediately before the War an open version, which looked horribly like the infamous TB14 Alvis of 1948, turned up at the Grossglöckner hill-climb. KMG 365, Wembley's demonstrator, was sold to Colonel Moore-Brabazon (Lord Brabazon of Tara), and a couple of years later the nation was treated to the spectacle of a Minister of the Crown going about his lawful occasions in a vehicle of 'enemy origin'. Britons, characteristically, were not shocked: they were merely envious.

1938 opened promisingly when Gordini won Paris-Nice outright in one of his competition Simcas, carrying ballast in lieu of a passenger: one wonders, in passing, whether the car was 'a genuine standard catalogued chassis' as enjoined by the rules! Da Costa's tuned 508C saloon annexed the 1,100 c.c. class at Vila Real in Portugal, and Gordini had no trouble at all

61. *Topolino* replacement. Steyr-Puch's version of the *Nuova* 500, 1959.

Steyr-Daimler-Puch A.G.

62. Ergonomic cab – or what could be done on 633 c.c. A fleet of Multiplas' in service in Watford, 1960.

(Woolf, Laing, Christie and Partners)

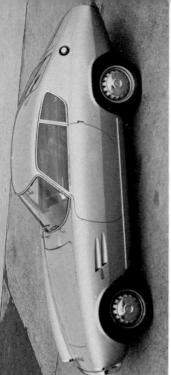

Shapes of the Sixties. **63.** The 2300S of 1962 was a Ghia design adopted for production by FIAT.

(FIAT)

64. Also from Ghia came the 1500/GT of 1963, a more sophisticated shape based on the mechanics of the 1500 cabriolet.

(National Motor Museum)

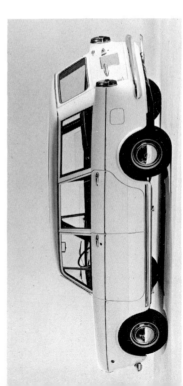

65. Typical of FIAT's own styling were the 1966 1100R station wagon (bottom left), last of a line dating back to 1953, and

(66) the uncompromisingly angular 1300 (**66**, bottom right) here seen in 1960 on pre-production trials in the Arctic Circle.

(FIAT)

in the *Bol d'Or*, winning outright at 63.38 m.p.h. from de Burnay's K3 M.G. and Polledry's Aston Martin. At Le Mans he fielded four entries: two of these were the new aerodynamic Simca-8s (Gordini/Scaron and Vernet/Breillet), while Molinari and Levy drove the 995 c.c. cars in 1937 trim. Scaron crashed *le sorcier*'s car, and Molinari charged a wall of sandbags, but the privately-entered Simcas of Debille/Lapchin and Camerano/Robert finished 9th and 11th respectively. If Le Mans was inauspicious, Spa was little short of a farce, all the competitors staging a sit-down strike on the last lap. But the Gordini/Scaron car won its class at 61.44 m.p.h., as well as going much faster than the Lancia 'Aprilias' which collected the 1½-litre honours. The *millecento* was succeeding where the *mille cinque* had failed.

Both Gordini and Tuson supported the T.T., Gordini himself and Breillet being down to drive the French 1100s, while A. P. Hamilton handled the British car. The Gordinis were shipped over from Calais overnight, arriving at Donington Park ten minutes after the end of the statutory practice period. Somehow *le sorcier* talked his way out of this one, and his cars were on the line a couple of hours later, though not before they had been forced to take on 110 lbs of ballast to bring their weight up to the permitted minimum of 1000 kilograms in running trim.

Once again, the results were disappointing. At the start the FIATs shot away from the now aged Singers, and at the end of the first hour Gordini led his class. Then his brakes became red-hot, and the pull-off springs fell into the drums with curious and expensive results. Even Gordini decided to give up after a spectacular spin which brought him slap into the path of 'Bira's' B.M.W. The rear brakes on the Tuson FIAT failed. Breillet carried on, discarding his goggles in the wet, but he was unwell, and his driving lacked the panache of Gordini's. Maybe it was his caution that gave Simca their class win. The season closed with another class victory for Molinari/Alin in the Twelve Hours of Paris at Montlhéry, but in far-away Brazil older FIATs were still making themselves felt. Landi's

'3½-litre' (possibly a rebuilt 525) was seventh in the Rio de Janeiro Grand Prix at Gavea, thus bringing to a close a distinguished run of performances. Caru had won the 1935 race, and had finished second in 1936, despite the presence of Pintacuda and Marinoni in a brace of Mille Miglia-type Alfa Romeo two-seaters.

Both Simcas and FIATs were out again in 1939, the Gordini/ Scaron partnership bringing a standard Simca-8 into 13th place in the Monte Carlo Rally, while the new Italian 508CMMs showed their form in the Tobruk-Tripoli marathon. Rossi collected his class at 74.49 m.p.h., a speed which compared interestingly with the 87.86 m.p.h. of the winning 2½-litre Alfa Romeo, and even more interestingly with the sedate 71.5 m.p.h. of the fastest 'Aprilia'. Gordini and Scaron had an improved streamliner for Le Mans, backed by Breillet and Anne Itier on the 1938 cars. Breillet inverted his Simca at Arnage, fortunately without serious damage to himself; the car was driven away by Gordini's mechanics. *Le sorcier*, however, was in cracking form, lapping at 80 m.p.h. and taking the Rudge-Whitworth Cup (and tenth overall) at 74.7 m.p.h. He also won the *Coupe de la Commission Sportive* from Brunot's 1½-litre Riley, but in the last few weeks of peace the leading FIAT exponent was no Italian on a *millecento* derivative, but an Englishman with a 29-year-old, Anthony Heal on his ex-Brooklands S61. In August he set a new Veteran Car record of 54.89 seconds at Prescott, following this with a brisk 23.52 seconds at Lewes, 'in a cloud of oil haze, so fast that the rubber dust on the road almost caught fire'. Two days before Britain went to War, he scored another win at Prescott, though drenching rain slowed the big FIAT to 62.3 seconds.

The 500, 1100 and 1500 covered most European requirements, but a general provider can never afford serious gaps in his range, and FIAT still lacked a replacement for the 527, not to mention a competitor for '8 h.p.' models like the roomy two-stroke D.K.W., Renault's new 'Juvaquatre', and the improved British Morrises and Standards. The first gap was plugged at the 1938 Paris Salon, with the 2800, a short-stroke

82 × 90 mm o.h.v. 'six' based on the 1500, though its cruciform-braced frame derived from the 508C. The four-speed box had a synchromesh second gear, and in addition to the headlamp flasher the new FIAT had self-cancelling direction indicators, which the smaller types lacked. No attempt was made to attract owner-drivers: the 2800 was a bulky affair on a 10 ft 6 in wheelbase which turned the scales at 41 cwt. Also new was the vee-grille, and Pininfarina made a few handsome 'parade cabriolets', a style beloved of totalitarian rulers. Of the 620 cars delivered between 1938 and 1944, the majority were short (9 ft 10 in) wheelbase 'Mil Cols' wearing tourer bodies as fitted to the Italian Army's 'colonial' 6C-2500 Alfa Romeo.

The second gap never was filled, though a small four-seater roll-top convertible not unlike a Renault 'Juvaquatre' in appearance was demonstrated to Mussolini when he opened Mirafiori in 1939. It had a 700 c.c. o.h.v. four-cylinder engine, and development was shelved when Italy entered the War a year later. It seems, though, that the design was finalised, and Dr Costantino of the *Centro Storico* recalls working on 700 plans in the Corso Dante drawing-office in 1939.

In the realm of exports, the major success story was Pigozzi's Simca firm, even if it was still a long way from challenging France's Big Three. The Simca-Cinq was an immediate success at 9,900 fr—the cheapest car on the French market. The Simca-8 (508C) took rather longer to establish itself, and did not appear in quantity until late in 1938. The French range included a pretty two-seater fixed-head coupé, and by June, 1939, Simca production reached its pre-War peak of two thousand a month. In Germany the 500 disappeared at the outbreak of War, but Heilbronn continued to deliver 1100s and 1500s in modest numbers until 1941. At the last pre-War Berlin Show, incidentally, the *topolino* actually undercut the bargain-basement Opel 'Kadett' by RM-15 (£1), though at RM-1,780 it could not approach the unrealistic 990 *reichsmarks* at which Hitler's new Volkswagen was being promoted. (It never did: in 1950, when Heilbronn started to make 500Cs once more, they charged DM-4,900 as against the DM-4,800 of the cheapest Beetle). Swedes found the 508C very much to their liking, though supplies dried up in 1940: the asking price was a competitive Kr-4,300, even if the small 2¼-litre Ford V8 could still be bought for less than Kr-5,000. In Switzerland, FIAT was once again 1939's best-seller, with 1,199 units sold by comparison with 1,160 Opels, 663 Peugeots, and 638 Fords.

Commercial-vehicle design took a further step forward with a modern range of forward-control diesels with five-speed gearboxes and compressed-air brakes. The 626N had a 5¾-litre six-cylinder engine and carried a payload of three tons, while the heavy-duty 666N had a 9.4-litre unit, which was also used for 4×4 and 6×6 army trucks on similar lines. In 1944 the company experimented with half-track troop-carriers of the type favoured by the *Wehrmacht*, but their 727, unlike Breda's rival model, did not progress beyond the prototype stage.

Italy did not enter World War II until May, 1940, and in the early War years private-car production continued at a fairly high level—23,502 in 1940, 13,799 in 1941, and 11,236 in 1942. 1940 versions of the 1100 and 1500 featured vee-grilles, while Count Lurani, though reduced to running his 1500 *berlina* on methane, was laying plans for a new *topolino*-based record machine to replace his 500 c.c. Guzzi-engined 'Nibbio'. There was also a final pre-War Mille Miglia, the thirteenth in the series, run over an abbreviated circuit (Brescia-Cremona-Mantua-Brescia). This was memorable for a German victory, by Hanstein's Superleggera-bodied 328 B.M.W. It was also memorable for the dramatic showing of the sports FIAT 1100s, now with long streamlined tails and wire wheels. As always they proved more than a match for the Lancias, even though the 'Aprilia' engine had been enlarged from 1,352 c.c. to 1,486 c.c. The fastest FIAT (Fioruzzi/Sola) set a record lap at 86.49 m.p.h. —on public roads, and allegedly on a mere 50 b.h.p., while the class-winning car averaged 82.47 m.p.h. A streamlined '500' won the 750 c.c. class at 70.8 m.p.h., its o.h.v. head giving it a maximum of 87 m.p.h.

Most interesting of all the entries were, however, a brace of 1½-litre straight-eight *Tipo*-815 Ferraris built in the Commendatore's garage at Modena, and driven by Alberto Ascari and the Marchese Rangoni-Machiavelli. Purists do not recognise these are true Ferraris, but it is even less correct to dismiss them as FIAT Specials. Indeed, these Massimino designs did not, as has often been stated, use FIAT 1100 blocks. Chassis frames, suspensions, gearboxes, differentials, steering-boxes and cylinder heads were authentic FIAT, but the blocks were cast in Modena by Calzoni, and the Ferraris raced with single Marelli distributors in place of the dual FIAT installation previously tried. One may suspect that FIAT components were used mainly in order to qualify for the prizes offered by Giovanni Agnelli to class-winning FIAT owners. The 815s showed great promise, but Ascari retired on the second lap with a rocker arm failure, while on the penultimate circuit Rangoni's timing chain broke. Though in the early 1950s Enzo Ferrari was still buying components from FIAT—unkind rumours linked frequent transmission failures with the unwise use of 1400 gearboxes!—his path and FIAT's were not to cross again officially until 1968.

The aircraft division continued to develop the G.50 monoplane fighter with retractable undercarriage and 840 h.p. A74 radial engine, of which 1,000-odd were made by the parent company and by C.M.A.S.A. at Marina di Pisa. The G.50's two-gun armament was no match for its British opponents, and its performance was inferior to that of the similarly powered Macchi MC200, also ordered by the Air Ministry. Other new Service models of the period were the RS14, a twin-engined torpedo seaplane with sleek lines which was later to serve with Marshal Badoglio's Co-Belligerent Air Force, and the CR25, a reconnaissance-bomber landplane on similar lines which was used in very small numbers.

Early in 1939, however, Rosatelli had brought out the last of his classic biplane fighters, the immortal CR42 'Freccia'. Of this Gianni Cattaneo has written: 'It was perhaps the best biplane in service anywhere, and it was well able to give a good account of itself against faster aircraft. Characterised by superb manoeuvrability, it combined all the qualities dear to the heart of the Italian pilot'. On the prototype there was the odd combination of a fixed oleo-pneumatic main undercarriage and a rectractable tailwheel, but the latter feature was abandoned on production aircraft. Neither armament (two fixed synchronised machine-guns firing through the airscrew) nor equipment (no radio was provided) were up to the standards of the 1940s, but the 'Freccia' was capable of 274 m.p.h., and could outfly and outfight the Gloster 'Gladiator', last of Britain's biplanes. FIAT planned to instal a Daimler-Benz DB601 liquid-cooled engine, which would have boosted speed to 320 m.p.h., but this version was never made. 'Freccias' served on all the Regia Aeronautica's fronts, and well over 1,500 were produced, including 72 sold to Sweden during the War. One of the East African squadrons made history when its aircraft were transported over hostile territory inside the fuselages of Savoia-Marchetti SM82 transports. In 1940 FIAT built the first of their G12 three-engined airliners, destined to be the mainstay of Italian services in the immediate post-War years, as well as joining Alfa Romeo in the manufacture of the Daimler-Benz inverted-vee aero-engine. This was adapted to all Italy's front-line monoplane fighters—the G.50, the MC200, and the Caproni-Reggiane Re2000. FIAT's version, the G.55, went into production in 1943, but was never made in large numbers.

But the clock was running down for Italy. The Piedmontese are rebels by nature, and FIAT workers had set the troubles of 1920 in train with the famous 'clock strike' against daylight saving. On 5 March, 1943, Lingotto and Mirafiori came out once more, 'for bread, peace and freedom'. After Badoglio's capitulation in September, of course, the Germans were in effective control of the North. Nazi reactions were immediate and predictable, in the form of a threat to transfer the FIAT works to the Fatherland. The threat was never implemented.

Giovanni Agnelli was an old man. He had lost both his two children—his daughter Tina died young in 1928, and his son Edoardo was killed in an air crash in 1935. Lingotto had not been neglected by the Allied Air Forces, and the test-track on the roof was peppered with holes. Italy was bankrupt, and facing defeat, not to mention schism between those who joined the Allies or the Partisans, and those who stayed with Mussolini to the bitter end. But though the founder lived to see peace restored, he died on 29 December, 1945, before the work of reconstruction could get under way.

10 Blossoming of the Wonder-flower

The output of FIAT during the year 1954 is represented by total invoices amounting to 275 billion lire, 30 more than in 1953, up 14.
The production of automobiles . . . increased in 1954 to 195,098 units, an increase of 34,500 against 1953, and represents 88 per cent of total sales.
These two data have been placed in evidence at the very beginning—total sales and autovehicle production—because they represent record figures which make people stop and consider the efforts, the ways and means which enabled FIAT to raise from the ashes of war to the present condition between 1946 and to-day. We think we are presently stabilised, but also full of vitality.

Report of the FIAT Directors, 29 April, 1955.

The English may be a little picturesque, but there is no mistaking the underlying jubilation in the report which Vittorio Valletta and his directors submitted to the shareholders after almost ten years of peace. With but one brief recession, in 1952, FIAT had grown steadily since 1945. Production had passed the six-figure mark in 1950, and 1953 had seen the first 150,000 year. In 1955 the new rear-engined 600 was to boost private-car deliveries to a new high of 232,000 units.

A defeated Italy had faced a dark and uncertain future in 1945. Two months after VE-Day, it is true, both FIAT and Lancia were back in production, but the latter was making only light lorries, and tyres were virtually unobtainable. *Topolino* were running about Rome on 'Spitfire' wheels, and even in 1947 seventy per cent of the Eternal City's 'buses were immobilised for lack of rubber, a state of affairs which manifested itself in unofficial services run by private individuals with an extraordinary assortment of vehicles—521s, 525s, straight-frame *Tipo Dues* dating back to 1916, and even *granturismo* 1,750 c.c. Alfa Romeos. New car prices were terrifying: a *topolino* listed at £125 in 1939 was now offered at £320, and the black market figure was no less than £1,125, with £2,375 being asked for a 1500. Officially there was no petrol for private cars till well into 1947, and steel was not freed until 1948: in the meantime manufacturers made do with what was going, which could mean surplus air-raid shelters. Italy had hoped to produce 30,000 private cars in 1946, and that June FIAT delivered 531, Lancia 134, and Alfa Romeo 9; but when the year drew to its close less than 11,000 had been made all told.

Italy was in a chaotic state. For one thing, a quarter of a century had passed since the last general election, and countless parties were battling for the nation's soul. On the far Right were the neo-Fascists of the M.S.I.: in the centre were Alcide de Gasperi's *democristiani*: and the Left was complicated by two brands of socialism—Pietro Nenni's P.S.I., which supported Palmiro Togliatti and the Communists, and Giuseppe Saragat's P.S.D.I., which did not, Togliatti himself campaigned under the figurehead of the great liberator, Giuseppe Garibaldi, a personality as far removed from Communism as the Afrikaners of Pretoria are from Mao-Tse-Tung, America was prepared to inject financial aid on a vast scale; but first Italy must decide her political destiny. She did, in April, 1948, when de Gasperi's centre-right group scored a resounding victory over the Communists and their allies. Thereafter Marshall Aid moved in. Import quotas were abolished in 1949, and though real prosperity did not reach the Italian working-class until the massive wage revisions of 1962, the far Left thenceforward fought a losing battle. The Communist unions lost control of FIAT for good in 1955. Between 1947 and 1948 Italian motor vehicle production all but doubled, rising from 25,375 to 44,221, with exports increased by 18.6 per cent. It was even hinted that the rate of growth could embarrass, and that Italian factories would be over-producing by 1951. In fact they were, but not for the reason anticipated by the economists.

By 1950 it was clear that Western Germany was recovering much too fast for anyone's comfort. A year later Belgium took 14,364 German cars, and only 1,100 from Italy, an awful warning of the recession that struck in 1952. Not only was the Italian discouraged from buying a car by the high price of petrol (at least twice English levels), and by a fiscal system which pegged the annual tax on a *millecento* at £70-odd. In addition his Government imposed levies on raw materials at each stage of their production, and by the time a car left the works these levies had inflated its price by some 35 per cent. Worse still, Rome, unlike Westminster, made no concessions to exporters, so that a customer in Stockholm or Sydney had to pay extra for the privilege of buying Italian. In 1951 only 22.9 per cent of Italy's new cars went abroad.

And increasingly the Italian motor industry spelt FIAT. Bianchi had abdicated into trucks and motorcycles, Isotta Fraschini's planned renaissance had fizzled ignominiously, and Alfa Romeo were not to become a major force until 1951, with the advent of the semi-mass-produced 1900. Lancia was good for perhaps 5,000 cars a year, and the new specialist makers, such as Ferrari and Maserati, manufactured in penny numbers until the 1960s. All but a thousand of the 25,000 Italian cars made in the first six months of 1948 were FIATs.

Neither Agnelli nor Valletta had approved of the War. Opel, Daimler-Benz, Morris and Vauxhall were proud of their war records: not so FIAT, who had continued to fulfil British and French contracts until Mussolini went to war, and whose subsequent record had been one of 'calculated inefficiency'. The strike of March, 1943, was only the first of a long series that was to interfere grievously with the Axis war effort. In 1945 alone the Nazis lost eight million man-hours through stoppages in the company's factories.

Actual damage had been less than catastrophic. True, not a

few workers had been deported to Germany and put to work for Hanomag in Hanover. Though Lingotto had been almost gutted, Mirafiori had escaped serious bombing, and a few lorries were already trickling off the lines in June, 1945. The worst disaster was the removal of Valletta, whom the Allied Military Government suspected of Fascist sympathies, but fortunately for all concerned he was safely back at the helm by the spring of 1946.

In the dark months while Italy hovered between Left and Right, Valletta showed his mettle. His policy, as he told Gabrielli when that great engineer assumed control of the *sezione aeronautica*, was 'to regain our former ascendancy, to re-establish the prestige of Italian technology, and to safeguard the jobs of our skilled labour force'. Before the days of Marshall Aid, he was off to the United States, securing loans for repayment in five, six, or even ten years. Marshall Aid itself furnished another $14 million for machine tools and other vital equipment, and one cynic estimated that FIAT alone received more U.S. assistance than either Greece or Turkey. In September, 1949, an order for £250,000 worth of tooling presaged FIAT's first new model since 1938, the 1400. Valletta's faith was rewarded; FIAT made 70,800 cars in 1949, 108,700 in 1950, and 120,000 in 1951. By 1954 his company had a payroll of 71,300, was paying over 69 billion lire annually in wages and salaries, producing 35,000 tons of steel a year, and exporting over 40,000 cars. Admittedly strikes had deprived FIAT of 277,000 man-hours in that year alone, but only 19,000 of these had been lost between July and December. Valletta had created his own monument.

For the present, empire-building ceased, though the Weber carburetter concern was absorbed in 1945. Nor were there any new models, the 500, 1100, and 1500 being reinstated in 1940 guise, joined in 1947 by a revised 508CMM, the 1100S, still Savio-bodied, but with a waterfall grille. With the aid of two Weber downdraught carburetters output was increased to 51 b.h.p. at 5,200 r.p.m., giving a maximum speed of 93 m.p.h. A price of 2,150,000 lire (£1,075) explains why only 401 were made, but it was an excellent little car, energetically raced by private owners. The S-types showed their form in the first stages of the 1947 Mille Miglia, Gilera averaging 83.1 m.p.h. as far as Padua, though he and his fellow-competitors were eventually swamped by the new FIAT-based Cisitalias. In August Auricchio, a wealthy cheese-manufacturer, won the Pescara race from Cortese on one of the first V-12 Ferraris, the 1948 Mille Miglia saw a victory for the 2-litre Ferrari of Biondetti/Navone, but the next three places went to 1100 FIATs, the tubular-framed 'special' of Comirato/Dumas beating a brace of S-models. The FIAT coupés also dominated their class at Spa, and 1949 was an excellent year. The FIATs beat the Cisitalias in the Targa Florio, the Mille Miglia, the Coppa Inter-Europa at Monza, and once again in the Belgian 24 Hours, where Brambilla and Bassi took their class at 70.9 m.p.h. from a sister car. They were, incidentally, faster than Britain's new lightweight $1\frac{1}{2}$-litre H.R.G.S.

Slightly improved 1100s and 1500s came out in 1948, while the *topolino* was brought up to date with a 16.5 b.h.p. pushrod engine. At the same time a torsion bar was incorporated in the rear suspension, and though the fuel tank remained on the dash, it now fed the carburetter by mechanical pump. A wood-framed 500B station wagon tested by *The Motor* in 1949 proved capable of 56 m.p.h., taking a good second less to reach 30 m.p.h. than had the side-valve four-seater cabriolet of ten years previously.

FIAT now covered 90–95 per cent of the Italian market with three basic models, and the specialist coachbuilders took their cue. Out of a lack of variety there sprang a brilliant industry dominated by such names as Pininfarina, Bertone, Castagna, Ghia, Vignale, and Zagato. As yet they tended to cloak standard FIAT chassis in their own creations, but with the advent of unitary construction in 1950 they started to work on special 'platforms' furnished by the factory—whence they progressed ultimately to the purchase of basic mechanical elements (engine, gearbox, and suspension units), and the end-product became a make in its own right. Sometimes they anticipated FIAT practice; steering-column change, first seen officially on the 1100E and 1500E late in 1949, appeared on a Monviso-bodied car at

Geneva in 1948. Sometimes they achieved an astonishing purity of line, as witness Pininfarina's 1946 Cisitalia coupé and his later, 1954 version of the 1100TV FIAT. Sometimes they perpetrated appalling extravaganzas such as Ghia's 1948 1500 two-door saloon—the grille was pure Buick, and all four wheels were spatted! Their thinking was advanced: Zagato used roof-doors in 1947, and a perspex roof in 1948. Castagna revived the pre-War French 'Vutotal' idiom , dispensing with screen pillars altogether on his 1950 1100 cabriolet, and tail fins, an American fad of 1958, were seen on a hideous two-door 1400 saloon by Ghia seven years earlier. Prices were high, and outputs small. In 1947 Italians paid only £625 for an 1100 saloon, but the same car with drophead coupé coachwork by Stabilimenti Farina cost a resounding £1,200. This inflation was to lead to greater restraint by the early 1950s. As one commentator observed: 'If a client is going to pay two million lire or more for a body, he wants an assurance that it will not be rendered unfashionable in a few months'. Unitary construction did not mean that the coachbuilders were forgotten. When the first 1400s were shown at Geneva in March, 1950, the stands of Balbo, Farina, Francis Lombardi, Ghia, Vignale and Viotti contained their ideas of how the latest FIAT should look. In addition there was SIATA's 'Daina' cabriolet, which was rather more than a 1400.

SIATA represented another class of FIAT-improver—those who acquired only the mechanics, and made sports cars of them. Some, like Nardi, Stanguellini, and the young house of Abarth, were mainly interested in competitions. Piero Dusio of Cisitalia had an exciting but unprofitable foot in both camps. By 1948 he was $87,000 in the red, and retired to Argentina, there to pursue the development of an abortive four-wheel Grand Prix car conceived by Ferry Porsche and his father. SIATA progressed steadily towards the role of manufacturers. In 1948 they were busily improving the pushrod 'Mouse' (which they had invented in 1937!) extracting fearsome outputs with the aid of roller-bearing crankshafts, and wedding *topolino* engines and suspensions to their own lightweight tubular frames, but a

year later they launched a new 'Amica' cabriolet in the fashionable slab-sided idiom, complete with steering-column change
and rear tank. It cost the equivalent of £700. The uninspired
1400 became a thing of beauty when cloaked with a body which
anticipated Alvis's Graber convertible. It was also a 90 m.p.h.
motor-car with the refinement of a five-speed gearbox. Subsequently they dressed it up to look like a 'TD' M.G. (the
'*Rallye*') or a Ferrari '*barchetta*' (*Tipo 'Gran Sport'*). Their
sports 1100s with Stanguellini camshafts and manifolding by
Abarth were quite effective, and in 1954 the American driver
John Bentley had an excellent season with such a car. He
summed it up as 'a simple, conventional, attractive machine of
modest weight and fairly brisk performance, responsive, tractable, and viceless, yet because of its enormous margin of
mechanical strength, eminently suited to racing'. In the early
post-War years Testa d'Oro, SIATA's erstwhile rivals in the field
of *topolino*-tweaking, sponsored some intriguing 500 specials.
These featured engines set well back in their frames, frontal
radiators, and 'stroked' 700 c.c. engines with alloy heads in
place of the bronze type hitherto used on their conversions.
They were seldom seen after 1949.

The Cisitalia was significant because it sought to be a poor
man's racer selling at around the £1,000 mark. The D46 of
1946 used a *millecento* engine with magneto ignition, developing
60 b.h.p. on a 9.5:1 compression, but the rest of the vehicle
was designed along aircraft lines, and consisted of a steel-
tube space-frame to which the light-alloy panels of the single-
seater body were attached. The fifteen-inch wheels were also
fabricated from light alloy, and the front ones were independ-
ently sprung by articulated arms concealed behind streamlined
fairings, with independent coils at the rear. Brakes were
hydraulic, and the gearbox was most ingenious. There were
only three forward speeds; first and reverse were selected by a
column-mounted lever, and the two upper ratios were obtained
by depressing the clutch pedal. Later cars had a conventional
four-speed affair. Final drive was by hypoid bevel, and on a
3.6:1 back axle 108 m.p.h. were claimed. *The Motor* was

unenthusiastic, admiring the car's engineering rather than its practical virtues. 'The one disappointing feature', said their contributor, 'was the almost complete lack of real power in the racing driver's meaning of the phrase, which meant that the exit from corners was completely lacking in that kick in the back or smooth surge which one expects'. The Cisitalia was at its best on short, twisting circuits like the Baths of Caracalla in Rome, or the Isle of Man, where Frank Kennington took second place in the 1949 Manx Cup.

A batch of twenty was laid down in 1946, and the Cisitalias were first seen in that year's Coppa Brezzi at Turin, where they were matched against Amedée Gordini's new 1,100 c.c. *monoposto* Simcas, now with Gordini-built chassis and his classic suspension, by independent coils at the front, and torsion bars at the rear. The Italians won the first round, Dusio himself taking first place at 64 m.p.h., from Cortese, Chiron and Sommer. The second round, at Forez, went to Simca, but throughout 1947 the battle raged strongly, Simca winning at Nîmes, Rheims, and Lausanne: on this last occasion Jean-Pierre Wimille was actually second in the 1,500 c.c. race, almost matching the speed of Luigi Villoresi's supercharged 4CLT Maserati. Simca also scored two more second places in Grands Prix proper, at Albi and Nice.

Dusio then attempted a one-make racing circus, with all-Cisitalia events featuring top Italian drivers. It proved an awful flop. The first and only race was run in Egypt at Cairo in March, 1947, with King Farouk acting as starter. Spectators were poorly catered for, in spite of paying £3 a seat. The crowd was thin, and not a few people felt (erroneously, as it turned out) that Franco Cortese's victory was rigged. Dusio allegedly lost 'several thousand of pounds', and repeats scheduled for Heliopolis and Alexandria were hurriedly cancelled. By 1948 Cisitalia finances were so shaky that their only major win was in the Prix de Berne, where Taruffi, Hans Stuck, and Macchieraldo finished 1–2–3 with 'Bira's' Simca trailing in fourth place. Subsequent Cisitalia successes were gained mainly by the sports cars.

These were also built up round multi-tubular frames and tuned FIAT 1100 engines, with transverse i.f.s. and quarter elliptics at the rear. Gear ratios were higher than those of the factory's 1100S, at 3.9, 5.2, 7.8, and 12.5 to 1, and on a compression ratio of 7.22:1 the competition coupés were said to have 65 b.h.p. under their bonnets, sufficient to propel them faster than the single-seaters. They cost more than the FIAT, at £1,250, but Pininfarina's uncluttered road-going model with its neat grille was one of the prettiest things of its era, and Cisitalia's second, third and fourth places in the 1947 Mille Miglia marked an auspicious start. 1948 saw class wins at Mantua and in Switzerland's Rheineck-Walzenhausen hill-climb, while Taruffi was second in the Targa Florio, behind Biondetti's Ferrari. After the South American *débacle* Dusio set up shop once more in Turin in 1951, trying his luck briefly with a clumsy-looking coupé powered by a 2.8-litre B.P.M. marine engine, before returning in 1954 to his old love. This time his '*Volo Radente*' had a fastback coupé body by Monviso mounted on a special cruciform-braced frame. The 1100-103 engine developed 68 b.h.p. with the aid of an 8.7:1 compression and oversize valves, and buyers had the choice of four or five speeds with floor or column change. It was said to do 105 m.p.h., but it never achieved the fame of Dusio's earlier creations. Though Cisitalia struggled on until 1964, making some handsome coupé and convertible versions of the rear-engined 600, they never rated more than a line or two in Turin Show reports.

By contrast Amedée Gordini went from strength to strength. True, Simca, his backers, still insisted on the inclusion of too many stock parts, vetoing such exciting projects as a vee-eight in 1948, and a V-12 in 1951. This policy eventually convinced *le sorcier* that he was better on his own, and from 1952 to 1957 he fought a losing battle against inadequate funds, until Renault persuaded him to give up and tune their engines instead. But while the going was good, it was very good indeed, and by the end of the 1940s his 1,221 c.c. Simca-based units were as fast as the full-house 1,500s, if seldom as reliable. They excelled, like the Cisitalias, on tortuous courses like the *Circuit des Ramparts* at Angoulême, which the *marque* won in 1948 and 1949. The sports cars won three *Bols d'Or* in succession: in 1947 the victor was Cayla, Gordini's bookkeeper, after the *monoposti* of Trintignant and Fièbvre (with jury-rigged central headlamps for night racing!) had retired, in 1948 Scaron won at 53.46 m.p.h., and in 1949 Manzon's 1100 was the outright winner, though Simcas also annexed every available class. In addition to Angoulême and the *Bol*, 1949's score included victories at Marseilles (for a still unknown Juan Manuel Fangio), Lausanne and Madrid, plus seconds at Aix-les-Bains and Comminges. In Czechoslovakia Zdenek Treybal won the national sports-car race at 69.33 m.p.h., from Sojka's rear-engined Tatraplan and Dobry's 2-litre Le Mans Frazer Nash.

Of course these latter-day racers with their hemispherical combustion chambers and five-bearing crankshafts were several times removed from anything in the catalogues of Nanterre or Turin. In 1950 Britons were allowed to inspect a sports-racer on the Simca stand at Earls Court: this had a twin-carburetter 1,491 c.c. engine of 'square' (78 × 78 mm) dimensions, a five-speed gearbox, and the usual Gordini suspension. The slab-sided light alloy body had central steering, and on a weight of $11\frac{3}{4}$ cwt it was said to do 136 m.p.h.

Much closer in concept to FIATs were the first 500 c.c. For-mula III cars built in Britain for that brand of 'poor man's racing' in 1946. The first successful example, that of Colin Strang, used a boxed-in *topolino* frame and suspension units, and Cooper started by cutting two chassis in half and joining them back to back, though later examples of this most successful 500 had no FIAT content. Among the other pioneers the Aikens, Cowlan, Cutler, Monaco, Parker, Smith and Spink drew on FIAT components, as did other early examples of the breed concocted in Belgium, France and Switzerland. A few makers, like Giaur in Italy, attempted to race linered-down editions of the 500 B/C unit, but their power-to-weight ratio never matched that of the air-cooled motorcycle engines favoured by Britons, and by 1951 Formula III was a British preserve, Italy's best showing being a solitary second place. Two years later the Italians set up a 750 c.c. formula of their own, with FIAT-based cars by such firms as Stanguellini, but once again they were in for a shock. In 1954 Stuart Lewis-Evans took a 500 c.c. Cooper to Italy, and beat the Giaurs and Stanguellinis comfortably at Castello di Teramo, and again at Senigallia. The FIAT-special brigade had to bide their time until the creation of Formula Junior in 1958.

There were countless other 'specials'. In Holland Maurice Gatsonides built and raced a flatiron sports car less than three feet high, using a tuned six-cylinder 1500 engine, while a glance at the 1951 season, when the 1100S was obsolescent and the 8V still under test, shows a curious assortment of machinery in orbit. Keller's 1100S collected a class award in the Six Hours of Sebring, Titterington's old 508S took a second place in an I.M.R.C. event at Phoenix Park, and Maderna won the 1½-litre category at Nice in a FIAT of unspecified type. At a Monza sports-car meeting in April there was a 1½-litre win for Cisitalia, and in the Mille Miglia the two 750 c.c. categories went respectively to Zagato and Giannini-prepared *topolini*.

The FIAT range was face-lifted again in 1949. The 1100 and 1500 emerged as the 'E' series with built-out rear boots and column change with synchromesh on second, though the long-chassis *millecento*, still the mainstay of Italian taxi-ranks, received no body modifications. The 1100S, however, was given a more drastic treatment, with a wider rear track and a new full-width 2+2 coupé body by Pininfarina in the Ferrari idiom. A heater/demister unit was standardised, weight and price went up, and overall gearing went down. Lamentably, FIAT saw fit to inflict the 1100E's column change upon it, but the car exhibited at Earls Court in 1949 would not have looked out of place there ten years later.

The principal efforts were, however, reserved for the 500, still a best-seller. The side-valvers had topped the 120,000 mark, and the 500B's short run had added another 21,000-odd 'mice' to the score. The 500C was to run for over five years, during which annual sales would average 65,000. Mechanically it differed little from the superseded B-type, but the stylists had given it a full-width front grille and a built-out rear boot, with a locker for the spare wheel concealed behind the number-plate mounting. Twin tail lamps and a heater were standard, and by 1951 it boasted overriders and winkers as well; at the same time *giardinietta* versions lost their timber trim. Traditionalists lamented the car's 'dollar grin', but it was still lighter than the entire opposition with the exception of Citroën's peculiar *deux chevaux*, largely because Giacosa kept it a two-seater. A convertible weighed in at $11\frac{3}{4}$ cwt, as against 12 cwt for Renault's 4CV, $14\frac{1}{2}$ cwt for a Morris 'Minor' tourer, and $14\frac{3}{4}$ cwt for the contemporary Volkswagen, already making uncomfortable inroads into such hitherto safe FIAT territory as Belgium and Switzerland. Its 61 m.p.h. top speed would see off the Renault and also the Morris— until the B.M.C. merger brought with it Austin's 803 c.c. pushrod engine, and its useful third-gear performance gave it an edge over the Renault with its wide-ratio three-speed box. Acceleration was still leisurely—even with the antiquated 1935-type 8 h.p. engine the Morris was a good five seconds quicker to 50, and lazy drivers might cavil at the *topolino*'s reluctance to attack any acclivity steeper than 1-in-22 without a downward change. On frugality, however, it had the whole bunch licked with the exception of the Citroën, a 500C tested by *The Motor* averaging 40.4 m.p.g. in hard driving, and turning in 58 m.p.g. at a steady 40—something that only an exceptional pre-War 500 could have achieved. Comparisons on a price-basis were less easy; of the 'foreigners' only the Renault was available in Britain, and the duty charged on its French-made components inflated the asking price to £635 at a time when a 'Minor' could still be bought for less than £400. It was, however, a sad commentary on Italian fiscal policy that home-market buyers paid £403, while defeated Germany could deliver standard Volkswagen for less than £450. None the less, the 500C was almost as modern as it had been in 1936, and *The Motor* confessed, rather sadly, that 'roadholding under braking and cornering conditions has no more than one equal among British light cars', a sentiment only too understandable when one reflects that in 1951 *le dernier cri* in the minimal class was the Austin A30, a reliable little creature spoilt by a deplorable penchant for lying down on its door handles.

The 500C also nearly involved itself in an unusual American project. In January, 1950, the Nash-Kelvinator Corporation announced a baby-car prototype, the N.X.I.: this was subjected to what they called 'surview', in other words a gigantic market-research programme in which a quarter of a million Americans were interviewed on the subject of sub-compacts. The car resembled a two-seater convertible edition of Nash's ugly 'Airflyte', the provisional price was quoted as $950, and along-side the N.X.I. were displayed two four-cylinder engines then under consideration—a side-valve Triumph 'Mayflower' and a FIAT 1100. The presence of both Vittorio Valletta (who hap-pened to be in New York at the time) and of E. G. Grinham from Standard-Triumph was taken as a further portent, while the project's internal codename was 'FIAT "Traveler".' When someone opened the little Nash's bonnet and found a 500C engine within, the rumours started to fly. John A. Conde of American Motors, however, doubts if the car ever ran under its own power, and when the N.X.I. finally reached buyers in 1954 as the 'Metropolitan', it was built by Austin and used Austin's 1,200 c.c. A40 power unit.

At Mirafiori the years of recovery were almost over. Valletta had raised his loans: truck and aircraft production were flowing once more. A new model was clearly indicated, for while the ageless *topolino* was good for several more years, and 'thoroughly modern *mille*' was certainly the equal of things like the Austin 'Devon' and Hillman 'Minx', the 1500 was becoming hard to sell. Only 4,790 had found buyers in the last two seasons, and FIAT, like other European makers, wanted something roomier and more utilitarian.

America had abdicated from the role of purveyor to the World. The War and the ensuing dollar shortage had cut her off from many a traditional market, and since 1951 American cars had been aimed at American buyers; thus Europe was ready to step into the breach with what Giacosa called 'an American car of European type', capable of coping with the corrugations of African highways and the thick dust of the Australian outback. FIAT's requirements, as stated in a directive of 1946, were 'good stability, good visibility; room for six people and their baggage; a speed of 75 m.p.h., and a fuel consumption of 28 m.p.g.'. Given these desiderata, the 1400 of 1950 makes sense.

It is easy now to regard the car as an appalling mistake, on a par with Britain's Standard 'Vanguard'. To-day nobody will admit to having liked the 1400, and a well-known journalist who tried it in its heyday recalls the suspension as 'sick-making'. It was outrageously overgeared, had a woolly steering-column change, and styling of such bulboid configuration that it is hard to believe it emanated from Pininfarina's home town of Turin. A Dutch owner remembers it as 'a lame dog, that didn't have enough power to fight its way out of a wet paper bag'. But what of its contemporaries? The 'Vanguard' handled badly, the Renault 'Frégate' had a dreadful all-indirect gearbox, and such lesser lights as the 1949 Borgward and Singer 1500s were uglier than any of the 1400 family—with the possible exception of the 1956 1900B *gran luce* coupé, over-chromed grille and all.

Such judgment from hindsight is, however natural to a generation who have encountered later FIATs—the 1100–103, the orthodox but outstanding 124, and the even more outstanding 128. In 1950 *The Autocar* could say this of the 1400:

> Performance on the indirect gears is extraordinary. The car runs smoothly and quietly up to the point where maximum power is developed, and if the throttle is held open the speed goes on building up slowly until, with any slight help from wind or gradient, the engine must be exceeding 5,000 r.p.m.

The Motor rated the 1400 'very comfortable, very controllable, entirely unaffected by hard driving', and the model's sales record is creditable when one considers that within two years of its introduction European customers were already demanding something smaller. No definitive 1400 production statistics are available, but Turin alone managed to sell approximately 134,000 units of all types between 1950 and 1958—a better record than that of the six-cylinder cars which replaced the 1400/1900 family. My unenthusiastic Dutch friend also rated the 1400 'really comfortable and sturdy, especially when compared with the majority of European cars in the same price category in our country', the Swiss (who could afford to be critical) took to it, and a Danish FIAT enthusiast told me that it was 'much better than its reputation'. Its tough build and soft suspension endeared it to Spaniards, and when the Italo-Spanish *Sociedad Español de Automoviles de Turismo* (SEAT) was set up in Barcelona in 1953 the 1400 was chosen as the new firm's initial staple. The mechanical elements, wedded to an 1800 hull, were still marketed for local consumption until the middle 'sixties.

The 1400 was entirely new. It even had a new type-serial—101—while it was also the first unitary-construction FIAT. The body structure was welded up to the cross-members of the 'chassis', the power unit was carried in an easily detachable 'wheelbarrow' modelled on Citroën practice, and the whole hull was fully dust-sealed and coated with sound-proofing compound. Steering was by worm and roller. The brakes followed established FIAT practice, but the hypoid back axle was a novelty, and though wishbones and coils were used for the front suspension, a combination of coil springs and a rigid axle was adopted at the rear. As owners of pre-War Buicks had discovered, this was not a felicitous arrangement, and *The Motor* tactfully glossed it over as 'not evidently superior to the best results obtainable with other designs'. Depressing as the body was, it was a comfortable six-seater.

Engine design featured a three-bearing crankshaft, wet liners and thinwall main and big-end bearings, while dimensions of 82×66 mm represented an all-time extreme in over-square power units for volume-production until the advent of Ford's 105E in 1959. Output was 44 b.h.p. at 4,400 r.p.m., and other details of the specification followed routine FIAT lines—12-volt coil ignition, mechanical pump feed, a single dry plate clutch, and a four-speed synchromesh gearbox with column change. The standard top-gear ratio was extremely high, at 4.44:1, and a saloon turned the scales at 22¼ cwt, or 2 cwt more than the original 1500 of 1935. The Italian list price was 1,275,000 lire (about £750), though the alternative model, a four-seater cabriolet, was a great deal more expensive. A tuned edition of this was supplied to the *polizia stradale* for road patrol work.

Viewed in the context of the early 1950s, the 1400 combined a respectable top speed of 75 m.p.h. with an easy cruising gait of 65–70, in both of which respects it was more than a match for Ford's 'Consul' or the Wolseley 4/50, for instance. The use of a high top called for a highish third on which 58 m.p.h. were possible, and fuel consumption, at 24–28 m.p.g., was adequate if unsensational. The same went for acceleration through the gears, but the FIAT's great weakness was revealed in the 23.7 seconds it took to accelerate from 20 to 40 m.p.h. in top: an 11 *légère* Citroën could do it in 11 seconds, and even the 1,442 c.c. Vauxhall 'Wyvern', a very lethargic performer by 1950 standards, managed 13.6 seconds. An 'American-type' car on which the gearbox had to be used all the time was surely a contradiction in terms!

The 1400, however, sold well as a taxi, and in 1953 the company fell into line with Mercedes-Benz and Borgward by offering a version with the 1.9-litre 305 diesel engine developed for use in light commercial vehicles. This 1400D was inevitably more lethargic, with a top speed of 64 m.p.h., but performance was not the objective, and a thirst of 35 m.p.g. on cheap fuel commended it to hire-car proprietors. Though no modifications were made to the chassis beyond the provision of larger-section tyres, the diesel's handling proved quite satisfactory, and *The Autocar* reported that 'it can be cornered fast with a feeling of complete safety'—in other words, the standard car's formidable degree of roll was not accentuated by an increase in weight.

FIAT were still questing a 1500 replacement, and the 1900 of 1952 was designed to appeal to a more discriminating market. The chassis-body structure was identical to that of the 1400, but in place of the oversquare 1,395 c.c. unit was a 1.9-litre undersquare affair developing 59 b.h.p. at 3,700 r.p.m. Within, the body was more luxuriously appointed; other distinguishing features were a bigger rear window and an over-elaborate radiator grille. An unusual item of equipment was the Tachimedion average-speed calculator. The use of a five-speed gearbox and a fluid coupling, however, singled the 1900 out from all its competitors. Fifth was very much an overdrive, at 3.23:1, while fourth (4.44:1) was also high.

Surprisingly, the 1900 proved capable of moving away from a standstill on fourth, second-gear starts were recommended practice, and clutchless changes presented no problems. Top speed was 86 m.p.h., and the car used no more petrol than a 1400. What militated against the big FIAT was its high price of 1,750,000 lire (£1,060)—too much for Italians, while on the European market the 1900 was up against such cars as the British Ford and Vauxhall 'sixes', and Mercedes-Benz's promising new 220. True, the Mercédès had a horrible steering-column change, and the miseries as well as the splendours of swing-axle rear suspension, but it was fast, smooth, and well-braked, and it cost very little more than the FIAT. Nearly 75,000 1400s were sold before the introduction of the revised 1400A series in 1954: in the same period 1900 sales were a paltry 8,060 units. By comparison Vauxhall sold 55,673 six-cylinder cars in their best year, 1955, and even the Renault 'Frégate', never anybody's favourite, accounted for 37,631 in the same season.

Nevertheless, the 1900 won the 1952 Algiers-Cape Rally: it also provided FIAT with something new for the autumn shows. It was, however, overshadowed by the model they had unveiled the previous spring at Geneva—their first all-new sports car since the 'Balilla' acquired overhead valves eighteen years previously. Dante Giacosa's 8V was a sensation, with its functional sports coupé body in powder blue, its unadorned grille flanked by inbuilt headlamps, and its Rudge-Whitworth wire wheels, even if these last were concealed behind unprepossessing clip-on soup-plate discs at the shows. Weight was quoted as less than one ton, and maximum speed as 120 m.p.h. Could this be the poor man's Ferrari?

It was not. Such a FIAT was not to make its appearance until 1961. The *Otto Vu*, as Italians called it, was a straight case of thinking aloud by the design department. Just as William Lyons and W. M. Heynes dreamed up the XK 120 as a test-bed for the Mk VII Jaguar's advanced twin o.h.c. engine, so did Giacosa envisage a prestige saloon powered by a vee-eight unit. Pundits pointed out, correctly, that the sports model's neat 2-litre (72 × 61.3 mm) engine would fit perfectly into the 1900's wide bonnet but this combination never happened. It was a pity: a 130 ancestor launched in 1953 might have furnished some very interesting competition for Mercedes-Benz and Jaguar.

The *Tipo* 104 engine was an intriguing piece of work with a light alloy block, cast iron liners, lead-indium bearings, and two dual-choke downdraught Weber carburetters, which gave 110 b.h.p. at a high 6,000 r.p.m. There was a reversion to central change for the four-speed close-ratio synchromesh box, but most important, FIAT's independent coil-and-wishbone suspension was applied at the rear as well as at the front. The hydraulic brakes worked in drums of $11\frac{1}{4}$-inch diameter. Unitary construction was now an integral part of FIAT's policy, and the 8V was built up round a steel-tube structure to which was welded a double skin of sheet steel—the bulkhead was so treated as well as the body proper. Other coachwork features included a curved screen, a sound-insulated roof, and bumpers, grille and mouldings of stainless steel. All the standard 8V coupés were finished in metallic cellulose, though as usual 'platforms' went to the specialists, Ghia basing a Pegaso-like coupé on SIATA's five-speed *derivazione*, while Zagato's version was lighter than FIAT's, and was raced to some purpose, Ovidio Capelli, the model's leading exponent, winning the Stella Alpina Rally, and adding class wins at Rocca di Papa, the Pescara 12 Hours, the *Coppa Internazionale di Monza*, and the *Giro dell'Umbria* in his first season. The Leto di Priolo brothers also campaigned an 8V Zagato to some purpose, taking 9th place in the 1954 Mille Miglia. Though only 114 8Vs were made, their record was long and distinguished including the 2-litre GT Championship of Italy in 1954, and they were still collecting awards in minor events at the end of the decade. In 1957 Ludovico Scarfiotti (grandson of a former President of FIAT) made f.t.d. in the Aosta-St Bernard hill-climb, and in 1958 an 8V finished 13th in the Targa Florio. Count Lurani recalls it as 'a simple chassis, a very good suspension and road-holding for its time; it would have been a really nice, powerful, inexpensive and attractive sports car'. On test it recorded 119, 89, 60 and 40 m.p.h. on the four forward gears, turned in an 0–60 m.p.h. time of 12.3 seconds (equalling that of the early DB2 Aston Martin, but fractionally slower than Jano's magnificent 2½-litre *granturismo* Lancia 'Aurelia'), and could reach the 'ton' faster than either Lancia or Aston, in 35 seconds. The testers found road behaviour good rather than outstanding, the gearbox slow, and the ride hard.

The 8V was destined to remain a test-bed. There were experiments with fibre-glass bodies and five-speed boxes, this latter installation being tried at Le Mans in 1953, when Lurani and Mahé drove a lightened, factory-bodied example. In practice it went down the Mulsanne Straight faster in fourth than in fifth, and the engine was detuned to make it more reliable. Fate was cruel; the FIAT started the race on seven cylinders and lasted a mere hour. Second-series 8Vs, incidentally, had a staggered 'Chinese' four-headlamp configuration which anticipated the Triumph 'Vitesse' of 1962. Most memorable of the model's derivatives was, however, the gas-turbine coupé now in Turin's *Museo dell'Automobile*.

This was a rush job. The frame was ready for body and mechanics at the close of February, 1954, everything was assembled by 10 April, and the turbine did its initial road trials four days later. Power—some 200 b.h.p. of it—came from a two-stage centrifugal compressor with two single-sided rotors, feeding three combustion chambers which supplied gas to a two-stage turbine: thence a single-stage power turbine drove the rear wheels. There was, of course, no gearbox, a 42/58 front-rear weight distribution called for larger-section rear tyres, and tail fins were provided to give extra stability at speeds of over 150 m.p.h. The chassis was largely 8V, and the press demonstration was staged on the Lingotto test-track, the driver being none other than Carlo Salamano, who confessed to having no idea of the turbine's potential when the taps were turned up. 'Perhaps', he quipped, 'I ought to wear a parachute, in case I make a mistake on the banking and drop a hundred feet down into the street'! Observers considered the FIAT quieter than Rover's original turbocar of 1950, but found the heat excessive both within and without. So far no further gas-turbine road vehicles have been seen around Turin: but both the *sezione aeronautica* and the *grandi motori* department have been closely concerned with such engines ever since.

1953 saw the completion of Giacosa's trilogy with his best to date—an 1100 replacement designated *Tipo* 103. Nobody would call this a qualified success. The first series sold over a quarter of a million units, and Italian production eventually ran to well over two million. Company officials used to call it 'the car that won't die'. It evolved into a fast saloon (the *turismo veloce*, or 1100TV), a less successful spyder, and an 18-cwt cab-over-engine van (1100T). For a while it ceased to be an 1100 at all, with the D-series of 1962, and towards the end the assembly lines were transferred to Lingotto. But, like the Morris 'Minor' in Britain, it went marching on, now with front disc brakes, a rear-wheel handbrake in place of the old transmission affair, and floor change for the first time since 1949. The last one did not leave Turin until early in 1970. Even then the *millecento* was not dead; certain assembly plants, notably that of FIAT (Ireland) in Dublin, needed extensive re-tooling to convert to the 124, so Eireann citizens went on buying 1100Rs. Indian production lasted even longer; on 3 February, 1972 Bombay's *Economic Times*, while announcing that the Indian Government were planning to adopt the 124 'for produc-tion to the public sector', reminded readers that Premier Motors had yet to replace the 1100 with the 128, as 'promised'.

But what the World saw in 1953 was an ugly little car resembl-ing a scaled-down Mk I Ford 'Consul'. Ugliness, however, spelt compact dimensions. The wheelbase was reduced to 7 ft 8 in, and overall length was down from the 13ft 7½ in of the original 508C to 12 ft 4½ in. It was also 56 lb lighter, thanks to the new unitary construction, and retained the old, taxi-like lock. Structurally, it derived directly from the 1400, and the engine followed accepted 1100 practice with such improvements as the latest type of diaphragm fuel pump. Other parallels with the 1950 idiom were found in the 'wheelbarrow' engine mounting, the steering-column change, the worm and roller steering, the coil-and-wishbone front suspension, and the hypoid back axle. Wisely, however, Giacosa reverted to orthodox semi-elliptic springing at the rear, while only two body styles were offered—standard and *lusso* saloons. The latter had a heater as factory equipment and cost £615 in Switzerland, £40 more than the basic type. A four-door station wagon (*familiare*) with sideways-opening tail-gate joined the range early in 1954. Also in the 1954 catalogue was the 1100TV, a 50 b.h.p. sports saloon with dual-choke Weber carburetter, distinguishable by its rear-hinged bonnet, enlarged rear window, two-tone colour scheme, and cyclops-eye central spotlamp *à la* Rover. This one would top the 80 mark, and its 0–60 m.p.h. acceleration time was down from 26.4 to 21.5 seconds, at the price of some flexibility.

The 1100 was a splendid little car, if not quite as revolutionary as its prototype had been in 1937. Overall standards had gone up. None the less, one must remember that the 1100-103's British equivalents were the Hillman 'Minx', still with side valves and selling on good finish and mechanical durability rather than on performance or handling: the spongy Austin 'Somerset'; and the 100E Fords, streets ahead of the 1932-type 'Anglia' and 'Prefect', but still three-speeders with a healthy appetite for fuel. European competition centred round the Volkswagen, cramped and slow, even though maximum speed was also cruising speed: the big and tough Peugeot 203; Panhard's eccentric front-wheel-drive 'Dyna 54'; and, ironically, Simca's all-French 'Aronde', a second cousin which was fast acquiring a personality and a following of its own.

The Autocar praised the low level of wind noise and found conversation possible at 70 m.p.h., while cruising speeds of 65 m.p.h. (which meant 4,300 r.p.m.) had no effect on the car.

> Opportunity was taken to sample the rear seats, and for such a small and light car it is unusually comfortable. The seating dimensions are quite adequate for occupants of normal stature even for a long journey, and there is sufficient width for an unusually long-legged passenger to vary his position by sitting somewhat sideways.

The Motor found a top speed of 77 m.p.h. 'a mechanical miracle' when allied to a fuel consumption of 45 m.p.g. at a steady 40, but thought that the gap between top (4.3:1) and third (6.75:1) was too wide. Their testers praised the flexibility, 10 m.p.h. being possible in direct drive without snatch—a practice which smacked of sadism and would never have been viable in the old days of fabric couplings. Suspension was so good that 'driver and passengers are entirely unconscious of the road surface, there being little obvious change between travelling at, say, 50 m.p.h. on an untarred, bumpy country lane, and 60 or even 70 m.p.h. on a smooth *autostrada*'. Steering characteristics were neutral, tail slides were easily controlled, and 'the general behaviour on both fast curves and sharp corners is greatly to be commended'. The column change was considered excellent of its kind.

In its day the 1100 was a successful rally car, the German driver Helmut Polensky summing it up as 'a wonder vehicle with the best road-holding I have met'. He and his co-driver Walter Schluter won the 1953 European Touring Challenge, using the FIAT to win the Travemünde event and to take second place in Norway's Viking. In 1954 the 103 collected a class victory in the Tulip, while Samsing was third in the Viking behind two Dagenham Fords.

Understandably there were no new models for 1954, but the 1400 and 1900 were improved, the A-series having revised cylinder heads (which boosted outputs to 50 and 70 b.h.p. respectively), dual-choke carburetters, new grilles and restyled rear window treatment. 1900As also came with twin foglamps and radios as standard equipment, and an ornate five-seater coupé, the *gran luce*, was offered as an alternative body style.

The first post-War decade saw an all-out export drive, with cars displayed at shows as far afield as Prague and Melbourne. As early as March, 1947 FIAT had invaded South Africa, with 500s at £290 undercutting the Eights of Morris and Austin at £375. The 1100 at £440 was both cheaper and better than the British opposition. It took rather longer to penetrate Sweden, thanks to what Tom Brahmer has described as 'a small, albeit enthusiastic agency somewhat awkwardly situated in Stockholm; and working on a shoe-string budget'. Sweden, be it said, was still a seller's market in days when the only native manufacturer, Volvo, was working off a two-year waiting-list. Anything sold; suddenly the streets of Stockholm were filled with exotics of the stamp of Lea-Francis or Salmson. By 1954 a FIAT 500C was good value at £385, even when compared with Standard's new 8 h.p. four-door saloon at £458. But Sweden highlighted FIAT's two headaches as an exporter: the inflationary levies and the uncomfortable rise, not only of Volkswagen, but of the British. In 1954 the entire Italian industry shipped less than 3,000 cars to Britain's 14,438 and West Germany's 15,935. The Netherlands presented a rather similar story, though in the 1949–50 period it was not Volkswagen who undercut FIAT, but Simca, thanks to an arrangement whereby Kaiser-Frazer's Dutch assembly plant handled 8CV models as well. Belgium, still living on the fat of colonialism, was a free market. It was also a Franco-German Utopia in the mass-production sector, with Britain (which meant Jaguar) taking the luxury honours. Italy sold 1,014 cars in 1949, but France unloaded 15,101 and Britain 12,635. Even Germany, which did not officially exist as a nation, shipped 5,865 units, most of them Volkswagen. Italy was later to pick up some sales from British industry, and things improved with the establishment of a FIAT assembly plant in 1954, but Valletta was still a very long way from beating the Beetle.

Switzerland was healthier. The Swiss liked FIATs. A census taken in September, 1952, showed that they outnumbered any other make of private car within the Confederacy. More interesting still, no fewer than 1,237 of the 19,611 examples in circulation were of pre-1935 manufacture. In the delivery van class the *marque* ran second only to Peugeot. As early as September, 1946 1100s were being imported in respectable numbers, and between 1947 and 1948 the company's Swiss sales doubled. As in Belgium, 1949 was to see the new German invasion, with Volkswagen undercutting the overhead-valve 500 at £370 (the FIAT retailed at £395). The Opel 'Olympia' might be rehashed 1938, but at £405 it was a real bargain: £60 less than was asked for a *millecento* of like vintage, and £5 cheaper than Morris's 'Minor', which must have infuriated Lord Nuffield! By 1950 Germany's share of the market had outstripped Italy's, albeit FIAT kept their head above water, ranking third in 1951, behind Volkswagen and Opel. Most popular model was the 1400, with 1,431 units sold. In 1954 the trend was still upward, with 3,853 new cars registered during the year, 2,486 of which were the well-loved 1100–103s.

America remained a British preserve. A generation nurtured on the classic individuality of the 'TC' M.G. wanted no part of the *topolino*, and pilot batches of 500Cs met with a cool reception. There were no FIATs at the 1953 New York Show—only SIATA's new five-speed 8V-based spyder, which they offered at $4,995. By Jaguar standards this was unrealistic, though it was authentic Woolworth when contrasted with the $29,220 asked for Wilfredo Ricart's Z102 Pegaso from Barcelona.

Still more doleful was the British scene. Renault and Citroën, with their old-established assembly plants at Acton and Slough, could circumvent the wholesale ban on imports, but even British cars were rationed, and new FIATs were seen only at Earls Court, where the company staged a comeback in 1949, displaying three 500Cs, an 1100E saloon, the 1100ES Pininfarina coupé, and a 1500E. The flag was kept flying by a small group of enthusiasts, mainly with *topolini* and 508Cs, which continued to run with the aid of dedicated specialists such as V. W. Derrington. Our little band improvised with Hardy Spicer propeller shafts, S.U. and Zenith carburetters, and Lucas electrics, mounts ranging from a SIATA-headed 500 said to have done 80 m.p.h. at Goodwood to a rare SIATA-Smith Special two-seater (now with side valves) conducted by the future Lord Snowdon. Good examples fetched impossible prices: I was happy to scrape up £550 for a 1938 508C saloon in 1952, and never regretted the extravagance. New models did not reappear until the autumn of 1954, and then they were priced for the fanatic only. None but a dyed-in-the-wool FIAT enthusiast would pay £575 for a 500C when an A30 two-door saloon retailed for a mere £476, and even the Morris 'Minor' (by this time an infinitely better proposition than the 'mouse') was dirt cheap at £530. The 1100 had handling, speed and fuel economy streets ahead of Austin's new 'Cambridge', but at £664 with the smaller 1,200 c.c. engine the Austin made sense. The FIAT at £789 did not. The 1900 (£1,389) was understandably, ignored in a market where just over £1,600 would buy a Mk VIIM Jaguar.

Of the foreign assemblers, Simca progressed rapidly towards independence, and from 1946 onwards they competed directly against FIAT throughout Europe. 1948 deliveries were 14,654 cars, and in 1949 they at last passed the 25,000 mark. For the time being FIAT designs were continued, but the *topolino* went modern, with o.h.v. and 'dollar grin', as early as the 1947 Paris Salon, Simca's 6CV version boasting a rear tank as well. In 1949 the Simca-Huit was enlarged to 1,221 c.c., complete with a new grille plus the 1100E's external boot and column change. At the same time the company introduced the '8 *Sport*', a Pininfarina-inspired two-seater coupé or cabriolet to challenge the 1100S. Bodies were built by Facel Metallon, and this 'jewel of the Simca range' weighed 18 cwt and was said to do 81 m.p.h. In April, 1951, Simca retooled their entire plant, making arrangements with an outside firm for continuing supplies of 6CV and 8CV spares, and that June saw the introduction of the all-French 'Aronde' saloon. The '*Sport*' was continued for the time being, but in October, 1952, even this was redesigned around the 'Aronde' engine. Hence-forward the FIAT-Simca connection was to be purely

850 variations – I.
67. (top) The Sport Spyder of 1965 was a Bertone design, standardised by FIAT, which became a best-seller in the U.S.A.

68. Francis Lombardi's 'Lucciola' (centre) was one of several four-door saloons produced, while **69** (bottom) is a 1967 factory shot of the standard styles – coupé and spyder with the sports engine, and the ordinary berlina.

(Author's Collection: Francis Lombardi. FIAT)

850 variations – II.
70. Lombardi's 1970 Grand Prix convertible (top) featured a roll-bar and a long rear deck whereas his 100G of 1969 (**71,** centre) was a pseudo-British effort inspired by Lotus or even Morgan on which the rear engine is cunningly camouflaged.

(Francis Lombardi: Moretti)

72. Moretti's 1967 'Sportiva' (bottom) subtly suggests a far bigger car in the G.T. class.

(author's collection)

financial, though Torinese technical influence was apparent in the 1300/1500 series of the 1960s.

In war-torn Germany Heilbronn's recovery was a slower process, and deliveries did not resume until 1950, when the first N.S.U.-FIAT 500Cs made their appearance. A few 1400s and 1900s were also made, but the first FIAT model to establish itself in West Germany was the 1100–103. Initially its impact was slow, but it had a long innings, and in its peak year (1963) no fewer than 24,690 were made.

SEAT began to build 1400s in Spain in 1953, and production had been worked up to twenty units a day by December. In Austria Steyr-Daimler-Puch, the country's sole surviving manufacturer of private cars, signed up with FIAT in 1949, turning out 1,477 assorted 1100B and 1100E models before turning their attention to the 1900 in 1953. Along with assembly of the parallel 1400, Steyr took time out to devise their 2000, a 1900 hull powered by a Steyr-designed 85 × 88 mm pushrod engine, considered by some to be a better unit than FIAT's 105-series. The car was made in modest numbers until 1958, when Steyr elected to concentrate on a version of the twin-cylinder 'Nuova 500', again with their own motor. By 1954 FIAT trucks and tractors were also being put together in Mexico, Argentina and Brazil, while the Argentinian Concord factory built locomotive diesel engines as well. There was an unsuccessful attempt to reinstate the Polski-FIAT operation in 1949, but Communist Poland was, understandably, reluctant to conclude a deal with Demo-Christian Italy, and for the time being Polish industry relied on Soviet designs and on the Renault-inspired 2½-ton Star lorry.

Truck production resumed its even tenor once Italy had absorbed the surplus Dodges and P.U.-type Hillmans left behind by the victorious Allies, spearheads of the post-War programme being the forward-control 626N and 666N diesels. Already Italian stylists were making their mark on coach design, with splendid full-fronted creations by firms like Viberti who were soon to adapt FIAT mechanical elements to their own chassisless structures, as did Van Hool in Belgium. In the realm of the 'heavies' the picture was the same as with the private cars: steadily increasing production, and a sharp tumble in export sales as the levies took their toll. 1948 saw a new 100-seater single-decker trolleybus, and there were two new forward-control diesel trucks in the 1950 range, the 4½-ton 640N with 6-litre six-cylinder engine, and the first of the famous 680 family, with a 10.2-litre unit developing 123 b.h.p., a double-reduction drive with eight forward speeds, and air-hydraulic brakes with an engine compression brake in reserve. Sleeper cabs were a factory option, and 'bus versions made their appearance at the same time, 680 derivatives including a 53-seater inter-urban type, an 80-seater for urban work, and a six-wheeler, the 672RN. At the other end of the scale was a revolutionary design, the 615 semi-forward-control lightweight for 30-cwt payloads. Synchromesh gearboxes were well established on commercial vehicles, of course, but the 615 also boasted the 1400's independent front suspension. In early forms it struggled along on the 1400's engine, but by 1953 this had given way to the 1.9-litre 305 diesel as fitted in the 1400D.

In 1951 FIAT entered the light 4 × 4 stakes with their version of the Jeep/Landrover theme. The 'Campagnola' was, in fact, the first model to use the 1900's 105 engine, and among its refinements were synchromesh, hydraulic brakes, hypoid final drive all round, and the 615's independent front suspension. Gear ratios ranged from 4.64:1 to 55.8:1, and in 1952 Paolo Butti set up a new Algiers-Cape record on a station wagon edition towing a trailer. Diesel 'Campagnolas' with the 305 unit were available from 1953, and the Italian Army selected the four-wheel-drive FIAT as their standard cross-country vehicle in preference to Alfa-Romeo's rival model with 1900 mechanics. It must hold FIAT's record for longevity, since it was still being made in small numbers in 1972. The 1954 commercial-vehicle range embraced the 'Campagnola', the 500C van, the one-ton 1100ELR based on the old-school *millecento*, the 615N, and three big forward-control oilers, the 642N, the 671N, and the 682N, as well as a comprehensive range of 'buses and trolleybuses. The company also controlled three 'bus lines—the old-established S.I.T.A. of Florence, now Italy's biggest network with 25,000 miles of routes and 900 vehicles: S.A.D.E.M. of Turin, with 1,500 miles; and Autostradale of Milan with a route-mileage of 6,200. This last-mentioned concern operated FIAT-Vibertis, 642s, and 682s, plus a few ten-seater 615Ns for private parties. Trailers, fashionable in Europe, were disliked because of their excessive side-sway, but the toughness of FIAT products was reflected in Autostradale's maintenance schedules. Engines were rebored at 62,000-mile intervals, resleeved at 125,000 miles, and had their crankshafts reground at 180,000. Tyres were not usually retreaded until they had covered 60,000 miles.

The aircraft division's recovery was of necessity slower, in the face of general disarmament and restrictions on Italy's air force. Gabrielli, however, implemented Valletta's instructions to the full.

Aero-engines were shelved, which meant the disappearance of a promising liquid-cooled inverted vee-sixteen developed during the War. Instead, employees were set to work reconditioning Rolls-Royce and Pratt and Whitney units for the Allies, and war-surplus 'Dakotas' were converted for airline use. Work was also resumed on Gabrielli's G12 three-engined transport, and twenty of these were in hand by 1947. G12s were sold to Alitalia and to S.A.I.D.E. of Egypt, in both of which concerns FIAT had a convenient financial interest. Tail units for these aircraft were made in the C.M.A.S.A. factory at Marina di Pisa. At the same time the G-55 fighter was resuscitated, with a Rolls-Royce 'Merlin' in place of the FIAT-built Daimler-Benz engine—this was marketed as a fighter trainer in single- and two-seater forms, which both Argentina and Egypt ordered. Entirely new was the G-46, a fully aerobatic low-wing monoplane for advanced flying training: several hundred of these were sold, both at home and for export, with six-cylinder in-line inverted engines by Alfa Romeo or de Havilland. 1951 saw a more sophisticated version powered by a 550 h.p. Alvis 'Leonides' radial motor, but this one never saw series production.

FIAT's turbocar was of course, anticipated by the *sezione aeronautica's* gas-turbine programme. In 1950 Italy acquired a manufacturing licence for de Havilland's 'Venom' and 'Vampire' jet fighters, and while the construction of airframes was shared between Macchi and FIAT, the latter firm made all the engines. In December, 1951, another landmark was passed, with the first test flight of Gabrielli's own jet 'plane, the G-80. This was a two-seater fighter trainer with swept-back wings, ejector seats, and a tricycle undercarriage. In 1953 FIAT won a NATO contract for the assembly of fifty North American F-86K fighters.

All in all, it was a good decade, masterminded by the wisdom of Vittorio Valletta. In 1955 the directors could point with pride to such items as the production of 15,000 tractors and 7,321 tons of spare parts. They were still hedging their bets with a new, if short-lived line in refrigerators and washing-machines. They might—and did—admit that 1954's output of 142,847 cars was small beer beside Detroit's contemporary performances. That year General Motors had delivered 1,417,453 Chevrolets and 358,692 Pontiacs. But FIAT were also on the way up. They, too, would join the million league.

11 General Provider

*Certain principles, of course, are established. The
driver of a 'Giulietta' or one of the larger FIATs takes
precedence of an 1100, a 600 of a 500, for the clear
mathematical reason that if car A, driven at full
throttle, is faster than Car B under similar conditions,
then Car A is bound to overtake, assuming (what else
can one assume) that there is enough road. Drivers of 600s
treat 500s with contempt and blow their horns at 1100s and
'Giuliettas', while the 500 driver just blows his horn.*

Richard Bensted-Smith, *The Motor*, June, 1958

In 1965 FIAT production passed the million mark for the first
time, with 1,013,588 deliveries: 994,300 cars and 19,000 trucks,
as well as 44,401 tractors. At Heilbronn the Neckar (formerly
N.S.U.-FIAT) works added another 21,609 units to the score,
and SEAT of Spain contributed 91,006, all private cars. French
sales had built up to over 20,000 a year, though Labour's
import surcharge had caused a slump to 7,010 units across the
Channel in England. The 1950s may not have been FIAT's
most illustrious decade, but in terms of physical expansion they
represented a major miracle, with deliveries of cars up by 750
per cent and an increase of 130 per cent in truck production.

The company's 1965 range might not match that of the
British Motor Corporation in sheer complexity, but it was
certainly comprehensive, with thirteen basic types—or fourteen
if one included the 600/850-based 'Multipla' family. There was
the twin-cylinder 500; two generations of modest rear-engined
four-seater in the shape of the 600 and 850; the indestructible
1100, currently a 'false' *millecento* with 1,221 c.c. engine; and

the angular 1300 and 1500 for the family man. The six-cylinder 1800B and 2300 rubbed shoulders with the British Ford 'Zodiac', the German Ford 20M, Vauxhall's 'Cresta' and Opel's 'Commodore', and had attracted the attention of Rover-fans since the demise of 'Auntie', the celebrated P4. For the open-air enthusiast there was a 1500 cabriolet, and if 95 m.p.h. were not enough this could be had with a hairy twin o.h.c. o.s.c.a.-based unit as the 1600S. Other sporting models included the 850 coupé and spyder, and the ultimate in poor man's Ferraris, the Ghia-styled 2300S 2+2 coupé, described by *The Motor* as 'long, noisy in an exhilarating way, not particularly easy to get into, and with rather heavy steering and controls'. A Briton paid £410 for a 500, and close on £3,000 for the sports 2300.

This range was orthodox, not to say conservative in character. After plunging into rear engines in 1955, it seemed, Giacosa had opted for tradition; the *système* Panhard, beam rear axles, manual gearboxes, all in the era of the Mini, the Hillman 'Imp', the Triumph 1300, and Auto-Union's new Audi. No front-wheel drive private car would be marketed under the FIAT name until 1969.

The early 1960s were, of course, the years of *la dolce vita* in Italy, with the industrial growth rate reaching astonishing proportions—in 1960 it was 20.3 per cent. Massive wage increases between 1962 and 1964 meant not only a recession, but more money in the hands of the working-class, and suddenly a whole generation nurtured on scooters graduated to FIAT 500s. As late as December, 1961, *Motor Cycle* could still point to a steady demand for scooters and mopeds, despite a slump in the sales of larger and more powerful motorcycles, but thereafter the trend changed, the 500 remaining, of course, Italy's best-selling car model. Even in the dark year of 1964 163,588 were delivered to home-market customers. By contrast, bigger types had a hard time: in 1960 Italians registered only 750 new Alfa Romeo 2000s and 600 Lancia 'Flaminias'. This concentration on the small and inexpensive benefited the specialist coachbuilders, whose output in 1959 was a formidable 14,511 cars.

An embarrassing side-issue of the new prosperity was a boom in imports, something Italy had not seen since the days of the San Giorgio and Fides in 1906. Between January and September, 1964, Italians registered 458,800 FIATS, 39,189 Alfa Romoes, 23,574 Autobianchis, 16,895 Lancias and 1,652 Abarths—but in third position overall was Volkswagen (24,524), with Opel and (ironically) Simca also disposing of over 18,000 units apiece. In addition, there were the 17,295 Innocentis made in Milan by the Lambretta scooter firm, which were B.M.C. designs with a sizeable British content, while Alfa Romeo's figures included the Renault 'Dauphine' which the firm had been building under licence since 1960. By 1965 national wage levels had reached the European mean, and firm fiscal action was taken, in the form of a purchase tax based on a car's dimensions, capacity and basic price. This was cruelty beyond even the machinations of Whitehall, and led to a serious slump. Commercial-vehicle sales dropped by 18 per cent, and at the same time Alfa Romeo and Lancia suffered a worse recession of over 30 per cent, though FIAT had a somewhat easier time, picking up some of the customers who could no longer afford Italy's 'class' cars. The troubles were short-lived, and Lancia were back on full time by the summer.

The industry had, however, to contend with a new opponent —Japan. In 1958 Japan made 50,643 private cars, and exported less than 2,500, most of these to Far Eastern countries and the Pacific. By 1962 her output of 990,705 units placed her fourth, behind the U.S.A., Western Germany, Britain and France, but ahead of Italy. Fortunately for FIAT, Japanese exports were still below the 80,000 level and had yet to gain a major foothold in any key market, but the menace was there to see.

The foreign imports were making inroads into their long-standing domination of the home market. In 1959 FIAT's share of the take was the traditional 87 per cent, but this was down to 65 per cent five years later, in spite of which the colossus continued to smash records of one kind or another. The £6 million invested in tooling up for 1955's rear-engined 600 brought an immediate reward in an all-time production record for Italian industry; 24,531 cars delivered that May. 1963 saw two two-million sellers in the FIAT catalogue—the 600 and the 1100–103. Expansion continued: 1956's Report of the Directors spoke of further extensions linking the central and southern blocks of Mirafiori, two new blast furnaces at Vado, and a new, computerised spare-parts division adjoining the S.P.A. factory at Stura. A new lightweight farm tractor, *Modello*-18, brought with it a chain of technical centres for power farming in eight Italian cities. The recession might still hover over Turin in 1965, but that year FIAT introduced a new antirust treatment, was conducting crash-tests with cars controlled by radio from low-flying helicopters, and had opened their *Centro Storico*, a factory museum rivalled only by that of Daimler-Benz at Stuttgart, and by Renault's subsequent display in their Champs-Elysées showrooms. Mirafiori blossomed more strongly than ever; in October, 1956 *The Motor* spoke in awed tones of 1,100 cars a day, but this had been doubled when William Boddy toured the FIAT complex five years later, to the accompaniment of the usual statistics—$46\frac{1}{2}$ miles of overhead conveyor lines, $2\frac{1}{2}$ miles of subways, and twelve of railway sidings. Nobody—except perhaps that far-sighted commentator Graham Turner—would have anticipated a daily output of 9,000 within ten years.

In 1956 FIAT joined forces with the Montecatini group to form the SORIN nuclear-energy consortium, and another car firm, Autobianchi, was added to the empire. Bianchi's car business had sunk to a trickle by 1939, and since the War only a prototype $1\frac{1}{2}$-litre had been made, though trucks and motorcycles were continued, and there was a brief and catastrophic essay into fibreglass boats. The two-wheelers were too conservative for Italian tastes, and by 1955 the firm was in a poor way. It was then that Ferruccio Quintavalle, a Milanese industrialist, persuaded FIAT and Pirelli to form a joint company with Bianchi to revive the cars. Valletta, always touchy on the subject of imperialism, announced that the new collaboration had as its object 'the production in common on a large scale of a car even smaller than the 600, which is presently being studied by us.

Such a collaboration will prove how unfounded are the attacks on FIAT claiming monopoly and regionalistic policies'.

In fact Bianchi were to produce nothing new or individual for eight years, which time FIAT had acquired the entire share capital. In the meanwhile the new venture enabled them to gain a foothold in the customised-FIAT business, and by 1964 the Desio works were turning out a healthy 32,000 cars a year. Later, like Ferrari, the factory would be utilised to deal with the overflow demand for FIATs proper.

The decade also saw a reversal of the empire-building game in France, where FIAT disposed of part of their 50 per cent stake in Simca to the Chrysler Corporation during 1962. They used these funds to buy into Simca Industries, a company formed by Pigozzi to administer his truck interests such as Unic of Puteaux, who were already building o.m. lorries under licence. In December, 1965, a further reshuffle saw FIAT's interest in the parent Simca concern reduced from 35 per cent to the 20 per cent they hold to this day, while Umberto Agnelli, Giovanni's grandson, became president of Simca Industries. Chrysler's virtual acquisition of Simca also brought to an end the reciprocal deal whereby FIAT and Simca sold each other's cars in their respective homelands. By 1964 FIAT-France was a *fait accompli*.

Even more noticeable was the absence of FIATs from major competitions. The last Mille Miglia was held in 1957, and thereafter most FIAT successes fell to the hotter Abarths, which had only a nominal FIAT content. True, there were exceptions; a Liège-Brescia-Liège Rally for minicars was staged in 1958, and the 'Nuova 500's duly collected first, second, fourth and fifth places. There was also the East African Safari, a tough exporters' selling-plate calculated to appeal to firms with a distaste for expensive competition departments. 1100s finished second and fourth in 1956, and in 1957 the Armstrong/Temple-Boreham car won its class, probably because a classification based on list price put it in a different category from the invincible Peugeots. In 1962 the 2300s beat the rival Mercedes-Benz, even though the redoubtable Singh brothers could manage nothing better than fourth—sufficient to keep sales in Kenya at a healthy level. 1965 was a good year for Abarth: it was also a good year for the Pole Sobieslaw Zasada and his incredible little 500-based Steyr-Puch 650TR, which beat the Minis in more than one European rally. All the *pur sang* FIATS achieved, however, were 5th, 6th and 7th places in the *Gran Premio Internacional,* an Argentinian touring-car marathon which Peugeot won.

The car division's activities followed two lines of development, the rear-engined family embracing the 600, the 'Nuova 500', and the 850, while there were three generations of the orthodox—the elderly 1400 and 1900, the 1100–103 in all its ramifications, and Giacosa's Pininfarina-shapes with Lampredi-designed engines, which had a ten-year span from 1959 to 1968, and covered everything from a modest 1300 up to a 2.3-litre executive saloon selling for over two million lire. The class of 1950 had served its purpose, and the B series of 1956 sold less than 30,000 units, most of which were 1400s. True, there were a few more brake horses, but two-tone paint and ornate trim told their own story, even steering-wheels being two-toned. One of the consequences of this face-lift was that it was now impossible to tell the two models apart, so the final series of 1900s was given the unpleasing grille hitherto reserved for *gran luce* coupés.

The 1100 ground inexorably on, even finding a niche with American buyers. 1955 saw a sports cabriolet edition of the 1100TV with wrap-round screen and divided grille, said to do 90 m.p.h. It looked like a scaled-down Ford 'Thunderbird', and only 571 were made. The 103E series of 1956 saw a raising of compression ratios: standard engines delivered 40 b.h.p., with 53 b.h.p. available on TV versions. At the same time the high-performance type was given twin fog-lamps instead of the 'cyclops' eye' of 1953. The D-models, unveiled at the 1957 Turin Show, boasted new heads with individual inlet ports and dual valve springs, while boots and rear windows alike were enlarged, and key-starting introduced. Two-tone paint was standardised, though the price was unchanged, at 920,000 lire.

In England, however, it sold for £869, over £100 more than a Hillman 'Minx', and £73 more than Wolseley's new 1500, a car which incorporated some of the traditional FIAT virtues. (In passing, I recall several 'dices' with 1500 prototypes on lonely Cotswold roads in the winter of 1956, and my astonishment at finding something that could show a clean pair of wheels to my tuned 1938 508C in such conditions!)

At the same time the TV gave way to the first of the 'false' 1100s, the 1200 with 72×75 mm (1,221 c.c.) 103C engine developing 55 b.h.p. at 5,300 r.p.m.—FIAT's answer to the growing challenge of the Simca 'Aronde'. This one retained the classic *millecento* specification, plus double-acting telescopic dampers all round, angular *gran luce* styling, and a wrap-round rear window. Appointments were more luxurious, and a car tested by *Motor Sport* could cruise at close to the 80 mark. A tidier edition of the original 1100TV cabriolet with the new power unit was introduced at Geneva in 1959, and in the same year the *millecento* marched on into the 103H series, offered in 'export', 'special' and '*lusso*' models, these last acquiring the 1200's body shape in 1960. Some 272,000 were sold up to 1962, when the entire 1100/1200 range was dropped in favour of the 1,221 c.c. 1100D, though foreign assembly plants continued to build the H-series for some time thereafter. A 103H engine was used to power Pininfarina's extraordinary PFX with diamond wheel formation, one of the sensations of the 1960 Turin Show. It actually ran under its own power.

All 1100Ds had angular lines with thin screen pillars, as well as 50 b.h.p. engines, new grilles and revised instruments. A Saxomat automatic clutch was a factory option, and a saloon now cost 960,000 lire. Weights and gear ratios were unchanged, and the 1100 in its latest guise was capable of an honest 83 m.p.h., accelerating to 50 m.p.h. in 15 seconds. I used a *familiale* version on snow and ice in the winter of 1963–4, and found it reassuringly sure-footed for a station wagon, but the model was beginning to show its age. *The Autocar* assessed it as a 'good example of a conventional car', criticising aerodynamics ill-suited to the motorway age, bumpy rear suspension, and awkward pedal angles, but nobody had a hard word to say of the column change, even when Rootes and B.M.C. were rediscovering the joys of 'four on the floor'.

The *topolino* had provided the raw material for Formula III in 1946, and now the *millecento* was to usher in another new formula. Such a step had been inevitable since the British had invaded Italy's national 750 c.c. category, and a solution became a matter of urgency when the country found herself short of front-rank Grand Prix drivers in 1957. The A.C.I. themselves sponsored a prototype with FIAT 1100 engine and two-speed gearbox, which looked horribly like an American dirt-track midget, and there was even talk of one-make racing, as typified by the Cisitalia fiasco of 1947, and later French experiments with Deutsch's and Bonnet's Panhard-engined Monomills. Fortunately Count Lurani dissuaded his fellow committee-members from such an unfortunate step, and what emerged in 1958 was Formula Junior. This laid down a capacity limit of 1,100 c.c., while cars had to be powered by 'homologated' engines, with clutches and gearboxes to match. Suspensions and brakes must come from the same model as the mechanical elements, overhead camshafts and self-locking differentials were barred, also fuel injection unless it was factory equipment on the standard car, and the minimum weight limit was 400 kilograms. These rules left Italians with the choice of two power units: the FIAT, and Lancia's more expensive V4 'Appia'.

By 1958 firms of the calibre of Foglietti, Raineri, Stanguellini, Taraschi, Volpini and Wainer had FJs running, but as yet performances were uninspired: at the Formula's début at Monza Lippi's winning Stanguellini was actually slower than a *sports* Alfa Romeo 'Giulietta'.

But the Formula soon caught on. The first foreign FJ event was a curtainraiser to the Portuguese Grand Prix in August, 1958, won by local driver Nogueira Pinto on a Stanguellini. In 1959 Wainer and Moretti were building rear-engined machines, and outputs averaged 75–80 b.h.p. At the same time Britain, France and Germany began to take an interest, and an ominous trend manifested itself in the Eifel Pokal. True, the Italians won again, but a D.K.W.-based car was third, and de Selincourt's Elva fourth. The Briton won at Cadours later in the year, and 1960 saw the old pattern of British domination, though Colin Davis did quite well with his O.S.C.A., and a youthful Alejandro de Tomaso was actually exporting his FIAT-based Isis models to America. 1961 saw the *millecento* units giving a reliable 85 b.h.p., while the Lancias offered as much as 95, but it was all over bar the shouting. The best a FIAT-type Junior could manage in 1962 was a solitary third place at Garda.

In the early 1950s Giacosa had been studying a replacement for the *topolino*, and his experiments had been extensive. Prototypes were built and tested with every possible configuration: water-cooled in-line engines, air-cooled flat-fours, front engine and rear drive, front engine and front drive, and rear engine and rear drive, this last being selected. The 600 eventually appeared in 1955 to the accompaniment of a fanfare unequalled since the days of the 509. 20 billion lire were invested in tooling, S.A.V.A. worked out a new and 'specially favourable' hire-purchase scheme, and an ingenious split model worked by an automatic telephone exchange formed the centre-piece of the 600's show début. Two production prototypes were driven the 6,240 miles from Rome to Calcutta at an overall average speed of 30 m.p.h. Italians queued to buy the cars, and at Geneva, once again chosen for the christening party, the specialist coachbuilders had their usual jamboree. Zagato and Monterosa showed sports coupés (on the latter's, the exhaust pipes were sunk into the rear wings), and Canta actually essayed a four-door saloon. Alongside the true 'specials' were a whole host of *elaborazioni*, with enlarged rear windows, special trim, built-in radios, reams of chromium strip and, overriders. In later years tuners such as Abarth and Giannini were to use such devices to distinguish their hotted-up saloons, but as yet the *elaborazioni* merely represented the cheapest way to be different, at £65–£90 above the list price.

Beneath all the ballyhoo, however, the 600 was a real achievement, in that four people were fitted into a car no bigger than the superseded 500C. In some respects the 600 was actually smaller; five inches less wheelbase and a roofline $1\frac{1}{4}$ in lower. The car was a unitary job based on a punt-type floor, reinforced by a rectangular backbone which also carried the gear, brake, and clutch linkages, and the hot-air ventilation system. The body sides were welded to this, and all wheels were now indepently sprung, by a transverse leaf and wishbone arrangement at the front, and by coils and trailing diagonal links at the rear. The dual-circuit hydraulic brakes worked in drums of 7.3-inch diameter and were supplemented by the familiar hand transmission brake.

The 60 × 56 mm (633 c.c.) engine was a far more robust affair with three-bearing crankshaft. Output was 22 b.h.p., there were pushrod-operated overhead valves, and the specification embraced pump and fan cooling, a downdraught carburetter, a combined air intake silencer and filter, and a FIAT diaphragm-type petrol pump. If the *topolino* had been a miracle of compactness, the 600 was even more so, for water spaces between the two end cylinders were eliminated, and the radiator was mounted alongside the engine. The four-speed all-indirect gearbox, with synchromesh on second, had ratios of 4.82, 7.15, 10.05 and 18.2 to 1, and the central lever possessed a pleasantly rigid linkage. Maintenance was reduced to a minimum, with chassis lubrication needed only at 3,000-mile intervals. Luggage accommodation was fair for a rear-engined car; the battery and spare wheel occupied all the space under the frontal bonnet, but when the 600 was used as a two-seater, the rear seat could be folded down to provide a wide platform.

The 600 was offered as a saloon or as a *tetto apribile* in the *topolino* idiom. On the road it revealed a degree of stability unmatched by contemporary rear-engined Renaults or Volkswagen. It weighed only $11\frac{1}{4}$ cwt, and proved capable of just under 60 m.p.h., with 40 available on third and 25 on second. An 0–50 m.p.h. acceleration time of 32.5 seconds showed little, if any improvement on the 500C; the fuel-consumption range of 45–55 m.p.h. was likewise much the same. Top was very much an overdrive, of course, but where the FIAT scored over the opposition was in its compact proportions. For sheer simplicity it could not match the 2CV Citroën (which was flat out at 45), and the Renault 'Dauphine' of 1956, if marred by a three-speed gearbox, was a faster, roomier machine with a 70 m.p.h. potential. But the front-wheel drive Citroën measured over twelve feet from stem to stern, as did the still competitive Morris 'Minor'. The Renault was almost a thirteen-footer, and even the modestly-proportioned Austin A30 was ten inches longer than the FIAT, at 11 ft 4 in. (It was also narrow, which made for interesting behaviour on tight turns!) In a free market the 600 was fairly priced, though this did not apply to the United Kingdom, where it sold for £585 against the £476 asked for the Austin. It was, however, cheaper than Renault's older 4CV. Germans paid DM–4,460 as against DM–4,600 for a bigger *de luxe* Volkswagen, but the FIAT was much better value than the Borgward Group's temperamental two-stroke Goliath, and it was to compete directly with Lloyd's 600 c.c. four-stroke 'Alexander' series introduced in 1957. In Switzerland the 600 and the 4CV both sold for £412, or appreciably less than an A30.

The press was enthusiastic. *The Motor* found the lack of acceleration embarrassing at times, while the ride was choppy at low speeds, and the suspension 'vintage' in feel. The brakes called for high pedal pressures, yet were entirely fade-free, the steering was direct and sensitive with a safe degree of under-steer, and above 50 the car was frankly noisy. *The Autocar* did not altogether agree on this last count: 'at the end of a day's journey during which the speedometer was more often than not hovering at the 50 mark, the 633 c.c. engine was as quiet and sweet as when it had been started some ten hours before'. Directional stability in cross-winds was rated in-different. *Motor Sport* emphasised the dual personality of a car on which the 'splendid' gearbox asked to be used to the full, yet which would pull down to 13 m.p.h. on top. Forty miles could be put into the hour with ease. Even in 1967, when the 600's main merit was a bargain price (£493 in England), *The Motor* could still sound an appreciative note:

Out of town it will buzz along at 60 m.p.h., and only when overtaking or struggling uphill with a load does the available horsepower seem inadequate. The compensation is exceptional economy, for it runs on the cheapest petrol, and does 40–45 m.p.g. provided you do not drive hard.

The essential soundness of the design is reflected in the few changes that punctuated its sixteen-year run. Winding windows replaced the *topolino*'s sliding type in 1956, and overriders and screenwashers came with the Fourth Series in 1957. A year later Fifth Series cars had 24.5 b.h.p. engines and more efficient dynamos, and in July, 1960 came the 600D with 32 b.h.p., 767 c.c. engine which made it a 70 m.p.h. car in favourable conditions. At the same time a rear-wheel handbrake was adopted, forward-hinged doors distinguished the class of 1964, and the fifth and last series of the 600D appeared at the end of 1965, this being identifiable by the absence of the chrome side trim first seen in 1957. Early in 1970 production ceased in Turin, but the demand continued, and in 1972 it was still selling in fair quantities in Germany, the Netherlands and Czechoslovakia—sufficient, at any rate, to keep production flowing in the SEAT factory at Barcelona. It would doubtless retain its following elsewhere—only, as a FIAT executive told me, 'there aren't enough to go round'.

Before 1955 was out, Giacosa had used his shoe-horn to even greater purpose. Not content to propel four people on 633 c.c., he now applied the same mechanical elements to a six-seater minibus. One of the advantages of a rear engine is that it permits full forward control without impeding *lebensraum*, and this characteristic was exploited on the 'Multipla'. The main mechanical difference was the coil-and-wishbone front suspension, and the wheelbase was lengthened slightly to 6 ft 7 in, in spite of which the car was only 139 inches long, 62 inches wide, and 62 inches high. Performance was, understandably, of little importance, though the 'Multipla' would stagger up to 57 m.p.h. and cruised at an easy 40, returning 44.5 m.p.g. at this speed. *The Motor* considered it a magnificent compromise, with a good ride at full load, a less good one when driven solo, and a safe and roll-free change from understeer to oversteer if pressed to the limit. *The Commercial Motor,* into whose preserve the 'Multipla' really fell, was more enthusiastic:

> It is a delightful little vehicle to drive. The seating position gives excellent all-round visibility, and does not become tiring on long journeys. All controls are light to operate, and the steering wheel is particularly well raked for comfort. The suspension provides a smooth ride over the worst surfaces, and fast cornering is possible without any noticeable roll or deviation from the set course on wet or dry roads.

Van versions were made by O.M., and the cars were widely used as taxis in Italy, as well as by a few British operators. One example, the property of an Aldershot firm, rapidly ran up a six-figure mileage and was then sold at an inflated figure. In 1963 the model was made available with roomier and more angular O.M. coachwork, and this version evolved into the 850T with 850 mechanical elements in 1965. Another interesting derivative was the 'Jolly', an open beach car with mahogany seats devised by Pininfarina and exhibited in 1956. A batch of 200 was laid down, among the customers being Henry Ford II. 'Multiplas' also formed the basis of the plexiglass-roofed sight-seeing 'buses used to transport visitors round the FIAT plants in Turin.

The tuners soon went to work on the 600, which became Carlo Abarth's speciality. By 1957 a 747 c.c. version with his own crankshaft was achieving 80 m.p.h. on 40 b.h.p., while the 850TC variant tested by *The Motor* in 1962 was a ferocious package involving a 62.5 ×89 mm (847 c.c.) unit with 9.8:1 compression, special camshaft, an Abarth divided exhaust system, a stronger clutch, higher gear ratios (top was now 4.084:1), lowered suspension, Michelin 'X' tyres, and Girling front disc brakes, with ribbed drums at the rear. Weight was still only 11¼ cwt, and what looked like a mildly doctored 600 proved a real bomb, screaming its way up to 60 in 15 seconds, and to 80 in just over half a minute. Modest driving returned 50 m.p.g., but conducted *à l'italienne* it could match the 32 m.p.g. of pre-War 508C saloons. Though a little spluttery at

1,500 r.p.m., it attained 7,000 on the indirects. Joseph Lowrey summarised it in inimitable style:

> At about £1,400 this miniature saloon with a true maximum of 93 m.p.h. is an expensive joke if you merely regard it as a means of driving big-car owners to suicide. But this sort of very lively, very controllable, and very compact car actually represents one of the quickest known ways of getting dry-shod to a lot of destinations—an E-type may be 56 m.p.h. faster, but it is surprising how often the car which is eleven inches narrower can offset that handicap on crowded roads.

Nor was this the limit if 600 saloon bodywork was essential. Carlo Abarth's 1967 catalogue contained something called the 1000TC *Corsa*, now with frontal radiator and an 86 b.h.p. 1-litre engine, which offered a staggering 117 m.p.h. for 2,400,000 lire, or more than the price of a *lusso* 2300. Far more attractive were the Zagato-bodied coupés, with bored-out 833 c.c. engines, standing less than four feet off the ground, this low line necessitating 'bubbles' in the roof for the passengers' heads. 'Chassis' and suspension were 600, and even the brakes were unchanged save for harder linings, but the result looked like nothing from Mirafiori or Lingotto, could attain 95 m.p.h., and cruised all day at 80. Its low build also gave it a stability in cross-winds beyond that of any 600, there was apparently no rev limit, and anyone with soul so dead as to hold the Abarth-Zagato down to 50 m.p.h. was rewarded with 70 m.p.g. Giacosa's solid 600 bottom end could even stand the ultimate in Abarthisation, the twin-cam *bialbero* unit which pushed out 90 b.h.p. in 1-litre form, but his brakes, alas! could not. John Bolster recalls exercising an early example on the *autostrada*:

> The moment I braked, there were four little bonfires, and there I was, darting in and out of the traffic without a brake to my name.

Other firms also worked on the 600, among them SIATA and O.S.C.A., who marketed a *testa rossa* version with raised compression and re-profiled camshaft for £84 in 1964.

With the 600 safely under way, Giacosa turned his attention to the minimal market, just as Sir Herbert Austin had attacked the motorcycle-and-sidecar brigade in 1922. The middle 'fifties were the era of the bubble-car, born of post-War economic stringency, and kept alive by the Suez Crisis of 1956. The handlebar-steered Messerschmitt, the Isetta with its swing-up nose-gate, and the Bond with its single, chain-driven front wheel represented cyclecar-type solutions, but FIAT's 'Nuova 500' had no motorcycle affiliations at all. Structurally it had a great deal in common with the 600, apart from the use of a rear-wheel handbrake, though it was substantially smaller. The wheelbase was 6 ft 0½ in, the length 8 ft 10 in, and overall width was 4 ft 4 in. Compared with the original *topolino* it was also a featherweight, at 9½ cwt dry.

Much of this weight-paring had been won by the use of a 'lawn-mower' engine; the 500's boot contained a 479 c.c. o.h.v. air-cooled in-line 'twin' with cast-iron liners, and block and head of aluminium. This was mounted in unit with a four-speed crash gearbox and the usual FIAT single-plate clutch, the whole assembly weighing only 200 lbs. The output, at 13 b.h.p., matched that of the original 1936 500 engine, and once again Giacosa opted for a two-seater, with room for two children on the luggage platform. The price was a real bargain, at 465,000 lire (about £300), though Britons had to pay £556 in 1957. Like the majority of truly successful models, the 500 got away to a shaky start.

The Autocar wondered 'whether reduction of size and power has not gone a little too far', and the first examples delivered in the summer of 1957 were completely gutless. Hastily they were recalled, two more brake horses were extracted from their engines, and the 500 emerged with a 55 m.p.h. top speed.

It was a controversial little car, even then. The beetle brows made for poor all-round vision, though the crash box presented no problems, the handling of the short and narrow vehicle was commendably roll-free, and the engine's ability to thrash away at over 4,000 r.p.m. for hours on end made up in part for the lack of urge—the 0–40 m.p.h. acceleration time was a painful

32 seconds. 'The main drawback on a long journey', said *The Motor*, 'was boredom rather than backache'. Elbow-room was limited, and leg-room impeded by the intrusive front wheel arches. William Boddy, however, commended the 500 to *Motor Sport*'s readers. He spoke of 'outstanding brakes and roadholding to offset a deficiency in speed. On dry and wet roads the little car goes round corners safely without the driver's having to back off much if at all, from cruising speed, and the brakes are entirely adequate, even to locking the wheels when powerfully applied'.

In 1958 a 499 c.c. sports version was added for enthusiasts, but by 1960 the enlarged unit was fitted to the standard article as well, producing a noisy but unquestionable 60 on the level. 1965's 500F has a bigger screen, forward-hinged doors, and enlarged fuel tank, a revised clutch and rear suspension, and thinner pillars. There were also eighteen horses in the boot. People still disagree on the pros and cons of the 500. A colleague regarded a thirty-mile run as her idea of purgatory, but my own experiences suggest a sporting 1½-litre of the 1920s with sophisticated springing. The heavy brakes, high noise-level, uncomfortable pedals, and the need to double-declutch for every change, up or down, are Vintage to the finger-tips, as is the remarkable top-gear flexibility provided one is in no hurry. The simple heater ducts can render the handbrake burning-hot to the touch, but a good 500 will sit at a speedometer 70 for hours on end, even if the 44 m.p.h. maximum in third is something of a handicap. 55 m.p.g. present no problem to any but the most brutal drivers.

1960 saw the ingenious *Tipo* 120 *giardiniera*, a baby station wagon on which the 499 c.c. engine was set horizontally (with air ducts in the rear quarters) to give a flat floor. The wheelbase was increased by four inches, but weight was still under 11 cwt, and performance was little impaired. Production of this model was transferred to Autobianchi's Desio works during 1969.

Autobianchi had, of course, entered on their new lease of life with the 'Bianchina', a roll-top convertible of some elegance mounted on a 500 platform, and the range was subsequently expanded to embrace a full cabriolet, a four-seater saloon, and a station wagon, as well as a 5-cwt van with the *Tipo* 120 engine installation and 35 cubic feet available for payload. This one sold quite well in Britain, albeit the first batch of a dozen r.h.d. 'Bianchina' coupés was also the last. The 500 c.c. Autobianchis remained in production throughout the 1960s, outliving an unsuccessful attempt to market a sports convertible version of the 600D, which they called the 'Stellina'.

All the other specialists went to work on the 500. There were 'Jollies', baby jeeps, and even a mock-Veteran resembling a 1908 single-cylinder de Dion, which rejoiced in the name of Venturina and flitted briefly across Turin's exhibition halls in 1962. In 1967 Vignale excelled themselves with a deplorable resuscitation of the 508S shape, the 'Gamine', which went on sale in London at £700 and was given the bird by FIAT-devotees. Of the tuners, Abarth offered the usual hot-camshaft and low-profile treatment, which culminated in a 695 c.c. version capable of close on 90. Giannini went a step further by concocting a flat-four out of two de-stroked (67×49 mm) 500 blocks on a common crankcase, installed in an Abarthised saloon hull. When Britain started to dominate Formula Junior, the Italians devised their own Formula Baby Junior (later Formula Monza) with 500-based single-seaters. A standard 500 motored round Scott Base in Antarctica with a New Zealand Government expedition in 1964, and a year later an attempt was made in Britain to do 100 m.p.g. on the road. The drivers shuttled up and down between Cheltenham and Evesham at 26 m.p.h., and although liberal coasting was used, they failed in their objective. At least their best figure of 96.59 m.p.g. improved on the 92.2 m.p.g. achieved on the same course by a 4CV Renault in 1954. Gordon Wilkins subsequently extracted 126 m.p.g. from a 500 at Silverstone.

The joke had vindicated itself, and nowhere was this better realised than in England, home of the baby car. A 1967 advertisement showed a 500F and a 600D side by side, with the by-line: 'Which of you costs under £500?' Pat came the answer: 'Me ... and Me'!—and this at a time when a Mini (without heater) retailed at £478, Ford's 105E 'Anglia' at £504, and the Hillman 'Imp' at £549.

The 500 and 600 were revolutionary enough in 1957, but by 1964 the *système* Panhard was no longer one of the designer's shibboleths, and the mass-producers, having explored both rear engines and f.w.d., were showing a marked preference for the latter layout. Aligned in the *traction avant* camp along with those veterans Auto Union and Citroën were B.M.C., Ford of Germany, Lancia, Panhard, SAAB and Wartburg, with Peugeot and Triumph already at work on f.w.d. models. The rear-engined brigade included B.M.W. (with their utility 700), Chevrolet, N.S.U., Simca, Skoda and Volkswagen, while Renault's catalogue contained both types. FIAT, however, surprised everyone by launching a *new* rear-engined car in 1964—the last such machine to be introduced by a volume-producer.

The 850 was in essence a revised 600, apart from such safety features as burst-proof locks and a rear tank, as well as other improvements; Porsche synchromesh for all forward gears, a rear-wheel handbrake, and a plastic cooling fan. Capacity was up to 843 c.c. (65 ×63.5 mm) and output was a satisfactory 34 b.h.p. (37 on 'special' versions as marketed in England). It was a bigger and roomier car, 11 ft 9 in long, and the rear seats were comfortable, while six-footers like myself no longer suffered from cramp in the right leg after a long journey. A 75 m.p.h. top speed brought the 850 into line with contemporary 1,098 c.c. versions of Morris's ageless 'Minor', the 105E Ford, and the new and cheap rear-engined Skoda 1000MB. Leisurely acceleration was offset by well-spaced ratios, controllable understeer made the car easy and safe to drive, and though there was still a tendency to pitch, directional stability was much improved by the lower build. The drum brakes were more than adequate.

The special-builders wasted no time. Boneschi produced a curious convertible with squared-off tail, and no fewer than three firms (Allemano, Caprera and Francis Lombardi) offered four-door saloons. As for Carlo Abarth, his OT 1600 was not for the squeamish. The regular *berlina* shell crouched low, its lines accentuated by the wide-rim cast-alloy wheels and Dunlop racing tyres, while the nose-radiator suggested one of Rosatelli's fighter biplanes. Power came from a 1.6-litre twin o.h.c. Abarth engine fed by two dual-choke downdraught Weber carburetters. On a weight of 15 cwt this bomb was persuaded to do 132 m.p.h., with the 'ton' in third, 75 in second, and 45 in bottom. An 0-100 m.p.h. time of 28 seconds was, astonishingly, almost identical with the 4.2-litre E-type Jaguar's 0-120 figure, and Bernard Cahier, who tried it for *The Autocar*, found the Abarth tractable in central Turin, though the noise level was frightening—shades of Nazzaro and the S76! The 'O' in the designation stood for *omologato*, guaranteeing a production of a thousand identical units and rendering the car eligible for saloon events. The price paid for all this ferocity was a tendency to wander at speed (chassis geometry was based on top speeds of 80-odd!) and a cool £2,580, even in Italy.

FIAT's own coupé and spyder, which arrived on the scene in 1965, were calculated to appeal to a much wider public. Engine modifications included a 9.3:1 compression, a 'hotter' camshaft, larger inlet valves, a dual-choke carburetter, and a four-branch exhaust manifold. The suspension was reinforced, there were disc brakes at the front, and 'proper' oval instruments were provided, though these were set in simulated wood. Coupés had 47 b.h.p. engines, the spyders being a little more potent, but made only with l.h.d. Bertone was responsible for the open bodies; the coupé, a genuine if somewhat cramped 2+2, was a FIAT creation. Top speed was an easy 85, and 70 came up in third with the rev counter sitting at 6,400. Gear-change was positive, and the car was not unduly tricky in cross-winds, though in driving rain on a motorway aquaplaning tendencies made themselves felt. *The Motor* found their test car a trifle thirsty when driven to capacity, but during a weekend's hard motoring with two up in the Peak District, my own fairly tired example returned 37 m.p.g. The noise level at 5,000 r.p.m. can be irritating, the gearbox demands constant use, and a heated rear window is really an essential in cold or damp weather, but FIAT had achieved almost the perfect 'personal car' for the congested roads of the 1960s. The adoption of a 903 c.c. engine during 1968 gave the 850 coupé a top speed of 90 plus, but even then a degree of Abarthisation was necessary to match the performance of a full-house Mini-Cooper 'S'. The original English list price was £865, but by 1971 inflation had raised this to over £1,000.

The Autocar considered the sports-model 850s 'something of a major departure from normal practice' on the strength of their factory-built bodies, but FIAT had never forgotten the enthusiast. Though the 8V ended its short run late in 1954, 1959 saw the first catalogued twin-camshaft FIAT, the 1500S. This was built up on the 'platform' of the existing 1200 cabriolet, but the engine was an adaptation of the successful O.S.C.A. unit, manufactured under licence by FIAT. These five-bearing motors had direct valve operation by inverted tappets, and chain-driven camshafts, though coil ignition and wet-sump lubrication were concessions to volume production. In twin-carburetter form 120 b.h.p. were claimed. Other parts of the car followed routine practice, and the rigid body, a Pininfarina product, boasted such embellishments as a Nardi wood-rimmed steering-wheel. As tested by *Motor Sport* it exceeded 100 m.p.h. without difficulty, could be wound up to 80 in third, and the engine 'ran like a turbine'. The retention of a beam rear axle made for considerable up-and-down movement on bad surfaces. Fuel consumption was a modest 24 m.p.g., but the O.S.C.A.-FIAT, like its contemporaries the Facel-Vega 'Facellia' and the MG-A Twin-Cam, was an oil-burner.

By 1961 it had acquired Girling disc brakes at the front, and 1963 models wore raised air intakes on their bonnets, indicative of more capacity (1,568 c.c.) together with thermostatically-controlled and clutched fans, and twin fuel pumps, electric and mechanical. Disc brakes were now fitted all round, as were paired headlamps. The last cars, made in 1965, had five forward speeds, as tried twelve years previously on the Le Mans 8V. Production was never on a big scale, and only l.h.d. versions were available. This, and a list price of £1,699, made the model a rarity in England, but the 1500S and 1600S have their significance as the ancestors of a much better and more popular car, the 124 Sport Special of 1966.

Also in the 1959 programme were a brace of six-cylinder saloons, supplanting the bulboid 1400B and 1900B. These, the 1800 and 2100, had robust four-bearing units from the drawing-board of Aurelio Lampredi, late of Ferrari. Dimensions were 72 × 73.5 mm for the smaller 112 unit, and 77 × 73.5 mm for the bigger, 2,054 c.c. 112A type. Fully-machined, poly-spherical combustion chambers, pump cooling, and dual-choke downdraught carburetters featured in their specification, and though column change was retained, they were the first FIATs to have synchromesh on all gears. The drum brakes incorporated a FIAT-Baldwin booster on the front, and, like the 500, the 1800 and 2100 had rear-wheel handbrakes from the start. Front suspension was by wishbones and torsion bars; unfortunately the 1400's beam axle and coils were perpetuated at the rear, which spoilt the handling. The unitary structure was very rigid, with box-section side-members and tubular cross-members, while the angular styling was a logical follow-up to the 1200 of 1957. Wheelbase was 8 ft 8¼ in, and saloons turned the scales at around 24 cwt. Station wagons were also offered; in addition, the 2100 could be had as a *berlina speciale* in monochrome finish, with four headlamps, a wrap-round grille, and a *de luxe* interior, which the catalogue termed 'a car well suited for use on formal occasions'.

The regular 'six' was almost as well equipped: a 2100 saloon came complete with oil pressure gauge, clock, thermometer, and seven assorted warning lights. It was exceedingly smooth and comfortable, would top 90 m.p.h., and would accelerate to 50 m.p.h. in 10.6 seconds. *The Autocar* spoke of 'outstanding adhesion in the wet', but *Motor Sport* sounded a note of caution:

> The car does not roll unduly, but the suspension is soggy, some surfaces cause either a floating or up-and-down motion, and too much work is called for by the indecisive, low-geared steering, although to its credit this transmits no kickback, little vibration,

and has powerful caster return action. But it is the sort of steering with which you can pretend to be Fangio trying hard, without much effect on the car.

Certainly a gentleman's carriage—but not quite a FIAT. Nevertheless, William Boddy obviously found much to commend in the 2300 which he sampled in January, 1963, as he concluded his report with the words: 'When I get older and enjoy straights more than corners I shall have nothing but praise for this FIAT.'

1961 saw servo-assisted disc brakes all round, an electromagnetic fan coupling, a sealed cooling system, and leaf springs at the rear. The 1800 was given more power, while the 2100 became the 2,279 c.c. 2300 with four headlamps. Optional on the larger car was a Laycock de Normanville overdrive made by Autobianchi, while automatics were at last seen on a FIAT. Plans were laid to use the Smiths' Easidrive box, but in the end the factory preferred the Anglo-American Borg-Warner. An overdrive-equipped 2300 sold for £1,510.50 in England in 1962, and both this and the 1800B survived until 1968.

The 2300 was hardly a driver's car: but this could not be said of the exciting 2300S, based on a Ghia-bodied prototype coupé shown at Geneva in March, 1961. Here at last was a poor man's Ferrari, with 135 b.h.p. twin-carburetter engine, floor change, a 3.9:1 top gear, and servo-assisted disc brakes. Like all special-bodied FIATs, this was a 'platform job', and the handsome package included such refinements as electric window lifts. Weight, at 25½ cwt, was slightly more than that of an E-type Jaguar. The 2300S offered a top speed of 120 m.p.h., an 0–100 m.p.h. time of 35 seconds, and a splendid, vintage feel. *The Motor* spoke of 'stability, comfort, and responsive handling at very high speeds', though its heavy brakes made it 'very much a masculine vehicle'. The vintage atmosphere, continued the report 'must go straight to the heart of many drivers prosperous enough to afford it. The feeling will go to their shoulders, too, for 3½ turns from lock to lock is not enough to make the steering light by modern standards, and the wheel is large, so that a ten-to-two grip keeps the driver's arms in the air'. The 'six-cylinder commotion' of Lampredi's engine was appreciated, though it probably rendered the two alarm bells (for overheating and the choke) essential as well as the usual plethora of warning lights. But even at £2,994 all on, the 2300S made many friends.

In this case the standard article performed better than the 'specials', and none of these lasted long. Abarth had a very expensive 135 b.h.p. coupé on show at Earls Court in 1960, while Moretti, who had abandoned their own designs in favour of customised FIATs made, a few elegant 2500SS spyders with 170 b.h.p. engines which they sold at 2,950,000 lire apiece. Top speed was said to be 130 m.p.h.

By contrast FIAT's 1300 and 1500, though closely resembling the 'sixes' in outward appearance, were 'average' family saloons with all-synchromesh gearboxes. Entirely new were the suspension arrangements, by coils at the front and conventional semi-elliptics at the rear. Engines retained Lampredi's polyspherical head design, and the company experimented with smaller 1.2-litre and 1.4-litre units before settling for capacities of 1,295 c.c. and 1,481 c.c. respectively. The bigger 1500 unit gave 72 b.h.p. at 5,200 r.p.m., and Italians paid the equivalent of £700 for a 1300, and £745 for a 1500. Once again, station wagons formed part of the production programme.

To-day these 1961 FIATs look foursquare and old-fashioned: one equates them with stalwarts of the stamp of the Peugeot 403 and the Austin A60. In actual fact the 1500 was appreciably faster than either, returning 92 m.p.h. on test, while the 1300 was nearly as quick. In acceleration and fuel consumption the FIAT had the edge on the Austin: its built-in toughness was the result of tests in which eighteen prototypes had covered vast mileages over the worst that Scandinavia and Equatorial Africa could offer. Road-test reports speak highly of the flexibility, the good gear-change, and the accurate steering. I remember a long trip to the North with a 1500 *familiare*, which cruised up the M6 Motorway at 80–85 m.p.h., and averaged 26 m.p.g. over a test route which included the crossing of the northern Pennines from Cockermouth to Newcastle-upon-Tyne. The column change was outstanding, surpassed only by that of the

Renault 16, while the 1500 was one of only two 'fours' I have handled which could genuinely be mistaken for a 'six', the other was the Rover 80 of 1962.

Subsequent developments included a long-chassis version, the 1500L, intended for hire work. This had all-disc brakes, and at the same time the standard 1300 and 1500 were improved with slightly longer wheelbases, higher-lift camshafts, revised timing, and stronger clutches. 1500 units now developed 75 b.h.p., and a car tried by *Autosport* in 1965 recorded a startling 96 m.p.h. There were also a few cabriolets, using the 1600S chassis, body and transmission, and a tuned edition of the 1500 engine. They would touch the 100 mark, but were not marketed after 1965. Saloons and station wagons were continued until 1968, about 600,000 finding buyers.

Of the foreign producers, Neckar of Heilbronn had a good decade, turning out close on 150,000 600s in the 1955–65 period, while the 1100 also sold well, 'Europa' variants being offered briefly in Britain for £34 less than was asked for the Turin-built model. In addition the firm offered special 500s with German coupé and 'limousette' coachwork, and some SIATA-tuned 1500 saloons and coupés. Heilbronn's banner year was 1962, with 50,297 cars delivered, and the 1800 did better in Germany than in other export markets, since it undercut B.M.W.'s new four-cylinder o.h.c. saloons. Thanks to FIAT, Italy sold more cars to Germany than she bought from her, and in 1965 the *marque* ranked fifth in total registrations within the *Bundesrepublik*, behind Volkswagen, Opel, Ford and Mercedes-Benz. 568,421 FIATs contrasted interestingly with the 'foreign' runners-up, Renault with 237,557 units. Of individual models, only the Volkswagen Beetle, the R3-series Opel 'Rekord', and the 12 M and 17M *Kölnische* Fords were used in greater numbers than the FIAT 600.

In Austria Steyr-Puch adopted the 500 in 1957, but fitted it with their own more powerful 493 c.c. engine as well as giving it bigger brakes and modifying the hull to take their own brand of swing-axle rear suspension. By 1965 their 650TR was distinguishing itself in European rallies: this was a 'hot' version with enlarged capacity, high-lift camshaft, dual-choke Zenith carburetter, Panhard rod at the front, Koni dampers, radial-ply tyres, and a bigger fuel tank, the spare wheel living behind the seats in the luggage space. It out-Abarthed Abarth. As *The Motor* said: 'It looks like a bright-red jelly mould, and went like a kind of saloon go-kart. This was a he-man vehicle, desperately noisy and demanding concentration to drive, but a funabout *par excellence*, and probably the fastest commuting car yet devised'. Ferdinand Porsche and Karl Rabe must have turned in their graves at the thought of this obstreperous successor to their 'Prince Henry' and 'Bergmeister' Austro-Daimlers, but its vogue was brief, and by 1969 Steyr-Daimler-Puch had reverted to limited production of the standard article.

SEAT of Barcelona expanded steadily, making 76,161 cars in 1964. They, too, produced 'local' FIATs with no exact Torinese equivalent. These included a four-door 600 and a cross-bred 1800/1500, using the hull of the 'six' and the 'four's' engine, while customers in quest of frugality were offered the old 1400 unit as an alternative. There were also a few Spanish SIATAS, using bored-out 735 c.c. 600 engines, and roadster bodies reminiscent of Renault's 'Floride' convertible. In Yugoslavia the Zastava works at Kragujevac had been making FIATS since October, 1954; initially these were 1400s and 1900s, but the 600 was adopted shortly afterward, and by 1962 an extended factory could cope with 82,000 vehicles a year.

The export picture remained patchy. Always the Germans had the upper hand, while in some markets (notably Norway and Finland) a sheer lack of foreign exchange forced buyers to draw heavily on the Iron Curtain republics with their penchant for barter deals. Czechoslovakia started to import cars from the West again in 1959, and the 600 soon found itself a niche despite inflated prices. Sweden faded from the picture, Italy's share of the market dropping to a miserable 1.4 per cent by 1964, and attempts to improve FIAT sales in Australia and Canada fizzled. In 1955 the Commonwealth imported only 1,444 Italian cars. Plans to assemble 1100s in Victoria and New South Wales never got off the ground, any more than did a deal with Chrysler whereby that concern was to distribute FIATS in Canada. A brighter corner of the New World was Argentina, where the Concord company started to assemble 600s and 1100s alongside their trucks and tractors in 1960, while there was a brief echo from the past when Autoar (successors to Piero Dusio's abortive South American adventure) adopted the FIAT 1900 engine in place of the traditional L-head four-cylinder Willys. Belgium was fast becoming a Franco-German preserve, with Britain and Italy the losers. By 1963 the 1100 was old-fashioned, the 1800 was too expensive, and the 1500 was fighting an inconclusive battle at 94,500 fr against a much improved Vauxhall 'Victor' (83,500 fr), the German Ford 17M (89,900 fr) and Volkswagen's 1500 (87,500 fr). The FIAT could match the Peugeot 404 on price, and was considered a better buy than the slower Hillman 'Super Minx'—some compensation for the fact that Milanese taxi-owners had re-equipped with this British model almost on FIAT's back doorstep!

Even Switzerland was not quite the paradise it had once been, though FIAT plugged the Swiss markets for all they were worth, launching model after model at the Geneva Show, and leaving seasonal improvements for Turin. By 1954 the 500C had run its race: sales were down to 578 units as against 1,264 in 1952, though the 1100 continued to hold its own. For the time being the 600 more than redressed the balance—5,232 of the 5,781 new Italian cars registered in 1955 were FIATS, but four years later the company's third place put them well behind Opel, and in 1960 they were actually beaten by Renault. Once again new models (the 1300 and 1500) had their effect, and in 1962 they were yapping at Opel's heels once more.

None the less, there were triumphs. One of these was New Zealand, hemmed in by successive governments with the same credo of austerity. Assembly of c.k.d. units was authorised on a strictly limited scale in 1961, and eventually FIAT were able to meet the stringent demands. The locally-produced content had to include batteries, brake hoses and cables, exhaust systems, rubber seals, hose-clips, wiring looms, springs, air filters, coils, interior trim, mirrors and visors, and speedometer cables, plus 'all glues, solvents, sealers and paints'. In these circumstances the achievement of Motor Holdings of Auckland is creditable—they put together 4,941 500s, 1,762 1500s and 576 1100T vans before passing on to more modern types.

In Britain the company worked hard to re-establish the strong position established by D'Arcy Baker and his pre-War successors. An exchange engine service was added to the facilities at Wembley in 1961, and a Test Day was staged at Brands Hatch in 1965. 1962 sales were 3,661 units, but in two years they had almost tripled, at 10,537.

Finally there was America, and in 1956 the car-carrier *M.V. Italterra* crossed the Atlantic with the first big shipment of 600s and 1100s. Initially the 1100 cost more (at £465) than the rival Renault 'Dauphine', but it was cheap beside such cut-price American models as the Studebaker 'Scotsman' (£722) and the basic six-cylinder Rambler (£784). 1959 was an excellent year, with 38,468 cars sold, but thereafter sales slumped. This was partly due to over-much stress on elderly types like the 1100, but FIAT, unlike many a British factory, has never relied too heavily on the capricious American market, and matters did not take an upturn until 1965, when the 850 spyder became available. FIATs were reintroduced to France after a long lapse in 1958, but again the build-up was slow. The establishment of FIAT's own French sales organisation (FFSA) in January, 1963, turned the *marque* into a major force. In 1965–66 Italy shipped 26,108 cars across the border—less than half West Germany's 52,638, but well above the British contribution—a promising start.

Commercial-vehicle production remained steady, the 1964 recession apart. This, however, was on a modest scale by British or French standards; the entire Italian industry could not match the production of a single British factory. In 1960, for instance, the Italians (FIAT, O.M., Alfa Romeo, Lancia, Bianchi, and a few small specialists) delivered 48,710 commercial vehicles. In the same year Vauxhall's Luton and Dunstable plants turned out 103,495 Bedfords.

Most of these trucks were, of course, of FIAT origin. The firm was top of the league in 1960, with 27,323 goods and 1,622 passenger models, while runners-up were their subsidiary company, O.M., who made 9,248 all told. The biggest of the independents, Alfa Romeo, could muster a mere 2,064.

The unitary-construction 'bus trade prospered. FIAT made their own models, and in 1959 these included the underfloor-engined 306/2, 309 and 314, as well as urban types, and parallel trolleybus variants seating up to 85 passengers. The big 306, a 51-seater coach, could be had with air springs and power-assisted steering, while outside firms such as Viberti and Aerfer offered enormous double-deckers. The 1960 Viberti was a 104-seater powered by a vertical underfloor-mounted 200 b.h.p. FIAT diesel engine, and the specification included an automatic gearbox and air-pressure brakes. Strictly a dream vehicle was the 'Golden Dolphin' shown at Turin in 1957: it was sumptuously fitted out with individual reading lamps, television, a radio-telephone, cloakrooms, refrigerator and bar, and the designed cruising speed was 125 m.p.h. The only thing missing was the FIAT gas turbine supposed to provide this formidable performance!

On the goods vehicle side the 1100 emerged in 1956 as a forward-control van, while in 1958 the range was augmented by the C40N and C50N, medium-capacity normal-control lorries with six-cylinder diesel engines. Forward control was, however, the order of the day. 1959 editions of the 682 series could be had with 180 b.h.p. supercharged engines, and a year later this theme was developed a stage further, into the 690N, a twin-steer six-wheeler for 10½-ton payloads. New models for 1965 included the 625N, a compact forward-control three-tonner with a five-speed synchromesh gearbox, powered by a new 2.7-litre four-cylinder diesel engine, and the 693N, a new six-wheeler with conventional double drive. Like most of the really big FIATs, it boasted a twin-plate clutch and eight forward speeds, while the 12,880 c.c. six-cylinder oil engine developed 226 b.h.p. at 1,900 r.p.m. A complete lorry cost £4,750 in Italy.

At the *sezione aeronautica* new models became less frequent.

73. Italian cars for New Zealand. 750 coupés on the assembly line at Auckland, 1971.
(John Tudehope and Harold D. Kidd)

74. Spanish cars for Great Britain: the first batch of SEAT 850s arrives at Brentford, January 1973.
(Woolf, Laing, Christie and Partners)

75, 76. Two faces of a best-seller – the standard 1,197 c.c. 124 as clothed by Francis Lombardi (top) in 1966

(Francis Lombardi)

and the twin overhead camshaft 125 in English export guise, 1970.

(Woolf, Laing, Christie and Partners)

Gone were the days when a fighter could be built for £5,000, or even £25,000, once the lines had been set up, and the Rolls-Royce bankruptcy of 1971 was to highlight the appalling problems of the aircraft industry. No longer could a single firm bear the entire burden of a major military project, and new designs might take years to get into the air. First particulars of FIAT's G-222 twin-engined light freighter were released in 1963; it did not fly until 1970. Thus the company had to keep going on NATO contracts, among them work on Sikorsky helicopters and North American F-86Ks. By 1958 they had built 231 of these latter, which went to France, Germany, the Netherlands and Norway as well as to the Italian Air Force.

None the less, the decade was to see one important new FIAT, the G-91 light tactical fighter designed for operation out of all-grass fields. Powered by a Bristol 'Orpheus' jet engine, it had a semi-monocoque all-metal fuselage, and swept-back wings, and could carry various armaments, from a battery of four 0.5-calibre Browning machine-guns to two rocket packs. It first flew in August, 1956, the second prototype was in the air by the following July, and operational trials began in February, 1958. The G-91 was a great success; photo-reconnaissance versions were developed alongside the original fighter models, while a big order came from the reconstituted *Luftwaffe*. Eventually Dornier, Heinkel and Messerschmitt collaborated to build 294 G-91s in Germany. Top speed of the aircraft was 668 m.p.h. at sea level.

By 1964 FIAT stood poised on the brink of a technical revolution. Dante Giacosa had long held a patent for an f.w.d. car with east-west engine, and in 1964 he put this idea into practice, though with a slightly apologetic air of 'trying it on the dog', the first *traction* he made was neither a FIAT nor produced in Turin.

Autobianchi's 'Primula' bore some outward resemblance to the Austin-Morris 1100 already being manufactured down the road by Innocenti, but under the surface it was quite different. The engine was the good old 1,221 c.c. FIAT 1100D, but unlike Alec Issigonis' creations it had an externally-mounted gearbox.

A single-plate diaphragm clutch with hydraulic actuation transmitted the power to an offset differential *via* a pair of gears, and Giacosa dispensed with a conventional fan, preferring an automatically-engaged electric affair operating over a third of the radiator's surface. The four-speed all-synchromesh gearbox had the traditional FIAT column change, front suspension was by transverse leaf with lower wishbones, and there were semi-elliptics at the rear. Rack and pinion steering, hitherto rejected by FIAT as too expensive to make in Italy, now featured. The result seems to have been something of a curate's egg, and its teething troubles suggest that FIAT were wise to use another brand-name in the formative years. Swiss sales were poor, and German owners suffered from indifferent service. A saloon cost 1,075,000 lire, and also in the range were a three-door station wagon and a sports coupé with 1,352 c.c. engine, wire wheels, and floor change, introduced during 1965.

Already the ingredients of a promising future were at hand. Neither the 'Primula' nor the 1600S were world-beaters, but their features were to put FIAT at the top of the league with the 124/125 range and the incredible 128 of 1969.

12 The New Italian Empire

Modena is famous for its military college, its cathedral,
and its position as the centre of Italy's exotic car
industry. This last mentioned distinction is confirmed by
FIAT's decision to move its sports car production
to nearby Maranello.

Ferrari's FIAT affiliation has, enigmatically, brought
much work and much trouble to Maranello in the way of
strikes. The workers employ the devastating technique
of working and striking alternate hours. Nevertheless,
it was possible to take a swift look into the
considerably enlarged factory where Ferraris, Ferrari
'Dinos', and FIAT 'Dinos' are coming off parallel lines.

The Autocar, July, 1971

Gianni Agnelli, grandson of the founder and to-day's FIAT
president, recently predicted that the world's motor industry
would soon be controlled by ten companies. He did not name
them; speculation could have sparked off a run on the *bourses*
of Europe in this era of mergers.

In Germany Glas was absorbed by B.M.W., the Hanomag
and Henschel truck firms joined forces, and Volkswagen built
themselves a consortium by acquiring N.S.U. and Auto Union.
Chrysler went empire-building for the first time since they
bought Dodge in 1928, emerging in control of France's Simca,
Britain's ailing Rootes Group, and Spain's Barreiros-Diesel.
They also concluded an alliance with Mitsubishi of Japan. At
the bottom end of a decimated American industry American
Motors swallowed the Kaiser Jeep Corporation. In January,
1968, the British Leyland Motor Corporation came into being
after a series of boardroom earthquakes, and after the dust had

settled the new group was found to embrace ten makes of private car and nine of commercial vehicle, even if some of these were masterpieces of badge-engineering. Japan's mushroom industry had begun to align itself in two major groups, with Prince Motors falling to Nissan-Datsun, and Toyota buying into Hino and Daihatsu.

Inevitably FIAT joined in the latest bout of empire-building. By 1965, of course, they already controlled Autobianchi and O.M., had a 36 per cent stake in SEAT, their Spanish licencees, and were well established in France with a minority holding in Simca and a majority interest in Unic.

Six years later the two Italian companies had been fully integrated, and FIAT had acquired a fifty per cent holding in Ferrari. In November, 1969, an even greater prize had fallen into their hands—Lancia, weakened by debts of 69 million lire. Long and bitter negotiations had won Agnelli a 15 per cent share in Citroën. As far as Italy was concerned, these transactions gave FIAT a virtual monopoly of heavy goods vehicles, while in the private-car sector they had only two major rivals— the state-owned Alfa Romeo concern and Innocenti. In 1969 these two factories had delivered 155,000 units to FIAT's 1,440,000, though Alfa Romeo, certainly, were out of Agnelli's reach. The future of Innocenti was less certain; their cars were Italianate versions of B.M.C. designs, and Lord Stokes had already shown a preference for channelling foreign sales through wholly owned subsidiaries rather than through licencees or concessionaires. FIAT, however, had plenty on their hands: a new plant at Rivalta started operations in 1967, and their contribution to the redevelopment of the impoverished South involved more than ten factories and 19,000 jobs.

FIAT, of course, was far more loosely-knit than the average empire, and badge-engineering was not part of their philosophy. O.M.'s trucks continued to be O.M.s and not FIATs, the firm introducing a new 270 b.h.p. Roots-blown vee-eight engine for their 'Titano' line, though by 1970 more and more FIAT elements were finding their way into O.M. designs. Autobianchi continued their policy of trying out new ideas 'before the West

End Run', the FIAT 127 being anticipated by their A112. 500
berline joined the station wagons they had been making since
1969. As for Lancia, it was made clear that they would continue
as 'small specialist manufacturers', though many people
would wonder how long an annual sale of less than 45,000
units would suit Agnelli's book. Even when FIAT started to
sponsor a rally team in 1970, their 124 Sport spyders were not
integrated into Lancia's existing and successful competition
set-up. A degree of integration was, however detectable by
the end of 1972, when Lancia's new 'Beta' saloon harboured a
twin-cam four-cylinder FIAT engine under its bonnet. When
Ferrari became an affiliate, there was talk of joint marketing
arrangements, but these have not eventuated, any more than
have fears that the association might reintroduce touring-type
FIAT gearboxes to Maranello's wares. Instead, FIAT boxes have
improved. When Ferruccio Lamborghini sold his old tractor
factory to FIAT, the inevitable rumours ensued, but Lamborghini remains independent and inviolate.

Citroën, of course, constituted a real coup. For years
Michelin, who had rescued the company from bankruptcy
in 1935, had been casting around for a buyer, but their proposed
deal with FIAT did not accord with Charles de Gaulle's nationalist views; he felt as strongly about Citroën as had Mussolini
when Henry Ford laid siege to Isotta Fraschini nearly forty
years before. The General was no match for Agnelli and his
advisers; they discovered a loophole whereby amounts to the
value of $11 million could be transferred to Italy without
Government permission, and suddenly de Gaulle was confronted by a French holding company in which FIAT had a
majority interest. John Bolster could not conceal his admiration
in *Autosport's* Paris Show report. 'At last', he proclaimed,
'General de Gaulle has tried to hit someone his own size, and
Agnelli has walked all over him'.

Everyone was happy. Michelin was free to concentrate on
tyres, and FIAT had a ready-made dealer-network in France.
What is more, they had a stake, not only in Citroën, but also
in Citroën's *Lyonnais* subsidiary Berliet, who were strong in

the heavy-vehicle field. Berliet and Unic between them made four-fifths of France's *poids lourds*, leaving the balance of 3,900 units a year in the hands of Saviem, itself a division of Renault.

1967 saw FIAT edge quietly ahead of Volkswagen, delivering 1,340,884 vehicles to Wolfsburg's 1,290,328. 1966 had been the Agnelli empire's first 'million year' in the private-car division, Italian buyers alone accounting for a quarter of a million 500s, 70,000 of the new 124s, and 55,000 600s. At the same time foreign imports took a tumble, from 20.8 to 10.74 per cent of new registrations. FIAT's 1968 figures were even higher, but though the growth rate was a disappointing 2½ per cent, they were faring better than the British factories who had cut so painfully into their favourite European markets in the late 1940s and early 1950s. A goodly proportion of Vauxhall's 329,000 units were Bedford trucks, while British Leyland had only just scraped in over the million mark; more than half their private cars were Minis and 1100/1300s, to which FIAT would soon have an answer. Ford of Dagenham (553,701) were worth watching, but even under Chrysler management Rootes were well down the second division on an output of less than 200,000. Far more ominous was a seven-figure performance by Toyota of Japan.

1969 was another poor year by FIAT standards, especially in view of a record performance by Renault—911,000 cars and 98,000 light commercials. Agnelli's annual report made gloomy reading; the national three-year wage agreement had come up for renewal, and not only was the wage bill up, but the company were 20 million man-hours and 277,000 cars to the bad thanks to a series of strikes. Small-car sales were falling, even though 500s were still being made to the tune of two thousand a day, and the new five-speed 125 Special was gaining many friends. On the credit side the f.w.d. 128 was going into production, and nearly one-and-a-half million vehicles had been delivered. 583,646 of these had gone for export. FIAT were manufacturing private cars in seven countries (Argentina, Austria, India, Poland, Spain, Turkey and Yugoslavia) and had assembly plants in another eighteen. The vast Togliattigrad complex was tooling up for the first FIAT derivatives to be made in Russia since the demise of the Amo F-15 truck in 1930. But two great personalities had gone. Vittorio Valletta had died in 1967, and now Dante Giacosa was stepping down from the design department, though he was retained as a consultant.

With Giacosa, certain conventions also departed. While he had been the architect of FIAT's rear-engined family, he was also an advocate of the conventional, maintaining that orthodoxy was justified in terms of low cost per copy, and ease of servicing. The 124 has vindicated this view both before and since his departure. Giacosa was also an opponent of automatic gear-boxes, which Italians did not want, and it is significant that before 1969 only a single model—the 2300 *berlina*—was marketed with other than a sliding-type box. One enthusiast has summed up Giacosa's FIAT as 'gentle and without temperament, like their creator', though it is a matter of opinion whether this description could be applied to the 1937 508C, his first independent effort for the company.

The old faithfuls saw the decade out, Turin delivering its last 600Ds in 1970, while the 850 appeared in a new guise in 1966. This 'Idromatic' version combined a torque converter and an automatic clutch with the regular all-synchromesh gearbox, and was popular with lady drivers, even if *The Autocar* considered it 'an awkward and not very satisfactory half-way stage to automatic control'. They did, however, recommend it for the handicapped. In 1968 an enlarged 903 c.c., 52 b.h.p. engine was offered for spyders and coupés. At the same time a bigger oil pump was provided, and a car tested by *Autosport* recorded a top speed of 92 m.p.h., and an 0–60 m.p.h. acceleration time of 11.4 seconds. By 1970 detuned 903 c.c. units were used in the 850T, a descendant of the O.M.-bodied 'Multipla' first seen in 1963. In 1969 the last new 850 variant went on sale in Britain. This was the 'Special', a *berlina* with the original 843 c.c. coupé engine and front disc brakes. It proved to be an 80 m.p.h. motor-car with better acceleration than the basic model, and an ability to keep station at a steady 70 on motorways.

As for the 1100, it just would not die, and the final R-series went into production at Lingotto in 1966. It sold another 300,000 before it was finally withdrawn in 1970. The 1100R had a 1,089 c.c. engine developing 48 b.h.p., a dual-choke carburetter, front disc brakes, and floor change, while the fuel tank was moved to the right rear wing in the interests of better luggage accommodation. To the end bottom gear was unsynchronised, but the veteran would do a respectable 78 m.p.h. and 32 m.p.g., being rated 'a durable workhorse suitable for a high-mileage, exacting owner'. The steering, however, emerged as 'dead and slightly vague', and a greasing schedule which called for attention to the front suspension, propeller shaft and steering at 1,500-mile intervals was considered 'vintage' by 1966.

The big news of that year was, of course, the 124, the work of Oscar Montabone, but with more than a hint of Dante Giacosa in its make-up. *Autovisie* in Holland and *Car* in Great Britain chose it as their 'car of the year'. Mauro Forghieri, Ferrari's chief engineer, drove one. 160,000 Italians bought 124s during the model's first eleven months of life. It formed the basis for new models introduced in Poland and in the Soviet Union. Unkind people called it 'Italy's Ford "Cortina",' and one critic told his readers that it was 'too cheap by £5'; a reference to the indifferent sound-damping of early 124s.

On paper it was as much an average family saloon as the 1500 which had preceded it, though in fact the two had but one feature in common—the all-synchromesh gearbox, used on the 124 with the important modification of a positive floor change. At 16.1 cwt the car was fractionally lighter than the 1100R, but increased body width made it a full five-seater. Entirely new was the five-bearing pushrod four-cylinder engine, with its wedge-shaped combustion chambers and pre-engaged starter motor. Cylinder dimensions were 73 × 71.5 mm (1,197 c.c.), and output was 60 b.h.p. Once again FIAT preferred a coil-and-wishbone arrangement at the front, but there was a surprising reversion to coil springs and a live axle at the rear. The new trailing-arm suspension was, however, a great improvement on the 1400/1900 and the early 'sixes' of 1959.

The 124 proved a taut and well-mannered machine, at its best on winding secondary roads, where its viceless behaviour enabled it to put up better averages than some faster members of its family. *Motor Sport* praised 'the life, the light controls, and the handling precision of a sporting car', while the example tried by *The Motor* attained 91 m.p.h., and accelerated to 50 m.p.h. in 9.2 seconds. In fact, this 'ordinary' saloon out-performed such contemporaries as the 1,300 c.c. Ford 'Cortina', the Hillman 'Minx', the Toyota 'Corona', and the front-wheel-drive Triumph 1300, while it was also more frugal, returning 28.3 m.p.g. to the Ford's 27.9 m.p.g., and the Toyota's 23. More leisured driving techniques gave an easy 30 m.p.g., and the English list price was a reasonable £774. A station wagon was also available.

The second step in 124 evolution was seen at the Turin Show in November, when the Sport Spyder with Pininfarina-styled open two-four seater body appeared, using the saloon's 'platform', suspension and all-disc brakes. Also in the range was a handsome and angular 2+2 coupé styled by FIAT themselves. A four-speed all-synchromesh gearbox was standard, with the option of five speeds at extra cost, but the engine was a new 1,438 c.c. unit with pent-roof combustion chambers and cogged-belt drive for its twin overhead camshafts. This developed 90 b.h.p. at 6,500 r.p.m., and could be pushed to 8,000 on the indirects. Preliminary tests showed a top speed of 106 m.p.h., and a standing quarter-mile in 18.2 seconds, more than three seconds quicker than the 1952 8V.

The coupés reached the English market during 1967, at a list price of under £1,400. Steering was somewhat heavy, though *Autosport* found the car 'very forgiving of driver errors and fundamentally safe'. Philip Turner, writing in *The Motor*, was conscious of 'a delightfully taut feeling', and could not resist likening the Sport Coupé to 'a baby Ferrari'. *The Autocar*'s testers almost went overboard:

> Seldom have our test staff been so unanimous in our praise of a car. Initial comments after a spell at the wheel ranged from 'I wonder if they would sell it to me', to 'No, you can't have the

key—I'm keeping it'. Here is a bang up to date sports car, not
from a specialist with a competition tradition, but from the
world's fourth largest mass producer. By all that is sacred to
the enthusiast the car has no right to be as good as it is. Yet
judged absolutely and objectively, it is outstanding if not exceptional, not so much for what it does, but in the way it does it.

Top speed was revealed as 105 m.p.h., 75 was possible on
third, and 48–50 on second, while the fuel consumption range
was a little heavy for a 1½-litre, at 21–26 m.p.g. The five-speed
version was even more delightful, the box being matched to
the car's character. The extra ratio found on 'Special' versions
of the 125 saloon was very much an overdrive, suitable only
for motorways, but on the 124 coupé it was there to be used,
with a quick and easy movement across the 'gate'. During
2,000 fast miles the only faults encountered were a sharply
cut-off dipped beam, irritating heater controls on the central
console, and some occasional, reproachful clonks from the
saloon-type rear suspension. Below 5,000 r.p.m. the engine
rarely made its presence felt, and the coupé lent itself to a
diversity of driving techniques. I remember sampling the back
seat (bearable for a six-footer) while the FIAT was conducted at
high speed by two different drivers. One of these, nurtured on
'30–98' Vauxhalls and the like, did all his motoring, including
tighter bends, in fifth and fourth. Of the other it could be said:
'Give her eight speeds and she'd use 'em all'; but the FIAT was
just as happy whichever way it was treated.

Next link in the chain was the 125, distinguishable externally
by its four-headlamp layout, though it was built up round a
much stiffer edition of the 124 structure, and had semi-elliptic
rear springs as well. The engine was based on that of the 124
Sport, but capacity was up to 1,608 c.c., and output was 94
b.h.p. at 5,600 r.p.m. Unlike the 124, it had a clutched fan, and
the disc brakes were servo-assisted. The wheelbase, at 8 ft
2½ in, was three inches longer, and it was amazing value in
Britain at £1,007. The top three ratios of the four-speed box
were delightfully close, at 4.1, 5.59, and 8.6 to 1, giving maxima
of 99, 82, and 53 m.p.h., and the 0–60 m.p.h. time ran the

coupé's very close. *Autosport* called it 'a safe car with no vices
. . . which persuades even a lazy driver to go faster than he
intended and invariably arrives at its destination a little sooner
than expected'. In terms of hard fact it was slower than the
superseded 2300, but it was a driver's car, which the 'six'
emphatically was not. Its worst faults were steering which was
too heavy at manoeuvring speeds, and a thirst of around 21
m.p.g. 1968 saw a Special version with square headlamps and a
five-speed gearbox, which was lapped up by *autostrada*-
conscious Italians.

1969 saw yet another permutation, the 124 Special, which had
the alternator ignition of the twin-cam cars, and inherited its
radial-ply tyres and four headlamps from the 125. Power came
from a 70 b.h.p. 1,438 c.c. pushrod engine, the rear suspension
was slightly revised, and it was a 95 m.p.h. machine, quieter
and appreciably more accelerative than the standard 124. It
was also a little 'too fast for chassis'. At the same time the
Sport Specials acquired two extra headlamps, and were offered
with the 1.6-litre 125 engine in 110 b.h.p. guise, in which
case a five-speed box was standard. At the £1,807 asked in
England this new coupé was excellent value, outperforming
such competition as the B.M.W. 2002, the 2-litre GT version of
Ford's best-selling 'Capri', and the Sunbeam 'Rapier' H120.
The 125 was unchanged, though it was now available with
a three-speed automatic transmission of General Motors
design.

Nor were the permutations at an end, for the 1970 catalogue
contained the 124 Special T, a Special with the 1,438 c.c. twin-
cam engine. The result was a 100 m.p.h. 124. At the same time
the Specials and Special Ts could be had with automatic,
and the basic 124 models were furnished with alternators
instead of coils. FIAT's coverage of the medium-sized sector
now rivalled that of Ford with their 'Cortinas' and 'Capris',
and in their 1,400 c.c. and 1,600 c.c. 124 Sport Spyders they
had the open models which Ford lacked.

Meanwhile FIAT had joined forces with Ferrari to produce an
out-and-out sports car, the 2-litre V-6 'Dino' announced in

1967. The underbonnet vista was pure Maranello—four chain-driven overhead camshafts, two inclined valves per cylinder actuated by inverted piston tappets, and an aluminium block and crankcase. The three dual-choke downdraught Weber carburetters were fed by electric pump, the cooling was assisted by an electric fan, and there was alternator ignition. The clutch was a single dry plate, and the five-speed gearbox had synchromesh on all its forward ratios. All this machinery lived in a unitary structure available in two guises—a spyder by Pininfarina or a fastback 2+2 coupé by Bertone. The suspension resembled that of the 125, brakes were servo-assisted discs, and the car rode on centre-lock wheels of magnesium alloy. A spyder turned the scales at 22½ cwt, and cost a swingeing 3,485,000 lire, though even this was a lot cheaper than Ferrari's own 'Dino' with rear engine, a spiral bevel back end in place of FIAT's hypoid unit, and the rack and pinion steering as yet unaccepted in FIAT circles. Further, the Commendatore extracted 180 b.h.p. from his version, whereas FIAT were content with a more conservative 172 b.h.p. at 7,200 r.p.m.

The 'Dino' was certainly the most complicated FIAT since the 519 of 1922. The engine proved to be turbine-smooth if noisy, *The Autocar* enthusing over 'the pure hum of mechanism running perfectly; no engine without a racing pedigree can make such a sound'. There was another parallel with the 519 in a brake servo mechanism which felt somewhat fierce, but when Charles Bulmer tried a 'Dino' for *The Motor* he found it 'difficult to think of any sports car engine more enjoyable to possess', with a top speed around the 130 mark. 'If' he continued, 'you didn't know that the "Dino" had a live axle at the rear you would think it had very good independent suspension all round'. Maintenance-free transistorised ignition arrived with 1968 models, and a year later both FIAT and Ferrari versions boasted 2.4-litre engines and cast-iron cylinder blocks based on FIAT's new 130, while the FIAT 'Dino 2400' acquired strut-type independent rear springing. Prices were up again, to 3,930,000 lire for open cars and 4,100,000 lire for coupés, but the FIAT still undercut the Ferrari at five-and-a-half million.

As for the traditional exotics, Maserati prices ran around the seven-million mark, and Lamborghinis were even costlier. Iso might save money by importing vee-eight Chevrolet engines from Detroit, but their latest 2+2 'Lele' was no bargain, either, at 6,300,000 lire. 'Dinos' were never made with right-hand steering.

The 1969 FIAT range embraced the 500F, the 600D, the 1100R, the complex 850 and 124/125 families, and the 'Dino'. As yet, however, there was no effective replacement for the *millecento*, though Autobianchi fans needed no crystal ball to see what was coming. 1968 'Primulas' had 124 engines, the 1,438 c.c. Special unit being earmarked for the coupés, and a year later Desio came up with the A112, a square box of a saloon on 'Primula' lines, powered once more by a detuned 903 c.c. 850 coupé engine. More interesting was the front suspension by Macpherson struts, but the Autobianchi was overshadowed at every turn by the latest FIAT, *Tipo* 128. Once again *Autovisie* voted it their 'car of the year', as did the Czechoslovak motoring press.

The 128 was entirely new, though every ingredient was well tried. The five-bearing crankshaft was a 124 heritage, as was the cogged-belt drive for the single upstairs camshaft. Diaphragm-type clutches and synchromesh bottom gears had long formed part of the FIAT credo, and at last the combination of an east/west engine driving the front wheels and rack-and-pinion steering gear found their way on to a real FIAT. Ignition was by 12-volt coil, final drive was by spur gears and a bevel differential, Macpherson struts were used for the front suspension, and a combination of leaf springs, wishbones and Macpherson struts took care of the back end. As on other inexpensive FIATs of the period, there were disc brakes at the front and drums at the rear.

The result was a miracle of compactness—taxes based on overall dimensions would never worry FIAT again. The over-square (80×55.5 mm) 1,116 c.c. engine gave an adequate 55 b.h.p., or little less than the company had been extracting from a 1.9-litre pushrod unit seventeen years previously. A further backward look was even more illuminating: in 1932 outputs in the 50–60 b.h.p. bracket had called for 2,516 c.c., in 1922 they represented the limit for the 3,446 c.c. 110S, also a 'six', while in 1910 such urge had called for *Tipo* 54's 5.7 litres of swept volume. Engine speeds had likewise gone up, from 1,600 r.p.m. in 1910 to 6,000 r.p.m. in 1969. On the new 128 the spare wheel lived under the bonnet to give an unobstructed boot within the confines of the fashionable box shape, and though the 128's wheelbase, at 8 ft, was longer than that of the original *millecento* or even the 124, it was a far shorter car, measuring 12 ft 7¾ in from stem to stern as against the 124's 13 ft 2½ in. Two- and four-door saloon versions were soon joined by a station wagon, while the tuners went to work. Giannini's 128NPS version with twin-carburetter engine could approach 110 m.p.h., on 76 b.h.p., and ex-Ferrari test driver Michael Parkes prepared saloon-car racers for the *Scuderia* Filipinetti. The 128 was lighter than all its f.w.d. rivals with the exception of the simpler Morris and Austin 1100s.

On the road it proved a formidable all-rounder. I found the pedals awkward and the 128 could 'float' disconcertingly on uneven surfaces. Also disappointing was the lock, which could not match the taxi-like characteristics of the old rear-drive FIATs. For all its high build, however, the 128 was refreshingly stable in cross-winds, and the performance was a revelation, even if the 4.24:1 top gear felt lower than it was, and made a driver reach instinctively for a fifth that was not there. The positive central change could not be faulted, and an 0–60 m.p.h. acceleration time of 16.3 seconds was entirely adequate. *The Autocar* subjected an early 128 to long-term assessment, and reported modest tyre wear—14,000 miles on the front and 22,000 on the back—but their mean fuel consumption of 27–30 m.p.g. erred on the pessimistic side. I can testify to an average of 34–37 m.p.g. on three different examples used over considerable distances. The adhesion on black ice was also superb.

In Yugoslavia Zastava introduced their own version with restyled rear panel. In the 1971 FIAT catalogue was a high-performance 1,290 c.c. 'Rallye' two-door saloon model; this had vastly improved handling and a top speed of 95 m.p.h. For 1972 the company unveiled a series of neat little coupés on a 7 ft 3½ in wheelbase. Standard variants had the 1,116 c.c. unit, but 'SL's' came with four headlamps and a 75 b.h.p. development of the 'Rallye' type. At the same time (October, 1971) FIAT proudly announced that they had built 700,000 128s in less than two years, and had exported 300,000 of these. Rivalta was turning out 1,600 units a day, though as yet the coupés were being put together in penny numbers at Lingotto. This, as Britons gloomily observed, meant no r.h.d. editions before 1973!

Front-wheel drive themes continued. There was an indication of things to come in Autobianchi's 1970 range; the 1,438 c.c. A111, an enlarged A112 with four-door bodywork, all-disc brakes, and the 124 Special engine. It was more expensive than the Special, at 1,385,000 lire. FIAT were trying it on the dog again.

A year later, however, Montabone came up with his 850 replacement, the 127, and by midsummer, 1971, the new small f.w.d. cars were leaving Mirafiori in respectable numbers. 850 saloons were now made in Barcelona, and sports types at Lingotto, a state of affairs which convinced rear-engine fans that the supply would slowly dry up.

Once again the faithful 903 c.c. engine was pressed into service, in A112 guise, and pleased by its ability to turn at a rousing 6,400 r.p.m. The rest of the car was scaled-down 128, with the same box styling. FIAT claimed that 80 per cent of the floor space was available for passengers and their luggage, this in spite of overall dimensions little greater than the 850's. An eight-inch increase in wheelbase added only just over an inch to the length, and the 127 was less than three-and-a-half inches wider than its predecessor. Safety had been conscientiously studied; the body was designed 'to deform progressively under impact from front and rear', and the floor was 'especially strengthened to resist outside forces on the body sides'. The critics were enthusiastic despite a driving position 'designed for the average Italian Ape' (as *The Autocar* put it), a notchy gear-change, and a bulkhead weak on sound insulation, letting in a lot of 'hard mechanical hammering noises', though this was not in any way indicative of distress. With 86 m.p.h. and available on top and 72 on third, the new car could match the 128 in straight-line speed, while the 0–60 m.p.h. time of 17.4 seconds compared interestingly with the 21.5 seconds taken by the 1100TV (then the fastest car in its class) in 1954. The ride on bumpy surfaces was considered superior to that of B.M.C.'s Hydrolastic, and the 127 became the third FIAT to collect an *Autovisie* award. The occasion called for a gold trophy, received in person by Gianni Agnelli at the Amsterdam Hilton in March 1972. At the same time a three-door estate version went on sale.

One gap in the sales picture had yet to be filled. The 2300 *lusso*'s departure in 1968 had left nothing for the well-to-do executive, but at Geneva in 1969 FIAT fans were given a preview of a new 2.9-litre 130, even if over a year was to elapse before they could buy it. The bottom end of the V6 engine was basically 'Dino', though in the interests of economy, simplicity and cost-cutting there was only one camshaft per block of cylinders, and FIAT's cogged-belt drive replaced Ferrari's chains. The blocks were of cast-iron, and the 130 had much in common with existing FIATs—notably the electrically-controlled fan, the alternator ignition, and the chassis-body structure. The suspension was new, with Macpherson struts at the front and torsion bars at the rear. Power steering was standardised, as was a Borg-Warner automatic box. By late 1971 some cars, however, were being delivered with the alternative five-speed manual transmission of German ZF type. Output, originally set at 140 b.h.p., was up to 160 b.h.p. by 1970, and when 130s started to appear in quantity a year later they had 102 ×66 mm (3,238 c.c.) power units which could all but match the 'Dino's brake horses. The range now included a sports coupé. At the beginning of 1972 Rivalta was turning out 100 saloons and 25 coupés a day, and the 130 had found its niche. It proved a far handier car than the 2300, and cruised happily down the length of the Milan–Turin *autostrada* in near-silence with the speedometer showing 160 k.p.h.

1972's principal novelty was, however, regarded in some circles as a retrograde step, for the 132, which replaced the 125 at the end of April, retained both rear-wheel drive and a live axle and coil springs at the rear. It was powered by new versions of the twin-cam four-cylinder engine, with capacities of 1,592 c.c. and 1,755 c.c.: the latter gave a respectable 105 b.h.p. at 6,000 r.p.m. Four forward speeds were standard, but both the admirable five-speed gearbox and a three-speed automatic of G.M. design were optional. A new and lower line met with a mixed reception, some people considering the 132's shape to be Japanese-inspired, but one thing was clear; FIAT were aiming at a more 'family' image for their new contender in the booming upper-middle class category. In Britain, £1,640 did not seem too much to pay for a five-speed *lusso* 1800, and the car promised to be competitive with the home team (now augmented by British Leyland's new front-wheel drive six-cylinder 2200 family) as well as with the single o.h.c. 2-litre offerings of Datsun and Toyota. It was, however, sobering to reflect that at the time of its introduction at the 1967 Show, the 125 saloon had retailed at a flat £999 inclusive of purchase tax.

Four months later the faithful 124 family received a face-list, which amounted to some extra brake horses for the pushrod engines, plus a cleaner front end treatment. Grilles were now of the same matt black mesh first seen on 'Rallye' editions of the 128, while a rectangular radiator badge was adopted. Both the Special T and the sports models used 132-type power units, a stock 1600 in the former case and a 118 b.h.p., edition of the 1800 in the latter.

Nor was the bridging of gaps in the range complete. Talk of a replacement for the 500 had been rife for years, and with Old Faithful's sales running at close on four million units it was surely time for a change. FIAT, however, were too canny a firm to discard a sure seller, and in any case they felt that world markets called for a four-seater city car. The 126, unveiled at the Turin Show in November, 1972, turned out to be a successor to the much-lamented 600, though its proportions were obviously inspired by the 127. Its overall dimensions were almost exactly those of the British Leyland Mini, long the exemplar of condensed four-seater design.

It was, however, FIAT's conservatism that startled the press. To all intents and purposes, front engines and front wheel drive had won the day (the same show season, indeed, had seen Peugeot's answer to the B.L.M.C. 1100, the 104), but across the Alps their design team remained faithful to a rear-mounted, air-cooled vertical-twin, maintaining that this layout made for ease of manufacture and servicing. This was certainly true of all Giacosa's previous babies, with the exception of the 850 Sport Special, on which the formidable Weber 'gasworks' dominated the scenery to the mechanic's detriment. FIAT's latest pushrod unit boasted oversquare dimensions of 73.5 × 70 mm, for a capacity of 594 c.c., and on 23 b.h.p. speeds of 65 m.p.h. were guaranteed. The all-independent suspension followed 500 lines, and dual-circuit drum brakes sufficed, but at long last synchromesh was offered to the company's marginal customers, even if they did not get it on bottom gear. In accordance with their accustomed policy, the first 126s were reserved for the home market, with two production lines in operation—at Mirafiori and in the new Southern plant at Cassino.

FIAT now offered such a diversity of models that the *trasformazione* and *elaborazione* industries began to feel the cold. SIATA were in liquidation by 1970, and Abarth were on the rocks a year later, thanks in part to a costly competition programme embracing such contrivances as a rear-engined 2-litre Group 6 car with sixteen-valve d.o.h.c. four-cylinder motor, and an even more formidable 2,968 c.c. vee-eight with four upstairs camshafts and Lucas indirect fuel injection. An agreement between the two companies dictated that these monsters should race as 'FIAT–Abarths', but there was very little FIAT in them! Those who rode out the storm prospered. Moretti, now no longer pretending to be anything but coach-builders, delivered 2,800 assorted 'specials' in 1968, and in 1971 Francis Lombardi's works at Vercelli were making 28 cars a day, even if fifteen of these were 128 'Smarts', in other words customised four-door saloons with four headlamps, fully adjustable seats, better sound-proofing, and some extra chromium plate. The eccentricities continued: at Turin in 1966 Ghia (soon to ally themselves with Alejandro de Tomaso, and therefore with Ford) displayed their 'Vanessa', a ladies' coupé based on the Idromatic 850. Electric windows and a clear plastic roof made sense, as did the collapsible shopping trolley, but the car was finished in mother o'pearl with lavender cloth upholstery, the dash was almost bare of instruments and padded in purple, and the fire-extinguisher could be used to inflate the tyres. FIAT mechanical elements lurked beneath most of the freaks evolved for the film *Monte Carlo or Bust*, a so-called SSK Mercédès-Benz being built up round an A.C. frame and a 2300 engine, and 1967 saw a rash of pseudo-thirties sports cars. In addition to Vignale's 500-based 'Gamine' there were Morgan-like 850s from Lombardi and Zanella, not to mention SIATA's swansong, the 'Spring'. This was a sports 850 masquerading as a sawn-off M.G. Top of Abarth's 1971 line was the 'Scorpione' with 1,280 c.c. pushrod engine and retractable headlamps. Moretti tried to make the 500 into an electric runabout (there was barely enough room for the necessary batteries!) and Giannini fielded a pair of exciting vee-eight engines in 1967. Capacities were 985 c.c. and 1,595 c.c., the big one was credited with 170 b.h.p., and it was intended to fit hem into the engine compartments of 850s. One may doubt, however, whether this particular heart transplant ever happened.

With FIAT concentrating their export sales in Europe, the licence producers were still doing well, though the Common Market had its effect. Belgian assembly was discontinued after 1967, and even Heilbronn's activities were now limited to the assembly of c.k.d. 124s, 125s, and 128s with sliding roofs to meet German requirements. Not that this indicated a drop in sales; FIAT's figures for the first four months of 1971, at 57,861 units, were 11,000 up on the corresponding period of 1970, and the *marque* was the *Bundesrepublik*'s fifth-ranking seller, ahead of Audi–N.S.U. and Mercédès-Benz, though still behind Renault. Top-selling British maker was British Leyland with a paltry 4,310 cars. There was also a slow-down in Austria with the demise of the savage little Steyr–Puch 650TR, but SEAT went marching on, with 17,000 hands turning out 180,007 cars in 1968. Everything was now made in Spain with the exception of 850 spyder bodies, and by 1971 Barcelona had become the sole European source of 600Ds and 850 saloons. Their range also included the 850 Special ('a happy car for the young family', as their English-language catalogue charmingly put it), the 850 sports models, three versions of the 124, a '1430' based on the 124 Special, the 124 Sport 1600, an updated edition of the old 1500, and a four-door 850 peculiar to Spain. By 1973 not only was 128 production in full swing, but SEAT-built 850s were being sold in Britain.

In the Communist republics, Yugoslavia's Zastavas outsold their locally-made rivals, Citroëns and N.S.U.s, and by 1971 128s were being delivered from Kragujevac. FIAT also signed up with the Bulgarian Government for the assembly of 124s and 850s in Sofia, though negotiations with Rumania proved abortive. FIAT, understandably, were not happy about terms which required Italy to take a proportion of Rumanian-built cars and the contract went to Renault. There was consolation, however, in the FIAT tractors being turned out by another state-owned plant in Brasov. In November, 1966, there was a rapprochement with Poland, and two years later the Polski–FIAT was a reality once more, in the shape of the 125P saloon.

The designation was a trifle misleading, for the car was basically a four-headlamp 124 fitted with either 1300 or 1500 engine, while the gearbox with its column change also followed 1961 practice, and the rear springs were semi-elliptic. By 1970 Poland was selling cars in Austria—some components, incidentally, were made in the old Stoewer works at Szeczin (Stettin).

Even more important were a series of agreements signed in 1965 and 1966 with the Soviet Government 'covering co-operation in the construction of motor vehicles'. This joint effort resulted in a huge factory at Togliattigrad on the Volga, near Kuibishev. The original contract was worth nearly £21 million to FIAT, and Russian engineers studied at Mirafiori, while Italian teams flew in and out of the u.s.s.r. supervising operations. In November, 1969 the first VAZ–2101 (sold as a Lada in the West) took the road, and deliveries began during 1970. To all outward appearances the VAZ was a 124 with a starting-handle added, but the structure had been considerably reinforced, and the 1,197 c.c. engine had an overhead camshaft. A special heater installation guaranteed an indoor temperature of 25 deg C when the thermometer stood at minus 25 deg out of doors. Ladas made their Western début at the 1971 Brussels Salon, and by the end of the year 700 cars a day were being turned out. The payroll of 34,000 workers was expected to double by 1973, when the Russians talked in terms of 660,000 cars a year. A station wagon edition was announced in January, 1972.

Special FIATs were also produced by Concord in Argentina, where 3,500 cars (600s and 1500s) were being made monthly in 1967: during the twelve-year period from 1959 to 1971 the 600 outsold any other individual model of private car in the Republic, with total deliveries of 166,803 units. Concord was also the country's second-ranking manufacturer, beaten only by the big IKA–Renault group. Local versions included coupés and spyders modelled on the sports 850, but with 62 ×66 mm (797 c.c.) engines developing 40 b.h p , and a 2+2 coupé derivative of the 1500 using a 1.6-litre pushrod unit. This was a curious stylistic synthesis of 850 and 1500 with superimposed double headlamps *à la* Triumph 'Vitesse', and could be had with saloon bodywork as well. Indians had less choice, Premier of Bombay building only the 1100 'Delight', basically a 1962-type 1100D with the 1,089 c.c. engine. Keener drivers, however, preferred it to the two local alternatives; the Hindusthan 'Ambassador' (*alias* 1957 Morris–Oxford), and a four-door Triumph 'Herald' marketed under the Standard name.

In Europe it was back to the halcyon days of the 501 and 509. In 1967 FIAT topped the foreign-import stakes in France and Belgium, and the company, as we have seen, was sitting pretty in Germany. At long last Belgian prices were competitive: the 124 comfortably undersold the less roomy B.M.C.

1100, while the 125 was cheaper than the sedate Humber 'Sceptre' and very little slower than cars like the Rover 2000 and Jaguar 240, which cost twice as much. Swedish sales took an upturn—in February, 1972 *The Autocar* reported 'an increasing number' of FIATS. In Portugal the 850 and 124 were firm favourites by 1971, the 124 Special T was making promising headway, and FIAT were fighting it out with Ford for first place, while anxiously watching the progress of Datsun and Toyota. Czechoslovak citizens could buy 500s, most 850 variants, the 125 and the 128, plus the Polski–FIAT and the VAZ–2101 for good measure, but prices were terrifying by Western standards: in 1972 59,000 crowns, or £3,370 at the official rate of exchange, were quoted for an 850 *berlina*! In the United Kingdom progress was steady. In 1967, when both 500F and 600D cost less than £500, 16,600 FIATS found buyers, and the following year new distribution depots were established at Dover and Warrington. In 1970 the company's English headquarters were moved to new premises on the Great West Road at Brentford, though the old Wembley works were retained for the time being. Sales had passed the 20,000 mark in 1969, when the best-sellers were the 124 and the 850: though Renault still held second place behind the ubiquitous Volkswagen, both these FIATS did better than any individual Renault model. The 124 was still Britain's favourite FIAT in 1970, but 4,021 128s were sold in the first nine months of the year, and by December the picture looked rosy, with a new record of 23,476 units in a twelvemonth, and FIAT in second place overall, less than a hundred behind Volkswagen. 1971 should have been even better, with Ford's English factories crippled by a long and bitter strike. Alas! FIAT also had their labour problems, and the *marque* was well behind Renault at the end of the year.

Switzerland, of course, continued to sell FIATS, though in 1968 they trailed some 70,000 cars behind Opel for their customary third place. The gap closed suddenly in 1969, and the company's position remains strong—the 1971/2 period was notable because Opel finally caught up with Volkswagen, and the Japanese drew level with the British. These two old adversaries, however, had only 10.9 per cent apiece of the market to Italy's 14.3. The 124 Sport Special became popular in Australia, while New Zealand's Auckland assembly plant had switched by 1971 to 850 coupés and 125 saloons, and the production of heavy trucks was contemplated. FIAT were hopeful; Britain's entry into the Common Market would, they suspected, lead to the end of duties calculated on a 'most favoured nation' basis, even if this would open the door still further to the Japanese menace.

In America, FIAT fought hard against a traditionally capricious market. 1966 offerings seemed to justify the jibe that 'the company never tries hard in English-speaking countries', consisting as they did of the 600D at $1,179 ($200 less than the asking price of a Mini), the 1100D at $1,490 ($17 less than a Volkswagen and well below Toyota's 'Corona'), and the 1500 cabriolet at $2,458. 1967, however, saw a sharp upturn; Americans took to the 850 spyder, and though FIAT still lay ninth in the foreign-import stakes, behind Datsun and Toyota, a sale of 15,223 units told its own story. A year later they had overtaken Renault and Mercedes-Benz, and they broke 40,000 for the first time in 1969, with only Volkswagen, Toyota, Opel and Datsun ahead of them. By 1970 the spyder was beginning to show its age, and only 36,642 cars were sold, but this still represented a 3 per cent share of the take, albeit the two Japanese giants accounted for 23 per cent between them. A report from Southern California in the spring of 1971 showed an up-and-down state of affairs. German Fords, M.G.s, Triumphs, Opels, and the Chrysler-backed Mitsubishi 'Colts' were fast-selling lines, but Volkswagen were feeling the effects of a car shortage, and Plymouth dealers were finding it difficult to move their 'Crickets', *alias* Hillman 'Avenger'. A bright future was, however, forecast for FIAT's latest contribution to the 'economy sedan game', the 128 at $1,800. It competed directly with the rear-engined Renault 10 at $1,845. Still, the United States had been directly responsible for another FIAT landmark—the 100,000th 850 spyder was delivered in March, 1971.

Also on the up-grade was the company's Canadian business,

based on the 850 spyder, the 124 Special and Sport, and the 128 range. A depot and service school were opened at Scarborough, Ontario, in September, 1968, and the 4,700 cars sold in 1969 were handled through a chain of ninety-odd dealers. Plans were being laid for a new handling terminal at Halifax, Nova Scotia.

The South American market was bedevilled by chronic currency problems, and local assembly plants represented the only effective remedy. In 1970, for instance, only Chile (4,596), Uruguay (1,414) and Venezuela (2,630) imported more than a thousand units, though FIATs were made or assembled in seven countries. The firm's Venezuelan offshoot, F.I.A.V., was partly FIAT-owned, and handled 124s, 125s, 125 Specials, 128s, and three commercial models—the 619, the 682, and the 697. Typical of the general picture was Uruguay, where the *marque* had been represented since 1914, though an endemic car shortage meant that 509s and 520s were still to be seen on the streets of Montevideo, the capital. A sales tax of 48 per cent on top of inflation had some disconcerting results: the cheapest car on the market was Citroën's jeep-like 'Méhari' at 1,150,000 pesos (£1,840 at par). A FIAT 850 came out at £2,384, and a 124 at over £3,500, in spite of which it was still cheaper than a Ford 'Escort'. FIAT, however, was the nation's best-selling make, with new registrations running at over a hundred a month.

Competitions remained an Abarth preserve, Schetty's 2-litre taking fourth place in the 1967 European Mountain Championship. FIATs still appeared occasionally in rallies, the Rubbieri/Cavriani 124 winning its class in the 1970 'Monte' and the 125 of Lindberg/Reinicke finishing fifth in the Acropolis. That winter's R.A.C. British Rally, however, saw a surprise entry of two works-supported 124 Sport Spyders, and in 1971 it became clear that FIAT were in earnest, even if the 1927 ruling had not been rescinded. They put up an impressive performance in the Monte Carlo Rally, Lindberg driving with immense verve in the scheduled sections. He was fastest at Burzet, and second fastest on the Col de Turini, while his seventh place in general classification was only just behind the best Lancia (Lampinen/Davenport). A fourth place in the Acropolis was, however, destined to be FIAT's best in the season, though the 124 Spyder of Pinto/Einsiedel took eighth place in the 1972 'Monte'. Lancias, by contrast, were first, fourth and sixth. The final break-through came a few months later in the Acropolis, when Lindberg/Eisendle scored an outright victory. As second place fell to the Lampinen/Reinicke Lancia, and FIATs also finished fourth and seventh, there was jubilation in the Corso Dante.

There was actually a FIAT stand at the 1966 British Commercial Vehicle Show—for the first time since 1929—but though Mercédès-Benz, Scania and Volvo established footholds on Leyland's home ground, the Italians stayed aloof. Not that their products were lacking in technical interest. In the light truck field the 1100T acquired a 1300 engine, and was joined by two more modern designs. The 25-30-cwt 241 of 1967 was a forward-control vehicle based on 124 mechanical elements and powered by a 1,438 c.c. pushrod engine, while the slightly smaller 238 was intended to compete with Volkswagen's Transporters, and was the first f.w.d. FIAT to go into production. It used an east/west edition of the 238's engine and vacuum-hydraulic brakes. The 615 was brought up to date as the 616N, available with two versions of the company's rationalised medium diesel engine—a 2.3-litre three-cylinder or a 3½-litre 'four' developing 90 b.h.p. In this latter form, with five-speed synchromesh gearbox and floor change, it was capable of 68 m.p.h. Further up the range, the 1971–2 catalogue included the six-ton 650, the seven-ton 662, the nine-ton 619, and the real 'heavies' in the shape of the ageless 684 and the 6×4 697N, now with 13.8 litres and 285 b.h.p. Newest of the 'bus and coach range was the 343, with horizontal, rear-mounted 9.8-litre six-cylinder engine, air suspension, and a ten-speed splitter gearbox.

The aircraft division, now absorbed into the Aeritalia group, provided work for 5,470 employees, and was making F-104 fighters for NATO as well as fighter-bomber versions of the G-91. The G-222 military transport was being test-flown, and there were joint programmes with v.f.w. of Bremen and Marcel Dassault of France. The end-product in the former case was a new v/stol fighter aircraft.

In 1972 FIAT's payroll was 189,800, and they turned out 1,661,500 cars and trucks, of which 646,500 were exported. On the debit side, the inevitable strikes lost them around 200,000 units, but almost all the southern plants were now in operation, notably the Cassino factory. Their progress in the past decade had fully justified Graham Turner's assessment of them as the company to watch.

13 Epilogue—Whither Fiat?

The American market is dangerous. It is a changing and capricious market. We sold up to 35,000 cars a year in the U.S. before dropping back to between 10 and 15,000 units. We are up again to about 30,000 cars a year and our export programme calls for 60,000 U.S. sales in 1972. Such a level is necessary to operate soundly and profitably. But you must split your risks.

Umberto Agnelli, 1969

FIAT rode into the 1970s determined to annex ten per cent of the world's car sales. Such a resolution is a healthy one, though it is well to remember that even an annual output of one-and-three-quarter million cars would not bring them within shouting distance of the all-time world's record: 2,587,490 units delivered by Chevrolet in 1965.

No one should underestimate the strength of FIAT. A firm which can supply jet fighters to Germany, ship-control systems to the U.S.S.R., 'buses to Thailand, tractors to Africa's emergent nations, and gas turbines for the electricity supplies of Belgrade and Bucharest stands in little peril. There does not seem much limit to the scope of a company whose civil engineers helped preserve the Abu Simbel Temples in Egypt, and built hydro-electric power plant in Pakistan.

FIAT is approaching monopoly in its native Italy. Yet at the same time the company is highly sensitive on this subject—the public speeches of Gianni Agnelli reflect the views both of his grandfather and of Vittorio Valletta. To-day the aircraft, nuclear energy and *grandi motori* divisions have been merged into consortia in which FIAT themselves are majority shareholders rather than outright owners. The transfer of marine engine activities to Trieste suggests that Gianni Agnelli remains loyal to another family dogma—that the duty of a capitalist is to provide work, not just to flood the market with goods or services.

What is more, if FIAT explores a new field, it does so with the intention of staying. Only twice has the company abdicated—from a short-lived bicycle venture in 1910, and from the domestic appliance business in the 1950s. Aero-engines were dropped in 1945, only to be resumed as soon as opportunity offered to enter the realm of gas turbines. This attitude in part explains their cautious approach to the regeneration of Italy's barren and impoverished South. Here the Government has tried to make up for generations of neglect, and there is a parallel in the endeavours of successive British administrations to channel profitable industries into the depressed areas of the North and Clydeside. Be the locale the Mezzogiorno or Motherwell and Coatbridge, the capitalist's counter-argument will be the same: you cannot operate efficiently when the work-force at your disposal has no knowledge or tradition of highly specialised labour of the right kind. And car-makers, especially, dislike the prospect of lapses in quality control while miners, textile workers or shipwrights settle down to a new routine.

FIAT has never enthused over the South. They have moved steadily away from urban Turin. Both Rivalta and the flight-test division at Caselle are a good twelve miles and more from the Via Roma. O.M. are based on Milan and Brescia, and Autobianchi on Milan, while 'Dinos' are put together in the Ferrari works at Maranello, near Modena. But the first southward moves were made by the state-owned Alfa Romeo company. Their Alfasud operation in Naples was set in train in 1968; it was certainly a dramatic gesture. Here were a new car, a new front-wheel drive configuration, a new sector of the market which impinged on FIAT's 128, and even a new name. When the little 1.3-litre saloon took its bow at the Turin Show in November, 1971, many a canny Piedmontese shook his head and said nothing.

Yet FIAT's own involvement in the South is not much smaller. Between 1970 and 1972 the company will have spent more than 250 thousand million lire in order to provide work for nineteen thousand people. Already some 500s, 850T minibuses and light trucks are being made in Naples, and 2,300 hands are employed at Bari making fuel-injection equipment and brakes for tractors. More cars are assembled by SicilFIAT at Termini Imerese in Sicily, and by 1973 there will be a gas-turbine works at Brindisi, a factory for earth-moving equipment at Lecce, a steering-gear plant at Sulmona, and two divisions of Marelli, another FIAT subsidiary, making electrical equipment at Vasto. A vehicle proving-ground is scheduled for Nardo, and yet another factory at Cassino will soon be in the car business. Where, however, FIAT's thinking differs from Alfa Romeo's is that these factories will start by being supplementary to the main complex in the North. Thus no major hitch in the new scheme can throw the whole operation out of gear.

One of the healthiest aspects of FIAT as a car maker is its attitude to competition. There has never been any badge-engineering. Even since the fall of the Stokes axe, British Leyland's 1100/1300 family still appears under three brand-names—Austin, Vanden Plas, and Wolseley. There are still Humbers as well as Hillmans in Chrysler–UK's 'Arrow' range, and in Japan there is an overlap between the bigger Daihatsus and the smallest Toyotas. The range-structures of America's Big Three are too complicated to explore in detail, but within an individual corporation it is the body-chassis combination that counts rather than the actual make.

Such tactics are foreign to FIAT. Admittedly a 600 can be a FIAT in Italy, a SEAT in Spain, or a Zastava in Yugoslavia, but each maker has his appointed part to play. Occasionally things get out of hand, and for a while in 1962–3 Britons were suddenly confronted with the illogical choice between a 600D and a Neckar 'Jagst 770', identical in all but the smallest details. In other markets, however the arrangement worked: France was supplied with Neckars from Heilbronn rather than with FIATS from Turin, as it was felt that this would help dispel the monopoly-image which the parent firm so dreads. It will come as a surprise to many people to find that in some countries one has the choice of more than one brand of FIAT. Czechoslovakia is one example, and Belgium another.

SEAT, as we have seen, acts as an auxiliary to Lingotto, Mirafiori and Rivalta, turning out obsolete models just as the *sezione ricambi* at Stura keeps stocks of spares flowing for five years after a model is withdrawn. The case of the Polski–FIAT is rather different: the official view is that it fills a small but significant gap between the 124 and the 132, which it would not be worth Turin's while to bridge. It is therefore allowed to compete against the native strain in Austria and France, and may conceivably do so in Britain. Yugoslav Zastavas are exported to certain markets, though the Russian situation is something else again. The Soviet Government signs a separate agreement every time it opens up a new market for its VAZ–2101s. FIAT is quite content for the Russians to use the car to help hold the bridgeheads they have gained with their Moskvitches in countries like Norway and Finland.

Nobody need fear for the car division's technical futu1e. Enrico and Fornaca, Zerbi and Giacosa have gone, but FIAT can afford the best that Italy can offer, and an organisation which sells more than eighty per cent of its output in Europe will continue to cater for Europe's needs. Their attitude to safety is 'a nice blend of sanity and sense', which should prevent an excess of hysterical Naderism.

What of the *marque*'s future in world markets? Whence will come that ten per cent promised by Gianni Agnelli? Anyone who has seen the *sezione ricambi* complex has seen a microcosm of FIAT efficiency, with 300 tons of parts going in and out, and 110,000 items sorted by computer and stored by an ingenious gravity system which protects against dead stock. A company that can perfect this can perfect anything. Unquestionably to-day the car's Italian nationality helps, as it hindered in the days of Mussolini's sabre-rattling. Italy may be firmly aligned with the West, both politically and economically, but she no longer plays power politics. Upheavals in Rhodesia or Ireland can lead to boycotts of British goods, a revolution in Czechoslovakia will have an adverse effect on Russian sales, and there are people who will never buy another Chevrolet or Plymouth until the last U.S. soldier has pulled out of South Vietnam. The Italians just go on quietly selling.

Further, Italy is no longer fiercely protectionist. She may be scared of foreign cars: a lot of people in Turin and Milan would sleep more easily if every Volkswagen were banished from Italian streets. But curiously the industry, long insulated from competition by Mussolinian nationalism and the stringencies of recovery under de Gasperi, has welcomed it with open arms.

What of the menace of Japan? Nobody minimises this. In 1970 the Japanese motor industry made over three million private cars, two million trucks, and 45,000-odd 'buses, and exports ran to seven figures. The 323,671 cars sold in the 'dangerous and capricious' U.S.A. represent six times FIAT's estimate of their own annual American potential, but they hardly constitute a major worry. Nor is New Zealand a pressing problem: the overall scope of the market is too small. But there are those 60,000 units sold to Australia, once excellent FIAT country. The Japanese have a long way to go in Britain, where memories of Singapore and the 'Railway of Death' die hard, and in any case Japan did not step up the tempo of her British sales drive until 1970.

There are other and more alarming symptoms, though. Belgium and Switzerland are solid FIAT markets—yet each took more than sixteen thousand Japanese cars in 1970. On the credit side, Japan is now the only major car-producing nation which adheres rigidly to protection. Hardly any foreign cars are imported; during the formative 1950s Hino made Renaults, Nissan–Datsun Austins, and Isuzu Hillman 'Minxes', but these had all gone by 1961. FIAT have penetrated Russian xenophobia and American Federal Safety Rules, but the nearest they have got to circumventing the Japanese embargo is a licence agreement whereby tractors are built in the Land of the Rising Sun. Maybe the best answer to protection is counter-protection, though one has a feeling that the top brass in the Corso Marconi would rather fight it out on a basis of merit.

Have FIAT finished their empire-building? Could they, for instance, swallow British Leyland if they felt so inclined? Nothing is beyond the realms of possibility, but experience has shown that the impetus for empire-building has come, not from the strong, but from the weak. The chain reaction that created British Leyland itself began when Standard, tottering at the bottom of the First Division, cast around for a partner. *Ergo*, FIAT will not make the first move. After all, they control as much of Italian industry as they want or are likely to get, have a finger in all manner of useful pies, and are careful to maintain holdings in their important foreign sales outlets. They even have an eight per cent interest in Yugoslavia's Zastava. But charity begins at home, and there are enough jobs to under-write in Italy without bothering about the foreign situation.

Perhaps the biggest question mark of all hangs over Turin, the 'company town'. Can any paternalism, however liberally administered, survive much longer? How far is FIAT removed from the old feudal estates, with whole families and villages working for the lord of the manor, and those recruited from outside housed in tied cottages, 'for the better performance of their duties'? A FIAT employee will find a FIAT club catering for his hobby, be it bowls or bridge; the flat he lives in, the medical centre he attends, and the convalescent home where he recovers from an illness, are all FIAT-owned. His children can while away the working hours in a FIAT crêche, spend holidays at FIAT camps by the sea or in the mountains, and if they attain the necessary educational standards they may enrol in the FIAT Technical School in the old Corso Dante works. After a quarter of a century's service he becomes eligible for a FIAT pension, and if he outlives his family circle he can spend the evening of life in a FIAT Retirement Home. One may well ask whether what has worked in Piedmont for over half a century will also work in the South with its different traditions, once the new

77. FIAT – Ferrari marriage: the 2-litre Dino coupé, 1967.

78. Competition revival: Lindberg's 124 Spyder winning the Acropolis Rally, 1972.

79, 80, 81. From a General Provider's repertoire. The 128 saloon (top) features the front wheel drive and east–west engine first tried in 1965 on the Autobianchi 'Primula'. The 130 coupé (centre) is a prestige car selling in Britain for over £5,500, and the twin o.h.c. 132 (bottom) is a 1972 introduction which is less obviously Italian than earlier models.
(Woolf, Laing, Christie and Partners: FIAT)

FIAT complex gets into its stride. And how much longer will it work in Turin, for that matter?

One may not predict the future of FIAT in the Mezzogiorno, but the Piedmontese is notoriously independent, and if he is beholden to anyone, it will be to a fellow-Piedmontese and not to a representative of officialdom in Rome. FIAT is part of his environment, so he will stay with FIAT. As one company official said to me: 'They pass through our school, and they go out. But most of them come back'.

The empire founded by Giovanni Agnelli in 1899 has withstood two world wars, industrial unrest, Mussolinian Fascism, and Palmiro Togliatti's bid to introduce eastern Communism. It has seen two occupations—by Nazi Germany, and by the Anglo-American forces. It has seen the fall of a monarchy. It has also withstood the influence of a uniformity that raised its head when Henry Ford created his first moving assembly line in 1911. Every FIAT is unmistakably a FIAT. My 1934 'Ardita 2000', my 1938 *millecento*, and my present 1966 850 coupé are three totally different cars; the first from the drawing-board of Tranquillo Zerbi, the second early Giacosa, and the 850 an example of late Giacosa—but they all possessed the same, indefinable feel.

'FIAT', said a company publication of 1966, 'has lived and is living the adventure of having to adapt its products to the needs of many people'. Sometimes their solutions have been exasperating, like the famous transmission handbrake. But I know of no other mass-producer whose wares have been stamped so indelibly with three distinct traditions; the dour independence of Piedmont, the liberal forward thinking of the Agnellis, and the Italian view of the motor-car as something to drive rather than as a status-symbol.

Technical Appendix

The numbered columns are

1	Dates of manufacture of the model	Years
2	Type designation assigned by the factory	Type
3	Cylinders and how arranged, number, arrangement, casting	Cylinders
4	Bore, stroke, capacity	Engine Dimensions
5	Output in b.h.p. at optimum r.p.m.	Output
6	Valves	Valves
7	Ignition	Ignition
8	Cooling	Cooling
9	Gears and lever location	Gears
10	Final Drive	Final Drive
11	Brakes, foot and hand	Brakes
12	Suspension, front and rear	Suspension
13	Wheelbase and track (mm)	Wheelbase, Track
14	Production	Number Built

Abbreviations The following have been used.

3 Cylinders	h/o	horizontally opposed.
6 Valves	AIV	automatic inlet valves
	OHV	overhead valves (pushrod)
	OHC	overhead camshaft
	DOHC	twin overhead camshafts
	4OHC	four overhead camshafts
7 Ignition	L.T.M.	low tension magneto
	H.T.M.	high tension magneto
	Alt.	alternator
9 Gears	Auto	automatic
	C	central change
	R	right-hand change
	S/C	steering-column change
	syn.	synchromesh
	all-syn	all-synchromesh
11 Brakes	Trans	on transmission
	4W	on four wheels
	R.W	on rear wheels
	Hy	hydraulic
12 Suspension	½-ell	half-elliptic
	¼-ell	quarter-elliptic
	¾-ell	three-quarter elliptic
	Cant.	Cantilever
	Ind.	Independent
	Tr.	Transverse
	McP	McPherson (strut)

Fiat Touring Models 1899-1972

1 Years	2 Type	3 Cylinders	4 Engine Dimensions	5 Output	6 Valves	7 Ignition	8 Cooling	9 Gears	10 Final Drive
1899–1900	3½ h.p.	2 h/o	65×99 679	4.2 at 800	AIV	Coil	Pump	3,C	Side chains
1900–01	8 h.p.	2 h/o	83×100 1,082	10 at 1,000	AIV	Coil	Pump	3,R	Side chains
1901–02	8 h.p.	2 inline pairs	83×100 1,082	10 at 1,100	AIV	Coil	Pump	3,R	Chain
1901–02	12 h.p.	4 inline pairs	100×120 3,768	20 at 1,200	AIV	L.T.M.	Pump	3,R	Side chains
1902	24 h.p.	4 inline pairs	120×160 7,238	30 at 1,100	AIV	L.T.M.	Pump	4,R	Side chains
1903–05	16–20 h.p.	4 inline pairs	110×110 4,181	20 at 1,200	T-head	L.T.M.	Pump	4,R	Side chains
1903	24–32 h.p.	4 inline pairs	130×120 6,371	34 at 1,200	T-head	L.T.M.	Pump	4,R	Side chains
1904	24–32 h.p.	4 inline pairs	130×130 6,902	34 at 1,200	T-head	L.T.M.	Pump	4,R	Side chains
1904	60 h.p.	4 inline pairs	150×150 10,597	60 at 1,200	T-head	L.T.M.	Pump	4,R	Side chains
1905–06	24–32 h.p.	4 inline pairs	125×150 7,363		T-head	L.T.M.	Pump	4,R	Side chains
1905–06	60 h.p.	4 inline pairs	145×160 10,566		T-head	L.T.M.	Pump	4,R	Side chains
1905–06	16–20 h.p.	4 inline pairs	105×130 4,500		T-head	L.T.M.	Pump	4,R	Side chains
1906–12	Brevetti	4 inline pairs	90×120 3,052		T-head	L.T.M.	Pump	3,R	Bevel
1907–08	28–40 h.p.	4 inline pairs	125×150 7,363		T-head	L.T.M.	Pump	4,R	Side chains
1907–08	50–60 h.p.	6 inline pairs	125×150 11,044		T-head	L.T.M.	Pump	4,R	Side chains
1908–10	Tipo 1	4 inline monobloc	80×100 2,009		L-head	H.T.M.	Pump	3,R	Bevel
1908–10	Tipo 3 20–30 h.p.	4 inline pairs	110×130 4,942		T-head	H.T.M.	Pump	4,R	Bevel

11 Brakes	12 Suspension	13 Wheelbase Track	14 Number Built	Remarks
Trans R.W	½-ell ½-ell	1470 1220	8	Tubular frame. Rear engine. No reverse gear. Later cars have 837 c.c. power unit.
Trans R.W	½-ell ½-ell	1750 1260	12	Reinforced wood frame. Rear engine. Also *sprinto* version (10 h.p.).
Trans R.W	½-ell ½-ell	1750 1260	56	Reinforced wood frame. Front vertical engine. 1902, 12 b.h.p. engine, honeycomb radiator in place of tubular type.
Trans R.W	½-ell ½-ell	2105 1250	11	Reinforced wood frame. 1902, wheelbase 2,120 mm honeycomb radiator.
Trans R.W	½-ell ½-ell	2350 1320	3	Reinforced wood frame. Honeycomb radiator. Also *corsa* with shorter wheelbase.
Trans R.W	½-ell ½-ell	2120 1250	230	Reinforced wood frame. 1904, pressed steel frame, 22 b.h.p. engine, choice of four wheelbases: 2,305, 2,615, 2,900, or 3,080 mm.
Trans R.W	½-ell ½-ell	2250 1250	35	Reinforced wood frame.
Trans R.W	½-ell ½-ell	2585 1350	121	Pressed steel frame. Alternative wheelbases 2,980 mm. or 3,100 mm.
Trans R.W	½-ell ½-ell	2585 1350	12	Pressed steel frame. Alternative wheelbase, 2,750 mm.
Trans R.W	½-ell ½-ell	2,900 1,350	850 (all models)	As 24–40 h.p., 1906, 40 b.h.p. at 1,200 r.p.m, wheelbase options 2,900, 3,100, or 3,350 mm.
Trans R.W	½-ell ½-ell	2,895 1,350	186	1096, available with alternative wheelbases 2,955, 3,335, 3,155, or 3,405 mm. Track on 1906 models 1,400 mm.
Trans R.W	½-ell ½-ell	2,830 1,400	412	Alternative wheelbases 3,030 or 3,280 mm. Continued into 1907–8 as 18–24 h.p., 26 b.h.p. engine, wheelbases 2,830, 3,130 or 3,330 mm 430 produced.
Trans R.W	½-ell ½-ell	2,880 1,350	681	Originally made (1905) by FIAT-Ansaldi with chain drive. 1909, output 26 b.h.p. at 1,400 r.p.m, four forward speeds, h.t. magneto ignition, wheelbase 3,020 or 3,065 mm.
Trans R.W	½-ell ½-ell	2,900 1,400	953	Wheelbase options, 3,200, 3,400, 3,700 mm. Another 557 made in 1906.
Trans R.W	½-ell ½-ell	3,540 1,450	116	
Trans R.W	½-ell ½-ell	2,700 1,370	1,623	1909, four forward speeds
Trans R.W	½-ell ¾-ell	3,090 1,400	763	

1 Years	2 Type	3 Cylinders	4 Engine Dimensions	5 Output	6 Valves	7 Ignition	8 Cooling	9 Gears	10 Final Drive
1908–09	Tipo 4 35– 45 h.p.	6 inline pairs	110×130 7,412		T-head	H.T.M.	Pump	4,R	Side chains
1908–09	Taunus 75– 90 h.p.	4 inline pairs	140×130 8,004		O.H.V.	L.T.M.	Pump	4,R	Side chains
1909–10	Tipo 5 35– 50 h.p.	4 inline pairs	130×140 7,429		L-head	H.T.M.	Pump	4,R	Bevel
1910–15	Tipo 1	4 inline monobloc	70×120 1,847	16 at 1,700	L-head	H.T.M.	Pump	4,R	Bevel
1910–11	Tipo 2	4 inline monobloc	80×130 2,614	22 at 1,700	L-head	H.T.M.	Pump	4,R	Bevel
1910–11	Tipo 3	4 inline monobloc	95×140 3,969	32 at 1,600	L-head	H.T.M.	Pump	4,R	Bevel
1910–18	Tipo 4	4 inline monobloc	110×150 5,702	53 at 1,600	L-head	H.T.M.	Pump	4,R	Bevel
1910–11	Tipo 7	6 inline monobloc	80×130 3,921		L-head	H.T.M.	Pump	4,R	Bevel
1911–15	Zero	4 inline monobloc	70×120 1,847	19 at 1,800	L-head	H.T.M.	Pump	4,R	Bevel
1911–13	S61	4 inline pairs	130×190 10,087	125 at 1,500	O.H.C.	H.T.M.	Pump	4,R	Side chains
1912–20	Tipo 2B	4 inline monobloc	80×140 2,816	26 at 1,800	L-head	H.T.M.	Pump	4,R	Bevel
1912–21	Tipo 3A	4 inline monobloc	100×140 4,398	40 at 1,800	L-head	H.T.M.	Pump	4,R	Bevel
1912–16	Tipo 5	4 inline monobloc	130×170 9,025	75 at 1,500	L-head	H.T.M.	Pump	4,R	Bevel
1915–20	70	4 inline monobloc	70×130 2,001	21 at 2,400	L-head	H.T.M.	Pump	4,R	Bevel
1919–26	501	4 inline monobloc	65×110 1,460	23 at 2,600	L-head	H.T.M.	Pump	4,R	Spiral bevel
1919–25	505	4 inline monobloc	75×130 2,297	33 at 2,600	L-head	H.T.M.	Pump	4,R	Spiral bevel
1919–25	510	6 inline monobloc	75×130 3,446	46 at 2,400	L-head	H.T.M.	Pump	4,R	Spiral bevel

11 Brakes	12 Suspension	13 Wheelbase Track	14 Number Built	Remarks
Trans R.W	½–ell ½–ell	3,300 1,400	107 (1908)	Optional wheelbase 3,500 mm.
Trans R.W	½–ell ½–ell	3,250 1,400		
Trans R.W	½–ell ½–ell	3,240 1,400	300	Chain drive optional.
Trans R.W	½–ell ¾–ell	2,740 1,400	3,450	Specifications for 1*bis* (1910). 1A (1912) had 18 b.h.p. Tipo 51A engine. Model revived as taxi, 1919–22.
Trans R.W	½–ell ¾–ell	2,740 1,400	999	
Trans R.W	½–ell ¾–ell	3,140 1,400	836	
Trans R.W	½–ell ¾–ell	3,140 1,400	838	Production figures for 1910–14 period only. Also made at Poughkeepsie, 1910–14.
Trans R.W	½–ell ¾–ell	3,140 1,400	50	Tipo 3 with 6-cylinder engine. Export only.
Trans R.W	½–ell ¾–ell	2,645 1,200	2,119 (1913/15)	Data for Zero-A, 1913. Earlier cars had 18 b.h.p. engines. Electric lighting, 1915. Brooklands model (78 made) had 21 b.h.p. engine, detachable wheels.
Trans R.W	½–ell ½–ell	3,140 1,400	*circa* 50	Also raced. Some with shaft drive.
Trans R.W	½–ell ½–ell	2,740 1,400	10,020	Electric lighting, 1915. Detachable wheels, electric starters, 28 b.h.p. engine, 2,840 mm wheelbase, 1916.
Trans R.W	½–ell ½–ell	3,140 1,400	2,167	Electrics, 1915. Tipo 3 (1912–15) had 45 b.h.p. engine, 2,915 mm. wheelbase. 681 built, as well as some in U.S.A., 1914–15. A few 3TERs made with S35B pushrod engine.
Trans R.W	½–ell ¾–ell	3,250 1,400	457	Electrics from 1915, made in U.S.A, 1913–18. Tipo 6 similar but with side-chain drive. 31,150 mm. wheelbase; 86 made, 1912–14.
R.W R.W	½–ell ½–ell	2,706 1,250	1,002	Production models had detachable cylinder heads. Electric lights and starter.
R.W R.W	½–ell ½–ell	2,650 1,250	80,000 approx	Also 501S sports model, 1921–26, 26.5 b.h.p., 2614 made, plus a handful with twin-cam engine (501SS). 1923 on, 501C (colonial) with wider track. 502 (1923) has 2,750 mm wheelbase: 6,753 made 1924–26. All models available with front wheel brakes (B-series), late 1924.
R.W R.W	½–ell ½–ell	3,050 1,410	17,753	Front-wheel brakes available, late 1924 (B-series). Some late cars completed to 507 specification.
R.W R.W	½–ell ½–ell	3,400 1,410	13,577	510S sports model with 3,100 mm wheelbase, 53 b.h.p. engine, available from 1920: 414 made. Front wheel brakes available, late 1924 (B-series) Some late cars completed to 512 specification.

Years	Type	Cylinders	Engine Dimensions	Output	Valves	Ignition	Cooling	Gears	Final Drive
1921–22	520	12 Vee	85 × 100 6,805	80 at 2,200	O.H.V.	Dual Coil	Pump	3,C	Spiral bevel
1922–27	519	6 inline monobloc	85 × 140 4,766	77 at 2,600	O.H.V.	H.T.M.	Pump	4,C	Spiral bevel
1925–29	509 509A	4 inline monobloc	57 × 97 990	22 at 3,400	O.H.C.	H.T.M.	Thermo	3,C	Spiral bevel
1926–27	503	4 inline monobloc	65 × 110 1,460	27 at 3,000	L-head	H.T.M.	Pump	4,R	Spiral bevel
1926–27	507	4 inline monobloc	75 × 130 2,297	35 at 2,600	L-head	H.T.M.	Pump	4,R	Spiral bevel
1926–28	512	6 inline monobloc	75 × 130 3,446	46 at 2,400	L-head	H.T.M.	Pump	4,R	Spiral bevel
1927–29	520	6 inline monobloc	68 × 103 2,234	46 at 3,400	L-head	Coil	Pump	4,C	Spiral bevel
1928–31	521	6 inline monobloc	72 × 103 2,516	50 at 3,400	L-head	Coil	Pump	4,C	Spiral bevel
1928–31	525	6 inline monobloc	82 × 118 3,740	68.5 at 3,200	L-head	Coil	Pump	4,C	Spiral bevel
1929–32	514	4 inline monobloc	67 × 102 1,438	28 at 3,400	L-head	Coil	Pump	4,C	Spiral bevel
1931–34	515	4 inline monobloc	67 × 102 1,438	28 at 3,400	L-head	Coil	Pump	4,C	Spiral bevel
1931–33	522	6 inline monobloc	72 × 103 2,516	52 at 3,300	L-head	Coil	Pump	4,C Syn	Spiral bevel
1931–34	524	6 inline monobloc	72 × 103 2,516	52 at 3,300	L-head	Coil	Pump	4,C Syn	Spiral bevel
1932–34	508	4 inline monobloc	65 × 75 995	20 at 3,400	L-head	Coil	Thermo	3,C	Spiral bevel
1933–37	518	4 inline monobloc	82 × 92 1,944	45 at 3,600	L-head	Coil	Pump	4,C Syn	Spiral bevel
1934–36	527	6 inline monobloc	72 × 103 2,516	52 at 3,600	L-head	Coil	Pump	4,C Syn	Spiral bevel
1934–37	508	4 inline monobloc	65 × 75 995	24 at 3,800	L-head	Coil	Thermo	4,C Syn	Spiral bevel

11 Brakes	12 Suspension	13 Wheelbase Track	14 Number Built	Remarks
4W, servo R.W	½–ell Cant.	3,860 1,500	5 (?)	Marketed as 'Superfiat', never under 220 designation
4W, servo R.W	½–ell Cant.	3,600 1,460	2,411	519S sports model has 3,300 mm wheelbase, 1,475 mm track. 519B (1925–27) with semi-elliptic rear suspension.
4W, R.W	½–ell ½–ell	2,550 1,200	92,214	509A (autumn 1926) accounted for 69,165 of total. Various sports versions, 1926–28, include 509S, 509SM, 509SC, outputs up to 36 b.h.p.
4W, R.W	½–ell ½–ell	2,750 1,400	42,421	Revised 501. Also 503S sports with cowled radiator.
4W, R.W	½–ell ½–ell	3,050 1,400	3,701	Revised 505.
4W, R.W	½–ell ½–ell	3,400 1,410	2,583	Revised 510.
4W, R.W	½–ell ½–ell	2,900 1,400	20,996	First FIAT with l.h.d. as standard. Also small-bore 1,866 c.c. 520T taxi.
4W RW	½–ell ½–ell	2,900 1,400	22,865 (all types)	Data for short chassis 521. Also 521 on 3,140 mm wheelbase. Also in Germany (N.S.U.) and Czechoslovakia (Walter).
4W R.W	½–ell ½–ell	3,400 1,460	4,513 (all types)	Data for original 1928 model. 1929–31 models are 525N on 3,260 mm. wheelbase, and 525S with 3000 mm. wheelbase. 525SS has 88 b.h.p. engine in short chassis. Hydraulic brakes, 1931.
4W 4W	½–ell ½–ell	2,555 1,220	36,970	Also sports models (514S, 514CA, 514MM) with outputs of up to 37 b.h.p., some with servo brakes. Early sports cars on 2,770 mm. w.b. commercial chassis. Also in Czechoslovakia (Walter) and Spain.
4W, Hy Trans	½–ell ½–ell	2,580 1,450	3,405	Simplified 514. Also made as taxi with 2,870 mm. wheelbase.
4W, Hy Trans	½–ell ½–ell	2,775 1,450	7,360 (all types)	Free wheel optional. Data for standard 522C. Also 522L with 3,070 mm. wheelbase, and (from 1932) 522S sports, 2,800 mm. wheelbase, 65 b.h.p. engine (of which 732 made).
4W, Hy Trans	½–ell ½–ell	3,230 1,460	2,775 (all types)	Long wheelbase 522. Free wheel optional. Data for 524L: also a 524C with 3,070 mm. wheelbase.
4W, Hy Trans	½–ell ½–ell	2,250 1,200	41,396	Production statistics include s.v. sports 508S, 1933/4. Options include free wheel, 24 b.h.p. and 28 b.h.p. engines. Also made in Germany (N.S.U.), Czechoslovakia (Walter), Poland (Polski-FIAT) and France.
4W, Hy Trans	½–ell ½–ell	2,700 1,430	7,452 (all types)	Details for standard 2-litre. Options include 78×92 mm. (1,758 c.c) engine, 40 b.h.p, and 54 b.h.p. version of 2 litre unit. 7-seaters have 3,000 mm. wheelbase. Made in France 1935–7 as Simca 11CV.
4W, Hy Trans	½–ell ½–ell	3,170 1,430	260	
4W, Hy Trans	½–ell ½–ell	2,300 1,200	72,769	Improved four-speed model: about 1,000 saloons made with 34 b.h.p. 108CS o.h.v. engine. Made in Germany (N.S.U.), Czechoslovakia (Walter), Poland (Polski-FIAT) and France (Simca).

1 Years	2 Type	3 Cylinders	4 Engine Dimensions	5 Output	6 Valves	7 Ignition	8 Cooling	9 Gears	10 Final Drive
1934–37	508S	4 inline monobloc	65×75 995	36 at 4,400	O.H.V.	Coil	Thermo	4,C Syn	Spiral bevel
1935–44	1500	6 inline monobloc	65×75 1,493	45 at 4,400	O.H.V.	Coil	Pump	4,C Syn	Spiral bevel
1936–48	500	4 inline monobloc	52×67 569	13 at 4,000	L-head	Coil	Thermo	4,C Syn	Spiral bevel
1937–48	508C	4 inline monobloc	68×75 1,089	32 at 4,400	O.H.V.	Coil	Thermo	4,C Syn	Spiral bevel
1938–44	2800	6 inline monobloc	82×90 2,852	85 at 4,000	O.H.V.	Coil	Pump	4,C Syn	Spiral bevel
1947–51	1100S	4 inline monobloc	68×75 1,089	51 at 5,200	O.H.V.	Coil	Thermo	4,C Syn	Spiral bevel
1948–53	1100B/E	4 inline monobloc	68×75 1,089	35 at 4,400	O.H.V.	Coil	Thermo	4,C Syn	Spiral bevel
1948–50	1500D/E	6 inline monobloc	65×75 1,493	47 at 4,400	O.H.V.	Coil	Pump	4,C Syn	Spiral bevel
1949–54	500C	4 inline monobloc	52×67 569	16.5 at 4,400	O.H.V.	Coil	Thermo	4,C Syn	Spiral bevel
1950–58	1400	4 inline monobloc	82×66 1,395	44 at 4,400	O.H.V.	Coil	Pump	4,S/C Syn	Hypoid
1951–73	Campagnola	4 inline monobloc	82×90 1,901	53 at 3,700	O.H.V.	Coil	Pump	4,C Syn	Hypoid
1952–54	8V	8, Vee	72×61.3 1,996	105 at 6,000	O.H.V.	Coil	Pump	4,C Syn	Hypoid
1952–58	1900	4 inline monobloc	82×90 1,901	60 at 4,300	O.H.V.	Coil	Pump	5,S/C Syn	Hypoid
1953–62	1100–103	4 inline monobloc	68×75 1,089	36 at 4,400	O.H.V.	Coil	Pump	4,S/C Syn	Hypoid
1953–56	1400D	4 inline monobloc	82×90 1,901	40 at 3,200	O.H.V.	Glow Plug	Pump	4,S/C Syn	Hypoid

11 Brakes	12 Suspension	13 Wheelbase Track	14 Number Built	Remarks
4W, Hy	½–ell	2,300		Also (1933/4) with 30 b.h.p. s.v. engine and three speeds.
Trans	½–ell	1,200		Made in Germany (N.S.U.) and Czechoslovakia (Walter).
4W, Hy	Ind coil	2,800	39,440	1500B (1938) and 1500C (1946/48) to similar specification. Made in Germany (N.S.U.).
Trans	½–ell	1,344		
4W, Hy	Ind Tr.	2,000	122,016	Semi-elliptic rear suspension from August 1938. Made in France (Simca-5) and Germany (N.S.U). 500B (1948–49) is
Trans	½–ell	1,116		similar except for 16.5 b.h.p. o.h.v. engine.
4W, Hy	Ind coil	2,420	121,947	Known as 1100 from 1939. Also 6-seater 508L (1100L) on 2,700 mm. wheelbase with 30 b.h.p. engine, and 508CMM
Trans	½–ell	1,226		sports coupé with 42 b.h.p. engine. Made in France (Simca-8), Germany (N.S.U.) and Poland (Polski-FIAT).
4W, Hy	Ind coil	3,200	620	Military-colonial tourers also made on 3,000 mm. wheelbase.
Trans	½–ell	1,460		
4W, Hy	Ind coil	2,420	401	Post-war edition of 508CMM. 1100ES (1949/52) has 2+2 Pininfarina body, steering column change.
Trans	½–ell	1,231		
4W, Hy	Ind coil	2,420	83,000	1100E (1949/53) has steering-column change. Also long-chassis 1100BL/EL with 30 b.h.p. engines. Made in
Trans	½–ell	1,231		Austria (Steyr-Daimler-Puch). French Simca-8 very similar, but with 1,221 c.c. engine.
4W, Hy	Ind coil	2,800	4,790	1500E (1949/50) has steering-column change.
Trans	½–ell	1,367		
4W, Hy	Ind Tr.	2,000	376,368	Also made in Germany (N.S.U.) French Simca-6 very similar.
Trans	½–ell	1,116		
4W, Hy	Ind coil	2,650	120,356	Unitary construction. Data for original version. 1400A (1954) with 50 b.h.p. engine, and 1400B (1956) with 58
Trans	Coil	1,326		b.h.p. Made in Austria (Steyr-Puch), Germany (N.S.U.), Spain (SEAT), and Yugoslavia (Zastava).
4W, Hy	Ind coil	2,250	circa 38,000	4×4 Jeep-type vehicle. Numerous variants, diesel-engined option from 1955.
Trans	½–ell	1,260	(to 1972)	
4W, Hy	Ind coil	2,400	114	Unitary construction, standard on all subsequent models.
Trans	Ind coil	1,290		Second series cars have 114 b.h.p. engines.
4W, Hy	Ind coil	2,650	15,759	1400 structure, 5-speed overdrive gearbox, fluid coupling. Data for original model, but production statistics cover
Trans	Coil	1,330		1900A (1954) with 70 b.h.p. and 1900B (1956) with 80 b.h.p. engine. Made in Yugoslavia (Zastava) and in Austria (Steyr-Puch), the latter using their own engine.
4W, Hy	Ind coil	2,340	1,019,378	Data for basic version, 1953/56. 1100TV (1953/6) has 50 b.h.p. engine, central cyclops' eye spotlamp. 1956, 1100E in
Trans	½–ell	1,232	(all types)	standard (40 b.h.p.) and TV (53 b.h.p.) versions. 1957, 1100D, 43 b.h.p., 1959, 1100H, 50 b.h.p. engine, handbrake on rear wheels. Also made in Germany, (N.S.U.), Yugoslavia (Zastava) and India (Premier). Still being made in Bombay, 1973.
4W, Hy	Ind coil	2,650	13,585	Diesel-engined 1400. 1400A series, 1954/6.
Trans	Coil	1,330	(1953/4)	

1 Years	2 Type	3 Cylinders	4 Engine Dimension	5 Output	6 Valves	7 Ignition	8 Cooling	9 Gears	10 Final Drive
1955–60	600	4 inline monobloc	60×56 633	24.5 at 4,600	O.H.V.	Coil	Pump	4,C Syn	Spiral bevel
1957–60	1200	4 inline monobloc	72×75 1,221	55 at 5,300	O.H.V.	Coil	Pump	4,S/C Syn	Hypoid
1957–60	500	2 inline separate	66×70 479	15 at 4,000	O.H.V.	Coil	Air	4,C	Spiral bevel
1959–62	1500S	4 inline monobloc	78×78 1,491	80 at 6,000	D.O.H.C.	Coil	Pump	4,C Syn	Hypoid
1959–68	1800	6 inline monobloc	72×73.5 1,795	75 at 5,000	O.H.V.	Coil	Pump	4,S/C all-syn	Hypoid
1959–61	2100	6 inline monobloc	77×73.5 2,054	82 at 5,000	O.H.V.	Coil	Pump	4,S/C all-syn	Hypoid
1960–73	500D	2 inline separate	67.4×70 499.5	17.5 at 4,400	O.H.V.	Coil	Air	4,C	Spiral bevel
1960–70	600D	4 inline monobloc	62×63.5 767	29 at 4,800	O.H.V.	Coil	Pump	4,C Syn	Spiral bevel
1961–67	1300	4 inline monobloc	72×79.5 1,295	65 at 5,200	O.H.V.	Coil	Pump	4,S/C, all-syn	Hypoid
1961–68	1500	4 inline monobloc	77×79.5 1,481	72 at 5,200	O.H.V.	Coil	Pump	4,S/C all-syn	Hypoid
1961–68	2300	6 inline monobloc	78×79.5 2,280	105 at 5,300	O.H.V.	Coil	Pump	4,S/C all-syn	Hypoid
1961–68	2300S	6 inline monobloc	78×79.5 2,280	136 at 5,300	O.H.V.	Coil	Pump	4,C all-syn	Hypoid
1962–66	1100D	4 inline monobloc	72×75 1,221	50 at 5,000	O.H.V.	Coil	Pump	4,S/C Syn	Hypoid

11 Brakes	12 Suspension	13 Wheelbase Track	14 Number Built	Remarks
4W, Hy Trans	Ind Tr Ind Coil	2,000 1,160	891,107	Rear engine. Data cover standard saloon and convertible, but also made as 6-seater station wagon/taxi) (Multipla), track 1,230 mm. Production of this model 76,371. Car versions also made in Germany (N.S.U.), Spain (SEAT), and Yugoslavia (Zastava).
4W, Hy Trans	Ind Coil ½-ell	2,340 1,232	400,066	1100 derivative, replacing TV, 1960, rear wheel handbrake 58 b.h.p. engine. 1960–63, 2,363 cabriolet versions also produced.
4W, Hy R.W.	Ind Tr Ind Coil	1,840 1,135	181,036	Rear engine. Production statistics cover all types to 1960. First cars had 13 b.h.p. engines, output increased further to 16.5 b.h.p. during 1958, 1958/9 limited production of 500 Sport with 499 c.c. 21 b.h.p. engine. Made in Austria by Steyr-Puch with own engine and suspension.
4W, Hy R.W.	Ind coil ½-ell	2,340 1,237		O.S.C.A.-designed engine, originally marketed as 1500. Front disc brakes from November, 1960. For production figures see under 1500 cabriolet (1963)
4W, Hy R.W.	Ind Coil Coil	2,650 1,340	185,000	Production figures cover all the 6-cylinder range (1800–2100–2300–2300S). Data for original version. 1800B (1961–68) has 1,345 mm track, semi-elliptic rear suspension, all-disc brakes, 85 b.h.p.
4W, Hy R.W.	Ind Coil Coil	2,650 1,340		For production figures, see under 1800, to which identical apart from engine. 78 b.h.p. engines in station wagons.
4W, Hy R.W.	Ind Tr Ind Coil	1,840 1,135	2,900,000 + (to 1972)	Rear engine. Improved F-series to same basic specifications, 1965. Also Giardiniera station wagon with horizontally mounted underfloor engine, wheelbase 1,940 mm., track 1,131mm, 1960–68, and since produced by Autobianchi at Desio. 500s also in Austria (Steyr-Puch).
4W, Hy R.W.	Ind Tr Ind Coil	2,000 1,160	1,561,000 (to and of 1969)	Rear engine. Also a Multipla version with 1,230 mm. track, made with 850T style body by O.M. 1964. Also made in Germany (Neckar), Yugoslavia (Zastava), Argentina (Concord), SEAT (Spain). All export markets supplied from Spain since 1970.
4W, Hy discs front: R.W.	Ind Coil ½-ell	2,420 1,295	600,000	Production figures also cover 1500, in standard form. Later cars with 2,425 mm. wheelbase. Made in Spain (SEAT) and Yugoslavia (Zastava).
4W, Hy discs front: R.W.	Ind Coil ½-ell	2,420 1,295		For production figures see also under 1300. 1965–7, wheelbase 2,505 mm. Standard cars discontinued 1967. Also 1500L, 66 b.h.p. engine, all-disc brakes, 2,650 mm. wheelbase, 88,000 made, 1963–68. Also in Spain (SEAT) and Yugoslavia (Zastava).
4W, Hy servo disc: R.W.	Ind Coil ½-ell	2,650 1,345		For production figures, see under 1800. Overdrive optional, automatic optional from 1963. *Speciale* (1961–63) with 2,730 mm. wheelbase, 1961–63, and thereafter on standard wheelbase.
4W, Hy servo disc: R.W.	Ind coil ½-ell	2,650 1,350		Ghia body design. Also available, 1961–64, with standard 2300 engine.
4W, Hy R.W.	Ind coil ½-ell	2,340 1,232	408,997	*Falsa 1100* with 1.2-litre engine. Also in Germany (Neckar)

Years	Type	Cylinders	Engine Dimensions	Output	Valves	Ignition	Cooling	Gears	Final Drive
1963–67	1500 Cabriolet	4 inline monobloc	77×79.5 1,481	72 at 5,200	O.H.V.	Coil	Pump	4,C all-syn	Hypoid
1963–66	1600S	4 inline monobloc	80×78 1,568	85 at 6,000	D.O.H.C.	Coil	Pump	4,C all-syn	Hypoid
1964–71	850	4 inline monobloc	65×63.5 843	34 at 5,000	O.H.V.	Coil	Pump	4,C all-syn	Hypoid
1965–73	850T	4 inline monobloc	65×63.5 843	40 at 5,000	O.H.V.	Coil	Pump	4,C all-syn	Hypoid
1965–73	850 Coupe/ spyder	4 inline monobloc	65×63.5 843	47 at 6,200	O.H.V.	Coil	Pump	4,C all-syn	Hypoid
1966–70	1100R	4 inline monobloc	68×75 1,089	48 at 5,200	O.H.V.	Coil	Pump	4,C Syn	Hypoid
1966–73	124	4 inline monobloc	73×71.5 1,197	60 at 5,600	O.H.V.	Coil	Pump	4,C all-syn	Hypoid
1966–72	124 Sport	4 inline monobloc	80×71.5 1,438	90 at 6,000	D.O.H.C.	Alt	Pump	4,C all-syn	Hypoid
1967–72	125	4 inline monobloc	80×80 1,608	90 at 5,600	D.O.H.C.	Alt	Pump	4,C all-syn	Hypoid
1967–69	Dino	6 vee	86×57 1,987	160 at 7,200	4.O.H.C.	Alt	Pump	5,C all-syn	Hypoid
1969–72	124 Sport 1600	4 inline monobloc	80×80 1,608	110 at 6,400	D.O.H.C.	Alt	Pump	5,C all-syn	Hypoid
1969–73	Dino 2400	6 vee	92.5×60 2,418	180 at 6,600	4.O.H.C.	Alt	Pump	5,C all-syn	Hypoid

11 Brakes	12 Suspension	13 Wheelbase Track	14 Number Built	Remarks
4W, Hy servo discs front: R.W.	Ind coil ½–ell	2,340 1,232	47,000 +	Derivative of 1960 1200 cabriolet. Later cars have 75 b.h.p. engines. From 1965, 5-speed all-synchromesh gearbox. Production figures include 1500s (1959) and 1600s (1963)
4W, Hy servo discs: R.W.	Ind coil ½–ell	2,340 1,242		Revised 1500S, O.S.C.A.-designed engine. 1965, four headlamps, engine 90 b.h.p. at 6,500 r.p.m., 5-speed all-synchromesh gearbox. For production figures, see 1500 cabriolet (1963)
4W, Hy R.W.	Ind Tr Ind Coil	2,027 1,211	1,300,000 to end of 1969	Rear engine. Super models, 37 b.h.p. at 5,100 r.p.m. From 1966, available with Idroconvert semi-automatic gearbox. From 1968, also 850 Special, 47 b.h.p. coupe engine, front disc brakes. Also made in Spain (SEAT), and produced by Barcelona factory for world markets. From 1973, SEAT versions available in England.
4W, Hy R.W.	Ind Tr Ind Coil	2,000 1,224		Rear engine. Styled on lines of O.M.'s version of 600 Multipla. Made at Naples plant. From 1970 with 903 c.c. engine.
4W, Hy discs front: R.W.	Ind Tr Ind Coil	2,027 1,212	512,000 + (to 1972)	Rear engine. Data are for original coupe. Spyder (l.h.d only) with 49 b.h.p. at 6,400 r.p.m, track 1,222 mm. 1968, both models with 903 c.c. (65×65 mm) engine developing 52 b.h.p. at 6,400 r.p.m., four headlamps on coupe. Idroconvert semi-automatic gearbox optional. Coupe also by SEAT to 1972: Spyder ceased 1973
4W, Hy discs front: R.W.	Ind Coil ½–ell	2,342 1,232	300,000 +	
4W, Hy discs: R.W.	Ind Coil Coil	2,420 1,330	circa 1,280,000 (all models) to 1972	Alternator ignition, 1970. From 1969, available also as 124 Special with 1,438 c.c., 70 b.h.p. engine, four headlamps, alternator ignition, automatic transmission option. (125,000 made to 1970). 1973, 65 b.h.p. standard engine, 75 b.h.p Special. Also in Spain (SEAT) and in modified form in Russia (VAZ)
4W, Hy servo discs: R.W.	Ind Coil Coil	2,280 1,346	280,000 + to 1972	FIAT-design d.o.h.c. engine with cogged-belt camshaft drive. Data for original spyder. Coupe (1967) has 2,420 mm. wheelbase. 1970, four headlamps, 5-speed gearbox optional. Also made in Spain (SEAT).
4W, Hy servo discs: R.W.	Ind Coil ½–ell	2,505 1,313		Four headlamps, automatic optional. From 1968, also 125 Special with 5-speed gearbox.
4W, Hy servo disc: R.W.	Ind coil ½–ell	2,550 1,378	7,500 + to 1972	Ferrari-based engine. Data are for 2+2 coupe. Spyder has wheelbase 2,280 mm., track 1,385 mm. Production figures include Dino 2400
4W, Hy servo discs: R.W.	Ind Coil Coil	2,420 1,346	(see 124 Sport, 1966)	4 headlamps. Data for coupe: spyder wheelbase 2,280 mm. 1973, with choice of 1,592 c.c. (108 b.h.p.) or 1,756 c.c. (118 b.h.p.) 132 engines. Also 128 b.h.p. FIAT-Abarth Rallye spyder.
4W, Hy servo discs: R.W.	Ind Coil Ind McP strut	2,550 1,390		Ferrari-based engine, cars built at Maranello. Data for coupe: spyder wheelbase 2,280 mm. For production figures, see Dino (1967)

1 Years	2 Type	3 Cylinders	4 Engine Dimensions	5 Output	6 Valves	7 Ignition	8 Cooling	9 Gears	10 Final Drive
1969–73	128	4 inline monobloc	80 × 55.5 1,116	55 at 6,000	O.H.C.	Alt	Pump	4,C all-syn	Spur gear
1969–73	130	6 vee	96 × 66 2,866	140 at 6,000	D.O.H.C.	Alt	Pump	Auto	Hypoid
1970–73	124 Special T	4 inline monobloc	80 × 71.5 1,438	80 at 6,000	D.O.H.C.	Alt	Pump	4,C all-syn	Hypoid
1971–73	127	4 inline monobloc	65 × 68 903	47 at 6,200	O.H.V.	Coil	Pump	4,C all-syn	Spur gear
1972–73	132	4 inline monobloc	80 × 79.2 1,592	98 at 6,000	D.O.H.C.	Alt	Pump	4,C all-syn	Hypoid
1972–73	126	2 inline separate	73.5 × 70 594	23 at 4,800	O.H.V.	Coil	Air	4,C syn	Spiral bevel

11 Brakes	12 Suspension	13 Wheelbase Track	14 Number Built	Remarks
4W, Hy disc front: R.W.	Ind McP strut Ind McP strut	2,448 1,420	1,270,000 + to 1972	Front-wheel drive, east/west engine. Also (1971) Rallye 2-door saloon, 1,290 c.c., 67 b.h.p. engine, servo-assisted brakes. 1972, range of coupes with 64 b.h.p. 1,116 c.c. or 75 b.h.p. 1,290 c.c. engines, four headlamps on SL variants. Range made in Egypt (El Nasr), Spain (SEAT) and Yugoslavia (Zastava)
4W, Hy servo discs R.W.	Ind McP strut Ind torsion bar	2,720 1,457		5-speed ZF all-synchromesh gearbox optional. Data for original model. 1970, output 160 b.h.p. at 6,000 r.p.m. 1971, coupe version available. 1972, engine 102 × 66 mm, 3,235 c.c., output 165 b.h.p. at 5,600 r.p.m.
W, Hy discs: R.W.	Ind coil Coil	2,420 1,330		124 with twin-cam engine. 5-speed or automatic gearboxes optional. 1973, engine 1,592 c.c. as fitted to 132. For production figures, see under 124 (1966).
W, Hy front discs: R.W.	Ind McP strut Ind McP strut	2,225 1,295	517,000 + to 1972	Front-wheel drive, east/west engine. Engine basically 1968 850 coupe type.
W, Hy servo disc: R.W.	Ind coil Coil	2,557 1,321		Available with 1,756 c.c., 105 b.h.p. engine, and choice of 5-speed manual or G.M. 3-speed automatic transmissions.
W, Hy R.W.	Ind, Tr Ind Coil	8140 1,203		Rear engine.

Index